THE ROMAN WORLD

FOR CAPPY, LUCKY, AND SUZI

THE ROMAN WORLD

A Sourcebook

Edited by
David Cherry

Blackwell
Publishing

BLACKWELL PUBLISHING
350 Main Street, Malden, MA 02148-5020, USA
9600 Garsington Road, Oxford OX4 2DQ, UK
550 Swanston Street, Carlton, Victoria 3053, Australia

First published 2001

4   2007

Library of Congress Cataloging-in-Publication Data

The Roman world: a sourcebook / edited by David Cherry.
    p. cm.
  Includes bibliographical references and index.
  ISBN 978-0-631-21783-1 (alk. paper) — ISBN 978-0-631-21784-8 (alk. paper)
  1. Rome—Civilization—Sources. I. Cherry, David, Dr.

DG77.R6716 2001
937—dc21
                                                      00–049428

A catalogue record for this title is available from the British Library.

Set in 10.5 on 12pt Sabon
by Ace Filmsetting Ltd, Frome, Somerset

For further information on
Blackwell Publishing, visit our website:
www.blackwellpublishing.com

CONTENTS

ILLUSTRATIONS

FIGURES

PLATES

PREFACE AND ACKNOWLEDGMENTS

It is, of course, impossible to encompass every aspect of Roman history in a single-volume collection of documents. The purpose of this book is a more limited one – to provide readers with a broad range of written material, over the whole of the period from the Twelve Tables to late antiquity, on topics that I think are important to understanding the shape of the Roman world: slavery and the structure of society (chapter 1); the position of women and the nature of family life (chapter 2); agriculture and farm management (chapter 3); the reach and the limitations of scientific and medical knowledge (chapter 4); government and political life from the mid-Republic to the fourth century AD (chapter 5); the nature of Roman provincial rule (chapter 6); the structure of the army and the experience of military life (chapter 7); the attitudes that the Romans harbored towards those who were, at one time or another, beyond the reach of military control (chapter 8); the practice of Roman religion, and the story of the persecutions of the Christians (chapter 9). The choice of material is, inevitably, idiosyncratic. It reflects both my own interests and what experience has taught me is likely to be of interest to non-specialists.

No attempt has been made to gloss over the brutality of Roman culture. Violence was commonplace and casual. Life, in every period, was cheap. The Romans, it is fairly clear, had a special aptitude for war and conquest, and for the practice of empire. At its height, the Roman empire stretched from northern Britain to Algeria, from Portugal to the Euphrates, and from the Danube to the Nile. It was an empire that brought peace to a world torn apart by war and by ancient animosities: the leisured and literate elite could claim, not without justification, that Rome had established a "common fatherland." It was also an empire built on the sacrifice of people who are rarely given voice in the sources that have come down to us – slaves, the rank-and-file soldiers of the legions, the ordinary men and women of the laboring class.

For permission to use previously published material, I am grateful to the following: selections 2, 18: I. Scott-Kilvert, *The Makers of Rome: Nine Lives by Plutarch*, translated by Ian Scott-Kilvert (Harmondsworth: Penguin Classics, 1965). Copyright © Ian Scott-Kilvert, 1965; selection 5: T. Wiedemann, *Greek and Roman Slavery* (Baltimore: Johns Hopkins University Press, 1981). Copyright Croom Helm, courtesy of Taylor and Francis; selection 6 (translation of parts of *L'Année Épigraphique*, 1971): J. F. Gardner and T. Wiedemann, *The Roman Household: A Sourcebook* (London and New York: Routledge, 1991); selections 11, 12, 48, 49, and figure 3.1: Jo-Ann Shelton, *As the Romans Did: A Source Book in Roman Social History*, 2nd edn (New York and Oxford: Oxford University Press, 1998), copyright © 1988, 1998 by Oxford University Press, Inc. Used by permission of Oxford University Press, Inc.; selection 13: Donald Russell, *Plutarch: Selected Essays and Dialogues* (Oxford: Oxford University Press, 1993), © Donald Russell, 1993. Reprinted from *Plutarch: Selected Essays and Dialogues*, translated by Donald Russell (World's Classics, 1993) by permission of Oxford University Press; selection 24: M. R. Lefkowitz and M. B. Fant, *Women's Life in Greece and Rome: A Source Book in Translation*, 2nd edn (Baltimore: Johns Hopkins University Press, 1992), pp. 243–6, © The Johns Hopkins University Press, 1992; selection 25: Owsei Temkin, *Soranus' Gynecology* (Baltimore: Johns Hopkins University Press, 1956), pp. 6–7, 27, 62–8, © The Johns Hopkins University Press, 1991; selections 26, 40: I. Scott-Kilvert, *The Rise and Fall of The Roman Empire by Polybius*, translated by Ian Scott-Kilvert (Harmondsworth: Penguin Classics, 1979). Translation copyright © Ian Scott-Kilvert, 1979; selection 36: N. Lewis and M. Reinhold, *Roman Civilization: Selected Readings*, 3rd edn (New York: Columbia University Press, 1990), adapted from Loeb Classical Library, courtesy of Harvard University Press, Cambridge, Mass.; selection 38: J. H. Oliver, "The ruling power: A study of the Roman empire in the second century after Christ through the Roman oration of Aelius Aristides," *Transactions of the American Philosophical Society*, n.s. 43 (1953), pt. 4; selection 39: N. P. Milner, *Vegetius: Epitome of Military Science*, 2nd edn (Liverpool: Liverpool University Press, 1996); selection 41 (translation of R. O. Fink, *Roman Military Records on Papyrus*, Cleveland, 1971): J. B. Campbell, *The Roman Army 31 BC–AD 337* (London and New York: Routledge, 1994); selection 56: G. A. Williamson, *The History of the Church from Christ to Constantine by Eusebius*, translated by G. A. Williamson, revised by Andrew Louth (Harmondsworth: Penguin Classics, 1965; rev. edn, 1989), copyright © G. A. Williamson, 1965, copyright © Andrew Louth, 1989; selection 57: H. Musurillo, *The Acts of the Christian Martyrs* (Oxford: Oxford University Press, 1972), © Oxford University Press, 1972. Reprinted from *The Acts of the Christian Martyrs*, introduction, texts and translations by Herbert Musurillo (1972), by permission of Oxford University Press; figure 7.1: Graham Webster, *The Roman Imperial Army of the First and Second Centuries AD*, 3rd edn (Totowa, NJ: Barnes and Noble, 1985).

I am grateful also to the College of Letters and Science at Montana State University, Bozeman, for its continued support, and to my editors at Blackwell, especially Tessa Harvey and Louise Spencely, whose help has been uncommonly generous. My greatest debt is to my daughter Katrina, whose companionship gives meaning to my everyday world.

One

THE SOCIAL ORDER

Editor's introduction

It is difficult now to describe, in any very precise way, the structure of Roman society. No systematic account of it has come down to us. Its characteristics must be reconstructed instead from the surviving literary sources, which are scattered across space and time, and which generally reflect the experiences and attitudes only of the leisured elite (who were never more than a tiny proportion of the population), or from inscriptions, which number in the tens of thousands, but are often short and formulaic.

What does emerge clearly from the historical record is that Roman society was characterized, in every period, by inequality, of wealth and of privilege. It is reasonably clear also that Roman society was, from the very beginning, almost obsessively concerned with rank and with status, and therefore also with defining and carefully guarding the means by which they might be demonstrated. In public, where it mattered, rank was advertised mainly through dress. From the time of Augustus (27 BC–AD 14), for example, only senators, their sons, and those who had been given permission to stand for public office were permitted to wear a toga with a broad purple border. Status, which was inextricably bound up with wealth, might be indicated by conspicuous expenditure, or by the differentiation of tasks in the large slave households of the wealthy.

The earliest division of society was into two classes: the patricians, an aristocracy of birth; and the plebeians, who comprised everyone else. By about the middle of the third century BC, however, an expanded aristocracy had emerged,

 means private law

which included the most distinguished and politically active plebeian families. Over time, a kind of dual nobility took shape, which counted among its members not only those who were of patrician birth, but also men who had been elected to the consulship.

Roman society was divided also into orders, the most prestigious of which was made up of senators and their families (wives, children, and grandchildren). It was the senatorial order – a small circle of perhaps several hundred families – that controlled politics and public life during the period of the Republic. Membership required election to political office, respectable birth, moral excellence, and wealth. The minimum property qualification in the late Republic was 400,000 sesterces.[1] Augustus, who was eager to shore up the prestige of the order, raised it to 1,000,000.

The second of the elite orders consisted of the equestrians (*equites*) or "knights." In the beginning, it seems, the title was assigned to men who had done their military service in the cavalry. Because it was expensive to purchase and to maintain a horse, it can be assumed that they were wealthy. Gradually, however, by a process that is impossible now to trace, equestrian rank was almost completely divorced from service in the cavalry; it came to be applied instead to any wealthy man who was not a senator. By the late Republic, the minimum property qualification had been set at 400,000 sesterces. Equestrians were expected also to possess the same qualities – of respectable birth and moral excellence – as were required of senators, but, as the historian Cassius Dio puts it (52.19), in "the second degree." Like senators, equestrians were distinguished by their dress, in their case, by the right to wear gold rings and a toga with a narrow purple border.

The *equites*, who numbered probably in the tens of thousands, were united by wealth, and to some degree, therefore, by similar interests. Many, perhaps the majority, were content to be part of the local elites who ruled the cities of the empire; some, like the publicans who contracted to collect taxes in the Republican era, were enormously wealthy and politically influential; others had no political ambitions at all. From the time of Augustus, the equestrian order was given an increasing number and variety of administrative and military responsibilities. It is characteristic of the Romans' determination to delineate status that by the end of the second century AD, office-holding equestrians had come to be subdivided according to their importance, which was now indicated by epithets: *egregius* ("excellent") for procurators; *perfectissimus* ("most accomplished") for senior prefects; *eminentissimus* ("most distinguished") for praetorian prefects.

The third of the elite orders was made up of decurions, which is what the Romans called those who served on municipal councils. They, too, were required to be of respectable birth, of upright character, and wealthy. The minimum property qualification varied over time and place; at Comum (modern Como) in northern Italy in the time of Pliny the Younger, it was 100,000 sesterces (*Letters* 1.19). Efforts were made to exclude the disreputable, such as men who had a criminal past, or those whose occupation was deemed to be dishonorable (auctioneers, for example).

Sometime early in the second century AD, a new way of differentiating status

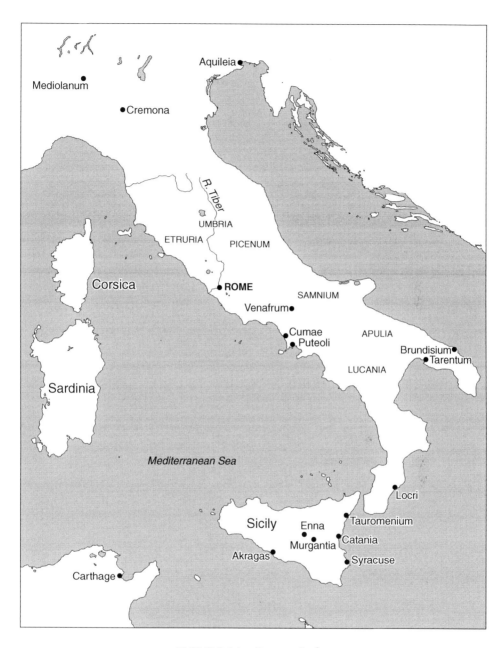

FIGURE 1.1 *Roman Italy.*

was introduced, according to which all citizens were classified either as *honestiores* ("more honorable") or *humiliores* ("more humble"). The *honestiores* included not only the three elite orders, but also veterans. In the criminal law, they were generally punished less harshly (which had no doubt always been true in practice). The *humiliores* will have consisted mostly of the freeborn, the majority of whom were poor. Their status varied mainly according to wealth and occupation. Most worked in agriculture.

Much of the rest of the population was made up of slaves, who were a significant part of the workforce from about the beginning of the second century BC. In the law, they were classified, not as persons, but as chattel. From the first century AD, they were protected against certain kinds of abusive treatment: the emperor Claudius (AD 41–54), for example, decreed that slaves who were abandoned because they were ill could not be re-enslaved if they recovered. It may be supposed that those who were employed in their owner's home, or put in charge of a workshop or other kind of commercial enterprise, were generally treated better than those who worked in the fields or in the mines. They were also more likely to be freed.

At law, the status of freedmen and women varied mainly according to whether they possessed the Roman citizenship, which was customarily awarded to those who were freed by a citizen owner. Ex-slaves were subject to a variety of legal disabilities, most of which are unlikely to have been of much practical importance: they were not allowed to serve in the legions, for example, and were forbidden to become senators, or to marry them. In fact, most appear to have married other ex-slaves. Many undoubtedly continued to be dependent, in some way, on their former owners.

It has often been remarked that, because of the wide divide between rich and poor in the Roman world, there was probably little opportunity for social mobility. Ironically, slaves who managed to win the favor of their owners probably had much better prospects of upward mobility than the freeborn.

1   THE TWELVE TABLES

Rome's first written code of law, the Twelve Tables are said to have been enacted in 451/450 BC. According to Roman tradition (see, e.g., Livy 3.32–8), they were drawn up by a specially appointed commission of ten men, all of them patricians, who generally behaved tyrannically, and illegally attempted to perpetuate their authority. What is reasonably clear is that the code was a product of plebeian agitation that aimed both at curbing the arbitrary exercise of the authority of the patrician magistrates and at establishing the principle of equality before the law. As such, it constitutes an important step in the class struggle (the so-called "Struggle of the Orders") that dominates much of the history of the early Republic.

Because the Twelve Tables were, for the most part, a codification of existing customs, they reflect the predominantly agricultural and pastoral character of the early Roman community. They also constitute easily our richest source of information about social and economic conditions in the fifth century BC. And though parts of them eventually became obsolete, and fell out of use, they were never formally repealed. Cicero remarks (*Laws* 2.59) that even in his own day children were required to memorize them.

The twelve, probably bronze, tablets on which the laws were originally inscribed have not survived. But their terms can be partially reconstructed from quotations in the works of later authors. The translation below is based on the text in M. H. Crawford (ed.), *Roman Statutes* (London, 1996), vol. 2, pp. 578–82.

Table I

If he [i.e., anyone] summons to law, he [the defendant] is to go; if he does not go, there shall be a call to witness; thereafter he [the plaintiff] is to take him.

If he [the defendant] acts deceitfully, or drags his feet, he [the plaintiff] is to lay his hands on (the defendant).

If there shall be illness or age, he [the plaintiff] is to provide a vehicle; if he shall be unwilling, he is not to arrange a covered carriage.

A property-owner is to be guarantor for a property-owner; whoever is willing is to be guarantor for an unpropertied citizen.

. . . .

He [the plaintiff] is to plead where they agree.

If they do not agree, they are to present their case in the Comitium[2] or the Forum before noon. They are to finish pleading together, with both present.

. . . .

If he has broken a limb, unless he settles with him [the victim], there is to be retaliation.

If he has broken the bone of a free man, the penalty is to be 300 (*asses*);[3] in the case of a slave, 150.

If he causes injury to another person, the penalty is to be 25 (*asses*).

If he has cut down a fruit-bearing tree, the penalty is to be 25 (*asses*).

If he has committed theft at night, and he [i.e., the property-owner] has killed him, he is (held) to be lawfully killed.

If he has committed theft during the day, and he has defended himself with a weapon, . . . and he is to call out.

If the theft is manifest, unless he settles, he [the magistrate] is to whip (him) and hand (him) over. If he is a slave, he is to whip (him) and throw (him) from the rock. If he is under the age of puberty, he is to whip (him), and he [the thief] is to repair the damage.

If he has searched with *lanx* and *licium*,[4] and has made discovery, the theft is to be (considered) manifest.

. . . .

Table II

Whoever lacks witness, he is to go before the house every other day to complain.

. . . .

Table III

. . . .

He [the creditor] is to bring (him) to court. Unless he [the debtor] does what has been decided or someone acts as his guarantor at law, he [the creditor] is to take (him) with him. He is to bind (him) with a rope or shackles. He is to bind (him) with not more than fifteen pounds or, if he wishes, with less.

If he [the debtor] wishes, he is to live off his own resources. If he does not live off his own, he who has bound him is to give him a pound of spelt[5] each day. If he wishes, he is to give (him) more.

On three consecutive market-days, he [the creditor] is to produce (him) in the Comitium.

Unless he [the debtor] settles, on the third market-day they [his creditors?] are to cut pieces.[6] If they cut more or less, it is to be without liability.

If he [the creditor] wishes, he is to sell (him) beyond the Tiber.

Table IV

If he [a child] is born deformed, and he [the father] does not pick him up, it is to be without liability.

If a father sells (his) son three times, the son is to be free from (his) father.

. . . .

Table V

A Vestal Virgin is to be free from guardianship.

For a woman, (her) guardian is to be (her) surety.

. . . .

If he dies without a will, for whom there is no proper heir,[7] the nearest agnate[8] is to have the family property and money[?].

If there is no agnate, the *gentiles*[9] are to have the family property and money[?].

If there is no guardian, the nearest agnate is to have guardianship.

If there is a lunatic or spendthrift[?], his agnates and *gentiles* are to have power over him and his family property and money[?].

. . . .

Table VI

. . . .

Right of possession is to be two years in the case of land, one year for other things[?].

Against a foreigner, right of possession is to be forever.

If she is absent for three nights a year. . . .

He is not to remove a connected beam from a joint in a house or vineyard.

. . . .

Table VII

The open space around a wall is to be two and a half feet.

The boundary between a garden or an estate is to be five feet. If they quarrel, they are to demand arbiters.

A road is to be eight feet; on a bend it is to be sixteen feet. They are to construct roads. Unless they have surfaced (them) with their own stone, he is to drive (his animals) wherever he wishes.

If rain-water causes damage, he is to contain (it).

If a tree hangs over onto another's property, he is to trim (it) above fifteen feet.

Table VIII

Whoever has chanted a magic formula ... or sung satirically or composed a song. . . .

If a quadruped has caused damage, unless he repairs (it), he is to hand over (the animal) as punishment.

. . . .

If he has grazed or cut down a crop at night, he is to be hanged for (the sake of) Ceres. If he is under the age of puberty, he [the magistrate] is to whip (him) and settle the penalty at double.

If he has burned a building or a pile of grain placed next to a house[?], he is to be bound and whipped and killed by fire. If by accident . . . , he is to repair the damage. . . .

. . . .

If a patron has defrauded a client, he is to be accursed.

Whoever has allowed himself to testify or be balance-holder,[10] unless he stands by[?] (his) testimony, is to be (considered) dishonest and unable to give testimony.

If he has given false testimony, he [the magistrate] is to cast (him) from the rock.

. . . .

He is not to hold an assembly.

Table IX

Concerning a citizen's rights, they are to declare under oath what they consider best for the community.

Concerning a citizen's rights, unless the assembly is very full, they are not to vote.

Table X

He is not to bury or burn a dead man in the city.

. . . .

Women are not to tear their cheeks or wail on account of a funeral.

He is not to gather a dead man's bones, for the purpose of holding a funeral afterwards, but. . . .

He is not to put perfumed liquid on a dead man. He is to sprinkle the funeral pyre with not more than . . . wine.

. . . .

. . . and he is not to add gold, but in the case of someone whose teeth are joined with gold, yet he buries or burns it with him, it is to be without liability.

He is not to locate a tomb within sixty feet of another's house.

A fore-court (of a tomb) or tomb is to be sacred.

Table XI

There is not to be intermarriage with the plebs.

Table XII

. . . .

If a slave has committed theft or caused damage, he is to be handed over as punishment.

2   PLUTARCH, *LIFE OF CATO THE ELDER*

A philosopher, priest (at Delphi), and occasional lecturer, Plutarch (ca. AD 50–120) lived for a time at Rome, but spent most of his life in his native Chaeronea, in central Greece. Besides the *Moralia*, a collection of more than sixty short essays on a variety of mostly ethical and religious topics (see also below, selection 13), his most important surviving work is the *Parallel Lives*, fifty biographies of Greek and Roman generals and political leaders, most of them organized in Greek–Roman pairs.

Marcus Porcius Cato was born at Tusculum, in central Italy, in 234 BC (he died in 149).

Spokesperson for a conservative and often reactionary ideology, he vehemently protested against the adoption of Greek culture. He was later regarded, in some quarters, at least, as a kind of paragon of Roman virtues – of austerity, frugality, and unyielding devotion to tradition. His only surviving work, *On Agriculture*, a guide to farming and estate-management written about 160 BC, is excerpted in selections 20 and 50.

The translation is from I. Scott-Kilvert, *Makers of Rome: Nine Lives by Plutarch* (Harmondsworth, 1965), pp. 123–4, 141–3, 145–6.

(4) He came to be known as the Roman Demosthenes, but what created an even more powerful impression than his eloquence was his manner of living. His powers of expression merely set a standard for young men, which many of them were already striving their utmost to attain. But a man who observed the ancestral custom of working his own land, who was content with a cold breakfast, a frugal dinner, the simplest clothing, and a humble cottage to live in, and who actually thought it more admirable to renounce luxuries than to acquire them – such a person was conspicuous by his rarity. The truth was that by this date the Roman republic had grown too large to preserve its original purity of spirit, and the very authority which it exercised over so many realms and peoples constantly brought it into contact with, and obliged it to adapt itself to, an extraordinary diversity of habits and modes of living. So it was natural enough that everybody should admire Cato when they saw others prostrated by their labors or enervated by their pleasures, while he remained unaffected by either. What was even more remarkable was that he followed the same habits, not merely while he was young and full of ambition, but even when he was old and gray-headed and had served as a consul and celebrated a triumph, and that he continued, like some champion athlete, to observe the rules of his training and maintain his self-discipline to the end.

He tells us that he never wore a garment which cost more than a hundred drachmas,[11] that even when he was praetor or consul he drank the same wine as his slaves, that he bought the fish or meat for his dinner in the public market and never paid more than thirty *asses* for it, and that he allowed himself this indulgence for the public good in order to strengthen his body for military service. He also mentions that when he was bequeathed an embroidered Babylonian robe, he immediately sold it, that none of his cottages had plastered walls, that he never paid more than 1,500 drachmas for a slave, since he was not looking for the exquisite or handsome type of domestic servant, but for sturdy laborers such as grooms and herdsmen, and that when they became too old to work, he felt it his duty to sell them rather than feed so many useless mouths. In general he considered that nothing is cheap if it is superfluous, that what a man does not need is dear even if it cost only a penny, and that one should buy land for tilling and grazing, not to make into gardens, where the object is merely to sprinkle the lawns and sweep the paths.

(20) He was also a good father, a kind husband, and a most capable manager of his own household, since he was far from regarding this side of his affairs as trivial or allowing it to suffer from neglect. For this reason I think I should give some examples of his conduct in his private life. He chose his wife for her family rather than her fortune, for he believed that while people of great wealth or high

position cherish their own pride and self-esteem, nevertheless women of noble birth are by nature more ashamed of any disgraceful action and so are more obedient to their husbands in everything that is honorable. He used to say that a man who beats his wife or child is laying sacrilegious hands on the most sacred thing in the world. He considered that it was more praiseworthy to be a good husband than a great senator, and was also of the opinion that there was nothing much else to admire in Socrates of old, except for the fact that he was always gentle and considerate in his dealings with his wife, who was a scold, and his children, who were half-witted.

When his son was born, Cato thought that nothing but the most important business of state should prevent him from being present when his wife gave the baby its bath and wrapped it in swaddling clothes. His wife suckled the child herself and often did the same for her slaves' children, so as to encourage brotherly feelings in them towards her own son. As soon as the boy was able to learn, his father took charge of his schooling and taught him to read, although he had in the household an educated slave called Chilo who was a schoolmaster and taught many other boys. However, Cato did not think it right, so he tells us, that his son should be scolded or have his ears pulled by a slave, if he were slow to learn, and still less that he should be indebted to his slave in such a vital matter as his education. So he took it upon himself to teach the boy, not only his letters, but also the principles of Roman law. He also trained him in athletics, and taught him how to throw the javelin, fight in armor, ride a horse, use his fists in boxing, endure the extremes of heat and cold, and swim across the roughest and most swiftly flowing stretches of the Tiber. He tells us that he composed his history of Rome,[12] writing it out with his own hand and in large characters, so that his son should possess in his own home the means of acquainting himself with the ancient annals and traditions of his country. He also mentions that he was as careful not to use any indecent expression before his son as he would have been in the presence of the Vestal Virgins, and that he never bathed with him. This last seems to have been the general custom among the Romans, and even fathers-in-law avoided bathing with their sons-in-law, because they were ashamed to show themselves naked. . . .

(21) . . . . Cato possessed a large number of slaves, whom he usually bought from among the prisoners captured in war, but it was his practice to choose those who, like puppies or colts, were young enough to be trained and taught their duties. None of them ever entered any house but his own, unless they were sent on an errand by Cato or his wife, and if they were asked what Cato was doing, the reply was always that they did not know. It was a rule of his establishment that a slave must either be doing something about the house, or else be asleep. He much preferred the slaves who slept well, because he believed that they were more even-tempered than the wakeful ones, and that those who had had enough sleep produced better results at any task than those who were short of it. And as he was convinced that slaves were led into mischief more often on account of love affairs than for any other reason, he made it a rule that the men could sleep with the women slaves of the establishment, for a fixed price, but must have nothing to do with any others.

At the beginning of his career, when he was a poor man and was frequently on

Handwritten margin note (left): Romans looked as a negative to what they would watch that was disturbing, including extreme acts of violence

1 Temple of Apollo (431 BC)   5 Temple of Ceres (493 BC)   9   Temple of Quirinus (293 BC)
2 Temple of Bellona (296 BC)   6 Temple of Saturn (497 BC)   10 Temple of Vesta
3 Aemilian bridge   7 Rostra (338 BC)   11 Regia
4 Sublician bridge   8 Temple of Janus   12 Tomb of the Scipios

FIGURE 1.2 *The city of Rome in the early third century* BC *(after F. W. Walbank et al. (eds),* The Cambridge Ancient History, *2nd edn, Cambridge, 1989, vol. 7, pt. 2).*

active service, he never complained of anything that he ate, and he used to say that it was ignoble to find fault with a servant for the food that he prepared. But in later life, when he had become more prosperous, he used to invite his friends and colleagues to dinner, and immediately after the meal he would beat with a leather thong any of the slaves who had been careless in preparing or serving it. He constantly contrived to provoke quarrels and dissensions among his slaves, and if they ever arrived at an understanding with one another he became alarmed

Handwritten margin notes (bottom): take that back; not treated well; didn't want them to get along or team up; cares v much about good; Romans lived in fear of slaves

and suspicious. If ever any of his slaves was suspected of committing a capital offense, he gave the culprit a formal trial in the presence of the rest, and if he was found guilty, he had him put to death.

(23) He was opposed on principle to the study of philosophy, and ... his patriotic fervor made him regard the whole of Greek culture and its methods of education with contempt. ... In the effort to turn his son against Greek culture, he allowed himself an utterance which was absurdly rash for an old man: he pronounced with all the solemnity of a prophet that if ever the Romans became infected with the literature of Greece, they would lose their empire. ... However, Cato's dislike of the Greeks was not confined to philosophers: he was also deeply suspicious of the Greek physicians who practiced in Rome. He had heard of Hippocrates' celebrated reply, when he was called upon to attend the king of Persia for a fee amounting to many talents, and declared that he would never give his services to barbarians who were enemies of Greece. Cato maintained that all Greek physicians had taken an oath of this kind, and urged his son not to trust any of them. He himself had compiled a book of recipes and used them for the diet or treatment of any members of his household who fell ill. He never made his patients fast, but allowed them to eat herbs and morsels of duck, pigeon, or hare. He maintained that this diet was light and thoroughly suitable for sick people, apart from the fact that it often produced nightmares, and he claimed that by following it he kept both himself and his family in perfect health.

3 JUVENAL, SATIRES 3

Decimus Iunius Iuvenalis, whose sixteen *Satires* ruthlessly ridicule what he considered to be the vices and vulgarities of his age, was born about AD 60 at Aquinum, in central Italy (he died sometime around 140). Very little is known with certainty about either his life or career. He is said to have been banished (perhaps by Domitian) for lampooning a favorite of the imperial court. It appears also that he was, at least for a time, miserably poor. It might be inferred, too, from *Satire* 3, in which his friend Umbricius explains that he is leaving Rome because he is too honest to make a living there, that Juvenal genuinely disliked foreigners, Greeks in particular.

Though disappointed at the going away of my old friend, I nonetheless approve his decision to locate his home at un-crowded Cumae,[13] and to give one citizen to the Sibyl. It is the doorway to Baiae,[14] a pleasant retreat on a lovely shore; I myself prefer even Prochyta[15] to the Subura.[16] For what place have we seen so miserable, so lonely, that you would consider it worse to be afraid of fires, the constant collapsing of buildings, and the thousand dangers of this cruel city, and poets reciting in the month of August?

But while his entire household was being packed on one wagon, he stopped at the old archway of the dripping Capena (gate).[17] Here, where Numa[18] used to meet his mistress every night, the grove of the holy fountain and the shrines are now rented to Jews, whose furnishings are a basket and hay (for every tree has to pay rent to the people, and, with the Muses ejected, the forest goes begging). We go down into the valley of Egeria,[19] and its unnatural caves. How much nearer would be the spirit of the water if a green border of grass enclosed its waves, and marble did not violate the native tufa.

Here Umbricius said: "Since there is no place in the city for honest pursuits, no reward for labor, my assets are less today than they were yesterday, and tomorrow will rub off something from the little that is left, I intend to go to the place where Daedalus[20] took off his tired wings, while my hair is newly white, while my old age is fresh and virtuous, while something is left for Lachesis[21] to spin, and I carry myself on my own feet without placing a staff beneath my hand. I yield my native land. Let Artorius live there, and Catulus; let those stay who turn black into white, for whom it's easy to contract for a temple, or rivers, or harbors, for draining flood-water, or transporting a corpse to the funeral pyre, or supplying a person for sale under the spear.[22] These men who once were horn-blowers, and habitués of the municipal amphitheater, and declaimers known in every town, now sponsor shows, and win popularity by killing whomever the mob requests with a turn of the thumb; from there they return to contract for public toilets, and why not for anything, since they are the sort that Fortune lifts from the gutter to great heights whenever she wants to jest?

What would I do at Rome? I don't know how to lie; if a book is bad, I can't praise and beg for it; I'm ignorant of the motions of the stars; I'm neither willing nor able to promise a father's funeral; I've never examined frogs' entrails; others are skilled at bringing a bride what her lover sends and confides; I will not be a thief's assistant, and so I'm no magistrate's attendant – I go forth like a maimed and useless body with dysfunctional hands. Who today is favored unless he's an accomplice whose seething soul burns with secrets that must never be disclosed? He who has let you in on an innocent secret thinks he owes you nothing, will never profit you: that man is loved by Verres who can indict Verres at any time he wishes. Let not all the sand of the shaded Tagus,[23] and the gold it rolls into the sea, be worth so much to you that you lose sleep, and accept gifts which must be sorrowfully put aside, and always be feared by your mighty friend.

I hasten to say something now about the race that is so favored by our wealthy, and which I avoid most of all; modesty will not stand in the way. I cannot stand, citizens, a city of Greeks; yet how large a measure of our dregs is Achaean? The Syrian Orontes[24] poured into the Tiber long ago, carrying with it its language and customs, its flute-players and slanting strings; even its native timbrels, and the girls ordered to sell themselves at the Circus. Be gone, you who take pleasure in a foreign whore with painted head-band! That peasant of yours, Quirinus, now dons a going-to-dinner coat, and wears victory-prizes on his wax-anointed neck. This one has come from lofty Sicyon, another from Amydon, this one from Andros, that one from Samos or Tralles or Alabanda; they head for the Esquiline,[25] and the hill named for the osier,[26] seeking the inner chambers of the great houses, about to become their masters. Quick-witted, hopelessly impudent, quick to speak and more torrential than Isaeus:[27] tell me, what do you think that man there is? He's brought with him any persona you wish: grammarian, orator, geometrician, painter, wrestling-trainer, augur,[28] rope-dancer, doctor, astrologer: a hungry Greekling knows everything; if you tell him to, he'll go to heaven. In short, it wasn't a Moor, or Sarmatian, or Thracian who took up wings, but one born in

the middle of Athens.[29] Should I not escape the purple clothes of men like these?
Will that man attach his seal before me, and recline on a better couch than mine,
who has been carried to Rome on the wind that brings plums and figs? Is it worth
nothing at all that as an infant I drank the air of the Aventine,[30] nurtured on the
Sabine berry?

What of the fact that this race, most skilled at flattery, praises the speech of an
unlearned friend, the appearance of a deformed one, equates an invalid's long
neck to that of Hercules holding Antaeus[31] high above the earth, and admires a
squeaky voice that sounds like a hen's when she's pecked by her husband? We
can certainly praise the same things, but in their case, it's believed. Could an
actor do better when he plays the part of Thais,[32] or of a wife, or of a Greek girl
without her cloak? An actual woman, not an actor, seems to be speaking; you
would suppose that everything below the belly is empty and flat, with even a hint
of the cleft. But not even Antiochus, or Stratocles, or Demetrius, or the gentle
Haemus[33] will be admired there: it is a nation of actors. You smile, he's shaken
with laughter; if he sees his friend's tears, he weeps, though he's not grieving; if
you request a bit of fire in winter-time, he puts on his cloak; if you say 'I'm hot,'
he sweats. So we're not equal; he's better, who's always prepared, night or day,
to take his expression from someone else's face, to throw up his hands, ready to
applaud, if his friend gives a good belch or pisses straight, or if his golden basin
emits a gurgle when turned upside down.

And nothing is sacred, nothing safe, from his lust, not the matron of the
family, or the virginal daughter, not her smooth-faced fiancé, not even the still-
virtuous son; if there are none of these, he'll violate his friend's grandmother.
They want to learn the family's secrets, and thereby make themselves feared. And
since I'm speaking of Greeks, forget about the gymnasium, and hear of a crime of
a deeper philosophical cloak: the old Stoic informer who killed his friend and
student Barea[34] was raised on that river bank where the Gorgon's winged horse
fell.[35] There's no place for any Roman here, where some Protogenes rules, or
Diphilus, or Hermarchus, who, because of the defect of his race never shares a
friend, but keeps him to himself. For when he has dripped a little of his country's
natural poison into a pliant ear, I'm thrust from the door, and long years of
servitude go to waste; nowhere is a client so readily thrown away.

Besides, not to flatter ourselves, what's the point of a poor man conscien-
tiously hurrying along in his toga in the dark, seeing that the praetor is urging on
his lictor,[36] and ordering him to go full speed, in case his colleague should be the
first to salute the childless Albina and Modia, who've long since been awake?
Here the son of freeborn parents gives way to the rich man's slave; to thrash
about on top of Calvina or Catiena once or twice, he'll pay as much as legionary
tribunes receive, but you, if the face of a covered-up whore captures your fancy,
you're paralyzed, and hesitate to bring down Chione[37] from her lofty perch. Produce a witness at Rome as venerable as the host of the Idaean goddess;[38] Numa
might come forward, or he who saved trembling Minerva from the blazing shrine:[39]
the questioning will be first about his wealth, lastly about his character. 'How
many slaves does he maintain?' 'How much land does he own?' 'How many and
how large are his dessert-dishes?' A man has as much credibility as he has money
in his strong-box. Though he swears on our altars and those of Samothrace,[40] the

poor man is thought to disdain thunderbolts and the gods, the gods themselves forgiving him.

And what of the fact that this same man furnishes the material and occasion of laughter for everyone, if his cloak is dirty and torn, if his toga's a little stained, and one shoe lies open where the leather is split, or if it shows more than one patch freshly sewn with coarse thread? There's nothing about luckless poverty that's harder to bear than this – that it makes men ridiculous. 'Get out,' he says, 'if you have any shame; all those whose assets don't qualify under the law must vacate the knights' seats; here shall sit pimps' sons, born in some brothel or other; here a sleek auctioneer's son shall applaud, between the cultivated sons of a gladiator and a trainer's young men.' Such was the purpose of that empty-headed Otho who assigned us our places.[41] Who has been approved as a son-in-law here if he lacks wealth, and can't match the girl's dowry? What poor man is appointed an heir? When is he an adviser to the aediles? Poor Romans ought to have marched out together long ago. It's hardly easy for those whose merits are impeded by poverty to raise themselves up, but the effort is harder at Rome: you pay a great deal for miserable housing, to fill your slaves' bellies, for a frugal meal. You're ashamed to eat off earthenware, though you would deny it was unseemly if suddenly transported to the Marsi[42] and a Sabine table, where you'd be pleased with a coarse Venetian cloak.

There's a large part of Italy, if we tell the truth, in which no one puts on a toga unless dead. Even on festival days, if a splendid show is presented in some grassy theater, and the well-known concluding-piece returns to the stage, when the countrified infant on its mother's lap is frightened by the open mouth of the pale-colored actor, you'll see senators and ordinary people dressed alike, and powerful aediles content with white tunics as the uniform of their distinguished office. Here everyone dresses sharply, beyond his means, and sometimes something more than what's enough is lifted from someone else's money-box. This vice is universal – here we all live in ostentatious poverty. Why detain you? Everything at Rome has a price. What does it cost you to be able to pay your respects now and then to Cossus, or that Veiento should glance at you, with his little lip shut? That one is cutting off his beard; this one's getting rid of his lover's hair; the house is full of cakes for sale. Take one, and let this eat away at you: we clients are compelled to pay tribute and add to the allowances of dandified slaves.

Who is afraid of his house collapsing at cool Praeneste, or at Volsinii situated amid its wooded hills, or at honest Gabii, or on the sloping hills of Tibur?[43] But we inhabit a city held up for the most part by slender pillars; for that's how the overseer shores up what's slipping, and, when he's patched up the opening of an old fissure, encourages the inmates to sleep with disaster hanging over them. I must live where there are no fires, no alarms at night. Ucalegon is already shouting for water and removing his lousy furniture; already your third floor is smoking – you're unaware; for if the alarm is raised on the ground floor, he will burn last whom only the roof-tiles shelter from the rain, where the gentle doves lay their eggs. Codrus possessed a bed smaller than Procula's, a sideboard decorated with six little pitchers, and a tiny drinking-cup, and Chiron[44] recumbent below the marble, and an old chest containing Greek books whose divine songs were being gnawed by uneducated mice. Unlucky Codrus had nothing, it's true: yet he lost that whole nothing. And the final addition to his misery is that, destitute and begging, no one will help him with something to eat, or with lodging and shelter. But if Asturicus' grand house is destroyed, mothers go unkempt, nobles wear black, the praetor postpones bail-hearings: then we bemoan the calamities of the city, then we abhor fire. And while it's still burning someone runs up to donate marble or building-materials, another will offer nude and shining statues, or some famous work of Euphranor or Polyclitus, or antique ornaments of the Asian gods; another will offer books and book-cases, and a portrait of Minerva, or a quantity of silver. Persicus, most elegant of childless men, replaces what he's lost with more and better things, and so is suspected, deservedly, of having set his own house on fire.

If you can tear yourself away from the circus-games, you can buy an excellent house at Sora, or Fabrateria, or Frusino,[45] for what you now pay annually to rent a dark room. Here there's a little garden, and a shallow well from which water's easily drawn, without need of a rope, to irrigate the tender plants. You might live there, a friend of the hoe, steward of a well-tended garden, from which you could feast a hundred Pythagoreans.[46] It is something, in any place, however remote, to have made yourself the owner of a single lizard.

At Rome the sick die mainly from lack of sleep (the illness itself having been caused by undigested food stuck fast to a feverish stomach), for what sleep is possible in a boarding-house? Only the very wealthy get sleep in the city. That's the cause of the disease. The crossing of wagons in the narrow bend of streets, the cries of cattle forced to halt, would snatch sleep from a Drusus,[47] or a sea-calf. If duty calls, the rich man is carried through the parting crowd, rushing ahead on a huge Liburnian sedan,[48] and he reads along the way or writes or sleeps inside, for the sedan's closed window makes him drowsy. But he'll arrive before us; hurrying along, we're blocked by a wave of people in front, and the great multitude of those who follow bear down on my back: one man strikes me with his elbow, another with a hard sedan-pole; this one bangs a beam on my head, that one a wine-cask. My legs are splattered with mud; I'm trampled by giant feet on every side, and a soldier's nailed boot sticks in my toe.

Do you not see how much smoke attends that handout? There are a hundred guests, each accompanied by his own portable kitchen. Corbulo[49] could hardly bear the weight of the many huge vessels and other things which that unfortunate little slave is carrying on his head, fanning the fire as he runs along. Freshly patched tunics are torn apart; a long fir-tree sways on a wagon as it approaches, and another cart carries a pine-tree; they totter aloft and threaten the people. For if that wagon-axle carrying Ligurian stone breaks down, and rains an overturned mountain on the crowd, what's left of their bodies? Who will identify the limbs and the bones? A poor man's crushed body wholly disappears, like his spirit. Meanwhile, his household, unaware, is washing the dishes, blowing on the fire, rattling about with the greasy flesh-scrapers, filling the flasks, and folding the linen. The slaves are busily engaged in their various tasks, but he is sitting newly arrived on the bank, and shuddering at the grim ferryman: forsaken, he has no hope of crossing the muddy waters, no coin in his mouth to pay his fare.

Consider now the other and different dangers of the night – how far it is to that towering roof from which a potsherd comes crashing down on my head whenever someone throws some cracked and broken vessels out the window; with what a weighty smash they strike and dent the stone. You may be deemed a fool, unprepared for sudden accident, if you go to dinner without having made your will: there's death in every open window as you pass along at night. So you hope, and carry a pitiful prayer with you, that they're content to rain down their waste-basins. That drunken bully, who happens not to have killed anyone, pays the penalty, suffers through the night like Achilles mourning his friend, lying now on his face, and then on his back; he'll not be able to sleep otherwise – some men can only sleep after a fight. But though he's young and flushed with wine, he's wary of the man whose scarlet cloak and long train of attendants, armed with torches and brass lamps, command him to keep his distance. But he despises me, whom the moon is accustomed to escort, or the flickering light of a candle, whose wick I carefully manage. Hear how the miserable fight begins, if it is a fight, when you strike, and I get beaten. He blocks my way, and orders me to stop: I have to obey, for what can you do when attacked by a madman stronger than yourself? 'Where are you coming from?' he shouts, 'whose vinegar, whose mussels swell you? What cobbler's been eating chopped leek and boiled ram's lips with you? You won't answer me? Either speak or take the boot. Say, where do you hang out? In what prayer-house do I look for you?' Whether you dare to say anything, or silently retreat, it's the same – he'll beat you either way, and then angrily take your bail-money. This is the freedom of the poor man: pounded and punched, he begs and prays that he be allowed to leave there with a few teeth.

Yet these are not the only things you should fear. After your house is locked up, and your shop is barred and chained, and everything everywhere is silent, a burglar will rob you. Or perhaps a mugger will do the deed quickly with his sword; whenever the Pontine marshes and the Gallinarian forest[50] are secured by an armed guard, they all run here as if to a game-preserve. What furnace doesn't groan with the forging of chains? That's mostly what iron is used for: you may fear there won't be enough left for plowshares, and weeding-hooks, and hoes. Happy, you would say, were the ancestors of our great-grandfathers, happy the days when, under kings and tribunes, they beheld a Rome satisfied with one prison.

To these I could add more and different reasons, but my cattle call, and the sun is setting – I must go; my mule-driver has long been signaling to me with his whip. So farewell; remember me; and whenever you hurry back from Rome to your Aquinum to recuperate, summon me also from Cumae to your Helvine[51] Ceres and Diana. I'll come to your cold country in my boots to hear your satires, unless it would embarrass them."

4   HORACE, *SATIRES* 2.8

Quintus Horatius Flaccus was born in 65 BC at Venusia, a small town in southern Italy. His father, an ex-slave, later moved him to Rome, where Horace eventually became part of the literary circle patronized by Augustus' friend and adviser, Maecenas. Besides the *Satires* (discussed below), his surviving works include the *Epodes*, seventeen poems written in the period

42–31 BC in imitation of the Greek poet, Archilochus; the *Odes*, the first three books of which were published probably about 24–23, and which range over a great variety of topics, including love, death, and the human condition; the *Epistles*, conversational set-pieces, published probably in 20, that warn against greed, and extol, among other things, the virtues of the "simple life;" a hymn, the *Carmen saeculare*, written for Augustus' celebration of the Secular games in 17; and the *Art of Poetry*. He died in 8 BC.

The *Satires*, published probably in 30 BC, are broadly autobiographical reflections on life, literature, food, family, and friends. *Satire* 2.8 describes a dinner-party attended by Horace's friend Fundanius, at which Maecenas was the guest of honor. Most of the other guests, like Porcius, who eats like a "pig" (*porcus*), are probably imaginary; the host, Nasidienus Rufus, is not otherwise attested. The seating arrangements at the party are described in figure 1.3.

Horace. How did you enjoy your dinner with the wealthy Nasidienus? Yesterday, when I wanted your company, I was told you had been dining there since noon.

Fundanius. So much so that I've never in my life had a better time.

Horace. Tell me, if you don't mind, what dish first soothed your angry stomach?

Fundanius. First there was Lucanian[52] boar; it was captured when there was a gentle south wind, as the father of the meal kept saying; around it were pungent turnips, lettuces, radishes (such things as arouse a bored appetite), skirwort, fish-pickle, Coan[53] burnt tartar. When these were removed, a slave with his belt worn high wiped the maple-wood table with a purple cloth, and another removed the scraps and anything that might offend the guests. Then, like an Athenian maiden with the sacred vessels of Ceres, swarthy Hydaspes appears

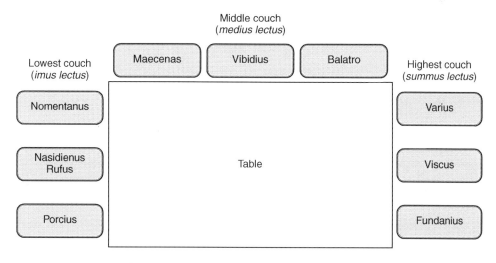

FIGURE 1.3   *The seating arrangements at Nasidienus Rufus' dinner-party (Horace, Satires 2.8).*

carrying Caecuban wine, and Alcon carrying Chian, unmixed with sea-water.[54] Then our host: "If Alban or Falernian is more to your taste, Maecenas, we have both."

Horace. The misery of wealth! But just who it was that dined with you so sumptuously, Fundanius, I'm eager to know.

Fundanius. I was at the top, and next to me Viscus of Thurii, and below, if I remember, Varius; Vibidius with Servilius Balatro, the shadows that Maecenas brought along. Nomentanus was above our host; Porcius below, who made us laugh by swallowing whole cakes at one bite. Nomentanus was there to point out with his index finger anything that might by chance go unnoticed; as for the rest of the crowd – we, I mean – we ate birds, oysters, fish, with a flavor much unlike anything we had experienced, as was made clear immediately, when he handed me liver of sparrow and turbot, which I'd not tasted before. After this he informed me that the honey-apples were red because they had been picked during a waning moon. What difference that makes, you'd learn better from him.

Then Vibidius said to Balatro, "Unless we drink him bankrupt, we shall die unavenged," and he demands larger goblets. Then paleness crossed our host's face, who feared nothing so much as ardent drinkers, either because they're more likely to speak abusively or because fiery wines dull a delicate palate. Vibidius and Balatro pour entire wine-flasks into Allifan goblets,[55] with everyone else following suit, except the guests on the lowest couch, who did no harm to the bottles.

Then a sea-fish is brought in, stretched out on a platter, surrounded by swimming shrimps. At this the host said: "This was caught before spawning; its flesh would otherwise be poorer. The recipe for the sauce is this: oil, of the first pressing at Venafrum;[56] fish-sauce from the juices of the Spanish mackerel; five-year-old wine, born this side of the sea, added while it's cooking (after cooking, there's no wine more suitable than Chian); white pepper; and vinegar, made from the fermenting of Lesbian[57] grapes. I was the first to demonstrate that you should add green cole-wort and bitter elecampane; Curtillus prefers unwashed sea-urchins, believing that the product of sea-shellfish is better than brine."

Meanwhile the canopy hanging over us fell with a weighty crash on the platter, trailing more black dust than the north wind stirs up on the fields of Campania. We were afraid of a greater disaster, but cheered up when we realized there was no further danger. Rufus wept, with his head down, as if his young son had died. That would have been the end, if Nomentanus, the wise, had not thus rallied his friend: "Ah, Fortune, what god is crueler to us than you. How you enjoy making sport of human affairs." Varius could hardly stifle a laugh with his napkin. Balatro, who thumbs his nose at everything, said: "This is the condition of life: the reward of fame is never equal to your labor. Consider that, in order to receive me lavishly, you are tortured and torn with every concern, that the bread not be burned, that the sauce not be served badly-seasoned, that all the slaves be properly dressed and neatly waiting.

Consider also these risks – that the canopy might collapse, as it did just a moment ago; that some lackey might trip and break a dish. But a host is like a general: adversity often reveals his genius, prosperity hides it." To this, Nasidienus replied: "May the gods grant you whatever favors you request; you are such a good man, and agreeable guest;" and he calls for his slippers. Then on each couch you would have noticed the buzz of whispers secretly exchanged.

Horace. There's no show that I would have preferred to see; but, come, tell me, what made you laugh next?

Fundanius. While Vibidius is asking the slaves whether the wine-flask was also broken, since cups weren't given to him when he asked, and while we were laughing at pretenses, egged on by Balatro, you return, Nasidienus, with forehead altered, as if intending to correct misfortune by art. Servants then followed, carrying on a giant dish the limbs of a crane, sprinkled with a lot of salt and some spelt, and the liver of a white goose raised on rich figs, and hares' limbs torn off, as being much more sophisticated than if one were to eat them with the loins. Then we saw blackbirds served with the breast singed, and pigeons without rumps – sophisticated treats, if the owner hadn't gone on describing their natures and properties. But we got our revenge by fleeing, without tasting anything at all, as if Canidia[58] had breathed on them, more deadly than African serpents.

5 DIODORUS OF SICILY, *HISTORICAL LIBRARY* 34.2

Diodorus was born in Sicily about 80 BC; he died sometime after 21. His *Historical Library*, of which Books 1–5 and 11–20 survive intact, is a rather pedestrian world history from mythological times to 54 BC. Book 34 is partially preserved, in a summary made of it by Photius, patriarch of Constantinople in the ninth century AD, and in a number of excerpts collected by Constantine VII (or Constantine Porphyrogenitus), a tenth-century Byzantine emperor. Chapter 2 (below) describes the course of a slave rebellion which began in Sicily in 135 BC, and lasted until 132, when it was crushed by the Roman army (the sources record two other large-scale rebellions, a second uprising in Sicily, 104–101 BC, and a revolt in Italy led by Spartacus, 73–71 BC). Diodorus' account is based largely on that of the Stoic philosopher Posidonius (ca. 135–50 BC), whose *Histories* survive only in fragments.

   The translation is from T. Wiedemann, *Greek and Roman Slavery* (Baltimore and London, 1981), pp. 200–7.

(Constantine Porphyrogenitus, exc. 2 (1), pp. 302f.) . . . . No civil conflict was ever so great as that of the slaves which took place in Sicily. Many cities suffered terrible catastrophes in the course of this conflict, and countless men, women and children experienced the greatest misfortunes, and there was a danger that the whole island might come under the control of the runaways. The only standard they set themselves for the exercise of their power was that it should cause the maximum harm to the free population. For most people these occurrences were surprising and unexpected; but for anyone able to judge things realistically they didn't appear to arise without due cause. Because of the extreme prosperity of the people who enjoyed the natural products of this very great island, almost everyone as he got richer adopted first a luxurious, and then an arrogant and provocative pattern of behavior. As a result of these developments, slaves were coming to be treated worse and worse, and were correspondingly more and more alienated from their owners. When a suitable opportunity occurred, this hatred broke out into the open. Consequently, many tens of thousands of slaves rallied together to destroy their masters without any need for incitement.

. . . . All the men who owned a lot of land bought up entire consignments of slaves to work their farms; . . . some were bound with chains, some were worn out by the hard work they were given to do; they branded all of them with humiliating brand-marks. As a result, such a huge number of slaves flooded the whole of Sicily that those who heard it thought it exaggerated and unbelievable. The Sicilians who controlled all this wealth were competing in arrogance, greed, and injustice with the Italians. Those Italians who owned a lot of slaves had accustomed their herdsmen to irresponsible behavior to such an extent that instead of providing them with rations they encouraged them to rob. This freedom was given to men who because of their physical power were able to put into practice anything they planned to do, men who because of under-employment and leisure could make the most of their opportunities, men who because of their lack of food were forced into risky undertakings; and this soon led to an increase in the crime-rate. They started by killing people who were traveling alone or in pairs in particularly out-of-the-way places. Then they got together in groups and attacked the farms of the weak by night, plundering their property and killing those who resisted. They became more and more bold, and Sicily was no longer passable for travelers at night. It ceased to be safe for those who had been living in the countryside to stay there; every place was affected by violence and robbery and murder of every kind. But because the herdsmen were used to living out in the open and were equipped like soldiers, they were (not surprisingly) full of courage and arrogance. They carried around clubs and spears and hefty sticks and wore the skins of wolves or wild boars, so their appearance was frightening and in itself not much less than a provocation to violence. A pack of trusty hounds accompanied each of them, and the great amount of milk and meat which was available for consumption dehumanized their minds as well as their bodies. So the whole country was, as it were, occupied by scattered groups of soldiers, since under their owners' maladministration these dangerous slaves had been armed. The governors did try to control the fury of the slaves, but because they didn't dare to punish them because of the power and importance of their masters, they were forced to overlook the fact that the province was being plundered. . . .

(Photius, *Bibliotheca*, p. 384) The slaves were exhausted by the hardships they had to put up with, and humiliated by beatings which were often quite unjustified. They could not take any more. They got together when they had the chance and talked about revolting, and in the end they put their plan into effect. Antigenes of Enna[59] owned a house-slave who was a Syrian by race, from Apamea. This man was something of a magician and wonder-worker. He pretended that he could foretell the future by means of commands that came to him from the gods when he was asleep, and because he was so good at this he managed to deceive a lot of people. He went on from there and didn't just prophesy on the basis of dreams, but even pretended to have visions of the gods while awake and hear from them what was going to happen. Of the many fantasies he invented some happened to come true. Since no one refuted those that didn't, while those that did turn out true were widely acclaimed, his reputation increased enormously. In the end he would produce fire and flame from his mouth while in a trance, by means of a trick of some sort, and in this way produce inspired utterances about the future. What he did was put some fire and the fuel needed to keep it going inside a walnut or something similar which had had holes bored into it at both ends; then he would put it into his mouth and breathe and thus produce sparks or even a flame.

Before the revolt he said that the Syrian goddess was appearing to him and promising him that he was going to be a king. He insisted on repeating this not just to others but even to his own master. The thing was treated as a joke, and Antigenes, bewitched by his marvelous trick, introduced Eunous to his dinner guests (that was the wizard's name) and asked him all about his kingdom and what his policy would be towards each of the people present. He had no hesitation in explaining the details, stating that he would have a very moderate policy towards the owners of slaves and generally producing an amazingly entertaining story, so that the guests were amused and some of them would take considerable portions of food from the table and give them to him, asking that when he became king he should remember the favor they were doing him. But indeed his magic-working had reserved a genuine kingship for him in the stars, and the favors received as a joke at these dinners were reciprocated under conditions which were serious indeed. The insurrection as a whole began like this.

(Constantine Porphyrogenitus, exc. 2 (1), p. 304) There was a citizen of Enna called Damophilos who was both extremely wealthy and extremely arrogant. He cultivated a huge area of land which he filled with herds of cattle owned by him and competed with the Italians living in Sicily not only as regards his luxurious lifestyle but also the number of his slaves and the harshness and inhumanity with which he treated them. He would proceed about the countryside accompanied by a retinue of expensive horses and four-wheeled carts and a paramilitary escort formed by his own slaves. In addition, he thought it very prestigious to have lots of beautiful boys and a crowd of uneducated hangers-on. Both at Enna and in his country houses he insisted on displaying his great wealth of embossed silverware and purple carpets, and served huge meals which were provocative and more suitable for kings; in terms of the expense and waste he surpassed the luxuriousness of Orientals. So did his arrogance. Here was a man who was totally uneducated, in possession of power without responsibility together with vast wealth, and it first made him bored, then made him behave insolently towards others, and in the end destroyed him and brought horrible disasters upon his country.

He bought large numbers of slaves and treated them in a humiliating way, marking with branding irons the bodies of men who had been of free birth in their own countries and experienced the misfortune of capture in war and enslavement. He bound some of them with chains and threw them into his prisons, and he appointed others as herdsmen without providing them with appropriate clothes or rations. Because of his willful and savage character, there wasn't a single day on which this same Damophilos didn't torture some of his slaves without just cause. His wife Me(g)allis took equal pleasure in these insolent punishments and treated her maids and those slaves who were under her jurisdiction with great brutality. The slaves developed the feelings of wild beasts towards their masters as a result of these humiliating punishments, and thought that nothing that could happen to them would be worse than the evil state they were in.

(Constantine Porphyrogenitus, exc. 3, pp. 206–7) The slaves got together to consider rebellion and the murder of their master and mistress. They went to Eunous, who lived nearby, and asked him whether their plan had the approval of the gods. He made a show of being divinely inspired and asked them why they had come, and pronounced that the gods would grant them their revolt if they didn't delay but put their plans into effect immediately. For Fate had decreed that Enna, the citadel of the whole island, should be their State. When they heard this they assumed that the spirit world was behind them in their undertaking, and their emotions were so intent on rebellion that nothing could delay their plans. So they immediately set free those slaves who were chained up and got together those of the others who were living nearby. About four hundred of them assembled in a field near Enna. They made a solemn agreement amongst themselves and exchanged oaths on the strength of nocturnal sacrifices, and then armed themselves as well as the occasion permitted. They all seized the most effective weapon of all, fury, directed towards the destruction of the master and mistress who had humiliated them. Eunous led them. Shouting to each other in encouragement they broke into the city about the middle of the night and killed many people.

(Photius, *Bibliotheca*, pp. 384–6) Eunous was leading them and working the miracle of the flames of fire to encourage them. They broke into the houses and committed much bloodshed; not even babes in arms were spared – they tore them from the breast and dashed them against the ground. I can't say how they humiliated and outraged the women, even in the sight of their husbands. A large number of slaves from inside the city joined them; they first did their worst to their masters and then turned to the slaughter of others. When Eunous' group heard that Damophilos was staying in an orchard near the city together with his wife, they sent some of their number to drag him and his wife away from there, with their hands tied behind their backs; they had to put up with all sorts of insults along the way.

(Constantine Porphyrogenitus, exc. 2 (1), p. 305) . . . . Damophilos had a grown-up but unmarried daughter, who had an extremely decent and humane character. She always used to be kind and comfort anyone her parents had whipped and help those slaves who had been chained up, and because she was so nice, she was extraordinarily popular with everybody. At this moment her previous kindness brought her unexpected help in the shape of those she had been kind to: not only did no one dare to lay a finger on the girl to humiliate her, but they all made sure that her virginity would remain untouched. They selected some suitable men from amongst themselves, including her particular friend Hermias, and escorted her to some relatives at (Catina).[60]

(Photius, *Bibliotheca*, pp. 385f.) . . . . Those who had been sent to get Damophilos and Megallis dragged them into the city and brought them to the theater, where the mass of insurgents had gathered together. Damophilos made an attempt to trick them into keeping him safe and was winning over many of the crowd with what he was saying. Hermias and Zeuxis hated him bitterly; they called him a deceiver, and instead of waiting for the formality of conviction by the People, one of them pushed a sword into his chest, the other struck his neck with an axe. Next, Eunous was elected king. This was not because he was particularly courageous or able as a commander, but simply because of his wonder-working and because he had started the revolt off, and also because his name seemed to symbolize that he would be well disposed towards those who would be subject to him. . . . Established as lord of the rebels in all matters, he summoned an assembly and killed off the people from Enna who had been captured, except for those who were skilled at making weapons; he forced these to carry out their work in chains. He gave Megallis to the female slaves to treat as they saw fit; they tortured her and threw her over a cliff. He personally killed his master and mistress, Antigenes and Python.

(Constantine Porphyrogenitus, exc. 2 (1), p. 305) . . . . There was also another insurrection by runaway slaves who concentrated in considerable numbers. There was a Cilician from the area of the Taurus mountains called Kleon, who was used to living as a bandit from childhood and had become a herder of horses in Sicily, but continued to commit highway robbery and murder of every kind. When he heard about Eunous' progress and the successes of the slaves with him, he revolted, persuaded some nearby slaves to share his madness and overran the city of Akragas[61] and the countryside round about.

(Photius, *Bibliotheca*, p. 386) Everyone had high hopes that the rival groups of slaves would start fighting amongst themselves so that by destroying each other the rebels would rid Sicily of the revolt. But they unexpectedly combined; at a bare word from Eunous, Kleon placed himself under his command and behaved towards him as a general would towards his king. He had a personal following of about five thousand soldiers. This happened about thirty days after the insurrection. Soon after, the rebels fought against Lucius Hypsaeus, who had been sent out from Rome as governor and had eight thousand soldiers from Sicily itself. They had twenty thousand troops, and were victorious. In a short time they managed to concentrate a force of up to two hundred thousand, and they were successful in many battles against the Romans and were rarely beaten. When news of this got around, a conspiracy of a hundred and fifty slaves was hatched at Rome, one of over a thousand in Attica, and others at Delos and in many other places. But in each place the authorities of the local communities quickly suppressed the insurrection by acting swiftly and inflicting harsh punishments; so they restrained anybody who was on the point of revolting. But in Sicily the situation continued to deteriorate.

(Constantine Porphyrogenitus, exc. 4, pp. 384f.) Eunous stationed his forces out of range of their missiles and directed insults at the Romans: it was not they, he pointed out, but the Romans who were runaways – runaways from danger. From some distance away, he put on a show of mimes for those in the city, in which the slaves performed the story of how they had revolted from their own particular masters, reproaching them for the arrogance and inordinate pride which was now leading them to their destruction. . . . The citizen masses not only failed to sympathize with (the rich), but on the contrary rejoiced because they were jealous at inequalities of wealth and differences in lifestyle. Their jealousy turned from the dumb grief it had previously been into open joy when they saw how the good fortune [of the wealthy] had been changed into a condition which would previously have been treated with utter contempt by the same people. What was most terrifying was that the insurgents were intelligent enough to think about the future and didn't set fire to farm buildings or destroy the equipment they contained or the harvests which had been stored there, and didn't touch any of the people working in agriculture; but the free masses, because of their jealousy, would go out into the countryside on the pretext of attacking the runaways and plunder the property there, and even burn down the farms.

(Photius, *Bibliotheca*, p. 386) Cities and their entire populations were captured and many armies were destroyed by the insurgents, until the Roman governor Rupilius[62] recaptured Taormina[63] for the Romans. He had besieged it so effectively that conditions of unspeakable and extreme hunger had been forced upon the insurgents – so that they began by eating their children, then their womenfolk, and in the end, they didn't even hesitate to eat each other. . . . In the end the Syrian Serapion betrayed the citadel and the governor was able to bring under his control all the runaways in the city. He tortured them and then threw them over a cliff. From there he went on to Enna, which he besieged in the same way; he forced the rebels to see that their hopes had come to a dead end. Their commander Kleon came out of the city and fought heroically with a few men until the Romans were able to display his corpse covered with wounds. This city too they captured through treachery, since it couldn't be taken by even the most powerful army. Eunous took his bodyguard of a thousand men and fled in a cowardly fashion to a region where there were lots of cliffs. But the men with him realized that they could not avoid their fate, since the governor Rupilius was already driving towards them, and they beheaded each other with their swords. The wonder-worker Eunous, the king who had fled through cowardice, was dragged out from the caves where he was hiding with four attendants – a cook, a baker, the man who massaged him in the bath, and a fourth who used to entertain him when he was drinking. He was put under guard; his body was eaten up by a mass of lice, and he ended his days at (Murgantia)[64] in a manner appropriate to his villainy. Afterwards Rupilius marched across the whole of Sicily with a few selected soldiers and freed it from every trace of brigandage sooner than anyone expected.

6   *L'Année Épigraphique* 1971, 88

The following stone inscription, the first part of which is fragmentary, dates probably to the first century AD. It is from the town of Puteoli (mod. Puzzuoli), a Roman colony on the coast of Campania, and a favorite resort of wealthy Romans. It describes the regulations that governed the conduct of funerals, which were normally carried out by professional undertakers, who could also be hired to torture or execute slaves, either by order of a court or at their owner's request. The translation is from J. F. Gardner and T. Wiedemann, *The Roman Household: A Sourcebook* (London and New York, 1991), pp. 24–6.

Then to the contractor or to his partner, as often as anyone shall throw out [a corpse unburied(?)], he shall pay a fine of sixty sesterces[65] per body, and the magistrate shall enforce judgment for recovery of this sum in accordance with the law of the colony.

The workforce which shall be provided for this undertaking is not to live on this side of the tower where the grove of Libitina[66] stands today. They are to take their bath after the first hour of the night. They are to enter the town only for the purpose of collecting or disposing of corpses, or inflicting punishment, and on condition that whenever any of them enters or is in the town, then he is to wear on his head a distinctive cap. None of them is to be over fifty years of age or under twenty, nor have any sores, nor be one-eyed, maimed, lame, blind, or branded. The contractor is to have no fewer than thirty-two operatives.

If anyone wishes to have a slave – male or female – punished privately, he who wishes to have the punishment inflicted shall do so as follows. If he wants to put the slave on the cross or fork, the contractor must supply the posts, chains, ropes for floggers, and the floggers themselves. The person having the punishment inflicted is to pay four sesterces for each of the operatives who carry the fork, and the same for the floggers and for the executioner.

The magistrate shall give orders for such punishments as he exacts in his public capacity, and when orders are given (the contractor) is to be ready to exact the punishment. He is to set up crosses and supply without charge nails, pitch, wax, tapers, and anything else that is necessary for this in order to deal with the condemned man. Again, if he is ordered to drag away the corpse with a hook, the work-gang is to be dressed in red and ring a bell while dragging away the body, or bodies if there are several.

Anyone who wishes any of the services listed in this regulation to be provided is to notify, or have notification made to the public contractor, or to his associate, or to the person responsible for the matter concerned, or, if he shall not be present, to such premises as he shall have hired or established for the conduct of the work of funeral director, as to the day, place, and nature of the service he wishes to have performed. Once notification is made, then the contractor or his associate or the person responsible shall carry out the commission for the person giving notice first, and then for the rest in order of receipt of notice, unless notice is received for the funeral of a decurion, or for a mass funeral. These are to be given precedence. . . .

If a commission is given [to remove] a hanged man, he (the contractor) is to see to its fulfillment and the removal (of the body) within the hour. If it is for a male or female slave, if the notification is received before the tenth hour, removal is to be effected the same day; if after the tenth hour, then before the second hour on the following day. . . .

7 PETRONIUS, *SATYRICON*

The author of the *Satyricon* is probably the same Petronius who is said by Tacitus (*Annals* 16.18) to have been the "arbiter of elegance" at the court of the emperor Nero (and to have "idled into fame"). He also wrote poetry, a small collection of which survives. The *Satyricon*, which is only partially preserved, recounts the adventures of three rather dissolute young men, a Greek freedman named Encolpius, who is the narrator, his boyfriend, Giton, and Ascyltos, with whom Encolpius frequently quarrels. The surviving story opens with the three somewhere in Italy (moderns have suggested Cumae or Puteoli), discussing declamation with Agamemnon, a teacher of rhetoric. All four are later invited to a fantastically extravagant dinner at the home of a wealthy, boorish, and comically vulgar ex-slave named Trimalchio. After relaxing in his private baths, they are brought to the door of the dining-room.

(28) . . . . A notice was attached to the door-post, with this inscription: "Any slave who goes outside without the master's permission will receive one hundred lashes." In the entrance-way itself stood a door-keeper in leek-green clothes, with a cherry-colored belt, shelling peas in a silver plate. Above the doorway hung a golden cage; a black and white magpie in it saluted those entering. (29) While I was staring at all this in wonder, I almost fell backwards and broke my leg. For on the wall on the left side of the entrance-way, not far from the door-keeper's room, there was a painting of a huge dog, tied up with a chain, and above it was written, in block letters, "BEWARE OF THE DOG." My friends laughed at me, but I caught my breath and continued to examine the whole wall. There was a painting of a slave-auction, with labels, and Trimalchio himself, with long hair, holding a staff of Mercury; Minerva was leading him into Rome. The painstaking artist had gone on to show, in detail, and with written comments, how Trimalchio had learned to make calculations, and how, finally, he had been made superintendent of the household. . . .

(30) We now went into the dining-room; inside the steward was receiving accounts. What I found especially astonishing was that *fasces*,[67] with axes, were attached to the door-posts of the dining-room, one part of them completed by a kind of bronze ship's beak, on which was written: "To Gaius Pompeius Trimalchio, priest of the college of Augustus, Cinnamus, superintendent of the household." Below it, a double lamp hung from the ceiling, and there were writing-tablets attached to each door-post, one of which, if I remember rightly, had this message: "On December 30th and 31st, our C. goes out to eat;" the other depicted the course of the moon, and the likenesses of the seven stars.[68] . . . . Full of these pleasures, we were trying to get into the dining-room, when one of the slaves, who had been assigned this duty, cried out, "With the right foot!" We were, for a moment, undeniably anxious, in case any of us had crossed the threshold contrary to the rules. But as we were all moving our right feet forward to go in, a naked slave fell at our feet, and began to beg us to save him from punishment: it was not a great sin that had put him in danger; the steward's clothes, which were hardly worth ten sesterces, had been stolen from him in the bath. So we withdrew our right feet, and pleaded with the steward, who was counting gold pieces in the entrance-way, to let the slave off. He looked up arrogantly, and said, "It's

not the loss that bothers me so much as the negligence of the wretched slave. He lost my dinner-clothes, which a client gave me on my birthday, Tyrian,[69] of course, but already washed once. What shall I do then? I give him to you."

(31) . . . . At last we sat down. Slave-boys from Alexandria poured snow-cooled water over our hands; others followed, knelt at our feet, and with great skill removed the abscesses under our toenails. And even at this unpleasant task, they were not silent, but kept singing as they worked. I wanted to find out whether the whole household sang, so I asked for a drink. A slave promptly repeated my request in a chant no less shrill; each of them did the same when asked to supply anything – you would have thought it was the chorus of a pantomime, not a gentleman's dining-room. But hearty and sumptuous hors d'œuvres arrived; for by now we had all sat down, except Trimalchio, for whom the first place was being reserved, in the new fashion. A donkey of Corinthian bronze had been placed on the relish-tray, with baskets holding white olives on one side, black on the other. The donkey was hidden by two plates, on the edges of which Trimalchio's name was engraved, and their weight in silver. Little bridges glued to the plate held dormice sprinkled with honey and poppy-seed; there were also hot sausages on a silver grill, and below it, Syrian plums and seeds of Punic apple. (32) We were busy with these luxuries, when Trimalchio himself was brought in, to the accompaniment of music, propped up on tiny pillows; a laugh escaped the imprudent, for his shaved head poked out of a scarlet cloak, and around his heavily draped neck he had placed a napkin with a broad purple stripe, and with fringes dangling from it all around. He also had a huge gold-plated ring on the little finger of his left hand, and, on the top joint of the next finger, a smaller one, which seemed to me to be entirely of gold, but was actually held together by what looked like iron stars. And so as not to display only these riches, he uncovered his right arm, which gleamed with a golden bracelet, to which an ivory hoop was connected by a shining piece of metal. . . .

More music follows, accompanied by wine and fantastic food. Trimalchio sings (badly), while his wife Fortunata bustles about the dining-room.

(37) I couldn't eat any more, so I turned to my neighbor to learn as much as I could: I proceeded to ask for far-fetched stories, and to enquire who that woman was who kept running around all over the place. "Trimalchio's wife," he said; "her name's Fortunata, and she counts her money by the *modius*.[70] And a little while ago, what was she? Forgive me: you would not have wanted to take bread from that woman's hand. Now, without rhyme or reason, she's gone to heaven, and is Trimalchio's everything. In fact, if she told him it was dark at noon, he'd believe it. He's so rich, he himself doesn't know what he has; but this wolf-bitch pays attention to everything, and even where you wouldn't expect it. She's sober, sensible, and prudent; but she has a wicked tongue – a magpie on the couch. Whom she likes, he likes; whom she doesn't like, he doesn't like. Trimalchio himself has estates wherever kites fly; he's richest of the rich. There's more silver lying in that door-keeper's room than anyone else has altogether. But his slaves! My god! I don't believe a tenth of them would recognize their own master. In fact, he could knock any one of those pretty boys he chooses into a rue-bed.

(38) And don't think that he buys anything. Everything's produced at home: wool, citrons, pepper; you'll get hen's milk, if you ask. When his wool wasn't good enough, he bought rams from Tarentum[71] and insinuated them into his flock. So that Attic honey could be produced at home, he ordered bees to be imported from Athens; the home-born bees, you see, will be improved a little by the Greek ones. And just in the last few days, he arranged for mushroom-stock to be sent from India. He doesn't have a single mule that isn't the offspring of a wild ass. You see all the cushions here: every one has purple or scarlet stuffing. Such is the felicity of his spirit. And don't look down on the others who are his fellow-freedmen. They are very succulent. See that one lying at the bottom of the lowest couch: he already has his 800,000. He grew from nothing. Just recently he was accustomed to carrying wood on his back. People say – I know nothing, but I've heard – that he snatched the cap off a goblin, and found its treasure. I envy no one, if the god has given him something. Still, he's subject to the slap,[72] and thinks highly of himself. And so he's put up this notice next to his shack: 'This attic is for rent from Gaius Pompeius Diogenes, beginning the 1st of July; for he has bought a house.' And that man who's lying in the freedman's spot is very pleased with himself. I don't blame him. He had his million sesterces, but he's been badly shaken. I don't think his hair's free from debt. Not his fault, by god! There's not a better man than him. But these damned freedmen have taken everything for themselves. You know how it is: a company's pot boils poorly, and just as soon as business declines, your friends are gone. You see him in this condition: and what an honorable profession he practiced! He was an undertaker. He used to eat like a king: boars wrapped in cloth, pastries, birds, chefs, and pastry-cooks. More wine was spilled under his table than anyone else has in his cellar. He was a notion, not a real man. And when his business was failing, and he was afraid that his creditors would think he was going bankrupt, he posted up this notice of an auction: 'Gaius Julius Proculus will offer for sale some items for which he has no further use.'"

Trimalchio discourses on astrology, then leaves with a stomach-ache. The guests talk excitedly, until he returns.

(47) . . . . Trimalchio came in, wiping his forehead, and washed his hands in perfume. After a short pause, he said, "Forgive me, friends; my bowels have been malfunctioning for many days. The doctors are at a loss. Still, pomegranate rind has helped me, and pine-wood boiled in vinegar. I hope now my stomach recovers its old modesty. Anyhow, with the noises it makes, you'd think there was a bull there. So if any of you wants to do his personal business, there's no reason to be ashamed. None of us is born solid. I think there's no greater torture than to hold it in. This is the one thing not even Jupiter can forbid. You laugh, Fortunata, you who routinely keep me awake at night? Of course, I don't forbid anyone to relieve himself in the dining-room; the doctors prohibit us from holding it in. But if something more is coming, everything's ready outside: water, chamber-pots, and the other little things. Believe me, vapors go to the brain, and cause a commotion throughout the body. I know many have died this way, unwilling to tell themselves the truth." We thanked him for his generosity and kindness, and then

suppressed our laughter by drinking quickly. We didn't yet realize that we were still in the middle of the luxuries, and that we were, as they say, working up-hill. . . .

(48) Trimalchio looked at us with a gentle expression and said, "If you don't like the wine, I'll change it. You'll admit that it's good. With the gods' kindness, I don't buy it: whatever's making you salivate is produced on a country estate with which I'm still not familiar. It's said to be on the boundary between Tarracina[73] and Tarentum. Now I want to join Sicily to my estates, so that when I decide to go to Africa, I'll travel through my own property. . . . " (49) He still had more to say, when the table was filled with a dish holding a giant pig. . . . Trimalchio, looking at it more and more closely, said, "What? What? Has this pig not been gutted? By god, it hasn't been. Call the cook in here." When the poor cook had arrived, he stood near the table, and said that he had forgotten to gut it. "What? Forgotten?" Trimalchio shouted; "you'd think he hadn't included the pepper and cumin. Strip him!" Immediately, the slave is stripped; he stands, despondent, between two executioners. But we all begin to intercede for him, saying, "Things happen; we beg you to let him go; if he does it again, none of us will speak up for him." Feeling very stern and severe, I couldn't restrain myself, but leaned over to Agamemnon, and said, "This slave must be hopeless; how does anyone forget to gut a pig? I sure as hell wouldn't forgive him, if he'd over-looked a fish that way." But not Trimalchio; his face softening into a smile, he said, "Well, since your memory's so bad, gut it here in front of us." The cook put his tunic back on, grabbed a knife, and, with a trembling hand, sliced the pig's belly in several places. Immediately, the incisions widened because of the pres-sure from inside, and out poured sausages and black puddings. (50) At this the slaves spontaneously applauded, and shouted, "Good fortune to Gaius!". . . .

Trimalchio discusses Corinthian plate; later a slave-boy who is about to be punished for drop-ping a cup is rescued by the intervention of the guests.

(52) . . . . Then Trimalchio shouted, "Out with water, in with wine!" We told jokes, especially Agamemnon, who knew what qualities would win him another invitation to dinner. Flattered, Trimalchio drank merrily, and soon, almost drunk, said, "Will none of you ask my Fortunata to dance? Believe me: no one dances the *cordax*[74] better." Then, with his hands held above his forehead, he imitated the actor Syrus, while all the slaves sang together: "Madeia! Perimadeia!"[75] And he would have gone into the middle of the room if Fortunata hadn't whispered in his ear. I imagine she told him that such abject foolishness was not in keeping with his importance. However, nothing was so changeable; at one moment he was afraid of Fortunata, and then he'd be restored to his true nature. (53) Now an accountant completely interrupted his passion for the dancing, by reading, as if from the city's register: "July 26th: thirty boys and forty girls were born on the estate at Cumae,[76] which belongs to Trimalchio; 500,000 *modii* of wheat were removed from the threshing-floor to the barn; 500 cattle were domesticated. On the same day: the slave Mithridates was led to crucifixion because he had slan-dered the spirit of our Gaius. On the same day: 10,000,000 sesterces which could not be invested were returned to the strong-box. On the same day: there was a

fire in the gardens at Pompeii, originating in the house of the bailiff, Nasta."
"What?" said Trimalchio, "when were gardens purchased for me at Pompeii?"
"Last year," the accountant said, "so they've not yet made it into the records."
Trimalchio glowed, and said, "I won't allow any property purchased for me to
be entered into my accounts unless I learn of it within six months." And now
decrees of the aediles were recited, and some stewards' wills, which contained a
clause disinheriting Trimalchio; then the names of bailiffs, and of a freedwoman
who had been caught in the act with a bath-attendant, and divorced by her husband, a watchman; and the name of a porter who had been banished to Baiae;[77]
then the name of a steward who was being prosecuted, and a lawsuit between
some chamber-servants. . . .

*Trimalchio is injured (but not badly hurt) in an accident involving some performing acrobats.
After a discussion about poetry, gifts are distributed to the guests. An argument ensues, which
is mediated by Trimalchio. Experts are then brought in to recite Homer.*

(60) . . . . Suddenly the ceiling began to rumble, and the whole dining-room shook.
I got up in a panic: I was afraid some acrobat was about to come down through
the roof. The other guests sat up with equal astonishment on their faces, wondering what new marvel was being announced from the heavens. Then suddenly, the
ceiling separated, and an enormous hoop, which appeared to have been hammered out of a giant cask, was let down; hanging all around it were golden crowns
and boxes of perfume. While we were being told to take these as presents, I
looked back at the table. . . . A plate with some cakes on it had now been placed
there. A Priapus[78] made by the pastry-chef was in the middle; in the conventional
style, it was holding fruit and grapes of every kind in its more than ample lap. We
greedily reached for the display, and the unexpected new fun restored our merri-
ment. For all the cakes and all the fruits, even at the slightest touch, began to
pour out saffron, and the annoying juice shot into our faces. Thinking, therefore,
that only a sacred dish would have been anointed with such holy material, we all
stood up straight, and said, "Good fortune to Augustus, father of his country."
But some grabbed the fruit even after this solemn event, and we filled our napkins with them, myself especially, because I thought that I could not fill Giton's
lap with too large a present. Meanwhile three slave-boys came in wearing belted
white tunics: two of them placed images of the *Lares*[79] with amulets around their
necks on the table; one carried around a bowl of wine and shouted, "May the
gods be propitious!". . . . (61) . . . . Trimalchio looked at Niceros and said, "You
used to be more agreeable at dinner; I don't know what it is that's made you silent.
Please, for my sake, tell us what happened to you." Delighted by his friend's kindness, Niceros said, "May every opportunity for profit pass me by, if I'm not bursting with joy to see you this way. So it will be an unmitigated pleasure, though I fear
that those rhetoricians of yours will laugh at me. Let them; I'll tell the story anyway, for what harm does it do me for someone to laugh? It's better to be laughed
at than sneered at." When he had said this, he began the following story:

"While I was still a slave, we were living in a narrow street; now it's the home of
Gavilla. There, as the gods willed it, I fell in love with the wife of the inn-keeper,

Terentius; you knew her – Melissa of Tarentum, a very pretty berry.[80] But I swear that I cared for her, not physically, or for sex, but because she was of noble character. If I asked her for anything, it was never denied me; if she made any money, I got half; whatever I had, I entrusted to her, and I was never deceived. Then her husband died in the country. And so I put on my shield and leg-guards, and planned how I might approach her; as you know, friends show up in tight places. (62) It happened that my owner had gone to Capua[81] to take care of business. Seizing the opportunity, I persuaded our house-guest to come with me to the fifth milestone. He was a soldier, as brave as Orcus.[82] So we headed off about the time the cock crows; the moon was shining as it if was noon. We came to some monuments: my man began to do his business near the gravestones; I sat down singing, and counted the gravestones. Then, as I looked back at my companion, he stripped and put all of his clothes beside the road. My heart was in my nose; I stood like a zombie. He urinated around his clothes, and suddenly turned into a wolf. Don't think I'm joking; there's no inheritance large enough to make me lie. But as I had started to say, after he had turned into a wolf, he began to howl, and ran off into the woods. At first, I didn't know where I was; then I went to gather up his clothes, but they had turned to stone. Could anyone be more frightened to death than I was? But I pulled out my sword and killed shadows all along the road, until I arrived at my girlfriend's country-house. I went in like a ghost, nearly breathed out my life; the sweat ran down my face; my eyes were lifeless; I could hardly be revived. My Melissa was astonished that I was out walking so late, and said, 'If you'd come earlier, at least you could have helped us. A wolf got on the property, and attacked all the cattle; it spilled their blood like a butcher. Still, it didn't make fools of us, even though it did get away, for our slave pierced its neck with a spear.' When I heard this, I couldn't shut my eyes any longer, but at first light I fled to the home of our Gaius like an inn-keeper who's been robbed, and when I came to where the clothes had been turned to stone, I found nothing but blood. But when I got home, my soldier was lying in bed like an ox, and a doctor was treating his neck. I realized that he was a were-wolf, and after that I was never able to sit down to eat with him, not if you had killed me. Others may think what they like about this; may your guardian spirits curse me if I'm lying."

After Trimalchio tells a story about witches, more food is served. Habinnas, a stone-mason, arrives with his wife Scintilla, and calls for Fortunata.

(67) . . . . She came in wearing a high yellow waist-band, so that a cherry-colored tunic appeared underneath it, and twisted anklets, and gilded white shoes. Then wiping her hands on the cloth that she had on her neck, she seated herself on the couch where Habinnas' wife, Scintilla, was lying, and clapping her hands, kissed her, and said, "Is it you I see?" Then she went so far as to take her bracelets off her fat arms and to display them to an admiring Scintilla. Eventually she removed even her anklets and her hair-net, which she said was pure gold. Trimalchio noticed this, and ordered everything to be brought to him, and said, "You're looking at a woman's shackles: this is how we fools are robbed. She must have six and a half pounds. I myself have a bracelet, made from the thousandth owed

to Mercury,[83] that weighs no less than ten pounds." And finally, in case we thought he was lying, he ordered a scale to be brought in, and the weight to be carried around and examined. Scintilla was no better: from her neck, she took a small gold box, which she called Felicio. Then she brought out two rattling earrings, and giving them to Fortunata to examine in turn, said, "Because of my master's kindness, no one has better." "What," said Habinnas, "you cleaned me out to buy you a glass bean? I swear, if I had a daughter, I would cut off her ears. If there were no women, we'd consider everything to be as valuable as mud; as it is now, we piss hot and drink cold." Meanwhile the giddy women laughed together, and exchanged drunken kisses, while one went on about her frugality, the other about her husband's sweethearts and carelessness. While they were clinging together, Habinnas got up stealthily, and grabbing Fortunata's feet, threw her up on the couch. "Oh! Oh!" she shouted, as her tunic rose above her knees. Recovering in Scintilla's embrace, she hid her burning red face in her napkin.

More entertainment follows, and more food.

(71) Trimalchio said, "Friends, slaves are human, too, and drink the same milk, even if cruel fate has oppressed them. But if I live, they will soon taste the water of freedom. In fact, I'm freeing all of them in my will. To Philargyrus, I'm also bequeathing a farm, and his slave-wife; to Cario, also an apartment-block, and his manumission-tax, and a bed, and blanket. I'm making Fortunata my heir, and commend her to all my friends. I'm making all this known so that my slaves may love me now as if I were dead." They all began to thank their master for his kindness, when he turned serious, and ordered that a copy of his will be brought in, and he read the whole thing beginning to end, while the slaves groaned. Then looking at Habinnas, he said, "What do you say, dear friend? You'll build my monument, just as I've directed? I beg you to put my little dog at the feet of my statue, and wreaths, and bottles of perfume, and all the fights of Patraites,[84] so that by your kindness I might be allowed to live after death; and it should be 100 feet across and 200 feet long. For I want there to be all kinds of fruit around my ashes, and plenty of vines. It's a serious mistake for someone to take care of his home while he's alive, but not to look after the one we must inhabit far longer. And so, above all, I want this to be added: 'This monument does not pass to my heir.' I shall certainly take care to provide in my will that no harm be done to me when I'm dead. For I'm appointing one of my freedmen to be guardian of my tomb, to see to it that people don't run up and crap on my monument. I beg you also to fashion ships, with full sails, going . . . [85] of my monument, and me, sitting on the magistrates' platform, wearing the official toga and five gold rings, and pouring money out of a bag for the public; you know that I paid for a feast costing two *denarii*[86] per person. And have dining-room couches made, if you can manage it. And show all the people enjoying themselves. On my right hand, place a statue of my Fortunata, holding a dove, and let her be walking a little dog with a waist-band; and my little boy; and large jars sealed with gypsum, so that the wine doesn't run out. And see to it that a broken urn is carved, and above it, a boy weeping. A sundial in the middle, so that anyone who looks at the time will read my name, whether he wants to or not. Also, consider carefully whether this

inscription seems suitable to you: 'Here lies Gaius Pompeius Trimalchio, freed-man of Maecenas. Membership in the priesthood of Augustus was conferred upon him in his absence. Though he could have been in all the decuries[87] at Rome, he preferred not to be. Pious, brave, loyal, he grew from little and left 30,000,000 sesterces, and he never listened to a philosopher. Fare well, and you too, passer-by.'" (72) After he said this, Trimalchio began to weep, copiously. And Fortunata wept, and Habinnas wept, and all the slaves filled the dining-room with lamentation, as if they'd been asked to a funeral. . . .

After the guests visit the baths, a violent quarrel breaks out between Trimalchio and Fortunata. He then addresses the guests.

(75) . . . . "Friends, I beg you to enjoy yourselves. For I was once as you are, but because of my virtues I've come to this. A little heart is what makes men; all the rest is rubbish. 'I buy well and I sell well;' someone else might tell you differently. I'm bursting with joy. But you, you snorer, are you still weeping? I'll soon see to it that you weep over your fate. But as I'd begun to say, it was my frugality that brought me into this fortune. When I came from Asia, I was as big as this candle-stick. In fact, I used to measure myself by it every day, and in order to grow a beard more quickly, I greased my lips from the lamp. Nevertheless, I was my master's pet for fourteen years. What your owner orders isn't shameful. Still, I satisfied my mistress also. You know what I mean; I won't say more, because I'm not boastful. (76) Well, as the gods willed, I became master of the house; I actu-ally had control of his brain. What then? He made me his co-heir with Caesar, and I received an inheritance worthy of a senator. But no one's satisfied with nothing. I became passionate about business. I won't keep you much longer: I built five ships, loaded them with wine – and at that time it was like gold – and sent them to Rome. You might think I'd arranged this: all the ships sank – it's the truth, not a tale. In a single day, Neptune devoured 30,000,000 sesterces. Do you think I gave up? No, by god: I no more tasted this loss than if nothing had hap-pened. I built others, larger and better and luckier, so that no one could say that I wasn't a brave man. You know, a large ship possesses great courage. I loaded them again with wine, and with bacon-fat, beans, perfume, and slaves. At that point, Fortunata did something loyal, for she sold all her gold and clothes, and put a hundred gold coins in my hand. This was the leaven of my savings. What the gods wish, quickly happens. On one trip, I made 10,000,000 sesterces. I immediately bought all the estates which had belonged to my patron. I built a house, bought slaves and cattle; whatever I touched grew like a honey-comb. When I began to have more than my whole country, I quit: I retired from busi-ness, and began to loan money to freedmen. And when I really didn't want to go on with my work, I was encouraged by an astrologer, who happened to have come to our colony, a little Greek whose name was Serapa, counselor to the gods. This man even told me things that I'd forgotten; explained everything to me from thread to needle; knew my insides; the only thing he didn't tell me was what I'd eaten the day before. You would have thought that he had always lived with me. (77) You recall, Habinnas? – I believe you were there – 'You got your wife from those profits. You're unlucky in your friends. No one ever thanks you

adequately. You own large estates. You're nourishing a viper under your arm,' and what I shouldn't tell you – that even now I have thirty years, four months, and two days to live. And soon I'll receive an inheritance. My oracle tells me this. But if I could join my estates to Apulia,[88] I'd have come far enough in my lifetime. Meanwhile, while Mercury was watching over me, I built this house. As you know, it was a hut: now it's a temple. It has four dining-rooms, twenty bed-rooms, two marble porticos, a dining-room upstairs, the bedroom where I myself sleep, this viper's quarters, a very fine room for the porter; the guest-room holds a hundred guests. In fact, when Scaurus came, there was nowhere he preferred to stay, and he has his father's guest-house by the sea. And there are many other things, which I'll show you in a moment. Believe me: if you have an *as*,[89] you're worth an *as*; you're judged by what you have. So your friend, who was a frog, is now a king. Meanwhile, Stichus, bring me the death-bed on which I wish to be carried out. Also bring perfume, and a sample from that amphora which I want to be poured over my bones."

(78) Stichus immediately brought in both a white burial-sheet and an official toga . . . and [Trimalchio] made us test whether they had been made with good wool. Then laughing a little, he said, "Make sure, Stichus, that neither mice nor moths touch them; otherwise, I'll burn you alive. I want to be carried out in style, so that the whole population calls down its blessings upon me." He immediately opened a flask of nard-oil and sprinkled it on all of us, and said, "I hope this pleases me as much when I'm dead as while I'm alive." He even ordered wine to be poured into a bowl, and said, "Imagine you've been asked to a festival in honor of my past life." The thing was becoming absolutely nauseating, when Trimalchio, now obnoxiously and disgracefully drunk, ordered a new entertain-ment – trumpeters – to be brought into the dining-room, and propped up on a pile of pillows, he stretched out on his death-bed, and said, "Pretend I'm dead. Play something pretty." The trumpeters blasted out a funeral song. One in par-ticular, a slave of the undertaker who was the most respectable of the bunch, played so loudly that he woke the whole neighborhood. So the night-watchmen, who were patrolling the streets of the neighborhood, thinking Trimalchio's house was on fire, suddenly broke down the door and dutifully began, with their water and axes, to cause a commotion. Seizing this most opportune occasion, we tricked Agamemnon, and fled as quickly as from a real fire. . . .

8   THEODOSIAN CODE

The *Theodosian Code* was published in AD 438 on the orders of Theodosius II, emperor at Constantinople, AD 408–50. Its purpose was to collect and to categorize all imperial edicts and decrees (*constitutiones*) issued since the empire had become Christian under the emperor Constantine. It is a rich source of information, not only about the law, but also about social and economic conditions in late antiquity.

3.3.1. Emperors Valentinian, Theodosius, and Arcadius, Augustuses, to Tatianus, Praetorian Prefect.

All whose parents have, because of their wretched misfortune, sold them into slavery at a time when they needed food,[90] are to be restored to their former freedom. Certainly, he who has profited from the servitude of a free man for a significant period of time ought not to demand repayment of the purchase price.

Issued at Mediolanum[91] the fifth day before the Ides of March in the consulship of Tatianus and Symmachus [March 11, AD 391].

5.9.1. Emperor Constantine Augustus to Ablavius, Praetorian Prefect.

Whoever has picked up a little boy or girl cast out of its home with the consent and knowledge of its father or owner, and has raised it at his own expense, shall keep it in the same status that he wanted it to have when it was picked up, that is, whether he preferred it to be a son or a slave: those who have knowingly and willingly cast infants out of their home, whether slave or free, are absolutely forbidden to make any kind of disturbance by trying to reclaim them.

Issued at Constantinople the fifteenth day before the Kalends of May in the consulship of Bassus and Ablavius [April 17, AD 331].

5.17.1.1. Emperor Constantine Augustus to the provincials.

It is appropriate also that *coloni*,[92] who are thinking about running away, be bound with chains like slaves, so that by virtue of their condemnation to slavery, they may be compelled to fulfill the duties that are suitable for free men.

Issued the third day before the Kalends of November in the consulship of Pacatianus and Hilarianus [October 30, AD 332].

9.31.1. Emperors Honorius and Theodosius, Augustuses, to Caecilianus, Praetorian Prefect.

No landowner of the curial or plebeian class is to hand over his children to be raised by shepherds, but we allow them to be given to other country-dwellers to raise, as often happens. Certainly, if anyone, after publication of the law, shall have given his children to shepherds to raise, he will be held to have acknowledged that he is an associate of brigands.

Issued at Ravenna the twelfth day before the Kalends of February in the consulship of the Augustuses, Honorius, for the eighth time, and Theodosius, for the
third time [January 21, AD 409].

SUGGESTIONS FOR FURTHER READING

On society in the time of the emperors, see P. Garnsey and R. Saller, *The Roman Empire:
Economy, Society and Culture* (Berkeley and Los Angeles, 1987), pp. 107–25. For the Republic, P. A. Brunt, *Social Conflicts in the Roman Republic* (New York and London, 1971). On
the period of late antiquity, see especially P. Brown, *The Making of Late Antiquity* (Cambridge, Mass., 1978), and *Society and the Holy in Late Antiquity* (Berkeley, 1982). Social
relations are examined in R. MacMullen, *Roman Social Relations, 50 BC to AD 284* (New
Haven, 1974). On patronage, see R. Saller, *Personal Patronage under the Early Empire* (Cambridge, 1982).

The best and most up-to-date account of slavery is K. R. Bradley, *Slavery and Society at
Rome* (Cambridge, 1994). See also Keith Hopkins' still valuable *Conquerors and Slaves: So-
ciological Studies in Roman History, Vol. 1* (Cambridge, 1978). On resistance to slavery, see
K. R. Bradley, *Slavery and Rebellion in the Roman World, 140 BC–70 BC* (Bloomington, 1989).
The decline of slavery in late antiquity is explained in C. R. Whittaker, "Circe's pigs: From
slavery to serfdom in the later Roman empire," *Slavery and Abolition*, 8 (1987), pp. 88–123.
The best work on freedmen is still S. Treggiari, *Roman Freedmen during the Late Republic*
(Oxford, 1969).

On the law of the Twelve Tables, see especially A. Watson, *Rome of the Twelve Tables:
Persons and Property* (Princeton, 1976). The most readable biography of Cato the Elder is A.
E. Astin, *Cato the Censor* (Oxford, 1978). On Juvenal, see E. Courtney, *A Commentary on the
Satires of Juvenal* (London, 1980). Probably the best introduction to Horace is D. West, *Read-
ing Horace* (Edinburgh, 1967). On Diodorus of Sicily and his work, see K. Sacks, *Diodorus
Siculus and the First Century* (Princeton, 1990). For Petronius, J. P. Sullivan, *The Satyricon of
Petronius: A Literary Study* (London, 1968).

Two

WOMEN, MARRIAGE, AND FAMILY

Editor's introduction

In the period of the late Republic, a number of women of the politically active class were able to assert themselves in ways that were highly visible, and that seem not to have been possible in an earlier age. Sempronia, for example, whose husband was consul in 77 BC, is said to have been involved in Catiline's conspiracy; she is described by Sallust (*Conspiracy of Catiline* 24–5) as smart, funny, and well-read, but altogether too skilled at singing and dancing. Male society, we might suppose, will have been more comfortable lauding the accomplishments of a woman like Turia, who is said to have risked her own safety to rescue her husband from the clutches of the triumvirs, and who is probably the unidentified woman who was memorialized in a eulogy delivered by her husband, and later inscribed on stone at Rome (the so-called *Laudatio Turiae*, which is reproduced below as selection 14), that also extols her more conventional attributes: modesty, obedience, agreeableness, sober dress, dedication to wool-working. What Turia, or any other woman, might have thought of her husband's characterization of her is, unfortunately, unknown.

It is also difficult to know whether the public conduct of women like Sempronia should be understood to signal a broader change in the roles of women who were not part of the wealthy, governing class. Lower-class women continued to scratch out a living as laundresses, weavers, butchers, and fish-sellers, or in one of the many occupations that are recorded on inscriptions at Pompeii: bean-dealer, nail-seller, brick-maker, stonecutter. For a lot of unskilled working-class women, prostitution was the only way to make a living, however inadequate. Many worked out-of-doors in the public archways (*fornices*).

Nothing is likely to have had a greater impact on the lives of upper-class women than the changes that occurred in marriage and divorce, mainly, it seems, in the period between about 150 and 50 BC. Where it had been customary for a woman to marry in such a way that she passed into the control of her husband, who then exercised over her a legal authority not unlike that of a father over his daughter, by the time of Cicero, if not earlier, most marriages were structured so that instead of becoming subject to her husband's authority, the wife remained under her father's power. Why the shift happened is unclear. It is tempting, but probably wishful thinking, to suggest that it occurred because women wanted it to. Whatever the explanation, the effect was to give women considerably more independence in marriage. It continued to be the case, however, even into the second century AD, that a woman's consent to marriage was not legally required (it was sufficient that her father, or guardian, approve).

An even more dramatic change took place in the rules governing divorce. For much of the period of the Republic, only husbands could initiate a divorce, and then only in certain circumstances. By the time of Cicero, however, divorce was easily accomplished, by either wife or husband, generally without financial penalties, and for almost any reason. It was, if the disapproving moralists of the Augustan age are to be believed, fairly common, at least in the political class. But though wives now possessed the right to end a marriage, few actually seem to have done so, maybe because women had very few opportunities to make an independent living, perhaps also because custody of children was normally awarded to their father.

The legal independence of women was somewhat constrained also by the institution of guardianship. Like prepubescent children whose fathers had died, every adult woman who was not in her husband's control, or under her father's power – either because she had outlived him, or been released from it – was required by law to have a guardian (*tutor*), whose main function was to authorize financial transactions she entered into (the signing of a contract, for example) that might result in loss to her. The legal sources are explicit about the reasons women were thought to need guardians: they lacked judgment, and were easily duped. In most cases, it appears that the guardian was either the woman's husband or a male relative (often, it seems, an uncle). By the time of the late Republic, however, guardianship had become something of a formality, at least in some cases, so that an increasing number of women were able to manage their financial affairs more or less independently. And from the time of Augustus (27 BC–AD 14), freeborn women who had given birth to three children, and freedwomen who had given birth to four, were released from guardianship altogether.

In law, and probably often in fact, women's place in the home was emphatically subordinate to that of the *paterfamilias*, the male head of household who possessed almost unlimited authority over everyone who lived in it. He had the right to dissolve his children's marriages, and even to execute them (few actual instances are recorded). Those who were under his power (*potestas*) owned nothing in their own name; anything they acquired belonged to him. In practice, however, the power of the *paterfamilias* was limited, perhaps most importantly by the demography of the Roman family, which can now be reconstructed thanks to the pioneering studies of Richard Saller[1] (and others), and which indicates that most Romans were probably not subject to their father's control at those times in their lives when they are most likely to have wanted to make independent decisions. Comparative evidence drawn from other, better documented, pre-industrial societies suggests that average life-expectancy at birth in the Roman world was probably in the order of twenty-five to thirty years. Infant mortality was undoubtedly very common – more than one-quarter of newborns are likely to have died before their first birthday. Half or more of all children probably did not survive past the age of ten. Those who did will have lived, on average, another thirty-five to forty years. It is reasonably clear also that men's average age at marriage in the Roman world was, compared to many other pre-industrial societies, relatively late. Analysis of funeral inscriptions suggests that most men probably married in their late twenties (most women in their late teens or early twenties). So the difference in age between father and child will often have been as much as forty years. This comparatively large generation gap, when combined with the figures given above for average life-expectancy at birth, means, among other things, that probably only one-fifth of men, and fewer than half of all women, were still under their father's power when they married.

It may be doubted also that the traditional picture of the Roman household, as consisting of several nuclear families ruled by an authoritarian, elderly patriarch, corresponds, in any very precise way, to the realities of Roman family life. The image is derived mainly from what survives of Roman private law, easily our largest source of information about the family. But legal rules only intermittently describe social practice. The literary sources suggest that it was very unusual for adult sons to live with their fathers. And the many surviving, funeral inscriptions on which the relationship between the commemorator and the deceased is identified rarely record extended relatives (grandparents, aunts and uncles, cousins). What really mattered to the Romans, it seems, were the relationships of the nuclear family, of husband and wife, and of parent and child.

It seems now to be fashionable to maintain that the Romans generally attached little value to children, and then mainly for the adults that they would grow up to be, or in the expectation that they would support their parents in old age. The philosophically minded, like the emperor Marcus Aurelius, were inclined to categorize children with barbarians, slaves, and animals, on the grounds that they were all irrational. But the grief expressed on tombstones set up to commemorate children is, in many cases, undeniably genuine. It was not uncommon for adults to show interest, and even to take pleasure, in the behaviors of childhood. Among the wealthy, about whom we are best informed, it seems to have been expected that fathers would play an active role in the education of their sons, especially when they were young. And small children were often referred to as *deliciae*, "sweethearts."

9 Livy, *History of Rome* 34.2–4

A skillful story-teller, with a fondness for idealized, and sometimes unhistorical, examples of old-fashioned heroism, Titus Livius was born at Patavium (now Padua) in northern Italy, probably in 59 BC. Of his *History of Rome*, from its origins to 9 BC, Books 1–10 (to 293 BC) and 21–45 (218–167 BC) are preserved more or less intact. He died probably in AD 17.

The following passage, taken from Book 34 of his history, is Livy's version of a speech which Cato the Elder (see selection 2) is said to have delivered in the Senate in 195 BC. The speech is directed against a proposal to repeal the Oppian law, which had been enacted in 215 BC, and which forbade women to possess more than half an ounce of gold, wear colored clothes, or ride in wheeled vehicles within a mile of Rome. Because Cato's efforts to prevent the repeal of the law were, in the end, unsuccessful, and because he was known to be somewhat eccentric – he once declared publicly that he made love to his wife only during thunderstorms[2] – the misogynist views that he expresses here should probably not be taken to be representative of his time.

(2) If each of us, citizens, had been resolved to assert a husband's rights and authority in relation to his own wife, we would have less trouble with women as a whole; now, our liberty, destroyed at home by female violence, is crushed and trampled even here in the Forum, and because we have not controlled them individually, we fear them collectively. For my part, I thought it a fairy-tale and a fiction that on a certain island all the men were utterly destroyed by a conspiracy of women;[3] but from no group is there not the greatest danger if you permit meetings, and gatherings, and secret consultations. And I can hardly decide in my own mind whether the act itself is worse or the precedent it sets; the one concerns us consuls and other magistrates; the other, citizens, concerns you more. For whether the proposal placed before you is in the public interest or not is to be determined by you who are about to vote; this womanly madness, whether it has arisen spontaneously or at your instigation, Marcus Fundanius and Lucius Valerius – but unquestionably to the discredit of the magistrates – I don't know whether it is more shameful for you, tribunes, or for the consuls: for you, if you have brought the women here to stir up tribunician intrigues; for us, if we are obliged to accept laws from a secession of women, as we did once from a secession of plebeians.[4] A little while ago, I couldn't get into the Forum through the crowd of women without blushing. Had I not been restrained by respect for their dignity and modesty as individuals, lest they appear to have been rebuked by a consul, I would have said, "What practice is this, of running around in public, and blocking the roads, and speaking to other women's husbands? Could you not have made the same request at home, each of your own husband? Or are you more attractive in public than in private and to other women's husbands than to your own? Though not even at home is it proper for you to be concerned about what laws are adopted or abrogated here, if modesty would keep wives within the limits of their proper rights." Our ancestors did not want women to conduct even personal business without a guardian to authorize it; they wanted them to be under the control of fathers, brothers, husbands; we, if it pleases the gods, now allow them to interfere even in public business, and to mingle in the Forum, and in meetings and

assemblies. For what are they doing now in the streets and at the intersections other than to promote the bill of the tribunes, and to urge that the law be repealed? Give rein to their unbridled nature and to their untamed spirit and hope that they themselves will set a limit to their license; unless you act, this is the least of those things imposed by custom or law to which women submit with a feeling of injustice. They want complete freedom, or rather, if we want to speak the truth, complete license.

(3) For if they win in this, what will they not try? Consider all the laws about women by which your ancestors restrained their license and made them subject to their husbands; even with all these constraints you can barely control them. What of it? If you allow them to grab hold of their bonds one by one and tear themselves free and, in the end, be made equal to their husbands, do you imagine that they will be bearable? Just as soon as they begin to be equal, they will be superior. But, by Hercules, they object to the enactment of any new provision against them, they complain not about law but about wrong-doing; in fact, what they want is that you repeal this law which you approved with your votes, and which, in the practice and experience of so many years, you have upheld – in other words, that by abolishing this one law you weaken all the rest. No law is wholly satisfactory for everyone; this alone is asked, whether it is beneficial for the majority and on the whole. If every law that harms someone in his personal life were to be repealed and discarded, what good will it do for everyone to pass laws which can immediately be abrogated by those against whom they have been enacted? Still, I want to know why it is that the agitated matrons have rushed out into the streets and barely refrain from entering the Forum and the assembly. That captives – fathers, husbands, sons, brothers – be ransomed from Hannibal? Such a misfortune of state is far removed, and may it always be so; but still, when it did occur, you refused this in the face of their pious prayers.[5] Yet it was not piety nor anxiety about their families which brought them together, but a religious rite: they were about to receive the Idaean Mother as she came from Pessinus in Phrygia.[6] What pretext, respectable even to mention, is given for this womanly insurrection? "That we may be resplendent in gold and purple," one says, "that we may be carried through the city in carriages on holidays and ordinary days, as if in triumph over the conquered and vanquished law and over the votes we wrested from you; that there be no limit to our spending and luxury."

(4) You have often heard me complaining, not only about the personal extravagance of women and of men, but also about that of the magistrates, and that the state is suffering from the two opposing vices, of greed and luxury, the diseases that have destroyed every great empire. As the fortune of the Republic becomes better and happier day by day, and the empire grows – and already we have crossed into Greece and Asia, places replete with all the allurements of vice, and we are handling even the treasures of kings – the greater my fear that those things will capture us more than we will capture them. A dangerous sign, believe me, were the statues brought to this city from Syracuse.[7] Now I hear far too many people praising the trinkets of Corinth and Athens and laughing with astonishment at the earthen antefixes of the Roman gods. I, for one, prefer that these gods be propitious, and I trust that they will be so, if we allow them to remain in their own dwelling-places. In our fathers' memory, Pyrrhus, through

his agent Cineas, tried to win over with gifts the hearts not only of men but also of women.[8] The Oppian law to restrain female extravagance had not yet been passed, but no woman took his gifts. What do you think was the reason? The same reason our ancestors had for passing no law on the subject: there was no extravagance to be restrained. In the same way that diseases must be known before their cures, so desires are born before the laws which restrain them. What provoked the Licinian law about 500 *iugera* except an uncontrolled desire to join fields together?[9] What prompted the Cincian law on gifts and donations except that the plebeians had already begun to be tributary to the Senate?[10] And so it is hardly surprising that no Oppian or any other law was needed to limit women's extravagance at a time when they would not accept gifts of gold and purple offered to them voluntarily. If Cineas were going around the city now with those presents, he would have found women standing in the streets to take them. And I, for one, can find no reason or explanation for some desires. For though there may be some natural shame or indignation in being denied what is permitted to another, still, when everyone's dress is made alike, what is it that any of you fears will not be conspicuous in herself? Certainly, the worst kind of shame is that caused by stinginess or poverty; but the law removes both from you, since you do not have what it is not permitted to have. "It is this very equality I object to," says that rich woman. "Why do I not stand out from the rest adorned with gold and purple? Why does other women's poverty lie concealed under this kind of law, so that it might appear that they would have owned, if it were permitted, what they don't have the means to possess?" Do you wish, citizens, to start a contest of this sort among your wives, so that the rich will want to own what no other woman can have, and the poor, lest they be scorned for this very reason, will spend beyond their means? As soon as these women begin to be ashamed of what they ought not to be ashamed, they will not be ashamed of what they should. She who can buy from her own funds will buy; she who cannot will badger her husband. That wretched husband – both the one who has been prevailed upon and the one who has not – when he sees another man giving what he himself will not give. Now they indiscriminately accost other women's husbands, and what is more, beg for a law and votes, and from certain men they get what they ask. Concerning yourself, your property, your children, you are easily moved; once the law has ceased to set a limit on your wife's expenditures, you yourself will never set one. Do not think, citizens, that the situation will be the same as that which existed before the law was passed. It is safer for a guilty man not to be accused than to be acquitted, and luxury undisturbed would have been more tolerable than it will be now, when, like a wild beast, it has been angered by its very chains, and then set loose. I think that the Oppian law should in no way be repealed; I pray that all the gods prosper whatever you decide.

10   JUVENAL, *SATIRES* 6

For Juvenal, see the introduction to selection 3. *Satire* 6, several parts of which are reproduced below, is a savage and often unfunny denunciation of women.

(1–37) I imagine that when Saturn was king, Chastity lingered on earth, and was seen for a while, when a frigid cave supplied a modest home, and under a common shelter enclosed fireplace and household gods, cattle and their owners; when the mountain-bred wife covered her forest bed with leaves and straw and the skins of her neighbors, the wild animals – not at all like you, Cynthia,[11] or you whose bright eyes were clouded by a sparrow's death,[12] but one endowed with breasts to suckle stout babies, often more unkempt than her acorn-belching husband. For men lived differently then, when the world was new, and the sky was young, men who were born of riven oak, or formed of dust, and had no parents. At least a few traces of ancient Chastity survived even under Jupiter; but that was before he had a beard, before the Greeks had learned to swear on someone else's head, when no one feared that his cabbages or fruit would be stolen, or lived with walled gardens. After that, Astraea[13] slowly withdrew to the heavens, with Chastity as her companion, and the two sisters fled together.

It is an ancient and long-established custom, Postumus, to shake another man's bed, and to scorn the *genius*[14] of the sacred couch. The iron age quickly produced every other crime; the silver age saw the first adulterers. Yet in these times of ours, you are preparing an agreement, a marriage-contract, and a betrothal; already you're getting your hair done by a master barber, and have given, perhaps, a pledge for her finger. You were unquestionably sane: now you're getting married, Postumus? Tell me, what Tisiphone,[15] what snakes are driving you mad? Can you stomach a woman as your master when there is so much rope available, when so many dizzyingly high windows stand open, when the Aemilian bridge offers itself to you close at hand? Or if none of these many means of exit pleases you, don't you think it better to sleep with a pretty little boy, who doesn't quarrel at night, doesn't ask you for little gifts when you're lying there, and neither complains that you're taking it easy nor tells you how much to pant.

(55–113) Some woman who lives on her father's farm has an excellent reputation? Let her live at Gabii,[16] or at Fidenae,[17] as she has lived in the country, and I will grant you your little paternal farm. Besides, who claims that nothing has happened in the mountains or in caves? Have Jupiter and Mars become so senile? Do the porticos show you a woman worthy of your allegiance? Do all the rows in the theater contain anyone whom you could pick out and love without misgiving? When soft Bathyllus[18] dances the role of gesticulating Leda,[19] Tuccia can't control her bladder; an Apulian woman emits a sudden and pitiable cry of ecstasy, as if embraced; Thymele is attentive – this is when rustic Thymele is educated. Still others, when all the stage-equipment has been put away, when the theater is empty and closed, and only the forums are noisy, and the Megalesian games are a long way from the Plebeian,[20] relieve their boredom by taking up acting, the thyrsus,[21] and the waist-band of Accius. Urbicus, in an Atellane satire,[22] gets a laugh with the gestures of Autonoe;[23] impoverished Aelia is in love with him. Some women undo a comedian's belt at great expense; others forbid Chrysogonus to sing. Hispulla takes pleasure in a tragedian; do you really think that anyone will love Quintilian?[24] You marry so that the lyre-player Echion or Glaphyrus, or the flute-player Ambrosius, may become a father. Let us construct a long stage in the narrow streets; let your doors and doorposts be adorned with wreaths of laurel, so that your noble son in his tortoiseshell cradle, may exhibit, Lentulus, the likeness of Euryalus or of a gladiator.[25]

Eppia, a senator's wife, ran off with a gladiator to Pharos,[26] and the Nile, and the infamous city of Lagus:[27] Canopus[28] itself condemned the monstrous morals of our city. Forgetful of home, of husband, and of sister, giving no thought to her country, she shamelessly deserted her weeping children, and, what's even more amazing, the games, and Paris.[29] And though, as an infant, she had slept, amid great wealth, in a tinsel-decorated cradle on her father's down, she made light of the sea; she had long made light of her reputation, the loss of which is of little importance among those accustomed to soft sedan-chairs. And so, with unflagging courage, she endured the tossing of the Tyrrhenian sea and the roaring of the Ionian, and the many seas she had to cross. For if danger arises in a just and honorable way, women grow cold with fear and dread, and can't stand up on their trembling feet; but they display a courageous spirit when they brave something shameful. When a husband insists, it's hard to board a ship – she's sick from the bilge-water, the sky's turned upside down. But she who's running off with her lover feels fine. Then she vomits on her husband; now she eats breakfast with the sailors, wanders about the deck, and delights in pulling on the rough ropes. And what's the youthful appearance by which Eppia is captivated? What did she see to allow herself to be called a "she-gladiator?" Little Sergius had already begun to shave, and to hope for a reprieve because of his wounded arm. There were many deformities in his face – a scar caused by his helmet, a huge swelling in the middle of his nose, an eye always oozing from a nasty injury. But he was a gladiator! This is what transforms them into Hyacinthuses,[30] this is what she preferred to children and to country, to sister and to husband – the sword is what they love. Had this same Sergius received his discharge, he would have begun to look like Veiento.[31]

(133–71) Why should I speak of love potions and incantations, of poison brewed and given to a stepson? Driven by the commanding power of their sex, they do worse things – lust is the least of their sins. "But why is Censennia, on her husband's testimony, the best?" She gave him a million sesterces:[32] that's the price at which he calls her chaste. He's not heartsick from Venus' quiver or burned by her torch: the arrows come from the dowry, the fires start there. Her freedom is purchased: she openly makes signals, and writes love-letters. The rich woman who marries a greedy man is unmarried. "Why does Sertorius burn with love for Bibula?" If you were to shake out the truth, it's the face, not the wife, he loves. Let three wrinkles appear; let her skin become dry and flabby; let her teeth turn black, and her eyes deteriorate; then his freedman will say, "Pack your bags and be gone! You've become a burden to us; you're always wiping your nose; go, and be quick about it! There's another woman coming, one with a dry nose." Meanwhile, she grows hot and imperious, demanding that her husband give her shepherds, and Canusian sheep,[33] and Falernian vines.[34] But that's nothing; she demands all his slave-boys, his entire work-house; whatever her neighbor has that's not in her house must be purchased. And in the winter, when the merchant Jason is barred, and the white stalls obstruct his armed sailors, huge crystal vases are carried off, still larger ones of agate, and finally a very famous diamond, made more precious by the finger of Berenice – it was once given by the barbarian Agrippa to his incestuous sister,[35] where kings celebrate festal sabbaths with bare feet, and a long-standing clemency is extended to elderly pigs. "Among such crowds of women, does there seem to be no one worthy of you?" Let her be beautiful, charming, rich, and fertile; let her display her ancestors in her halls; let her be more chaste than every disheveled Sabine who stopped the war – a prodigy on earth not unlike a black swan. And who could endure a wife equipped with everything? I would rather have a Venusian[36] woman than you, Cornelia, mother of the Gracchi, if, along with your great virtues, you bring me an over-proud countenance, and reckon triumphs as part of your dowry. Away with your Hannibal, I beg you, and Syphax[37] overcome in his camp! Leave, and take all of Carthage with you!

(184–99) Some small things are intolerable to husbands. For what's more offensive than that no woman considers herself beautiful unless transformed from a Tuscan into a Greekling, or from a woman of Sulmo[38] into a true woman of Athens? Everything's in Greek, though it is a greater shame for us not to know Latin. Their fears and anger, joys and troubles – all the secrets of their souls – they pour forth in Greek: they even have sex in Greek. Still, you might pardon all that in a girl; but will you, who are approaching your eighty-sixth year, still talk in Greek? Such speech is not decent in an old woman: whenever that lascivious phrase – "my life, my soul" – is uttered, you're using in public what should be left under the blankets. For whose groin is not excited by a caressing and naughty voice? He has fingers. But though you say these things more tenderly than a Haemus or a Carpophorus,[39] all fluttering of the heart subsides – your face counts up your years!

(231–78) Forget about harmony as long as your mother-in-law is alive. She teaches her daughter to delight in the spoils of her destitute husband; she teaches her to reply to her seducer's love-letters in a way that's not at all unskilled or innocent; she deceives or bribes your guards; then she summons Archigenes[40] when your wife is well, and tossing around the heavy blankets; meanwhile, the lover, hidden away, lies waiting; impatient at the delay, he silently plays with himself. Do you honestly expect the mother to hand down habits that are honorable, and different from her own? Actually, it's profitable for the shameless old woman to bring up a shameless daughter.

There is hardly any court-case in which the proceedings were not started by a woman. Manilia brings an accusation, if she's not the defendant. They themselves construct and shape the pleadings; they are ready to tell Celsus[41] himself how to begin his case, and how to make his points.

Who doesn't know of Tyrian[42] cloaks and female wrestling-oil? Who hasn't seen the wounds of the training-stake, which she pierces through and through with her sword, attacking it with a shield, completing all the correct steps? A matron fully qualified to blow a trumpet at the Floralia,[43] unless she's harboring some further ambition in her breast, and is preparing for the real arena. What modesty can be displayed in a woman who wears a helmet, and abjures her own sex? She loves strength; yet she wouldn't want to become a man, knowing how meager is our pleasure. How dignified for a husband, at an auction of his wife's belongings, to see her belt and tunic-sleeves, and helmet-plumes, and leg-covering; or if she fights a different sort of battle, you'll have the pleasure of seeing your young wife selling her greaves. These are the women who sweat in a thin robe, whose delicate skin is irritated by silk clothes. See how she groans as she completes her prescribed exercises; how she's bent by the weight of her helmet; how large and thick are the bandages wrapped round her knees; then laugh when she puts down her weapons and picks up a chamber-pot. Tell us, grand-daughters of Lepidus,[44] or of the blind Metellus,[45] or of Fabius Gurges,[46] what gladiator's wife ever put on such attire? When did the wife of Asylus[47] groan against a training-stake?

The bed in which a wife sleeps always has bickering and mutual quarrels; there's little sleep to be got there. It's there that she harasses her husband, worse than a tigress that has lost her cubs; she pretends to have a complaint, conscious of her own secret doings; she either criticizes his slave-boys, or weeps about an imagined mistress, with an abundance of tears always ready in their place, waiting for her to tell them when to flow. You believe it to be love; you're delighted, you worm, and you kiss away her tears – what notes, what letters you'd find, if you opened the desk of the jealous adulteress!

(300–65) What does Venus worry about when she's drunk? That woman can't tell head from tail who eats giant oysters in the middle of the night, pours foaming perfumes into her unmixed Falernian wine, and drinks from a shell-flask, while the roof spins round, the table rises, and the lights appear double. Go now and wonder why Tullia sneers as she sniffs the air, or what Maura is saying to her infamous foster-sister when she passes by the ancient altar of Chastity. Here they set down their sedans at night, and splash the statue of the goddess with long bursts of urine, and take turns riding each other, with the moon looking down on their motions. From there they go home. You, when daylight comes, and you're on your way to visit your mighty friends, will tread on your wife's piss.

Well-known are the secret rites of the Good Goddess,[48] when the flute stirs the loins and the maenads of Priapus[49] are carried along, aroused equally by the horn-blowing and the wine, tossing their hair and howling. What lustful longing is in their hearts! What sounds they make when their passion is aroused! What a torrent of old wine flows through their limbs! Saufeia challenges the pimps' slave-girls to a contest, and wins the prize for gyrations; she herself admires the undulations of Medullina, but the prize remains with Saufeia, whose virtue matches her birth. Nothing is done there as if it were a game; everything is carried out as in real life, in ways that would warm the age-chilled crotch of Priam or Nestor.[50] Then lust shows itself, impatient of delay, and women's true nature is revealed, as the cry is repeated from every corner, "Now's the time! Let in the men!" If one young adulterer is asleep, she orders another to put on his cloak and hurry; if there's no one else, a run is made on the slaves; if there's no hope of finding slaves, the water-carrier will be paid to come in; if he can't be found, and men are lacking, she doesn't hesitate to take on a donkey. Would that our ancient rituals, or at least our public rites, be preserved from this sort of pollution! But every Moor and Indian knows which she-lutist brought a penis bigger than the two Anticatos of Caesar[51] into that place in which every representation of the other sex must be covered, and from which even a mouse flees, conscious of its testicles.

Who in the past was ever contemptuous of the Gods? Who would have dared to laugh at the earthen-ware bowls and black pots of Numa,[52] or the fragile plates made of Vatican clay? But nowadays at what altar is there not a Clodius?[53] I hear what my old friends used to advise – "Put on a lock and keep her inside." But who will guard the guards? The wife makes arrangements, beginning with them. And the passions of the humble are those of the high and mighty: she who wears out the black pavement with her feet is no better than she who's carried on the necks of tall Syrians. Ogulnia rents clothes to see the games; she hires attendants, a sedan-chair, cushions, female friends, a nurse, and a blond slave-girl to carry her messages; but whatever's left of her father's silver, down to the very last utensil, she'll give to some smooth athlete. Many of these women are poor, but none of them exercises any restraint, or measures herself by the limits that her poverty prescribes. Men, on the other hand, do sometimes have regard for what's useful; the ant has taught some of them to fear cold and hunger. But an extravagant woman takes no notice of her dwindling resources: as if money was always sprouting up from her exhausted strong-box, and she always had a full pile to draw from, she never considers what her pleasures cost her.

(434–510) More intolerable still is the woman who, as soon as she has sat down to eat, praises Vergil, pardons the dying Dido, and compares rival poets, weighing Vergil suspended in one scale against Homer in the other. Grammarians surrender; rhetoricians are routed; the whole crowd is silenced; no lawyer or auctioneer will speak, nor any other woman; such is the cascade of words that you'd think all the pots and bells were being clashed together. There's no need now for trumpets or brass – a single woman can bring help to the laboring moon.[54] But wisdom sets a limit even on virtue, and if she wants to be considered both learned and eloquent, she ought to raise her tunic knee-high,[55] sacrifice a pig to Silvanus,[56] and bathe in the public baths.[57] Let not the matron who reclines next to you at dinner affect a special style of speaking, or hurl crooked arguments at you in her whirling speech! Let her not know all history; let there be some things in her reading that she doesn't understand. I hate the woman who is always consulting and thumbing through the *Ars* of Palaemon,[58] who observes every rule and law of speaking, who, like an antiquarian, quotes verses that I've never heard of, and upbraids her uneducated female friends for solecisms that even men needn't worry about: at least allow husbands to make grammatical mistakes!

There's nothing that a woman won't permit herself, nothing she considers shameful, once she's encircled her neck with green emeralds, and attached huge pearls to her elongated ears. There's nothing more intolerable than a wealthy woman. Meanwhile her face takes on a disagreeable and ridiculous appearance, swelling with lumps of dough. Or she reeks of Poppaean cosmetics[59] that stick to the lips of her unfortunate husband; her lover she meets with clean-washed skin. When does she bother to look nice at home? It's for her lovers that she purchases perfumes, for them that she buys whatever the slender Indians send here. Eventually, she reveals her face, removes the first layer of plaster, and begins to be recognizable. Then she freshens herself with the milk of young she-asses; she'd take a herd of them along with her if sent away north, into Hyperborean exile. But when she's been plastered over and treated with so many medicaments, including those lumps of wet dough, should it be called a face, or a sore?

It's worthwhile to ascertain what they do all day. If her husband has turned his back on her the night before, the wool-maid will perish, the cosmeticians will be stripped of their tunics, the sedan-carrier will be accused of coming late, and will be forced to pay for her husband's sleepiness. One has rods broken over his back, another bleeds from the strap, a third from the whip – there are women who pay their torturers an annual salary. During the beating, she fixes her face, listens to her girl-friends, or inspects the hem of a gold-embroidered robe. As the flogging continues, she skims the lengthy entries of the daily gazette,[60] and it continues until, the floggers exhausted, and the inquisition finally at an end, she gruffly shouts "Get out!" The governance of her household is as savage as that of a Sicilian court.[61] If she has an appointment and wants to look better than usual, and is in a hurry to meet someone waiting for her in the gardens, or more likely near the shrine of Isis[62] the procurer, unfortunate Psecas will do her hair with her own hair torn out, and her clothes torn off her shoulders and her breasts. "Why is this curl standing up?" A rawhide whip exacts punishment for the offending ringlet. What was Psecas' crime? How is it the slave-girl's fault if the shape of your nose displeases you? Another girl combs out the hair on the left side and rolls it into a curl; also part of the council is a maid who used to belong to her mother, and who, having retired from sewing, has been promoted to wool-working. She will be the first to give her opinion; after her, those who are inferior in age or skill will state their views, as if some issue of honor or life itself were at stake: so serious is the attention paid to beautification; so many are the tiers and layers piled up on her head! From the front, you'd see an Andromache;[63] she's not as tall from behind – you'd think it was a different woman. What if she happens to be so short that, without the help of high heels, she looks no bigger than a pigmy-girl, and has to rise nimbly on tip-toe for a kiss? Meanwhile, she pays no attention to her husband, and never considers what she costs him. She lives with him like a neighbor, closer to him only in this – that she hates his friends and his slaves, and weighs heavily on his money.

(582–601) If she's of lower rank, she'll promenade between the turning-posts of the race-track; she'll have her fortune told, presenting her forehead and her hand to the prophet who asks for many smacks of the lips.[64] Wealthy women hire their own Phrygian or Indian fortune-teller, skilled in the stars and the heavens, or one of the older men who's paid to expiate thunderbolts. Plebeian fates are determined in the Circus or on the ramparts;[65] she who displays a long gold chain on her bare neck inquires before the pillars and the dolphin-columns[66] whether she should dump the tavern-keeper and marry the rag-seller. But these poor women at least undergo the dangers of child-birth, and endure all the troubles of nursing to which their status condemns them; but there are hardly any pregnant women lying in gilded beds. Such are the skills, so powerful are the drugs, of those who make women sterile, and kill mankind in the womb. Rejoice, poor friend; give it to her to drink, whatever it may be, with your own hand, for if she were willing to grow big and trouble her womb with bouncing babies, you might perhaps find yourself the father of an Ethiopian, and some day a dark-colored heir, whom you'd rather not see in daylight, would fill all the places in your will.

11 OXYRHYNCHUS PAPYRUS 744

It was, it seems, not unusual for new-born children to be abandoned (in the Roman term, "exposed"), left in public places, like the town garbage-dump, either because their parents were unable to care for them, or because they were unwanted. Many undoubtedly died. It has sometimes been supposed that the practice was uncommon.[67] But the evidence shows that it was both widespread and widely accepted.[68] It is reasonably clear also that boys were abandoned less often than girls, who in many parts of the Roman world would need to be supplied with a dowry, and might therefore be considered to be a financial burden. It could be argued, then, that the practice itself is evidence, not of callousness, or of the undervaluation of children, but of widespread poverty.

The following letter, written by a man named Hilarion to his wife Alis in 1 BC, was found at Oxyrhynchus, Egypt. The translation is from J. Shelton, *As the Romans Did: A Sourcebook in Roman Social History*, 2nd edn (New York and Oxford, 1998), p. 28.

I send you my warmest greetings. I want you to know that we are still in Alexandria. And please don't worry if all the others come home but I remain in Alexandria. I beg you and entreat you to take care of the child and, if I receive my pay soon, I will send it up to you. If you have the baby before I return, if it is a boy, let it live; if it is a girl, expose it. You sent a message with Aphrodisias, "Don't forget me." How can I forget you? I beg you, then, not to worry.

12 BERLINER GRIECHISCHE URKUNDEN 1052

Husbands and wives sometimes drew up contracts spelling out their respective duties and obligations. The following example, which comes from Egypt, dates to 13 BC. The translation is from J. Shelton, *As the Romans Did: A Sourcebook in Roman Social History*, 2nd edn (New York and Oxford, 1998), p. 43.

To Protarchus,[69] from Thermion, daughter of Apion, accompanied by her guardian Apollonius, son of Chaereas, and from Apollonius, son of Ptolemaeus:

Thermion and Apollonius, son of Ptolemaeus, agree that they have come together for the purpose of sharing their lives with one another. The above-mentioned Apollonius, son of Ptolemaeus, agrees that he has received from Thermion – handed over from her household as a dowry – a pair of gold earrings. . . . From now on he will furnish Thermion, as his wedded wife, with all necessities and clothing according to his means, and he will not mistreat her or cast her out or insult her or bring in another wife; otherwise he must at once return the dowry and, in addition, half again as much.

. . . . And Thermion will fulfill her duties toward her husband and her marriage, and will not sleep away from the house or be absent one day without the consent of Apollonius, son of Ptolemaeus, and will not damage or injure their common home and will not consort with another man; otherwise she, if judged guilty of these actions, will be deprived of her dowry, and, in addition, the transgressor will be liable to the prescribed fine. Dated the seventeenth year of Caesar.[70]

13   PLUTARCH, *PRECEPTS OF MARRIAGE*

The *Precepts of Marriage* is one of the more than sixty essays that make up Plutarch's *Moralia* (on Plutarch, see also the introduction to selection 2). It was written as a wedding-present for a young woman named Eurydice and her husband Pollianus. Though Plutarch, like some of the Stoic philosophers (notably Musonius Rufus),[71] insisted that wives should be educated, in philosophy and even in mathematics, his ideal of marriage conforms broadly to the more conventional notion that a wife ought to subordinate her interests to those of her husband, have no friends other than his, and generally arrange her life in accordance with his needs. The translation is from D. Russell, *Plutarch: Selected Essays and Dialogues* (Oxford and New York, 1993), pp. 284–96.

(preface) . . . . In philosophy too there are many fine subjects of discourse, but none more important than this discourse of marriage, whereby philosophy charms those who come together to share their lives, and makes them gentle and amenable to each other. I have therefore put together in the form of some brief similitudes, so that they are the more easily remembered, the main points of the teaching you have often heard in the course of your education in philosophy. These I send as a gift to you both. . . .

(4) As fire is easily kindled in chaff or tinder or rabbit fur, but also easily extinguished unless it takes hold of some other material capable of protecting and feeding it, so one must realize that the love of the newly married, blazing up quickly out of physical attraction, is not persistent or secure unless it settles in the character, lays hold of the mind, and acquires a life of its own.

(9) We see the moon bright and conspicuous when she is far from the sun; when near, she vanishes and is hidden. A good woman, on the other hand, should be seen most when she is with her husband, and stay at home and be hidden when he is away.

(14) There is no usefulness in a mirror ornamented with gold and jewels, unless it shows a likeness. Similarly, there is no profit in a rich wife, unless she makes her life and character resemble and harmonize with her husband's. If a mirror shows a scowling image of a happy face, or a cheery, grinning image of an angry sullen face, it is faulty and worthless. And so, if a wife puts on a glum look when her husband wants to be playful and affectionate, or if she laughs and jokes when he is serious, she is a poor wife, and has no sense of occasion; she proves herself in the first case disagreeable, in the second insensitive. Mathematicians tell us that lines and surfaces do not move on their own, but only in conjunction with bodies. Similarly, a wife should have no feelings of her own, but share her husband's seriousness and sport, his anxiety and his laughter.

(19) A wife ought not to have friends of her own, but use her husband's as their common stock. And the first and most important of our friends are the

gods. A married woman should therefore worship and recognize the gods whom her husband holds dear, and these alone. The door must be closed to strange cults and foreign superstitions. No god takes pleasure in cult performed furtively and in secret by a woman.

(20) Plato says that the happy and blessed city is one in which the words "mine" and "not mine" are least to be heard, because the citizens treat everything of importance, so far as possible, as their common property. Even more firmly should these words be banished from a marriage. Doctors tell us that an injury on the left side refers the sensation to the right. Similarly, it is good for a wife to share her husband's feelings, and a husband his wife's, so that, just as ropes gain strength from the twisting of the strands, so their communion may be the better preserved by their joint efforts, through mutual exchanges of goodwill. Nature joins you together in your bodies, so that she may take a part of each, and by mixing them together give you a child that belongs to you both, such that neither of you can say what is his or her own, and what the other's. Community of resources also is particularly appropriate for the married; they should pour everything into one fund, mix it all together, and not think of one part as belonging to one and another to the other, but of the whole as their own, and none of it anyone else's. We call our mixed drink "wine" though there is more water than wine in it; similarly, the property and the house should be called the husband's even if the wife contributes the greater part.

(22) The Roman who was reproached by his friends for divorcing his chaste, rich, and beautiful wife, replied by holding up his shoe. "This shoe," he said, "is new and beautiful, but no one knows where it pinches me."[72] A wife should not rely on her dowry, her birth, or her beauty, but ensure by her conversation, manners, and behavior, which are the points that most touch a husband, that there is nothing in their daily life harsh or hurtful, but only painless and harmonious affection. Doctors are more alarmed by fevers that come from obscure and gradually developing causes than they are by those that have an obvious and conspicuous origin. Similarly, repeated, trivial, daily annoyances that go unnoticed cause more damage and disruption to the joint life of husband and wife.

(30) According to the old custom, Egyptian women did not wear shoes; this was so that they should spend all day at home. With most women, if you take away their gilded shoes and bracelets and anklets, their purple dresses and their pearls, they too will stay at home.

(33) Rich men and kings who honor philosophers adorn both themselves and their beneficiaries; but philosophers courting the rich do nothing to increase the reputation of these people, but merely diminish their own. It is the same with wives. If they submit to their husbands, they are praised. If they try to rule them, they cut a worse figure than their subjects. But the husband should rule the wife, not as a master rules a slave, but as the soul rules the body, sharing her feelings and growing together with her in affection. That is the just way. One can care for one's body without being a slave to its pleasures and desires; and one can rule a wife while giving her enjoyment and kindness.

(34) Philosophers distinguish three classes of bodies: those made up of separate units, like a fleet or an army; those made of units connected together, like a house or a ship; and those which have a natural unity, such as animals have. A

marriage between lovers has this natural unity; a marriage for money or children is made of units connected together; a marriage based simply on the pleasure of sleeping together is made of separate units, and should be called cohabitation rather than a shared life. . . .

(37) Cyrus' Greek troops[73] were ordered by their generals to receive the enemy attack in silence if the enemy advanced shouting, and to shout if the enemy was silent. Sensible wives keep quiet when their husbands shout in anger, but speak and try to calm them down if their anger is silent.

(46) A woman said to Philip,[74] when he tried to lay hands on her against her will, "Let go: every woman is the same when the lamp is taken away." This was a good rejoinder to a vicious adulterer, but for a married woman, it is precisely when the lamp has been removed that she needs to be different from ordinary women; when her body is not seen, her chastity, her faithfulness, her discipline, and her affection must be apparent to her husband.

(48) Eurydice, I would have you read what Timoxena[75] wrote to Aristylla about the love of ornament, and try to memorize it. As for you, Pollianus, do not think that your wife will avoid extravagance and expense if she sees that you do not despise it in other matters, but take pleasure yourself in gilded cups, painted rooms, or elaborate collars for your horses and mules. If extravagance is abroad in the men's quarters, it cannot be driven out of the women's. You are old enough now to study philosophy; use its demonstrations and arguments to improve your character, conversing and associating with those who can help you. Gather whatever is valuable from every quarter, like a bee; carry it yourself to your wife, share it with her, discuss it with her, making the best arguments her friends and familiars. You are her "father" and her "mother" and her "brother;" but it is just as honorable to hear a wife say, "Husband, you are my guide and philosopher, my teacher of the noblest and divinest lessons." Such studies, in the first place, keep women away from absurd behavior: a woman who understands mathematics will be ashamed to dance; if she hears the magic of Plato's or Xenophon's words, she will not let the magic of witchcraft into her life.

14 *LAUDATIO TURIAE (INSCRIPTIONES LATINAE SELECTAE* 8393)

The so-called "Eulogy of Turia" is the funeral speech which an upper-class Roman delivered in honor of his wife, probably in the last decade of the first century BC, and which he subsequently arranged to be inscribed on a memorial to her. She is praised, not only for the conventional virtues – of modesty, piety, sobriety, selfless devotion to husband and family – that were expected of every Roman wife, but also for her courage and intelligence. Because the part of the inscription that is likely to have recorded their names is missing, the identity of both the speaker and his wife are uncertain.[76] They are sometimes assumed to be Quintus Lucretius Vespillo, consul in 19 BC, and his wife Turia, because some of the events which are described in the speech are similar to ones that are elsewhere recorded as having happened to them.[77]

Left column

. . . . You were orphaned suddenly before the day of our wedding, when both of your parents were murdered together in the solitude of the countryside. Since I had gone away to Macedonia, and your sister's husband Cluvius to the province of Africa, it was mostly because of you that the death of your parents was not left unavenged. So assiduously did you fulfill your duty by asserting your demands and claims that we could not have done more if we had been present. But these are things you have in common with that most virtuous woman, your sister.

While you were doing this, having secured the punishment of the murderers, you immediately left your father's house to guard your modesty, and came to my mother's house, where you awaited my return. Then you and your sister were pressured to agree that your father's will, in which you and I had been appointed heirs, had been rendered invalid, because he had contracted a *coemptio*[78] with his wife, as a result of which you, together with all your father's property, would necessarily have come under the guardianship of those who were pursuing the matter; your sister would have been entirely excluded from that inheritance, since she had been emancipated to Cluvius. With what intelligence you handled this, with what presence of mind you resisted them, I know full well, though I was absent.

You safeguarded our common interests by asserting the truth, that the will had not been broken, so that we should both take the inheritance, rather than you getting all of it. And you resolutely defended your father's intentions, to such an extent that you declared that you would share the inheritance with your sister, if you were unable to uphold the validity of the will, and that you would not come under the condition of legal guardianship, since there was no such right against you in the law, for no *gens*[79] could be produced that could lawfully compel you to do this. For even if your father's will had been invalidated, those who were bringing the prosecution had no such right, since they did not belong to the same *gens*. They yielded to your determination and did not pursue the matter further. And so alone you successfully upheld the defense you had undertaken of your duty to your father, your devotion to your sister, and your loyalty to me.

Marriages as long as ours are rare, ended by death, not broken by divorce. For we were fortunate enough to be together for forty years without quarrel. Would that our long partnership had come to an end because of something that had happened to me; it would have been more just for the older one to yield to fate.

Why should I recall your domestic virtues, of modesty, obedience, affability, reasonableness, diligence at wool-working, religion without superstition, sobriety of dress, modesty of appearance? Why should I speak about your concern for your relatives, your devotion to your family, that you looked after my mother as you did your own parents, that you worked to provide the same quiet life for her as you did for your own relatives, and the innumerable other virtues you have in common with all married women who cultivate a good reputation? It is your own special virtues that I am championing, and very few women have encountered similar circumstances, so as to oblige them to endure and to accomplish such things, which fortune has made rare for women.

Through our common diligence we have preserved all the property you received from your parents, for you were not concerned to acquire for yourself what you had handed over entirely to me. We divided our duties in such a way that I exercised guardianship of your property and you managed the care of mine. I shall pass over much concerning this part of our relationship, so as not to interject myself into what is properly yours. Let it be enough for me to have indicated how you felt.

You have demonstrated your generosity to many friends and especially to your relatives. Someone might praise other women, but the only equal you have had . . . is your sister. Your female relatives . . . you brought up in your own houses with us. You also supplied them with dowries, so that they could obtain a status worthy of your family. The dowries that you had constituted, Cluvius and I agreed to pay, and because we approved of your generosity, and did not want your patrimony to be diminished, we substituted our own resources, and contributed our own property to the dowries. I have mentioned this not for the purpose of commending ourselves, but to show that it was a matter of honor for us to carry out with our means what you had conceived in a spirit of pious generosity.

Many other kindnesses of yours I have chosen not to mention. . . .

Several lines are missing.

Right column

You furnished abundant assistance during my flight – you provided me with the means of a dignified life, when you sent me all the gold and jewelry you had taken from your body – and thereafter enriched me in my absence with servants, money, and provisions, craftily deceiving the guards posted by our adversaries. You begged for my life when I was absent – it was your courage that urged you to make the attempt – and because of your entreaties I was protected by the clemency of those against whom you prepared your arguments. But you always spoke with undaunted courage.

Meanwhile, when a gang of men collected by Milo,[80] whose house I had acquired by purchase when he was in exile, tried to profit from the opportunities provided by civil war by breaking into our house to plunder it, you drove them back and defended our home.

Several lines are missing.

. . . . that I was restored to my country by him,[81] for if you had not provided for my safety, by arranging what he could save, his support would have been promised in vain. So I owe my life no less to your devotion than to Caesar.

Why should I now reveal our intimate and secret plans and private conversations? How I was saved by your advice when I had been roused by startling news to meet sudden and imminent dangers. How you did not allow me rashly to tempt fate by acting too boldly, and prepared a safe hiding-place for me, when I had begun to think more modestly, choosing as partners in your plans to save me your sister and her husband, Gaius Cluvius, all of you sharing in the danger. If I tried to relate everything, there would be no end to it. It is enough for me and for you that I was safely hidden.

But I confess that the most bitter thing that has happened to me in my life was something that happened to you. When I had been restored to my country as a citizen, because of the kindness and wisdom of Caesar Augustus, who was absent, Marcus Lepidus,[82] his colleague, who was present, was confronted with your request concerning my recall, and you lay prostrate at his feet, and not only were you not raised up, but you were dragged away and carried off like a slave, your body full of bruises, but your spirit unbroken, and yet you kept reminding him of Caesar's edict with its expression of pleasure at my recall, and though you had to listen to insulting words and to suffer cruel wounds, you loudly proclaimed the words of the edict, so that the author of my dangers should be known. This matter soon proved harmful to him. What could have been more effective than the virtue you displayed? You provided an opportunity for Caesar to show his clemency, and not only to safeguard my life, but also to censure Lepidus' insolent cruelty by your admirable steadfastness.

But why go on? Let me wrap up my speech, which should and can be brief, lest by dwelling on your great deeds I treat them unworthily. In return for your great services towards me, let me acknowledge before the eyes of all that you saved my life.

When peace had been re-established throughout the world, and the state had been restored, quiet and happy times befell us. We hoped to have children, who for a long time fate had begrudged us. If it had pleased fortune to continue to be favorable to us, as it was accustomed to be, what would have been lacking for either of us? But taking a different course, it put an end to our hopes. What you considered and what you tried to do because of this would perhaps be remarkable and praiseworthy in other women, but because in you they are hardly remarkable when compared to your other virtues, I will pass over them.

Despairing of your ability to have children, and grieving over my childlessness, lest by staying married to you I might lose hope of having children, and for that reason be unhappy, you spoke of divorce, and said that you would leave our house, surrendering it to another woman's fertility, intending nothing else than that you yourself, trusting in our well-documented like-mindedness, would search out and provide someone who was worthy and suitable for me, and you declared that you would treat future children as common to us, and as your own, and that you would not effect a separation of our property, which up until then had been held in common, but that it would continue to be under my control and, if I so wished, under your administration: you would have nothing apart, nothing separate, and you would thereafter display towards me the dutiful devotion of a sister or a mother-in-law.

I must confess that I was so angry I lost my mind, so horrified by what you had tried to do that I was barely able to regain my composure. To think that we could be separated before it had been decreed by fate; to think that you could conceive in your mind that you might cease to be my wife while I was still alive, though you had been utterly faithful to me when I was in exile, and almost dead! How could my desire or need to have children have been so great that I would have broken faith because of it, and exchanged certainty for uncertainty? But what more can I say? You remained with me as my wife. For I could not have given in to you without disgrace for me and unhappiness for us both. But on your part, what could have been more memorable than that you devoted yourself to my interests, that when I could not have children by you, and you despaired of having your own, you wanted to arrange for me to have them through another woman's fertility.

Would that the time allotted to each of us had allowed our marriage to continue until I, the older one, had been carried away – that would have been more just – and you had performed for me the last rites, and that I had died while you were alive, and that you had become like a daughter to me in place of my childlessness. It was fated that you should go ahead of me. You have bequeathed me sorrow, born of my longing for you, and left me miserable, without hope of children. I, for my part, shall conform my feelings to your judgment, and follow your admonitions. But all your ideas and instructions ought to yield to your praises, so that they may be a comfort to me, that I may not miss as much what I have consecrated to immortality as a permanent memorial.

The accomplishments of your life will not be forgotten by me. The thought of your fame gives me courage, and from your achievements I have learned how to resist fortune, which did not rob me of everything, since it has allowed your memory to be enlarged by praise. But with you I have lost the tranquility of my existence. Recalling how you used to foresee and protect me from dangers, I am overcome by calamity, and cannot hold to what I promised. Natural grief wrests away my power of self-control. I am drowned by sorrow, and tormented by grief and fear – I stand firm against neither. Remembering my previous misfortunes and afraid of what the future may bring, my heart sinks. Deprived of such defenses, the thought of your fame does not prepare me to endure patiently; I seem destined instead to suffer longing and grief.

The conclusion of my speech will be that you deserved everything, but it was not my destiny to give it to you. Your last wishes I consider to be law; whatever I shall be able to do in addition, I shall do. I pray that the gods of the underworld grant you rest and protect you.

15   PLINY, *LETTERS* 4.19

Gaius Plinius Caecilius Secundus, nephew and adopted son of Pliny the Elder (see selection 22), was born at Comum (now Como), in northern Italy, about AD 61. He had a long and distinguished career as a lawyer and public servant, culminating in his appointment as governor of the province of Bithynia-Pontus (in what is now northern Turkey) in about 111–12. His surviving works include the *Panegyricus*, a ponderously effusive speech in praise of Trajan that he delivered in the Senate in 100, and 368 *Letters* (in ten books), most of them written for a public audience. When Pliny was about forty, he married a young woman named Calpurnia (it was his third marriage). The following letter is addressed to Calpurnia's aunt, who raised her after the death of her mother.

Gaius Plinius to Calpurnia Hispulla.

Since you are a model of family devotion, and cherished your excellent and loving brother as much as he cherished you, and love his daughter as if she were your own, displaying the affection not only of an aunt but also of the father she lost, I know how pleased you will be to learn that she has turned out to be worthy of her father, of you, and of her grandfather. She is very intelligent and frugal; she loves me, which is an indication of her virtue. In addition, because of her fondness for me, she has developed an interest in literature. She has copies of my works, which she reads again and again, and even learns by heart. How concerned she is when I am about to speak in court, how happy when it's done! She stations someone to keep her informed about the kind of reception and applause I get, and about the outcome of the case. Whenever I read from my work, she sits close by behind a curtain and avidly listens to my praises. She even sings my verses, to the accompaniment of her lyre, instructed not by some musician, but by love, which is the best teacher.

All this gives me the greatest hope that our mutual happiness will grow each day and last forever. For she does not love my age or my person, which gradually decays and grows old, but my passion for fame. Nothing else would be suitable for one brought up by your hands, and trained in your precepts, who has seen nothing in your company except what was pure and honorable, and learned to love me on your recommendation. For you respected my mother like a daughter, and have guided and encouraged me since my boyhood; you used to predict that I would become such as I am now in the eyes of my wife. So we eagerly thank you, I because you gave her to me, she because you gave me to her, as if you chose us for each other. Farewell.

16 *Corpus Inscriptionum Latinarum* 13.1983

Something in the order of 250,000 inscriptions, many of them fragmentary, have been recovered from different parts of the Roman world, most of them from the period 100 BC–AD 200. They were written mostly on stone, sometimes on metal (especially bronze). They are published in a number of collections, the largest of which is the *Corpus Inscriptionum Latinarum* (Berlin, 1863–).

Many of the inscriptions are funeral epitaphs, which, in appearance, are not unlike modern tombstones. The following example, which was found at Lugdunum in Gaul (mod. Lyons, France), commemorates a young woman named Blandinia Martiola, who married at thirteen. The sentiments expressed by her husband are not untypical of those recorded on other epitaphs.

To the gods of the underworld.

To the eternal memory of Blandinia Martiola, a most blameless girl, who lived eighteen years, nine months, and five days. Pompeius Catussa, a Sequanian citi-

PLATE 2.1 *The funerary monument of Tiberius Claudius Dionysius and
Claudia Prepontis, Rome, ca.* AD *40–50 (Vatican Museum XXXI.14.70). The
clasped hands symbolize marriage. The inscription reads: "To the spirits of
Tiberius Claudius Dionysius. Claudia Prepontis made (this) for her deserving
patron and for herself."*

zen,[83] a plasterer, to his incomparable wife, who was very kind to him, and who lived with me for five years, six months, and eighteen days, without any hint of wrong-doing.

During his lifetime, he saw to the erection of this memorial for himself and for his wife; he consecrated it while it was still under the mason's trowel.

You who read this, go bathe in the baths of Apollo, as I used to do with my wife. I wish that I still could.

17 VALERIUS MAXIMUS, MEMORABLE DEEDS AND SAYINGS 6.3.9–12

Almost nothing is known about the life or career of Valerius Maximus. His *Memorable Deeds and Sayings*, published probably soon after AD 31, is a collection of moralizing anecdotes – about famous people and about Roman institutions – that was meant to be used by teachers and rhetoricians. The following passage collects several examples of stern and unforgiving husbands.

(9) Severity in exacting vengeance is sometimes a response to great wickedness, as in the case of Egnatius Mecennius, who beat his wife to death with a club, because she had been drinking wine. Not only was he not prosecuted for his actions, but he wasn't even criticized, for everyone agreed that she was a perfect example of someone who had paid the penalty for violating her sobriety. Certainly, any woman who drinks too much wine closes the door to every virtue, and opens it to sinfulness.

(10) Savage also was the marital sternness of Gaius Sulpicius Galus, who abruptly divorced his wife, not without cause, because he had seen her outside with her head uncovered. "For the law," he said, "dictates that your appearance is to be approved by my eyes alone. You're to dress suitably for them, be attractive for them, trust that their judgment is more reliable than yours. Furthermore, that you've made your appearance needlessly provocative is, in itself, grounds for suspicion of immorality."

(11) Quintus Antistius Vetus felt the same way when he repudiated his wife because he had seen her in public speaking intimately and secretively with a certain freedwoman: alarmed, as it were, by the first signs and stirrings of wrong-doing, not by any wrong-doing itself, he swiftly punished her misbehavior so as to protect himself from injury rather than to avenge it.

(12) To these should be added Publius Sempronius Sophus, who repudiated his wife by letter for no other reason than that she had dared to watch the games without his knowledge. So women used to be treated this way even when they had no intention of misbehaving.

Suggestions for Further Reading

On women, see especially E. Fantham, H. P. Foley, N. B. Kampen, S. B. Pomeroy, and H. A. Shapiro, *Women in the Classical World: Image and Text* (Oxford, 1994). S. Pomeroy, *Goddesses, Whores, Wives and Slaves: Women in Classical Antiquity* (New York, 1975) is still valuable. On women in the period of the later empire, G. Clark, *Women in Late Antiquity: Pagan and Christian Life-Styles* (Oxford, 1993). Much has been written about women and the law. The best introduction is J. F. Gardner, *Women in Roman Law and Society* (London, 1986); for the later empire, A. Arjava, *Women and Law in Late Antiquity* (Oxford, 1996). On Livy, see P. G. Walsh, *Livy: His Historical Aims and Methods*, 2nd edn (Bristol, 1989). For Juvenal, E. Courtney, *A Commentary on the Satires of Juvenal* (London, 1980).

The definitive work on marriage is S. Treggiari, *Iusti Coniuges: Roman Marriage from the Time of Cicero to the Time of Ulpian* (Oxford, 1993). There are a number of important essays in B. Rawson (ed.), *Marriage, Divorce and Children in Ancient Rome* (Oxford, 1992). On Plutarch, see D. A. Russell, *Plutarch* (London, 1973). There is a comprehensive discussion of the *Laudatio Turiae* in E. Wistrand, *The So-called Laudatio Turiae: Introduction, Text, Translation, Commentary* (Gothenburg, 1976). On inscriptions, L. Keppie, *Understanding Roman Inscriptions* (Baltimore, 1991).

On family life, see especially K. R. Bradley, *Discovering the Roman Family: Studies in Roman Social History* (New York, 1991); S. Dixon, *The Roman Family* (Baltimore, 1992); and the essays collected in B. Rawson (ed.), *The Family in Ancient Rome: New Perspectives* (Ithaca, NY, 1986), and in B. Rawson and P. Weaver (eds), *The Roman Family in Italy: Status, Sentiment, Space* (Canberra and Oxford, 1997). On the family in late antiquity, there are two excellent articles by Brent Shaw: "Latin funerary epigraphy and family life in the later Roman empire," *Historia: Zeitschrift für alte Geschichte*, 33 (1984), pp. 457–97; "The family in late antiquity: The experience of Augustine," *Past and Present*, 115 (1987), pp. 3–51. J. F. Gardner and T. Wiedemann, *The Roman Household: A Sourcebook* (London and New York, 1991), is a wonderfully rich collection of primary sources. On patriarchy (and much else), see R. Saller, *Patriarchy, Property and Death in the Roman Family* (Cambridge, 1994). For mothers, S. Dixon, *The Roman Mother* (London, 1988). On children, see especially T. Wiedemann, *Adults and Children in the Roman Empire* (New Haven, 1989).

Three

ECONOMY

Editor's introduction

In the almost complete absence of reliable quantitative data, it is impossible now to construct a detailed picture of the Roman economy. What is reasonably clear is that the economy as a whole was, broadly speaking, underdeveloped, in the sense that the vast majority of the population lived at or near the level of subsistence.[1] Most people made a living, in some fashion, from agriculture, which was the basis of the personal fortunes of the governing class, and the main source of wealth in the empire, probably in every period. Surplus capital was usually invested in land, ownership of which conferred both social status and political power.

The vast majority of agriculturalists were peasants, about whom distressingly little is known (difficult to detect in the artefact record, they are generally ignored by the literate elite). In most years, they are unlikely to have produced more than what they needed to feed themselves and their families. It is sometimes supposed that there was a decline in the number of small-holding, independent peasants, at least in Italy, from about the period of the late Republic. But there is really no evidence for it.

More is known about the agricultural practices of the wealthy, most of whom, it seems, did not possess the sort of vast estates (*latifundia*) that moralists were inclined to criticize, but rather a number of smaller and often somewhat scattered properties, sometimes grouped around a large, central farm. Normally, they either leased their land to be worked by tenants (whose rent was exacted sometimes as a fixed payment, sometimes as a proportion of the harvest) or worked it directly with a permanent labor force of slaves, with temporary labor, slave or free, brought in at busy times such as the harvest and the vintage. There is no way now to determine whether tenancy or agricultural slavery was more common.

All that can safely be said is that slave labor appears to have been most prevalent, at least in central and southern Italy, in the period between about 150 BC and the middle of the first century AD, and that in other parts of the empire, tenancy is likely to have been predominant in every period.

Not much is known either about industry, which, with the exception of textiles and pottery, appears to have been generally small-scale. There was never any significant demand for manufactured goods, probably because most people were too poor to buy them. Most products, it seems, were made at home or by local craftsmen. There were few technological improvements. And entrepreneurship was uncommon. Senators and equestrians are known to have invested in workshops and warehouses. But they were more likely to consume wealth than to invest it. Capital was sometimes loaned out at interest. But a lot of loans were unproductive, taken out to finance political campaigns, for example, and only rarely for the purpose of investing in potentially profit-making enterprises. Trade, too, was never more than a small part of the economy, at least in part because methods of transportation were primitive and inefficient. The transportation of bulk commodities over land (by ox-drawn cart, for example) was slow and costly. Water transportation was generally faster and cheaper. But transporting cargoes long distances by sea was risky (because of storms and pirates), and limited by the length of the sailing season, which normally lasted only from April to October.

It is unclear whether the economy was capable of achieving any significant measure of growth. There is plenty of evidence to show that cultivation was expanded, in some cases dramatically, across parts of the western provinces in the first two centuries AD, a period which is widely agreed to have been unusually prosperous. But we might imagine that it was a case mostly of the rich getting richer.

18   PLUTARCH, *LIFE OF CATO THE ELDER* 21

On Plutarch and on Cato the Elder, see the introduction to selection 2. The following passage describes Cato's schemes for making money, which were widely regarded as unconventional. The translation is from I. Scott-Kilvert, *Makers of Rome: Nine Lives by Plutarch* (Harmondsworth, 1965), pp. 143–4.

.... When [Cato] began to devote himself more energetically to making money, he came to regard agriculture as a pastime rather than as a source of income, and he invested his capital in solid enterprises which involved the minimum of risk. He bought up ponds, hot springs, land devoted to producing fuller's earth, pitch factories, and estates which were rich in pasture-land or forest. All these undertakings brought in large profits and could not, to use his own phrase, be ruined by the whims of Jupiter. He also used to lend money in what is surely the most disreputable form of speculation, that is, the underwriting of ships. Those who wished to borrow money from him were obliged to form a large association, and when this reached the number of fifty, representing as many ships, he would take one share in the company. His interests were looked after by Quintio, one of his freedmen, who used to accompany Cato's clients on their voyages and transact their business. In this way he drew a handsome profit, while at the same time spreading his risk and never venturing more than a fraction of his capital.

He would also lend money to any of his slaves who wished it. They used these sums to buy young slaves, and after training them and teaching them a trade for a year at Cato's expense, they would sell them again. Often Cato would keep these boys for himself, and he would then credit to the slave the price offered by the highest bidder. He tried to encourage his son to imitate these methods, and told him that to diminish one's capital was something that might be expected of a widow, but not of a man. But he certainly went too far when he ventured once to declare that the man who deserved the highest praise, indeed who should be honored almost as a god, was the one who at the end of his life was found to have added to his property more than he had inherited.

19 CICERO, *ON DUTIES* 1.150–1

Marcus Tullius Cicero was born at Arpinum, in central Italy, in 106 BC. An outspoken champion of Republican institutions, he was elected consul, as a "new man,"[2] in 63. He is probably better known through his own works than any other writer of classical antiquity. In addition to his extensive collection of letters (864 in all, 774 written by Cicero, 90 by his correspondents), we possess fifty-seven of his speeches, from the period 81–43. Most deal with civil and criminal cases, and with the doings of the politically active. He also wrote extensively about political theory, rhetoric, and philosophy. He was killed, on the orders of Mark Antony, in 43.

The following passage is from his work *On Duties*, which he wrote in 44 BC for his son. The prejudice that he expresses against working-class occupations is typical of his class, which generally lived off the income of inherited property, and which considered all paid labor, and manual labor in particular, to be demeaning.

Now concerning trades and means of livelihood, which ones are to be considered suitable for free men, and which are sordid, we generally hold to the following. First, those means of livelihood are rejected as unsuitable which incur men's hatred, such as those of tax-collector and money-lender. Unsuitable also for free men, and sordid, are the means of livelihood of all hired workers, whom we pay for labor, not for skill, for in their case, their very wages are a token of their servitude. They must be considered sordid also who buy from merchants in order to re-sell immediately, for they would not make a profit other than by routinely lying, and there is certainly nothing more base than misrepresentation. And all craftsmen are engaged in a vulgar trade, for a workshop cannot contain anything suitable for a free man. Least respectable of all are those trades which cater to sensual pleasures: "fish-mongers, butchers, cooks, poulterers, fishermen," as Terence says. Add to this, if you please, perfumers, dancers, and all garden-variety entertainers.

But the trades in which either a greater intelligence is required or from which no small benefit is derived, such as medicine, architecture, and teaching – these are respectable for those whose rank they suit. Trade, if it is on a small scale, is to be considered sordid. But if it is plentiful and on a large scale, importing many things from all over, and distributing to many without misrepresentation, it is not to be greatly disparaged, and can even be thought to deserve the greatest respect, if it conveys those who are involved in it, satiated or satisfied with their profits, from the port to a country estate, as it has often conveyed them from the sea into port. But of all things by which something is acquired, nothing is better than agriculture, nothing more profitable, nothing more pleasurable, nothing more worthy of a free man.

20   CATO, ON AGRICULTURE

On Cato, see the introduction to selection 2. His only surviving work is *On Agriculture*,[3] which was written about 160 BC to advise wealthy landowners how to organize and run their estates. It is an important source of information both about farming practices and about the economics of estate-management. Cato assumed that farms would normally be supervised by slave overseers and worked by slave labor.

(Preface) It would sometimes be better to acquire wealth by trade, if it were not so hazardous, and similarly by money-lending, if it were as honorable. Our ancestors believed, and embodied in their laws, that a thief should be fined double, and a money-lender fourfold: to what extent they considered a money-lender to be a worse citizen than a thief can be inferred from this. And when they praised a good man, they said he was a good farmer, a good tiller of the soil; he who was praised in this way was judged to have received the highest commendation. I consider the merchant to be energetic, and devoted to money-making; but, as I said above, it is dangerous, and subject to disaster. But the bravest men and the sturdiest soldiers come from those who farm; their profession is most honorable, most stable, and least despised; and those who are engaged in that pursuit are least inclined to be disaffected. . . .

(1.7) If you were to ask me what the best farm is, I would say: 100 *iugera*[4] of land, comprising every kind of soil, and in the best location; a vineyard is best if it produces a lot of good wine; an irrigated garden is in second place; third, a willow-plantation; fourth, an olive-plantation; fifth, a meadow; sixth, grain-land; seventh, a stand of timber; eighth, an orchard; ninth, an acorn-grove.

(2) When the owner[5] arrives at the farm-house, after paying his respects to the household gods, he should, on the same day, go around the whole property; if not on the same day, at least on the next. When he has learned how the farm is being maintained, what work has been accomplished, and what remains to be done, he should, on the following day, summon the overseer and ask him how much work has been done, what remains, whether what has been completed was done in a timely way, whether it's possible to finish what's left, and what the yield has been of wine, of grain, and of everything else. When he has learned this,

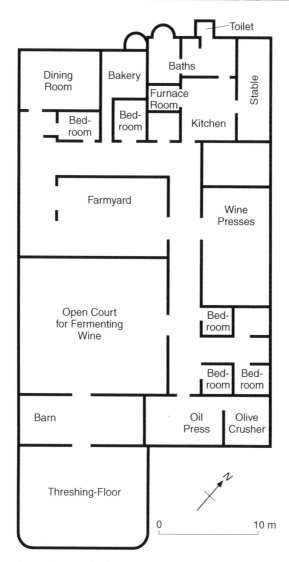

FIGURE 3.1 *Plan of a rural villa at Boscoreale, Italy (from J. Shelton,* As the
Romans Did: A Sourcebook in Roman Social History, *2nd edn, New York
and Oxford, 1998).*

he should make a list of the work done and the time taken to do it. If the work
does not seem satisfactory, the overseer claims that he has worked diligently, but
the slaves have not been well, the weather has been bad, slaves have run away, he
has had to do public work – when he has given these and many other excuses,
call him back to your calculation of the work done and the workers employed.
When the weather has been wet, point out what work could have been done on
rainy days: scrubbing and applying pitch to the wine-jars, cleaning the farm-
house, transporting grain, carrying out manure, making a manure-pit, cleaning

seed, mending ropes, and making new ones; and that the slaves ought to have mended their smocks and hoods. Point out, also, that on feast days old ditches could have been cleared, the public roadway shored up, brambles cut back, the garden dug, the meadow cleared, twigs bundled, thorns dug out, grain[6] ground, cleaning done. Point out that such large rations ought not to have been given to the slaves when they were sick. When this has been gone over calmly, see to it that what work remains is completed; examine the accounts of cash, of grain, and of what has been purchased as fodder; examine the accounts of wine, and of olive-oil – what has been sold, what has been collected, what is still owed, and what remains for sale; where security should be taken,[7] let it be taken; arrange for what remains to be checked over. If anything is in short supply for the current year, see to it that it's provided; that what is superfluous is sold; that whatever work should be hired out is hired out. He [i.e., the owner] should give directions as to what work is to be done, and what work is to be hired out, and leave these in writing. He should look over the cattle and hold a sale. He should sell the olive-oil, if the price is right, and sell any surplus of wine and grain. He should sell worn-out oxen, substandard cattle, substandard sheep, wool, hides, an old wagon, old tools, an old slave, a sick slave, and anything else that's not needed. The owner ought to be a seller, not a buyer.

(4) You should have good stalls, good pens, and latticed feed-racks: the bars should be one foot apart; if you make them in this way, the cattle will not scatter their feed. Build your house in proportion to your means. If you build well on a good farm, situating the house in a good place, if you can live properly in the country, you will go there more willingly, and more often; the farm will get better, there'll be less wrong-doing, and you'll receive a greater profit; the forehead is better than the back of the head. Be a good neighbor; do not allow your slaves to misbehave. If your neighbors view you favorably, you'll sell your produce more easily, hire out your work more easily, hire workers more easily; if you build, they will help with their labor, their animals, and their materials. If – knock on wood – it should ever be necessary, they will gladly defend you.

(5.1–5) The duties of an overseer are these. He should use good practices. Feast days must be observed. He should keep his hands off of other people's property, while diligently preserving his own. He should settle disputes among the slaves; if any of them does something wrong, he must punish him properly in proportion to the offense. He should see to it that the slaves are not troubled, or cold, or hungry. He should keep them busy with work, by which he'll more easily keep them from wrong-doing and meddling. If the overseer is determined that they will not behave badly, they will not do it; if he allows it, the owner must not allow him to go unpunished. He should show his appreciation for good work, so that the others may take pleasure in behaving properly. The overseer should not lounge about; he should always be sober; he should not go out to eat. He should keep the slaves busy, and see to it that what the owner has ordered is done. He should not think that he knows more than the owner. He should consider the owner's friends to be his own. He must listen to anyone he's been told to heed. He should not perform any religious rites, except at the time of the Compitalia,[8] at the cross-roads, or at the hearth. He should extend credit to no one without the owner's permission; what the owner has loaned, he must collect. He should not lend anyone seed, fodder, grain, wine, or olive-oil. He ought to have no more than two or three households from which he borrows and to which he lends. He should routinely go over the accounts with the owner. He should not have the same laborer or servant or caretaker for longer than a day. He should not want to buy anything without the owner's knowledge, nor want to hide anything from the owner. He should have no hangers-on. He should not want to consult any fortune-teller, or prophet, or diviner, or astrologer. He must not be stingy with the seed, for that is bad luck. He should see to it that he knows how to do every kind of farm-work, and does it often, but not to the point of exhaustion; if he does, he'll learn what's on the minds of the slaves, and they will do their work more contentedly. If he does this, he will be less likely to lounge about; he will be in better health, and will sleep more easily. He should be the first to get out of bed, and the last to go to bed, before which he should see that the farm-house is closed, that everyone is asleep in his proper place, and that the cattle have feed.

(6.1–3) As to what you should plant, and in what places, the following ought to be observed. Where the soil is heavy, rich, and treeless, it's best that grain be planted; if the same soil is vaporous, it should be sown ideally with rape, turnips, millet, and panic-grass. In soil that's heavy and warm, plant olives – those for pickling, the longer variety, the Sallentine, the oblong-shaped variety, the posea, the Sergian, the Colminian, the waxy-white; choose especially whatever variety is said to be best in those areas. Plant this type of olive at intervals of twenty-five or thirty feet. Land which is suitable for olive-planting is that which faces the west and is exposed to the sun; anything else will be no good. Where the soil is colder and thinner, it's best to plant the Licinian olive. If you plant it in heavy or warm soil, the yield will be worthless, the tree will die from bearing, and a reddish moss will harm it. Around the boundaries, and along the roads, plant elms and some poplars, so as to have leaves for the sheep and cattle; and timber will be available, if you should need it. Wherever there is a river bank or wet ground, plant poplar shoots and a reed-thicket. The method of planting is as follows: turn over the soil with a double-mattock, then plant the eyes of the reed three feet apart. Plant wild asparagus there, from which you can get asparagus.

(10) An olive-plantation of 240 *iugera*[9] should be equipped in the following way: an overseer, the overseer's wife, five laborers, three plowmen, one muleteer, one swineherd, one shepherd – thirteen people in all; three teams of oxen, three asses equipped with pack-saddles to carry manure, one mill-ass, one hundred sheep; five assembled oil-presses, one copper vessel that holds five *quadrantales*,[10] with a copper lid, three iron hooks, three water-pitchers, two funnels, one copper vessel that holds five *quadrantales*, with a copper lid, three hooks, one small bowl, two olive-oil amphoras, one jar that holds fifty (*heminae?*),[11] three ladles, one water-bucket, one basin, one pot, one wash-basin, one little dish, one chamber-pot, one watering-pot, one ladle, one candlestick, one *sextarius*[12]-measure; three large carts, six plows with plowshares, three yokes equipped with straps, six harnesses for the oxen; one large rake, four manure-hampers, three manure-baskets, three *semuncias*,[13] three blankets for the asses; tools – eight iron pitch-forks(?), eight hoes, four spades, five shovels, two four-toothed rakes, eight hay-sickles, five straw-sickles, five pruning-hooks, three axes, three wedges, one hand-mill, two tongs, one poker, two braziers; one hundred olive-oil jars, twelve

pots, ten jars for storing grape-pulp, ten for storing olive-oil dregs, ten wine jars, twenty grain jars, one jar for lupines, ten large jars, one wash-tub, one bath-tub, two water-basins, one lid each for the jars and pots; one donkey-mill, one hand-mill, one Spanish mill, three sets of traces, one side-board, two copper disks, two tables, three large benches, one bench in the bedroom, three stools, four chairs, two fancy chairs, one bed in the bedroom, four beds held up by ropes, and three ordinary beds; one wooden mortar, one fuller's mortar, one loom, two mortars, one pestle for beans, one for grain, one for seed, one for cracking olive-pits; one *modius*-measure,[14] one half-*modius*-measure; eight mattresses, eight blankets, sixteen cushions, ten table-cloths, three napkins, six hoods for the slaves.

(56) Rations for the slaves. For those who work through the winter, four *modii* of wheat; in summer, four and a half; for the overseer, the overseer's wife, the foreman, and the shepherd, three *modii*; for the chain-gang, four pounds of bread during the winter, five pounds of bread when they begin to dig up the vines, until the figs ripen – then go back to four.

(57) Wine for the slaves. For three months after the vintage is complete, they should drink after-wine.[15] In the fourth month, give them one *hemina* a day, that is, two and a half *congii*[16] a month; in the fifth, sixth, seventh, and eighth months, give them one *sextarius* a day, that is, five *congii* a month; in the ninth, tenth, eleventh, and twelfth, give them three *heminae* a day, that is, one *amphora*[17] a month. In addition to this, issue three and a half *congii* per person for the Saturnalia[18] and the Compitalia. The annual total of wine for each person is seven *quadrantales*. Add proportionately more for the chain-gang, according to the type of work they're doing; for them to drink ten *quadrantales* of wine in a year is not excessive.

(58) Relish for the slaves. Store as many fallen olives as possible. Later, store the mature olives from which very little oil can be made; give them sparingly, so that they will last as long as possible. When the olives have been consumed, give them fish-pickle and vinegar. Give each person one pint of olive-oil a month. One *modius* of salt per person each year is sufficient.

(59) Clothes for the slaves. A tunic three and a half feet long; a blanket every other year. When you give anyone a tunic or a blanket, first take the old one, and have smocks made from it. You ought to give them a good pair of wooden shoes every other year.

(83) A sacrifice for the health of the cattle should be done in the following way. For each head of cattle, make an offering to Mars Silvanus[19] in the forest during the day: three pounds of meal, four and a half pounds of bacon, four and a half pounds of meat, which you may place in one vessel, and three pints of wine, which likewise may be placed in one vessel. Both slaves and free men are allowed to make this offering. When the ceremony is over, immediately consume the offering on the spot. A woman must not be present at this offering or see how it is done. You may make this vow every year, if you wish.

(123) Make wine as a remedy for hip-gout in the following way. Cut a half-foot thick piece of juniper-wood into small pieces. Boil it with a *congius* of old wine. When it has cooled, pour it into a bottle. Take one *cyathus*[20] in the morning before eating. It will be helpful.

(136) On what terms cultivation should be assigned to a share-cropper. In the

region of Casinum[21] and Venafrum,[22] on good land, he should be given one-eighth of the un-threshed grain, on reasonably good land, one-seventh, on third-quality land, one-sixth; if he receives threshed grain, one-fifth. In the region of Venafrum, on the best land, he should receive one-ninth of the un-threshed grain. If they mill the grain in common, the cultivator should pay for the milling in proportion to his share. He should receive one-fifth of the barley, and one-fifth of the beans.

The following admonitions are addressed to the overseer.

(143) See to it that your wife performs her duties. If the owner has given her to you as your wife, be content with her. Make her fear you. Do not allow her to be extravagant. She should visit the neighbors and other women as little as possible, and should have them neither in the house nor in her part of it. She should never go out to eat, or lounge about. She should not perform any religious rites, or arrange for someone to do it for her, without the permission of the owner or the owner's wife; let her remember that the owner performs religious rites for the whole household. She should be clean; she should keep the farm-house neat and clean; she should clean the hearth every day before she goes to bed. On the Kalends,[23] Ides,[24] and Nones,[25] and whenever there is a feast day, she should hang a wreath over the hearth, and on those same days pray to the household gods for prosperity. She should see to it that she has food cooked for you and for the slaves. She should have many hens and lots of eggs. She should have dried pears, sorb-apples, figs, raisins, sorb-apples in must, and pears, and grapes, and sparrow-apples in jars, grapes in grape-pulp and in pots buried in the ground, and fresh Praenestine nuts in a pot buried in the ground. Scantian apples in jars, and the other things that it's customary to store, and wild fruits – all these she should diligently store away every year. She should know how to make good flour, and finely ground grain.

21   COLUMELLA, *ON FARMING*

Lucius Iunius Moderatus Columella was born to a land-owning family at Gades (mod. Cádiz), Spain. He became an army officer,[26] and, later, the owner of several estates in Italy. His work *On Farming* (*De re rustica*), which was written probably AD 60–5, and which draws mainly on his own experience, is easily our most comprehensive account of Roman agricultural practices.[27] It also provides valuable information about the profitability of slave labor in the first century AD. It is addressed to a man named Publius Silvinus, who is not otherwise known.

(1.preface.1–3) Very often I hear the leaders of our state blaming the infertility of the soil, or the inclemency of the weather for the past several years, as being harmful to crops; and I even hear certain men downplaying the above-mentioned complaints (in their view, for good reason), because they think that the soil has been worn out and exhausted by the over-production of an earlier age, and that it can no longer provide nourishment to mortals with its former generosity. For my part, Publius Silvinus, I am convinced that such reasons are far from the truth, for it is wrong to suppose that Nature, which that creator of the world endowed with permanent fertility, is afflicted with barrenness, as if with some disease; nor is it appropriate for a man of good judgment to believe that Earth, which was allotted a divine and everlasting youth, and is said to be the common parent of all things – because it has always brought forth everything, and will continue to bring forth everything – has grown old like a person. Nor do I believe that such things have happened to us because of the violent behavior of the skies, but rather as a result of our own faults, for agriculture, which the best of our ancestors had treated with the best of care, we have given to all the worst of our slaves, as if to the executioner for punishment.

(1.preface.7–10) .... What has happened is all the more amazing – that something of the greatest importance to our bodies and to the needs of life should have made, up to this time, the least progress, and that this method of increasing and of bequeathing our patrimony, which is entirely free of immorality, should be scorned. For other methods – which are various and in conflict, so to speak, with each other – are not in agreement with justice, unless we think it more equitable to have acquired booty as a result of military service, which benefits us nothing without bloodshed and the misfortune of others. Or, for those who hate war, would the dangers of the sea and of trade be more desirable, so that man, a terrestrial creature, violating the laws of nature and exposed to the anger of the winds and the sea, should hang on the waves and always wander over an unknown world, in the manner of birds, a stranger on a far-off shore? Or is money-lending more commendable, a thing hated even by those whom it seems to help? But no more admirable is the "canine" occupation, as the ancients called it, of barking at every millionaire, or of practicing banditry against the innocent and in defense of the guilty, something despised by our ancestors, but allowed by us within the walls of the city and in the very Forum itself. Or should I consider to be more honorable the hypocritical fawning of the paid morning-caller, who hovers around the doorways of the powerful, relying on rumors to predict how long his master will sleep? For the slaves do not condescend to reply to his questions about what's going on inside. Or should I think it more fortunate for someone, driven away by a door-keeper in chains, to loiter at those ungrateful doors, often until late at night, and, by the most demeaning servility, to purchase the honor and authority of the *fasces*[28] at the price of his own dishonor and the dissipation of his inheritance? For public office is purchased, not with voluntary servitude, but with gifts. If good men ought to shun these and similar things, there remains, as I have said, one method of increasing one's wealth that is honorable and suitable for a free man, and this is found in agriculture.

(1.preface.17–18) .... Those true descendants of Romulus,[29] exercised in constant hunting and no less by working in the fields, were distinguished by extraordinary physical strength, and hardened by peace-time labors, they easily endured the hardships of war when called upon to do so, and always esteemed the ordinary people of the countryside more highly than those of the city. For just as those who stayed within the boundaries of the farm-houses were judged to be lazier than those who worked the land outside, so those who idly lingered within the walls, under shelter of the city, were considered to be more indolent than those who cultivated the fields or supervised the work of the cultivators. It is clear, also, that their market-day assemblies were employed for this purpose – that urban business might be conducted only on every ninth day, and rural business on the others. For in those days, as I have said before, the leaders of the state used to spend their time in the fields, and when their advice on matters of state was desired, they were summoned from their farm-houses to the Senate, and it was for this reason that those who summoned them were called "travelers."

(1.2) I think that land should be purchased in the immediate area, so that the owner may both visit it more often, and announce that he will visit it more frequently than he actually intends to visit it; for under this apprehension, both the overseer and the slaves will stick to their duties. But whenever he has the chance, he should spend time in the country, and his stay there should not be idle nor spent in the shade. For the careful owner ought to go around every little part of his estate rather frequently, and at every time of the year, so that he may observe more carefully the nature of the soil, whether in foliage and grass or in already mature crops, and not be unaware of anything that could properly be done on it. For it is an old saying of Cato that that land is most badly treated whose owner does not give directions as to what should be done on it, but listens to the overseer. For that reason, special care is to be taken, in the case either of one who possesses an estate inherited from his ancestors, or of one who intends to buy an estate, to know what kind of farm is considered best in the region, so that he may either dispose of one that's unprofitable or buy one that's praiseworthy. But if fortune underwrites our prayer, we will have a farm in a healthy climate, with fertile soil, partly level, elsewhere with hills gently sloping to the east or to the south; with some parts of the land cultivable, and others wooded and rough, not far from the sea or a navigable river, by which its products may be sent off and supplies brought in. The level ground, divided into meadows, arable land, willow-groves, and reed-thickets, should be next to the farm-house. Some of the hills should be bare of trees, to serve only for grain-crops, which do better, however, in moderately dry and fertile plains than in steep places, and so even the higher grain-fields ought to have level ground, and be sloped as gently as possible, and very much like flat land. Next, other hills should be covered with olive-groves and vineyards, and with what will provide props for the vines; they should be able to supply wood and stone, if the need to build requires it, and grazing-land for the cattle; they should send down falling streams into the meadows, gardens, and willow-plantations, and running water for the farm-house. There should be herds of cattle and of other four-footed animals grazing the cultivated land and the thorn-bushes. But such a situation as we desire is hard to find and, being rare, is seldom come across; next best is one which has as many as possible of these qualities; acceptable is one that has more than a few.

(1.7.1–6) . . . . An owner is required to be careful especially in respect to people. And these are either tenant-farmers or slaves, either unfettered or in chains. He should behave agreeably with his tenants, and show himself to be easy to get along with, and be more insistent in exacting labor services than payments, since this is both less offensive, and yet, generally speaking, more profitable. For when land is carefully cultivated, it usually yields a profit, never a loss, unless unusually severe weather or robbers attack it, in which case the tenant does not dare to ask for a remission of his rent. But the owner should not insist on his rights in every matter in which his tenant is obligated, such as the exact days for payment, or the demanding of firewood, and other small services, attention to which causes country-people more bother than expense; in fact, we should not claim everything that's allowed, for the ancients considered the extremes of the law to be extreme oppression. Still, we must not allow the whole to be remitted, for, as the money-lender Alfius is said to have remarked, very truthfully, "even the best debts become bad ones if they are not called in." But I myself recall having heard Publius Volusius, an old man and former consul who was very wealthy, declare that the most fortunate estate was one which had tenants who were native to it, and which held onto them even from the cradle, by reason of long-standing familiarity, as if born on their father's property. So it is my decided opinion that the frequent renting out of a farm is a bad thing, but that the tenant-farmer who lives in town and prefers to cultivate the land through his slaves, rather than by his own hand, is worse. Saserna used to say that from a man of this kind the usual return was a lawsuit instead of revenue, and that for that reason we should work to hold onto rural-bred and hard-working tenants, when it is not possible for us to cultivate the land ourselves or when it is not feasible to cultivate it with our slaves, something which does not happen, however, except in areas which are under-populated because of the severity of the climate and the barrenness of the soil. But when both the climate and the soil are moderately good, his personal attention always brings a greater return from the land than that of a tenant, always than that even of an overseer, unless the most egregious carelessness or greed on the part of the slave gets in the way. There is no doubt that both of these offenses are normally either committed or encouraged through the fault of the owner, given that he has the authority to see to it that such a person is not put in charge of his affairs, or that he is removed, if he has already been put there. On distant estates, however, which the owner cannot easily get to, it is better for every kind of land, and especially for grain-land, to be under free tenant-farmers rather than slave overseers. A tenant-farmer cannot do much harm to grain-land, as he can to vineyards and trees, but slaves do it tremendous damage: they rent out the oxen, and keep them and the other animals poorly fed, and do not plow the ground carefully, and they claim to have sown far more seed than they have actually sown; but what they have entrusted to the earth, they do not look after in such a way as to make it grow properly, and when they have gathered it together on the threshing-floor, every day during the threshing they lessen it either by fraud or by negligence.

(1.8.1–2) Our next concern is in regard to slaves – what duties and what sorts of tasks should be assigned to each. So my advice at the beginning is not to appoint an overseer from among those slaves who are physically attractive, and certainly not from that class which has been involved in the sensuous occupations of the city! This lazy and sleepy-headed class of slaves, accustomed to lounging about, to the Campus,[30] the Circus,[31] the theaters, to gambling, taverns, and brothels, is always dreaming of the same silliness; and when they carry it over into farming, the owner suffers loss, not so much in the slave himself, as in his whole property. He should be chosen who has been hardened by farm-work from infancy, and has been tested by experience.

(1.8.5–6) But whatever kind of overseer you choose, a woman companion should be assigned to him, to keep him in line, and yet in certain matters to help him; and this same overseer should be warned not to become intimate with any of the household slaves, still less with an outsider. Sometimes, however, he may consider someone whom he has observed to be constantly busy and vigorous in carrying out his tasks as being worthy of being invited to his table on a feast day, as a mark of distinction. He should not make a sacrifice except on the orders of the owner. Soothsayers and witches, two types of people who rely on empty superstition to induce ignorant minds to spend money and then to behave shamefully, ought not to be allowed in. Nor should he have knowledge of the city or of the markets, other than to buy or sell things in connection with his responsibilities.

(1.8.15–19) In regard to the other slaves, the precepts that ought to be observed are, in general, as follows, and I do not regret having applied them myself: to talk rather familiarly with the rural-bred slaves, provided that they have not conducted themselves inappropriately, more often than with the city-bred slaves; and when I perceived that their unending labor was lightened by this friendliness on the part of their owner, I would even joke with them sometimes, and allow them to joke more often. Now I make it a practice to consult them on any new work, as if they were more knowledgeable, and in this way to learn what talents each of them possesses, and how intelligent each of them is. In addition, I notice that they are more willing to undertake work when they think that they have been consulted and that their advice has been taken. Certainly, it is customary for all who are cautious to inspect the slaves who are in prison, to determine whether they are carefully chained, whether the places of confinement are safe and adequately guarded, whether the overseer has either put anyone in chains or released someone without his owner's knowledge. For the overseer should be very careful to uphold both principles: that he not release from shackles anyone whom the owner has punished in that way, unless with his permission, and that he not release anyone whom he himself has chained up on his own initiative until the owner knows about it; and the investigation conducted by the owner should be more painstaking on behalf of slaves of this type, so that they may not be badly treated in respect to clothing or other allowances, seeing as they are more liable to suffer unjust punishment because they are subject to more people, such as overseers, foremen, and jail-keepers, and when wounded by cruelty and greed, are more to be feared. And so a careful owner inquires not only of them, but also of those who are not chained, and who are more trustworthy, whether they are receiving what they ought to according to his instructions, and he tests the quality of their food and drink by tasting it himself, and examines their clothing, their gloves, and their foot-coverings. He should also give them plenty of opportunities to complain about those who cruelly or fraudulently mistreat them. And I sometimes stand up for those who have a legitimate grievance, and punish those who incite the slaves to rebel, or who slander their keepers, and on the other hand, I reward those who conduct themselves energetically and industriously. And to unusually fertile women, who ought to be rewarded for bearing a certain number of offspring, I have granted exemption from work, and sometimes even freedom, after they had raised a large number of children. For exemption from work was awarded to any woman who had three children, freedom also to any who had more. Such justice and consideration on the part of the owner contributes greatly to increasing his estate.

(3.3.1–6) Now, before I discuss the planting of vines, I do not think it out of place to lay down, as a sort of foundation for the coming discussion, the principle that we should first weigh up and investigate whether viticulture enriches an owner. For it is almost pointless to give directions about planting vines, as long as what is prior is not yet agreed upon – whether vines should be kept at all. And most people would be so uncertain about this that they would avoid and fear such an arrangement of their land, and would consider it better to have meadows and pastures, or timber-land; for in regard to vineyards planted with trees, there has been no small dispute even among authorities, with Saserna denigrating this kind of land, Tremelius very much approving it. But we shall assess this opinion in its proper place. Meanwhile, students of agriculture should first be taught this – that the return from vineyards is a very rich one. And not to dwell on that past fertility of the land, about which Marcus Cato long ago, and Terentius Varro[32] more recently, have written – that each *iugerum* planted with vines yielded 600 *urnae*[33] of wine (for Varro emphatically declares this in the first book of his *Res rusticae*), and that this is what was customarily produced, not just in one region, but also in the district of Faventia,[34] and in the Gallic territory which is now annexed to Picenum;[35] certainly, in our own times, the region around Nomentum[36] is distinguished by a very celebrated reputation, and especially the part of it that Seneca[37] owns, a man of great ingenuity and learning, on whose estates, it has been reported, each *iugerum* of vineyards has normally yielded eight *cullei*.[38] For what happened in our Ceretanum[39] seems to have been a kind of prodigy – that a certain vine on your property produced more than 2,000 grapes, and that on my property, 800 grafted vines yielded seven *cullei* in less than two years; that first-class vineyards produced 100 *amphorae* per *iugerum*, when meadows and pastures and woodland are judged to do very well by their owner if they bring in 100 sesterces for each *iugerum*. For I can scarcely recall a time when grain-crops returned a yield of four to one throughout at least the greater part of Italy. So why is viticulture disparaged? Certainly not through its own fault, but, Graecinus says, because of human mistakes: first, because no one bothers to search carefully for cuttings, and so most people plant vineyards of the worst kind; also because they do not nourish the vines they have planted in such a way that they gain strength and grow before they wither; but even if they do happen to grow, they cultivate them carelessly. From the very beginning, they think that it makes no difference what kind of land they plant; in fact, they even select the very worst part of their lands, as if such ground alone were suitable for this plant, because it could not produce anything else. But they either do not understand the method of planting or fail to put into practice what they do understand. Then too, they rarely have the dowry – that is, the equipment – ready for their vineyards, though this, if overlooked, wastes a great deal of work, as well as the owner's financial resources. In fact, most people try to get the richest possible yield immediately, and do not provide for the future, but as if they were living simply day to day, put such demands on their vines, and burden them with so many young shoots, that they give no thought to future generations. When they have done all this, or at any rate most of it, they prefer anything to admitting that it's their fault; they complain that their vineyards are not providing a return for them, vineyards which they have ruined through greed, or stupidity, or neglect.

(11.1.13–19) When he who is about to take up the duties of an overseer has been instructed in the skills of many different farmers, he should, first of all, avoid intimacy with any of the domestic slaves, and even more so with outsiders. He should be abstemious in regard to sleep and wine, both of which are very incompatible with diligence; for a drunk man's attention to duty declines as he loses his memory, and a great many things escape the notice of the sleepy-headed. For what can anyone do, or order anyone else to do, while he's asleep? He should also be averse to sexual passion, for if he gives himself up to it, he will not be able to think of anything other than what he loves; for his mind, enticed by vices of this sort, thinks that there is no reward more agreeable than the gratification of his lust, nor any punishment more serious than the frustration of his desire.

So he should be the first to wake up and, according to the time of year, always lead the recalcitrant slaves to their work, himself walking briskly in front of them. For it is of the greatest importance that farm-laborers get to work at the break of dawn, and not proceed slowly with their work because of laziness. Indeed, Ischomachus, who has already been mentioned, says: "I prefer the prompt and conscientious work of one man to the slow and negligent work of ten."[40] It certainly causes a great deal of harm if a worker is given the opportunity to trifle away his time. For as often happens in completing a journey, he who proceeds energetically and without any lingering arrives much sooner than he who, having set out at the same time, has searched for shady trees, and pleasant springs, or cool breezes. In the business of farming, it is difficult to say how much better an active worker is than one who is lazy and recalcitrant. The overseer, therefore, must see to it that the slaves go out immediately at first light, not in a slow and half-hearted way, but that they follow him, as if into battle, with vigor and eagerness of spirit, as he marches energetically in front of them like a general, and he should encourage them with various exhortations as they labor at their work; and sometimes, as if coming to the aid of one whose strength is failing, he should take his iron tool for a while, and himself do the work for him, and tell him that it ought to be done in the vigorous way in which he himself has done it.

And when twilight has come, he should leave no one behind him, but follow behind them, like a good shepherd, who allows no member of the flock to be left in the field. Then, when he has come inside, he should do the same as that careful shepherd, and not immediately hide himself in his house, but exercise the greatest care for each of them; and if, as often happens, one of them has received some injury in the course of his work, and is wounded, he should apply lotions, or if anyone is rather sick in some other way, he should immediately bring him to the infirmary, and order that any other treatment appropriate to him be applied. No less consideration should be shown for those who are healthy, that their food and drink be supplied honestly by those in charge of provisions; and he should accustom the farm-workers to eat always at their master's home and household hearth; and he himself should eat in their presence, and be an example of frugality. Nor should he eat lying down, except on holidays, and he should celebrate feast days by bestowing gifts on the strongest and most frugal among them, and sometimes even invite them to his table, and be prepared to grant them other honors also.

(11.1.21–4) He should keep the slaves groomed and clothed in a way that's more serviceable than dainty, that is, carefully protected from the cold and rain, both of which are best kept off by long-sleeved coats made of skin and by thick hoods: and if this is done, almost every winter day can be endured while they work. Therefore the overseer ought to examine the slaves' clothes just as he examines their iron tools, as I have already said, twice a month. For frequent inspection offers no hope of impunity and no opportunity for wrong-doing. And so he ought to call out every day the names of the slaves who are chained in the prison, and investigate whether they are carefully fettered, and also whether the places of confinement are secured and properly fortified; nor should he release anyone whom the owner or he himself has put in chains, except on the owner's orders. He should not consider making a sacrifice except on his owner's orders; and he should not on his own initiative have any knowledge of soothsayers or fortune-tellers, both of which types of people assail ignorant minds with empty superstition. He should not visit the city or any markets except for the purpose of selling or buying something necessary. For he ought not to go beyond the boundaries of the estate, nor by his absence give the slaves the opportunity to stop working or to get into trouble. He should prevent paths and new boundaries from being made on the land. Except for the owner's friends, he should receive visitors as infrequently as possible. He should not use his fellow-slaves to his own advantage, nor allow any of them to go beyond the boundaries of the estate, unless great necessity compels them to do so. He should not spend his owner's money on cattle or any other commercial product, for such things divert him from his duties as an overseer, and make him a trader rather than a farmer, and do not allow him ever to balance the owner's accounts; but when the money is to be counted up, goods are displayed instead of cash. And so he will consider it something to be avoided, in the same way that enthusiasm for hunting and fowling is to be avoided – things by which many workers are distracted from their duties.

(12.1.1–5) . . . . The overseer's wife ought to be youthful, that is, not too much of a girl. . . . She should be of sound health, not ugly in appearance, nor on the other hand very beautiful, for unimpaired strength will be required both for staying awake and for other tasks; ugliness will disgust her partner, while excessive beauty will make him lazy. And so care must be taken that we do not have an overseer who is inclined to wander or averse to his wife's company, nor, on the other hand, one who is inclined to lounge about inside, never far from her embrace. But these things which I have spoken of are not the only ones to be looked for in an overseer's wife. For in the first place, it must be considered whether she is far removed from wine, greediness, superstition, sleepiness, and the company of men, and whether she readily understands what she ought to remember and what she ought to provide for the future, so that she might display nearly the same character as we prescribed for the overseer; for between husband and wife there ought to be many things in common, and they should avoid wrong-doing just as much as they hope for a reward for work well done. Then she should exert herself so that the overseer has to do as little as possible inside the house, since he ought to go out with the slaves at first light, and return at twilight, exhausted by the work he has done.

But by putting the overseer's wife in charge of domestic matters, we are not releasing the overseer from responsibility for them, but lighten his task by giving him a helper. In fact, the duties which are undertaken at home should not be left entirely to the woman, but delegated to her in such a way that they are at the same time watched over by the eyes of the overseer. For the overseer's wife will be more diligent if she remembers that there is someone there to whom an accounting must frequently be rendered. Moreover, she will have to be absolutely convinced that she should always, or certainly most of the time, remain inside the house; and that she should send outside those slaves who have something to do in the fields, and keep within the walls those who appear to have something to do in the farm-house; and she must see to it that the daily tasks are not left undone because of inaction. What is brought into the house, she should carefully inspect, in case it is damaged, and accept only what has been examined and found to be intact; then she ought to separate what is to be consumed, and guard what can be stored, so that the expenses for the year are not used up in a month.

Suggestions for Further Reading

The best introduction to the Roman economy is P. Garnsey and R. P. Saller, *The Roman Empire: Economy, Society and Culture* (Berkeley, 1987); see also R. Duncan-Jones, *The Economy of the Roman Empire: Quantitative Studies*, 2nd edn (Cambridge, 1982); *Structure and Scale in the Roman Economy* (Cambridge, 1990). M. Rostovtzeff, *The Social and Economic History of the Roman Empire*, 2nd edn, ed. P. M. Fraser (Oxford, 1957), is still fundamental. On the economic importance of slavery, see especially M. I. Finley, *The Ancient Economy*, 2nd edn (Berkeley, 1985). On money, M. H. Crawford, *Coinage and Money under the Roman Republic: Italy and the Mediterranean Economy* (London, 1985); R. Duncan-Jones, *Money and Government in the Roman Empire* (Cambridge, 1994).

On agricultural techniques and practices, see M. S. Spurr, *Arable Cultivation in Roman Italy, c. 200 BC–AD 100* (London, 1986); K. D. White, *Roman Farming* (Ithaca, NY, 1970). For the period of the later empire, C. E. Stevens, "Agriculture and rural life in the later Roman empire," in *The Cambridge Economic History of Europe*, 2nd edn, ed. M. M. Postan (Cambridge, 1971), vol. 1, pp. 92–124. On patterns of land-holding, see M. I. Finley (ed.), *Studies in Roman Property* (Cambridge, 1976). For imperial estates, D. P. Kehoe, *The Economics of Agriculture on Roman Imperial Estates in North Africa* (Göttingen, 1988). The best introduction to pastoralism is C. R. Whittaker (ed.), *Pastoral Economies in Classical Antiquity* (Cambridge, 1988).

On trade, see J. D'Arms and E. C. Kopff (eds), *The Seaborne Commerce of Ancient Rome: Studies in Archaeology and History* (Rome, 1980); P. Garnsey, K. Hopkins, and C. R. Whittaker (eds), *Trade in the Ancient Economy* (Berkeley, 1983); P. Garnsey and C. R. Whittaker (eds), *Trade and Famine in Classical Antiquity* (Cambridge, 1983); K. Hopkins, "Taxes and trade in the Roman empire (200 BC–AD 400)," *Journal of Roman Studies*, 70 (1980), pp. 101–25; C. R. Whittaker, *Land, City and Trade in the Roman Empire* (Brookfield, Vt., 1993). For the later empire, F. W. Walbank, "Trade and industry under the later Roman empire in the West," in *The Cambridge Economic History of Europe*, 2nd edn, ed. M. M. Postan and E. Miller (Cambridge, 1987), vol. 2, pp. 71–131. On the role of pottery, D. P. S. Peacock and D. F. Williams, *Amphorae and the Roman Economy: An Introductory Guide* (London, 1986).

Four

SCIENCE AND MEDICINE

Editor's introduction

The Romans never attached much importance to science or to scientific research. Much of what passed for scientific knowledge was instead taken over from the Greeks. The chief value of science, it was widely believed, was in its application. It might also be inferred from Pliny the Elder (selection 22) that the study of natural phenomena was considered to be a means of moral improvement. Technical advances, many of which had a military application, were made mostly in the fields of engineering and architecture – the development of concrete; the extensive use of wood and metal screws; improved techniques of dome and vault construction.

It seems to be widely agreed that the Romans also contributed little to the development of medicine. Galen of Pergamum (selection 24), who became court-physician under the emperor Marcus Aurelius, made a number of important discoveries in physiology and anatomy. But most Roman medical writers were cataloguers and encyclopedists. Medical theory was constructed on Greek and Hellenistic ideas, especially, it seems, from about the time of Asclepiades of Prusa (mod. Bursa, Turkey), who was the first Greek medical teacher to practice at Rome, where he founded a school around 40 BC. The most widely accepted theory of pathology, for example, which understood disease to be a consequence of imbalance among the four humors – blood, phlegm, yellow bile, and black bile – was borrowed directly from the Greeks. Even Celsus (selection 23), who wrote in Latin, and who seems to have had surgical experience, preferred to rely on Hellenistic doctrines.

Where the Romans made probably their most important contribution to medical practice was in military medicine, in the treatment of battle-wounds, for example, and in the development of legionary hospitals, the remains of which have been unearthed at Vetera (mod. Xanten) and Novaesium (mod. Neuss) in Germany, and at Inchtuthil in Scotland. They can also be credited with the development (or improvement) of a wide variety of medical instruments, almost 200 of which have been recovered at Pompeii alone.

With the exception of court-physicians like Galen, medical practitioners were never very highly esteemed, maybe because, at least until the time of the late Republic, most seem to have come from what the elite considered to be the socially inferior classes, including slaves. Magic, superstition, and charlatanry were common in every period.

22   PLINY THE ELDER, *NATURAL HISTORY*

Uncle and adoptive father of Pliny the Younger (selection 15), Gaius Plinius Secundus was born in AD 23 at Comum (mod. Como), in northern Italy. After commanding a cavalry squadron on the Rhine, he held a series of posts under the emperors Vespasian and Titus, culminating in his appointment as commander of the fleet stationed at Misenum, on the bay of Naples. He died while observing the eruption of Mt. Vesuvius in AD 79. His only surviving work is the *Natural History*, an encyclopedic collection of wondrous, and often fanciful, stories about natural phenomena, people, animals, plants, metals, and stones.

(2.5) That the shape of the world has the rounded appearance of a perfect sphere is shown, in the first place, by the fact that people have agreed to call it "orb," but also by the evidence of the facts, for not only does such a figure in all its parts bend into itself, and not only must it be held up by itself, enclosing and holding itself together without the need of any joints, and without experiencing an end or a beginning in any of its parts, and not only is such a shape best suited to the motion by which, as will soon appear, it is constantly turned, but also by the testimony of our eyes, because it is seen to be concave and the same length in every direction, something which could not happen in the case of any other figure.

(2.32–6) . . . . Let us now examine the remaining bodies between the sky and the earth. It is clear that what they call the star of Saturn is the highest and therefore looks the smallest, and that it goes around in the largest circle, returning to the beginning of its position in no less than thirty years. The motions of all the wandering stars, including the sun and the moon,[1] follow a course that is contrary to that of the world, that is, to the left, while the world is always heading to the right. . . . The star of Saturn is of a cold and frozen nature. The orbit of Jupiter is much below it, and it therefore revolves much faster, going around once in twelve years. The third star is Mars, which some call Hercules; because of its proximity to the sun, it glows with fire; it revolves about every two years. Because of its excessive heat and Saturn's cold, Jupiter, lying between them, is moderated by both, and rendered healthy. Next, the motion of the sun is of 360 parts, but in order that an observation made of its shadows may return to the starting-point, five and one-quarter days are added each year; for that reason,

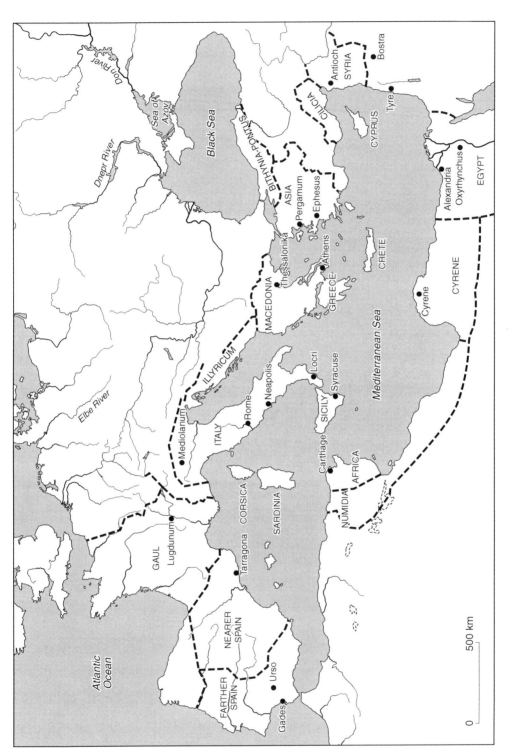

FIGURE 4.1 *The Roman world in the time of Augustus.*

one intercalary day is added to every fourth year, so that our reckoning of time might agree with the course of the sun. Below the sun revolves a huge star called Venus, which wanders with an alternating motion, and is shown by its very names to be a rival of the sun and the moon: for when advancing and rising before dawn, it takes the name of Lucifer, as being another sun and hastening the dawn, but when shining after sunset is called Vesper, as prolonging the light and acting in place of the moon.

(2.41–3) But everyone's admiration is overcome by the last star, the one most familiar to the earth, and fashioned by nature to be a remedy for darkness – the moon. By its multi-shaped transformations it has tortured the minds of observers, who are embarrassed that the nearest star is the one that is least known – always waxing or waning, and now curved into the horns of a sickle, now divided in half, now bent into a circle; spotted and then suddenly shining clear; huge and full-orbed, and then suddenly not there; sometimes shining all night, sometimes rising late and for part of the day augmenting the light of the sun; failing[2] and yet visible while it is failing; hiding at the end of the month when it is not thought to be struggling; at one time low, at another high, and not even this in a consistent way, but sometimes raised to the sky, sometimes touching the mountains, now carried up to the north, now thrust down to the south. The first human being to notice these facts about it was Endymion – hence the traditional story of his love for it. We certainly feel no gratitude towards those who have worked diligently to shed light on this light, while by a curious disease of the human mind it pleases us to fashion a record of bloodshed and slaughter, so that the crimes of mankind might be known by those who are ignorant of the world itself.

(2.147) . . . . It is recorded that in the consulship of Manius Acilius and Gaius Porcius[3] it rained milk and blood, and that often on other occasions it has rained flesh, for example in the consulship of Publius Volumnius and Servius Sulpicius,[4] and that of the flesh that wasn't torn to pieces by birds, none went bad; similarly, that it rained iron in the region of Lucania[5] the year before Marcus Crassus was killed by the Parthians,[6] and with him all the Lucanian soldiers, of which there were a great many in his army: the shape of the iron that fell was similar to sponges; the seers prophesied wounds from above. But in the consulship of Lucius Paullus and Gaius Marcellus[7] it rained wool near Compsa castle,[8] close to where Titus Annius Milo[9] was killed a year later. It is recorded in the accounts of that year that while Milo was pleading a case in court, it rained baked bricks.

(2.189–90) . . . . There is no doubt that Ethiopians are scorched by the heat of the star near them, and are born with a singed appearance, with curly beard and hair, and that races in the opposite regions of the world have white and frosty skin, with straight yellow hair; that the latter are fierce because of the rigidity of their climate, the former wise because of the fluidity of theirs; and their very legs demonstrate that in the case of the former the juice is called back into the upper parts of the body by the nature of heat, while in the case of the latter it is driven down to the lower parts by falling moisture; in the latter place, dangerous wild beasts abound, in the former, a great variety of animals and especially of birds; but in both places people are tall, in the former because of the pressure of the fires, in the latter because of the nourishing effect of the moisture. But in the

middle of the earth, because of a healthy mixture of both, there are regions that
are fertile for everything, and people are of medium height, with a strong mixture
even in their complexion; customs are gentle, senses clear, intellects fertile and
capable of understanding the whole of nature; and they also have governments,
which have never existed in the case of the outer races, any more than they have
ever been subject to the central races, being separate and solitary as a result of the
savagery of the nature that presses upon them.

(3.1.3–5) The whole circuit of the earth is divided into three parts, Europe,
Asia, and Africa. It begins from the west, from the Straits of Gibraltar, where the
Atlantic Ocean bursts in and is spread out into the inland seas. As you enter from
here, Africa is on the right, Europe on the left, Asia between them; the boundaries are the river Tanais[10] and the Nile. The ocean straits which I mentioned are
fifteen miles long and five miles wide, from the village of Mellaria in Spain to
Cape White in Africa, according to Turranius Gracilis, who was born in the
region; Livy and Cornelius Nepos give its width at the narrowest point as seven
miles, but ten where it's widest: so narrow is the mouth through which such a
vast amount of water pours. Nor does great depth lessen the miracle, for many
white-water reefs terrify passing boats, as a result of which many have called it
the threshold of the internal sea.[11] At the narrowest part of the straits, the mountains standing on both sides – Abyla in Africa, Calpe[12] in Europe – enclose the
channel; these were the limits of Hercules' labors, which is why the natives call
them the pillars of that god, and believe that by digging through them he let in
the sea which had been shut out until then, and changed the face of nature.

I shall begin then with Europe, wet-nurse of the conquerors of all nations, and
by far the most beautiful part of the earth, which many have rightly considered
to be, not a third part, but half of the world, dividing the whole circle into two
parts from the river Tanais to the straits of Gades.[13] The ocean, pouring the
Atlantic sea through the space that has been described, and in its eager progress
overwhelming all the lands that were afraid of its coming, also washes those that
resist it with a winding and broken shoreline: Europe especially it hollows out
with a large number of bays, but into four main gulfs, the first of which bends in
an immense curve from Mount Calpe, which, as was said, is the extremity of
Spain, all the way to Locri[14] on Cape Bruttium.

(7.9–12) I indicated that some tribes of Scythians,[15] and in fact many of them,
feed on human bodies – this perhaps may seem incredible, unless we consider
that such monstrous races have existed in the middle part of the world, the Cyc-
lopes[16] and Laestrygones,[17] and that not long ago it was customary for the tribes
beyond the Alps to practice human sacrifice, which is not far removed from eating people. But next to these [that is, the Scythians], towards the north, not far at
all from where the North Wind rises or from the cave that bears its name, a place
they call the Door-bolt of the earth, dwell the Arimaspi, whom we have spoken
of already, and who are remarkable for having one eye in the middle of their
foreheads. Many writers, the most distinguished being Herodotus[18] and Aristeas
of Proconnesus, report that around their mines they constantly wage war with
griffins, a kind of wild beast with wings, as is commonly reported, that digs gold
out of mines, which the beasts guard and the Arimaspi try to seize, both with
remarkable greed.

But beyond the other Scythian cannibals, in a certain large valley in the Imaus mountains,[19] there is a region called Abarimon, home to a forest-dwelling people who have their feet turned back behind their legs, and who are extremely fast, wandering all over with the wild animals. Baeton, Alexander the Great's route-surveyor on his journeys, records that these men cannot breathe in another climate, and so could not be brought to the neighboring kings, and had not been brought to Alexander. According to Isogonus of Nicaea, the cannibals whom we described earlier as being to the north, ten days' journey beyond the Borysthenes river,[20] drink out of human skulls and use the hair-covered scalps as napkins around their necks. The same man declares that certain people in Albania are born with keen gray eyes, and are gray-haired from childhood, and that they see better at night than during the day. He also says that the Sauromatae, thirteen days' journey beyond the Borysthenes, always take food every third day.

(7.21–3) India especially and parts of Ethiopia abound with marvels. The biggest animals are produced in India; for example, Indian dogs are bigger than others. In fact, the trees are said to be so tall that arrows cannot be shot over them, and that, if you're prepared to believe it, squadrons of cavalry may be concealed under a single fig-tree; that reeds are of such height that sometimes a single piece between two knots will make a boat that carries three people. It is agreed that many people are more than five cubits[21] high, that they do not spit, and that they do not suffer from headaches or toothaches or pain in the eyes, and rarely from pain in other parts of the body – so toughened are they by the moderate heat of the sun; and that their philosophers, whom they call Gymnosophists, stand gazing at the sun without moving their eyes from sunrise to sunset, standing all day first on one foot and then on the other in the glowing sand. Megasthenes reports that on the mountain named Nulus there are people with their feet turned backwards who have eight toes on each foot, and that on many of the mountains there is a race of people with dogs' heads, who are covered with the skins of wild animals, who bark instead of speaking, and who live by hunting and fowling, using their nails as weapons; he says that there were more than 120,000 of them. Ctesias writes also that among a certain race of India the women give birth once in their life-time, and that the new-borns immediately begin to grow old; he also describes a race of men who are called the Monocoli, who have only one leg, and jump with remarkable speed; they are also called the Umbrella-foot people, because in hotter weather they lie on their backs on the ground and protect themselves with the shadow of their feet; and that they are not far away from the Troglodytes; and that westward again from these are some people without necks, who have eyes in their shoulders.

(7.36–42) That females are changed into males is not a fable. We find in the annals[22] that at Casinum,[23] in the consulship of Publius Licinius Crassus and Gaius Cassius Longinus,[24] a girl's parents witnessed her transformation into a boy, who at the order of the sooth-sayers was sent away to a deserted island. Licinius Mucianus recorded that at Argos he saw a man named Arescon, who had had the name Arescusa, and had even married, and had then developed a beard and male genitals, and had married a wife; and that he had also seen a boy of the same type at Smyrna.[25] In Africa, I myself saw Lucius Constitius, a citizen of Thysdritum, who had been turned into a male on the day of his marriage....

For other animals there is a prescribed time both for sex and for giving birth, but humans are born all year, and the period of gestation varies – in one case it lasts into the seventh month, in another into the eighth, and right up to the beginning of the eleventh; a child born before the seventh month is rarely alive. No one is born in the seventh month unless conceived the day before or the day after a full moon, or in the period between moons. In Egypt, it is common for children to be born even in the eighth month, and indeed for such cases to live also in Italy, contrary to past opinion. These things vary in other ways: Vistilia, the wife of Glitius, and afterwards of the very distinguished citizens, Pomponius and Orfitius, had four children by them, always in the seventh month, but subsequently gave birth to Suillius Rufus in the eleventh, Corbulo in the seventh (both of them consuls), and later Caesonia, wife of the emperor Gaius, in the eighth. Those born in this number of months experience the greatest difficulty during the first forty days, but the mothers in the fourth and eighth months of pregnancy; and abortion in these cases is fatal. . . .

On the tenth day from conception, pain in the head, dizziness and dim vision, distaste for food, and vomiting are evidence of the formation of an embryo. If the child is male, the mother has a better color and an easier delivery; movement in the womb begins on the fortieth day. Everything is opposite in the case of the other sex: the burden is hard to carry, there is a slight swelling of the legs and the groin; the first movement, moreover, is on the ninetieth day. But in the case of either sex, there is the greatest feebleness when the embryo begins to grow hair, and also at the full moon, a period which is especially harmful also to infants after birth. And her pace in walking and everything else that can be mentioned are so important during pregnancy that those who eat food that is too salty give birth to children lacking nails, and if they breathe, the delivery is more difficult; in fact, yawning during delivery is fatal, just as sneezing after sex causes abortion.

(7.63–6) Woman is the only animal, however, that menstruates; consequently, she alone has what they call moles in her womb. This is shapeless, inanimate flesh that resists the point and the edge of a knife; it is moved around, and it holds back menstruation, as it also holds back delivery: sometimes it is fatal; sometimes it grows old with her; sometimes it falls out when the bowels are moved violently. Something similar is produced also in the stomach of males, which they call a tumor, as in the case of the praetorian, Oppius Capito. But nothing could readily be found that is more remarkable than the menses of women. New wine touched by it turns sour, crops that come in contact with it become sterile, grafts die, seeds in gardens are dried up, the fruit of trees falls off; by its very reflection, the brightness of mirrors is dimmed; the edge of steel and the gleam of ivory are dulled, hives of bees die, rust immediately attacks even bronze and iron, and there is a horrible smell in the air; dogs who taste it are driven mad and their bite is infected with an incurable poison. Furthermore, bitumen, which is generally sticky and viscous, and which, at a certain time of the year, floats in a lake in Judaea which is called Lake Asphalt,[26] adheres to everything it touches, and cannot be pulled apart, except by a thread that has been soaked in the above-mentioned poison. They say that even the ant, the smallest of creatures, is sensitive to it, and throws away grain that tastes of it, and does not afterwards touch it. And this great mischief occurs in a woman every month, and in larger quantity every three months; but for some women it comes more often than once a month, just as in some women it never occurs. But such women do not give birth, since this material is the means of human generation, with seed from the males acting like a coagulant, and collecting this substance within it, which at that very moment is given life and body.

(25.9–11) Nothing else will be found that aroused greater wonder in antiquity than botany. A method was discovered long ago of predicting, not only the day or night, but the very hour, of solar and lunar eclipses. But there still exists among a great many of the common people a long-standing conviction that this is caused by sorcery and by herbs, and that this is the one science that is most prevalent among women. Certainly, there are stories everywhere about Medea of Colchis and other women, and especially about Circe of Italy, who has even been enrolled among the gods. It was for this reason, I think, that Aeschylus, one of the earliest poets, declared that Italy is full of powerful herbs, and many have said the same of Circeii,[27] where that woman lived. Strong evidence exists even now in connection with the Marsi, a people descended from Circe's son, since it is well known that they are snake-tamers.

(25.16) But the reason why more herbs are not well-known is because illiterate country-folk, who are the only ones living among them, are the only ones to have experience of them; and no one bothers to look for them with a crowd of physicians standing in the way. Many that have been discovered still lack names, such as that which I mentioned when discussing the cultivation of crops, and which we know, if buried at the corners of a grain-field, ensures that no birds will enter. The most disgraceful reason why they are few in number is that even those who possess such knowledge are unwilling to share it, as if they themselves would lose what they have passed on to others. It happens also that there is no certain method of discovery, for even in the case of those that are already known, it was sometimes chance that did the discovering, at other times, to tell the truth, a god.

(28.33–6) .... Moths do not touch clothing that has been worn at a funeral, and snakes are pulled up with difficulty except with the left hand. You will not easily be led wrong by one of the discoveries of Pythagoras – that an uneven number of vowels in given names portends lameness, blindness, or similar disabilities on the right side of the body, an even number on the left. They say that a difficult delivery is immediately brought to an end if someone throws over the house where the pregnant woman is located a stone or missile that has killed three animals – a human being, a boar, and a bear – each with one stroke. A light spear, pulled out of a human body, is more likely to accomplish this, provided that it has not touched the ground. The result is in fact the same if it is carried inside. So also, Orpheus and Archelaus[28] write, arrows drawn out of a body, and not allowed to touch the ground, arouse the passion of those lying in a bed when placed under it. They also say that epilepsy is cured by food taken from the flesh of a wild beast that has been killed by the same sword by which a human being has been killed. The parts of certain people have healing powers, as I have said already of the thumb of King Pyrrhus; and at Elis,[29] there used to be shown a shoulder blade of Pelops,[30] which they claimed was made of ivory. Even now many have scruples about shaving the moles on their face.

But as I have already pointed out, the best defense of all against snakes is the saliva of someone who is fasting. Daily experience, however, may identify still other valuable uses of it. We spit on epileptics, that is, we throw back the disease. In a similar way we repel witchcraft and the bad luck that results from having come in contact with someone who is lame in the right leg. We also ask forgiveness from the gods for some overly bold request by spitting into our lap. For the same reason, it is customary to spit three times as a ritual in using any remedy, and so to increase its efficacy; and to mark incipient boils three times with the saliva of someone who is fasting. It is surprising, but easily tested, that if someone regrets a blow, inflicted by hand or by a missile, and immediately spits into the palm of the hand by which it was delivered, the resentment of the one who has been struck is instantly lessened.

(29.112–13) There are the following remedies for headache: attaching the hard, stony material – it's the width of a pebble – that is extracted from snails which have been found without shells (being not yet complete), and which have had their heads removed; and small snails are crushed, and rubbed on the forehead; there is also wool-grease; attaching bones taken from the head of a vulture; or its brain with oil and cedar resin rubbed all over the head and smeared on the inner part of the nostrils; the brain of a crow or owl cooked and taken in food; a rooster shut up without food for a day and a night, the sufferer fasting with him at the same time, with feathers plucked from the neck, or the comb, being tied around the head; applying the ashes of a weasel; a twig from a kite's nest placed under the pillow; mouse-skin ashes applied in vinegar; the little bone of a slug found between two wheel-tracks, passed through gold, silver, and ivory, and attached in dog-skin, a remedy that always benefits many.

23   CELSUS, ON MEDICINE

Little is known about Aulus Cornelius Celsus other than that he lived in the time of the emperor Tiberius (AD 14–37). He wrote an encyclopedia of agriculture, medicine, rhetoric, and military science (probably also of philosophy and law), of which only the medical books are preserved. Written mainly to instruct other laymen, they borrow heavily from Hellenistic medical theories and practice.

(1.2.1–3) It is necessary for the weak, who include most town-dwellers, and almost all of those who are devoted to literature, to take greater precautions, so that care might restore what the nature of their body or location or profession takes away. So any of these who has digested well may safely get out of bed early; if he has digested a little, he ought to stay in bed, and if he was obliged to get up early, he should go back to sleep; he who has not digested should just stay in bed, and neither work nor exercise nor attend to business. He who vomits undigested food when he does not have heartburn should drink cold water at intervals and nonetheless restrain himself. He should also live in a house that is light, airy in summer, sunny in winter; he should avoid the midday sun, the morning and evening cold, and vapors from rivers and marshes; and he should rarely expose himself to the sun when it is breaking through a cloudy sky, so as not to be affected first by cold and then by heat – a thing which especially excites plugged nostrils and running colds. These things ought to be observed especially in unhealthy places, where they even cause pestilence.

(1.4) The next thing is to speak of those who have some weak parts of the body. He whose head is weak should, if he has digested well, rub it gently in the morning with his hands; he should, if possible, never cover it with cloth; he should have it shaved to the skin. It is best to avoid moonlight, especially before the actual conjunction of the moon and sun, and not to walk anywhere after eating. If he has hair, he should comb it every day, walk a lot, but, if possible, not under cover or in the sun; everywhere he should avoid the heat of the sun, and especially after eating and drinking; he should be rubbed with oil rather than washed, but never rubbed in front of a burning fire. . . . If he goes to the baths, he should first sweat for a little while in the lukewarm bath, while wrapped up, and then be rubbed with oil; then go into the hot bath; when he has sweated, he should not get into the tub, but pour hot water all over himself from his head down, then lukewarm water, then cold water, which he should pour longer on his head than on his other parts; then he should rub his head for a while, then wipe it off and rub it with oil. Nothing is as beneficial for the head as cold water, and so he who has a weak head should hold it for a while under a large water-pipe every day during the summer. But even if he is rubbed with oil and does not go into the baths, and cannot stand to cool his whole body, he should nevertheless always pour cold water over his head; but since he doesn't want it to touch the rest of his body, he should lean down so that the water does not run down his neck, and use his hands to direct the flowing water to his face, so that he does not injure his eyes or other parts. It is essential for him to eat moderately, and what he can easily digest; if fasting hurts his head, he should also eat in the middle of the day; if it does not hurt, he should eat only once. It is better for him to drink a light, undiluted wine, rather than water, so that he may have something to take refuge in when his head begins to worsen; and on the whole, neither wine nor water is always suitable for him; each is a remedy when taken in turn. To write, to read, to argue, is not good for him, especially after eating; after this even thinking is not sufficiently safe; however vomiting is worst of all.

(2.1.1–4) Spring is most healthful, next after that winter; summer is more dangerous than healthful; autumn is by far the most dangerous. But the best type of weather is that which is settled, whether cold or hot; the worst is that which is the most variable; and it's for that reason that autumn overwhelms the most people. For it is usually hot in the middle of the day, but cold at night and in the early morning, and also in the evening. So the body, relaxed by the summer, and subsequently by the midday heat, is seized by the sudden cold. But though this occurs mainly at this time, whenever it happens, it is harmful. When the weather is settled, clear days are the most healthful; rainy days are better than foggy or cloudy ones; in winter the best days are those on which there is no wind at all, in summer those on which the west winds are blowing. If there is another kind of wind, those from the north are more healthful than those from the direction of the sunrise or from the south; but these vary somewhat according to the nature of the region. For almost everywhere wind is healthful when coming from inland, harmful when from the sea. And not only is good health more likely in settled weather, but existing diseases also, if there are any, are milder and more quickly ended. The worst weather for the sick man is what made him sick, to such an extent that if the weather changes to a type that is naturally worse, in his situation it may be healthful.

(2.6.1–6) [*Indications of impending death.*] . . . . The nose is pointed, the temples sunken, the eyes hollowed, and the ears cold and flaccid with the tips turned down a little; the skin around the forehead is hard and tight. The color is dark or very pale, much more so if the following is true: there has been neither insomnia, nor diarrhea, nor loss of appetite. Sometimes these causes give rise to the appearance of death, but last only one day: and so when they last longer, it is an indication of death. But in the case of a long-standing disease, if such signs have lasted already for three days, death is at hand, and the more so if, in addition to these things, the eyes also avoid the light and shed tears, and are red where they should be white, and the veins in them are pale, and phlegm floating in them begins to stick to the corners, and one of them is smaller, and both are either deep-sunken or swollen, and the eyelids are not closed during sleep, but some of the white of the eyes shows between them, where this has not been caused by diarrhea; and the same is true when the eyelids are pale, and a similar color affects the lips and nostrils; so also when the lips and nostrils and eyes and eyelids and eyebrows or any one of them become distorted; and because of weakness the patient neither hears nor sees. Death is likewise announced when the patient lies on his back with his knees bent; when he keeps slipping down to the foot of the bed; when he uncovers his arms and legs and tosses them about, and they lack warmth; when he opens his mouth wide; when he sleeps a great deal; when one who is not of sound mind grinds his teeth, if he did not do it when he was healthy; when a sore, which arose either before or during the illness, has become dry and either pale or livid. The following are also indications of death: the nails and fingers are pale; the breath is cold; or if someone, in a fever or acute disease, or insane, or with pain in the lung or the head, uses his hands to pick at a piece of wool or to pull on the threads of his clothes, or grabs at anything small projecting from the opposite wall. Pains arising around the hips and lower parts, if they spread to the internal organs, and then suddenly subside, are evidence that death is approaching, and the more so if there are other signs in addition.

(3.23.1–3) Among the best known illnesses is the one that is called *comitialis*, or "the greater."[31] The sufferer suddenly falls down, foam emerges from his mouth, then after a period of time he returns to himself, and gets up all on his own. This type of disease affects men more often than women. And it usually lasts right up until the day of death without danger to life; but sometimes, when it is recent, it destroys the patient. And it often happens that, if remedies have not helped, it is removed by the onset of puberty in boys and of menstruation in girls. When someone falls down, there is sometimes a stretching of the tendons; sometimes there is none. Some try to rouse them by the same methods that are used with those who are lethargic, which is altogether pointless, because not even the lethargic patient is cured by these methods, and because, though it may be impossible ever to awaken the lethargic patient and he may therefore die from starvation, the epileptic, on the other hand, returns to himself. If someone falls down, and there is no stretching of the tendons, blood should definitely not be let out; if there is stretching of the tendons, it should not be let out unless other things suggest it. It is, however, necessary to move the bowels, or to purge them with black hellebore, or to do both, if the patient's strength allows it. It is necessary next to shave his head, and to rub it thoroughly with oil and vinegar; to give him food after the third day, as soon as the hour has passed at which he fell down. But gruel and other soft and easily digested food, or meat, least of all pork, are not suitable for such patients, but food-materials of the middle type: for he both needs strength and must avoid indigestion; in addition, it is best for him to avoid the sun, the baths, fire, and all heating-agents; also cold, wine, sex, looking down from a steep place, and everything that is terrifying; vomiting, fatigue, anxiety, and all business.

(5.19.11) Among remedies which are suitable for a broken head, some include the following, which is ascribed to Iudaeus. It consists of these things: salt, 16 grams; scales of red copper, copper rust, 48 grams each; ammoniacum[32] for fumigation; frankincense soot, dry resin, 64 grams each; Colophon[33] resin, wax, prepared calf's suet, 80 grams each; vinegar, one and a half *cyathi*;[34] olive-oil, less than a *cyathus*.

(5.27.1–2) I should speak next of wounds that are caused by a bite, sometimes of a man, sometimes of an ape, often of a dog, occasionally of wild animals or of snakes. Almost every bite has some sort of poison; and so, if the wound is severe, a cupping-glass should be applied to it; if the wound is less severe, a plaster should be applied immediately, especially that of Diogenes. If that is not available, use one of those that I recommended against bites; if those are not available, the green Alexandrian; if not even that is available, then any one of those that are suitable for fresh wounds, provided that it is not greasy. Salt is also a remedy for bites, especially for one made by a dog, if a hand is placed over the wound and struck with two fingers, for it draws out the poison; and it is also correct to bandage the wound with fish-pickle. Certainly, if the dog was rabid, the poison must be drawn out with a cupping-glass; further, if the wound is not associated with the tendons or muscles, it should be cauterized; if it cannot be cauterized, it is not a mistake to let out the man's blood. Then after the wound has been cauterized, those things should be applied to it that are used for other burns; but for a wound that has not been subjected to flame, those medicines that are strongly corrosive. After this, the sore should be filled in and brought to healing. . . . Some send those bitten by a mad dog immediately to the baths, and allow them to sweat there as long as the strength of their body permits, with the wound kept open so that the poison may drip out of it more easily; then they administer a lot of undiluted wine, which is an antidote to all poisons. And when this has been done for three days, the patient is judged to be safe from danger.

(7.5.3–4) If a broad weapon has been embedded, it is not a good idea to extract it from the opposite side, in case we add a second large wound to an already large one. It ought to be pulled out, therefore, by some type of instrument, such as that which the Greeks call the Dioclean cyathiscus, because it was invented by Diocles, whom I have already said was among the best of the early physicians. It has two iron or even copper blades; one has hooks, turned downwards, at each end; the other has raised sides, so that it forms a groove; also, its end is turned up a little, and is perforated by a hole. This blade is passed down cross-wise to the weapon; then, when it has reached the point of the weapon, the blade is twisted a little so that it takes hold of the weapon with its perforation. When the point of the weapon is in the hole, with the hooks of the other blade fitted to the one below it, the fingers draw out the instrument and the weapon at the same time.

There is a third type of weapon which sometimes has to be extracted – a lead bullet, or a stone, or something similar, which, having penetrated the skin, rests unbroken inside. In all these cases, the wound should be opened wider, and the object in there extracted by forceps along the path by which it entered. But it is more difficult, in every injury, if the weapon is fixed in bone, or has embedded itself in the joint between two bones. When in a bone, it should be moved around until the place which is gripping the point is loosened; and then the weapon should be extracted either by hand or by forceps; this is also the method for extracting teeth. It hardly ever happens that the weapon does not come out, but if it is stuck, a blow can also be delivered with some instrument. The last resort, when it cannot be pulled out, is to bore a hole next to it with a trephine, and to cut away the bone from the weapon in the shape of the letter [V], in such a way that the lines of the letter which diverge face the weapon; when that has been done, it must be loosened, and is easily removed. But if it has forced its way into the joint between two bones, the two limbs around the wound should be wrapped with bandages or straps, and by means of these pulled in opposite directions, so that the tendons are stretched; because of this stretching, the space between the bones is widened, with the result that the weapon can be removed without difficulty. Care must be taken, as I indicated elsewhere, not to injure any tendon, or vein, or artery with the weapon while it is being extracted. . . . But if anyone has been struck by a weapon which is also poisoned, after doing all the same things, and even more quickly, if possible, that treatment should also be applied which is given to one who has drunk poison, or been bitten by a snake.

24   GALEN, *ON THE USEFULNESS OF THE PARTS OF THE BODY* 14.6–7

Claudius Galen (ca. AD 129–200) was born and educated at Pergamum, in what is now Turkey. After working as a gladiators' doctor, he moved to Rome in 162, where he became court-physician under the emperor Marcus Aurelius. He is said to have published more than 300 works, of which roughly a third survive.

The theory that he advances in the following passage, in which the male and female generative organs are assimilated, and the "failure" of the female organs to project outwards is made a consequence of insufficient heat, was taken to indicate that women could be considered to be less "perfect" than men. The translation is from M. R. Lefkowitz and M. B. Fant, *Women's Life in Greece and Rome: A Source Book in Translation*, 2nd edn (Baltimore, 1992), pp. 243–6.

The female is less perfect than the male for one principal reason, because she is colder, for if among animals the warm one is the more active, a colder animal would be less perfect than a warmer. . . . All the parts, then, that men have, women have too, the difference between them lying in only one thing, which must be kept in mind throughout the discussion, namely, that in women the parts are within, whereas in men they are outside, in the region called the perineum. Consider first whichever ones you please, turn outward the woman's, turn inward, so to speak, and fold double the man's, and you will find them the same in both in every respect. . . . In fact, you could not find a single male part left over that had not simply changed its position; for the parts that are inside in woman are outside in man. . . .

So, too, the woman is less perfect than the man in respect to the generative parts. For the parts were formed within her when she was still a fetus, but could not, because of the defect in the heat, emerge and project on the outside, and this, though making the animal itself that was being formed less perfect than one that is complete in all respects, provided no small advantage for the race; for there needs must be a female. Indeed, you ought not to think that our creator would purposely make half the whole race imperfect and, as it were, mutilated, unless there was to be some great advantage in such a mutilation. . . . This is the reason why the female was made cold, and the immediate consequence of this is the imperfection of the parts, which cannot emerge on the outside on account of the defect in the heat, another very great advantage for the continuance of the race. For, remaining within, that which would have become the scrotum if it had emerged on the outside was made into the substance of the uterus, an instrument fitted to receive and retain the semen and to nourish and perfect the fetus.

Thus, from one principle devised by the creator in his wisdom, that principle in accordance with which the female has been made less perfect than the male, have stemmed all these things useful for the generation of the animal: that the parts of the female cannot escape to the outside; that she accumulates an excess of useful nutriment and has imperfect semen and a hollow instrument to receive the perfect semen; that since everything in the male is the opposite [of what it is in the female], the male member has been elongated to be most suitable for coitus and the excretion of semen; and that his semen itself has been made thick, abundant, and warm. . . .

25 SORANUS, GYNECOLOGY

Soranus was born at Ephesus, in what is now Turkey, probably in the second half of the first century AD. He eventually moved to Rome, where he is known to have practiced medicine in the time of the emperors Trajan and Hadrian (AD 98–138). Of the more than twenty works that he is credited with writing, we have only the partially preserved Gynecology and two very short treatises, "On Bandages" and "On Fractures."

Gynecology deals mainly with midwifery, pregnancy, labor, infant care, and diseases, both those treated by diet (Book 3), and those treated by surgery and drugs (Book 4). It seems to have been written for midwives and physicians. The translation is from O. Temkin, Soranus' Gynecology (Baltimore and London, 1956), pp. 6–7, 27, 62–8.

(1.4) *Who Are the Best Midwives?* It is necessary to tell what makes the best midwives, so that on the one hand the best may recognize themselves, and on the other hand, beginners may look upon them as models, and the public in time of need may know whom to summon. Now generally speaking, we call a midwife faultless if she merely carries out her medical task; whereas we call her the best midwife if she goes further and in addition to her management of cases is well versed in theory. And more particularly, we call a person the best midwife if she is trained in all branches of therapy (for some cases must be treated by diet, others by surgery, while still others must be cured by drugs); if she is, moreover, able to prescribe hygienic regulations for her patients, to observe the general and the individual features of the case, and from this to find out what is expedient, not from the causes or from the repeated observations of what usually occurs or something of the kind.

Now to go into detail: she will not change her methods when the symptoms change, but will give her advice in accordance with the course of the disease; she will be unperturbed, unafraid in danger, able to state clearly the reasons for her measures; she will bring reassurance to her patients, and be sympathetic. And it is not absolutely essential for her to have had children, as some people contend, in order that she may sympathize with the mother, because of her experience with pain; for [to have sympathy] is [not] more characteristic of a person who has given birth to a child. She must be robust on account of her duties but not necessarily young as some people maintain, for sometimes young persons are weak, whereas on the contrary older persons may be robust. She will be well disciplined and always sober, since it is uncertain when she may be summoned to those in danger. She will have a quiet disposition, for she will have to share many secrets of life. She must not be greedy for money, lest she give an abortive wickedly for payment; she will be free from superstition so as not to overlook salutary measures on account of a dream or omen or some customary rite or vulgar superstition. She must also keep her hands soft, abstaining from such wool-working as may make them hard, and she must acquire softness by means of ointments if it is not present naturally. Such persons will be the best midwives.

(1.30) *Whether Permanent Virginity Is Healthful.* Some have pronounced permanent virginity healthful, others, however, not healthful. The former contend that the body is made ill by desire. Indeed, they say, we see the bodies of lovers pale, weak, and thin, while virginity, because of inexperience with sexual pleasures, is unacquainted with desire. Furthermore, all excretion of seed is harmful in females as in males. Virginity, therefore, is healthful, since it prevents the excretion of seed. Dumb animals also bear witness to what has been said, for of mares, those not covered excel at running, and of sows, those whose uteri have been cut out are bigger, better nourished, stronger, and firm like males. And this is evident in humans too: since men who remain chaste are stronger and bigger than the others and pass their lives in better health, correspondingly it follows that for women too virginity in general is healthful. For pregnancy and childbirth exhaust the female body and make it waste greatly away, whereas virginity, safeguarding women from such injuries, may suitably be called healthful.

(1.60–5) *Whether One Ought to Make Use of Abortives and Contraceptives and How?* A contraceptive differs from an abortive, for the first does not let conception take place, while the latter destroys what has been conceived. Let us, therefore, call the one "abortive" and the other "contraceptive." And an "expulsive" some people say is synonymous with an abortive; others, however, say that there is a difference because an expulsive does not mean drugs but shaking and leaping. . . . For this reason they say that Hippocrates, although prohibiting abortives, yet in his book "On the Nature of the Child" employs leaping with the heels to the buttocks for the sake of expulsion. But a controversy has arisen. For one party banishes abortives, citing the testimony of Hippocrates who says: "I will give no one an abortive;" moreover, because it is the specific task of medicine to guard and preserve what has been engendered by nature. The other party prescribes abortives, but with discrimination, that is, they do not prescribe them when a person wishes to destroy the embryo because of adultery or out of consideration for youthful beauty, but only to prevent subsequent danger in childbirth if the uterus is small and not capable of accommodating the complete development, or if the uterus at its orifice has knobby swellings and fissures, or if some similar difficulty is involved. And they say the same about contraceptives as well, and we too agree with them. And since it is safer to prevent conception from taking place than to destroy the fetus, we shall now first discourse upon such prevention.

For if it is much more advantageous not to conceive than to destroy the embryo, one must consequently beware of having sexual intercourse at those periods which we said[35] were suitable for conception. And during the sexual act, at the critical moment of intercourse when the man is about to discharge the seed, the woman must hold her breath and draw herself away a little, so that the seed may not be hurled too deep into the cavity of the uterus. And getting up immediately and squatting down, she should induce sneezing and carefully wipe the vagina all round; she might even drink something cold. It also aids in preventing conception to smear the opening of the uterus all over before with old olive-oil or honey or cedar-resin or juice of the balsam tree, alone or together with white lead; or with a moist cerate containing myrtle-oil and white lead; or before the act with moist alum, or with galbanum together with wine; or to put a lock of fine wool into the opening of the uterus; or, before sexual relations to use vaginal suppositories which have the power to contract and to condense. . . .

And we shall make specific mention of some. Pine bark, tanning sumach, equal quantities of each, rub with wine, and apply in due measure before intercourse after wool has been wrapped around; and after two or three hours she may remove it and have intercourse. Another: of Cimolian earth,[36] root of panax, equal quantities, rub with water separately and together, and when sticky apply in like manner. Or: grind the inside of fresh pomegranate peel with water, and apply. Or: grind two parts of pomegranate peel and one part of oak galls, form small suppositories and insert after the cessation of menstruation. Or: moist alum, the inside of pomegranate rind; mix with water, and apply with wool. Or: of unripe oak galls, of the inside of pomegranate peel, of ginger, of each two drachmas;[37] mold it with wine to the size of vetch peas and dry indoors and give before intercourse; to be applied as a vaginal suppository. Or: grind the flesh of dried figs and apply together with natron. Or: apply pomegranate peel with an equal amount of gum and an equal amount of oil of roses. Then one should always follow with a drink of honey-water. . . .

Moreover, to some people it seems advisable: once during the month to drink Cyrenaic balm to the amount of a chick-pea in two *cyathi* of water for the purpose of inducing menstruation. Or: of panax balm and Cyrenaic balm and rue seed, of each two obols;[38] [grind] and coat with wax and give to swallow; then follow with a drink of diluted wine or let it be drunk in diluted wine. [Or:] of wallflower seed and myrtle, of each three obols, of myrrh a drachm, of white pepper two seeds; give to drink with wine for three days. Or: of rocket-seed one obol, of cow parsnip one-half obol; drink with oxymel. However, these things not only prevent conception, but also destroy any already existing. In our opinion, moreover, the evil from these things is too great, since they damage and upset the stomach, and besides cause congestion of the head and induce sympathetic reactions. Others, however, have even made use of amulets which on grounds of antipathy they believe to have great effect; such are uteri of mules and the dirt in their ears and more things of this kind which according to the outcome reveal themselves as falsehoods.

Yet if conception has taken place . . . , in order that the embryo be separated, the woman should have [more violent exercise], walking about energetically and being shaken by means of draught animals; she should also leap energetically and carry things which are heavy beyond her strength. . . .

For a woman who intends to have an abortion, it is necessary for two or even three days beforehand to take protracted baths, little food, and to use softening vaginal suppositories; also to abstain from wine; then to be bled and a relatively great quantity taken away. For the dictum of Hippocrates in the "Aphorisms," even if not true in a case of constriction, is yet true of a healthy woman: "A pregnant woman if bled, miscarries." For just as sweat, urine, or feces are excreted if the parts containing these substances slacken very much, so the fetus falls out after the uterus dilates. Following the venesection, one must shake her by means of draught animals (for now the shaking is more effective on the parts which previously have been relaxed) and one must use softening vaginal suppositories. But if a woman reacts unfavorably to venesection and is languid, one must first relax the parts by means of sitz baths, full baths, softening vaginal suppositories, by keeping her on water and limited food, and by means of aperients and the application of a softening clyster; afterwards one must apply an abortive vaginal suppository. . . . In addition, many different things have been mentioned by others; one must, however, beware of things that are too powerful and of separating the embryo by means of something sharp-edged, for danger arises that some of the adjacent parts be wounded. After the abortion one must treat as for inflammation.

SUGGESTIONS FOR FURTHER READING

On Roman science, see J. L. Harris, *Science in Ancient Rome* (New York, 1988). On Pliny the Elder, see now J. F. Healy, *Pliny the Elder on Science and Technology* (Oxford, 1999). Other books on Pliny: M. Beagon, *Roman Nature: The Thought of Pliny the Elder* (Oxford, 1992); R. French and F. Greenaway (eds), *Science in the Early Roman Empire: Pliny the Elder, His Sources and Influence* (Totowa, NJ, 1986).

The standard work on Roman medicine is J. Scarborough, *Roman Medicine* (London and Ithaca, NY, 1969); see also his brief history of Greek and Roman medicine in *Civilization of the Ancient Mediterranean: Greece and Rome*, ed. M. Grant and R. Kitzinger (New York, 1988), vol. 2, pp. 1227–48. The best introduction to Soranus is O. Temkin, *Soranus' Gynecology* (Baltimore, 1956).

Five

POLITICS AND GOVERNMENT

Editor's introduction

In the beginning, Rome was ruled by kings, the last of whom was overthrown sometime around 500 BC. In the Republican government that was established to replace them, the authority of the kings was assigned to a pair of elected officials called consuls, who held office for a year, and who were expected, then and later, to exercise a kind of general stewardship over the business of state. Other magistracies were created later, as and when they were needed. Like the consulship, most were collegial and annual. The main exception was the dictatorship, which placed extraordinary, though not unlimited, power in the hands of a single man, and which, according to tradition, was to be held only for as long as it took to accomplish a specific task, and never for more than six months. Dictators were appointed often in the fifth and fourth centuries BC, rarely in the third (except during the wars against Carthage), and then not at all until Sulla assumed the position in 82.

From about 443 BC, two former consuls were chosen every five years to hold the office of censor, which lasted for eighteen months. The duties of the censors were to compile an official list of citizens (*census*), revise the rolls of the Senate, and supervise both public morality and the leasing of publicly owned land (*ager publicus*) and buildings. The office of praetor was established in 366 BC to oversee the administration of justice at Rome. A second praetor (*praetor peregrinus*) was added about 242 BC to handle lawsuits in which one or both parties were not Roman citizens. Other praetorships were created later to help govern the provinces. Tribunes of the plebs were first elected in the early part of the fifth century BC to protect citizens against the arbitrary exercise of government authority. From 449, ten were elected every year. They possessed the right to veto any action taken by a magistrate or by any of their fellow tribunes. The office of plebeian aedile was established originally to assist the tribunes. A second type, called the curule aedileship, which at first only patricians were eligible to hold, was created in 367 BC. The aediles were charged eventually with maintaining public order, supervising the grain-supply, streets, and markets (including weights and measures), and organizing the public games. The most junior of the magistracies was the quaestorship, which was created in 447 BC to oversee the public treasury (*aerarium*).

Almost from the beginning of the Republic, office-holding was monopolized, first by the patricians, and later by a small group of wealthy families. But individuals generally held office only at intervals, in part because elections were fiercely competitive, so much so that friendships and even marriages were sometimes contracted, or dissolved, as a matter of political convenience. Campaigning tended also, as Quintus Cicero's *Handbook on Campaigning for Office* (selection 28) indicates, to be mainly about standing and personality, not policy or platform. For voting and other, mostly legislative, purposes, the citizen body was organized into four assemblies, each of which had different functions. The oldest was the Curiate Assembly, which grouped citizens into thirty *curiae*. It quickly became obsolete, meeting, for the most part, only to witness wills and adoptions. The Centuriate Assembly divided the citizen population into five classes, according to wealth, and into 193 centuries, which functioned as voting units. It voted on legislation and elected senior magistrates, including consuls. Because the wealthiest classes controlled an absolute majority of the centuries, and because voting stopped as soon as a majority was reached, the poor, it can be assumed, probably never got to vote. And because voting took place only in Rome, many of those who lived in distant parts of Italy or in the provinces were effectively disqualified also. The Tribal Assembly (*comitia tributa*) grouped the same citizens into thirty-five tribes, which, like the centuries of the Centuriate Assembly, acted as voting units, but which, unlike them, voted simultaneously. Originally, it seems, the tribes were based on ethnicity. By about the middle of the third century BC, however, they had come to be organized around geographic location. The main functions of the assembly were to elect junior magistrates, like the quaestors, and to enact laws. The fourth of the popular assemblies was the Council of the Plebs (*concilium plebis*). It was established in the fifth century BC to counter the overwhelming influence wielded by the patricians, who were not permitted to attend it. It elected the tribunes and some of the aediles, and made resolutions (*plebiscita*), which after 287 BC were considered to be binding on the community as a whole, patricians included.

The most important part of Republican government was the Senate. Originally a council of elders, it came to be composed instead of former magistrates, who joined it after they had completed their year in office (no one, therefore, was ever elected directly to the Senate). Membership was lifelong. The formal powers of the Senate were limited: it set financial and military policy, directed the administration of Italy, and handled relations with foreign governments. In practice, however, it controlled virtually every aspect of government, and much of the legislation enacted in the assemblies, by monopolizing its traditional role of advising the magistrates, and by the issuing of decrees (*senatus consulta*).

So the history of Republican government is in many ways the story of the collective rule of an aristocracy, which was highly competitive, and which, in theory, and occasionally in practice, was dependent on the will of the people.[1] That the system as a whole heavily favored the interests of the elite may help to explain why Augustus was so careful to preserve (or at least to give the appearance of preserving) its institutions, while he gradually took over many of their functions. The objectives of government remained the same: to maintain order, and to collect taxes. Its size was increased, by the creation of new posts reserved for senators, like the two prefects Augustus appointed to oversee the treasury, by the founding of new institutions, like the military treasury (*aerarium militare*) that Augustus established in AD 6 to provide benefits to veterans, and by the employment of non-elected officials in positions of public responsibility, above all, equestrians, and, increasingly, the freedmen and slaves of the emperor's household. But relative to the size of the empire, which had a population of perhaps 50–60 million, the government was conspicuously small: at the end of the second century AD, there were probably fewer than 350 senior officials in Rome, in Italy, and in all of the provinces.[2]

The basic structure of the civil service was developed by the emperor Claudius, who divided the routine business of government into five departments, each of which he placed under the supervision of one of his freedmen: one (*ab epistulis*), whose head functioned as a kind of general secretary to the emperor, handled all of his correspondence; a second (*a rationibus*), which came eventually to be directed by a procurator of equestrian rank, oversaw the record-keeping operations of the fisc (*fiscus*), the treasury that collected revenues from the emperor's estates, from the imperial provinces, and, increasingly, from the senatorial provinces also; a third department (*a libellis*) dealt with requests and petitions to the emperor; another (*a cognitionibus*) handled paperwork associated with legal cases brought before the emperor; the fifth (*a studiis*), which maintained the emperor's private library, was probably expected also to provide him with material for edicts and for public speeches. The higher levels of the administration continued to be made up mostly of amateurs – senators and equestrians who spent only a part of their working lives in office, and received no special training for their duties. For the most part, they reported, and were accountable, to the emperor. Mid-level administrative and military positions were filled increasingly by equestrians.

The city of Rome and Italy continued to be governed by the consuls and by the Senate, until late in the second century AD, when they were placed under the jurisdiction of two officials with closer ties to the emperor: the urban prefect, whose authority extended 100 miles from Rome, and the prefect of the Praetorian Guard, who administered the rest of Italy. From the time of Augustus (27 BC–AD 14), Rome also had a kind of police force and fire department (the *vigiles*), which was made up of freedmen and commanded by a prefect of equestrian rank (*praefectus vigilum*). Another equestrian prefect (*praefectus annonae*) was charged with overseeing the supply of grain to the city.

The emperors themselves were expected to make policy decisions, to reply to letters and petitions, to try cases, both in the first instance and on appeal, and to introduce legislation. Their official position rested primarily on two powers, which were awarded first to Augustus in 23 BC: *imperium maius*, which gave them a military authority superior to that of anyone else, and *tribunicia potestas*, the power of a tribune, by virtue of which they were entitled both to veto the acts of magistrates and to propose laws. From a fragmentary inscription (*Inscriptiones Latinae Selectae* 244) which dates to the time of Vespasian (AD 70–9), it appears that their power was formally granted to them by a decree of the Senate, which was thereafter ratified by popular vote. Emperors who expected to maintain the support of the aristocracy were careful also to consult a council of advisers (*consilium principis*) made up of senators and equestrians.

The Senate as a whole was gradually stripped of its control of fiscal, military, and foreign policy. Having relinquished most of its authority, it also lost much of its prestige. Under the emperors, its principal functions were to enact legislation, and, on occasion, to try cases. Elections, which were transferred from the assemblies to the Senate in AD 15 (Tacitus, *Annals* 1.15, below), were steadily brought under the control of the emperors.

26 POLYBIUS, *HISTORIES*

Polybius was born to a land-owning and politically active family at Megalopolis in Greece. He was one of a thousand Greeks taken hostage in 167 BC after the battle of Pydna and deported to Rome, where he was befriended by the Roman general and statesman, Publius Cornelius Scipio Aemilianus. Of the several works that he is known to have written, we possess only his *Histories*, a universal history of the Mediterranean world, 264–146 BC, written mainly to explain the rise of Rome to his fellow Greeks. Only the first five books (to 216 BC) are preserved intact (the rest survive in excerpts).

In the following passages, taken from Book 6 of his *Histories*, Polybius presents an idealized view of the practice of Republican government, which he portrays as an effective system of checks and balances. In practice, ordinary Romans had little influence on political decisions. The translation is from I. Scott-Kilvert, *Polybius: The Rise of the Roman Empire* (Harmondsworth, 1979), pp. 302–5, 312–17.

(6.2) . . . . The best and most useful aim of my work is to explain to my readers by what means and by virtue of what political institutions almost the whole world fell under the rule of one power, that of Rome, an event which is absolutely without parallel in earlier history. . . . In private life, if you wish to pass judgment on the characters of good or of bad men, you would not, assuming that your opinion is to be subjected to a genuine test, examine their actions only at periods of unclouded tranquility, but rather at times of conspicuous success or failure. The test of true virtue in a man surely resides in his capacity to bear with spirit and with dignity the most complete transformations of fortune, and the same principle should apply to our judgment of states. And so, since I could find no greater or more violent changes of fortune in our time than those which befell the Romans, I have reserved this place in my history for my study of their constitution. The particular aspect of history which both attracts and benefits its readers is the examination of causes and the capacity, which is the reward of this study, to decide in each case the best policy to follow. Now in all political situations we must understand that the principal factor which makes for success or failure is the form of a state's constitution: it is from this source, as if from a fountain-head, that all designs and plans of action not only originate but reach their fulfillment.

(6.11.11–6.17.9) Now the elements by which the Roman constitution was controlled were three in number, all of which I have mentioned before, and all the aspects of the administration were, taken separately, so fairly and so suitably ordered and regulated through the agency of these three elements that it was impossible even for the Romans themselves to declare with certainty whether the whole system was an aristocracy, a democracy, or a monarchy. In fact, it was quite natural that this should be so, for if we were to fix our eyes only upon the power of the consuls, the constitution might give the impression of being completely monarchical and royal; if we confined our attention to the Senate it would seem to be aristocratic; and if we looked at the power of the people it would appear to be a clear example of a democracy. The powers of these three elements over the various parts of the state were, and with a few modifications still are, as follows.

The consuls, until such time as they are required to lead out the legions, remain in Rome and exercise supreme authority over all public affairs. All other magistrates with the exception of the tribunes are subordinate to them and are bound to obey them, and it is they who present foreign embassies to the Senate. Besides these duties, they refer urgent business to the Senate for discussion and are entirely responsible for implementing its decisions. It is also their duty to supervise all those affairs of state which are administered by the people; in such cases they summon meetings of the popular assembly, introduce measures, and execute the decrees of the people. As for preparations for war and the general conduct of operations in the field, their power is almost absolute. They are entitled to make whatever demands they consider appropriate upon the allies, appoint military tribunes, enroll soldiers, and select those who are suitable for service. They also have the power to inflict punishment when on active service upon anyone under their command, and authority to spend any sum they think fit from the public funds; in this matter of finance they are accompanied by a quaestor, who complies wholly with their instructions. Thus, if anyone were to consider this element in the constitution alone, he could reasonably say that it is a pure example of monarchy or kingship. Here I may add that any changes which may take place now or in the future in the functions I have just described, or am about to describe, do not alter the truth of my analysis.

Let us now consider the Senate. This body has control of the treasury and regulates the flow of all revenue and expenditure; the quaestors require a decree of the Senate to enable them to authorize expenditure on any given project, with the exception only of payments made to the consuls. The Senate also controls what is by far the largest and most important item of expenditure – that is, the programme which is laid down by the censors every five years to provide for the repair and construction of public buildings – and it makes a grant to the censors for this purpose. Similarly, any crimes committed in Italy which require a public investigation, such as treason, conspiracy, poisoning, and assassination, also come under the jurisdiction of the Senate. Again, if any private person or community in Italy requires arbitration for a dispute, or is in need of formal censure, or seeks help or protection, it is the Senate which deals with all such cases. It is also responsible for dispatching embassies or commissions to countries outside Italy, either to settle differences, to offer advice, to impose demands, to receive submissions, or to declare war; and in the same way, whenever any foreign delegations arrive in Rome, it decides how they should be received, and what answer should be given them. All these matters are in the hands of the Senate and the people have nothing to do with them. Thus, to anyone who happened to be living in Rome when the consuls were away from the city, the constitution might well appear to be completely aristocratic, and this is the impression which prevails among many of the Greek states and of the kings of other countries, since the Senate handles almost all the business of state which concerns them.

So when we consider that the Senate exercises authority over all the detailed functions which I have described, and, most important of all, has complete control of expenditure and revenue, and that the consuls hold absolute power in respect of military preparations and operations in the field, we are naturally inclined to ask what place in the constitution is left for the people. The answer is that there is undoubtedly a role for the people to play, and a very important one at that. For it is the people alone who have the right to award both honors and punishments, the only bonds whereby kingdoms, states, and human society in general are held together. The fact is that in states where the distinction between these is not recognized, or is recognized in theory but ill-applied in practice, none of the business in hand can be properly administered, for how can this be done if the good and the wicked are held in equal estimation? The people, then, are empowered to try many of the cases in which the offense is punishable by a fine, when the penalty for an offense is a serious one and especially when the accused have held the highest offices of state; and they are the only court which may try on capital charges. As regards this last, they have one custom which is particularly praiseworthy and deserves mention. This allows men who are on trial for their lives, if they are in the process of being condemned, to leave the country openly and thus to inflict a voluntary exile upon themselves – so long as one of the tribes which pronounce the verdict has not yet voted. Such exiles may take refuge in the territories of Neapolis,[3] Praeneste,[4] Tibur,[5] and certain other towns, with which this arrangement has been made by treaty. On the same principle it is also the people who bestow offices on those who deserve them, and these are the noblest rewards of virtue the state can provide. Besides this, the people have the power to approve or reject laws, and most important of all, they deliberate and decide on questions of peace or war. Furthermore, on such issues as the making of alliances, the termination of hostilities, and the making of treaties, it is the people who ratify or reject all of these. And so, from this point of view, one could reasonably argue that the people have the greatest share of power in the government, and that the constitution is a democracy.

I have described how political power is divided between these three elements in the state, and I shall now explain how each of the three can, if it chooses, work with or against the other. The consul, when he sets out with his army, equipped with the powers I have mentioned, appears to hold absolute authority for the execution of his purpose, but in practice he needs the support both of the people and of the Senate, and cannot bring his operations to a successful conclusion without them. It is obvious, for example, that the legions require a constant flow of supplies, but without the approval of the Senate neither grain nor clothing nor pay can be provided, so that a commander's plans can be completely frustrated if the Senate chooses to be antipathetic or obstructive. It also rests with the Senate to decide whether a general can execute all his plans and designs, since it has the right either to send out another general when the former's term of office has expired, or to retain him in command for another year. Again, it is in the power of the Senate either to celebrate a general's successes with pomp and magnify them, or to obscure and belittle them. For the processions which they call triumphs, in which the spectacle of what they have achieved in the field is actually brought before the eyes of their fellow-citizens, cannot be properly staged, or in some cases enacted at all, unless the Senate agrees and grants the necessary funds. As for the people, it is a matter of prime necessity for the consuls to consider their interests, however far away from home they may be, for as I have explained above, it is the sovereign people which ratifies or rejects the suspension of hostilities and the making of treaties. But most important of all is the fact that on laying down their office the consuls are obliged to account for their actions to the people; so under no circumstances is it safe for the consuls to neglect to cultivate the good-will both of the Senate and of the people.

The Senate, again, although it possesses such great power, is obliged first of all to pay attention in public affairs to the views of the people and to respect their wishes. Besides this, it cannot carry out inquiries into the most serious and far-reaching offenses against the state – such as involve the death penalty – and take steps to control them, unless its decree is confirmed by the people. The same is the case in matters which directly concern the Senate itself. For if anyone introduces a law which aims to remove from the Senate some of its traditional authority, or to abolish the precedence or other dignities of the senators, or even to reduce some of their property, in all such cases it is the people alone who are empowered to pass the measure or to reject it. It is also a fact that if a single one of the tribunes interposes his veto, the Senate is not only prevented from reaching a final decision on any subject, but cannot even meet and hold sittings. Now the tribunes are always bound to carry out the decrees of the people, and above all, to pay attention to their wishes. For all these reasons, therefore, the Senate stands in awe of the masses and takes heed of the popular will.

On the same principle, however, the people also have obligations towards the Senate and must take its wishes into account both individually and collectively. All over Italy an immense number of contracts, far too numerous to specify, are awarded by the censors for the construction and repair of public buildings, and besides this the collection of revenues from navigable rivers, harbors, gardens, mines, lands – in a word, every transaction which comes under the control of the Roman government – is farmed out to contractors. All these activities are carried on by the people, and there is scarcely a soul, one might say, who does not have some interest in these contracts and the profits which are derived from them. Some people actually purchase the contracts from the censors for themselves, others act as their partners, others provide security for the contractors, while others may pledge their property to the treasury for this purpose. All these trans-actions come under the authority of the Senate. It can grant an extension of time, it can lighten the contractor's liability in the event of some unforeseen accident, or release him altogether if it proves impossible for him to fulfill his contract. There are in fact many ways in which the Senate can either inflict great hardship or ease the burden for those who manage public property, for in every case the appeal is referred to it. More important still is the fact that the judges in the majority of civil trials where the action involves large interests are drawn from the Senate. The result is that all citizens, being bound to the Senate by ties which ensure their protection, and being also uncertain and afraid that they may need its help, are very cautious about obstructing or resisting its will. In the same way, people would think twice about opposing the projects of the consuls, since they will come both individually and collectively under their authority while on a campaign.

27   CICERO, *IN DEFENSE OF SESTIUS*

On Cicero, see the introduction to selection 19. The following passages are taken from a speech that he delivered in 56 BC in defense of a man named Publius Sestius, who had been charged with public violence (he was acquitted). Cicero divides the Roman political class into two camps – the *optimates* ("best men"), who, like Cicero, championed the authority of the Senate, and the *populares* ("men of the people"), who, because they courted the support of ordinary Romans, he considered to be disreputable and dangerous.

(96–9) In this state, there have always been two kinds of men who have sought to engage in public affairs and to distinguish themselves in them. One of these types has wanted to be considered as, and actually to be, *populares*, the other, *optimates*. Those who wanted what they did and said to be pleasing to the multitude were judged to be *populares*, but those who conducted themselves in such a way that their policies would be approved by each of the best citizens were reckoned to be *optimates*. "Who then are these *optimates* of yours?" In number, if you ask, they are uncountable (for we could not otherwise exist); they are the leaders of public policy, and those who follow their lead; they are drawn from those very large classes to which the Senate is open; they are Romans who live in municipal towns and in the countryside; they are managers of business; the *optimates* are also freedmen. In number, as I've said, this type is spread widely and across various groups; but so that there is no misunderstanding, the whole type can be briefly summed up and defined. All are *optimates* who are not criminals, or wicked, or mad, or encumbered by troubles at home. It follows, therefore, that they are those whom you have called a "race," who are upright, of sound mind, and well-off in respect to their domestic affairs. Those who, in governing the state, serve the wishes, interests, and principles of these men are considered to be champions of the *optimates*, and are themselves *optimates*, and the most eminent and distinguished citizens, and leaders of the state. What then is the guiding principle for those who govern the state, which they ought to focus on, and towards which they ought to direct their course? It is that which is best and most desirable for all who are sound and good and prosperous – peace with dignity. Those who desire this are all considered to be *optimates*; those who bring it about are judged to be the best men and the saviors of the state. For in the same way that it is unsuitable for men to be so carried away by the dignity of a public career that they do not exercise foresight in times of peace, so too it is unsuitable for them to embrace any peace which is inconsistent with dignity.

Of this "peace with dignity," these are the foundations, these are the elements, which must be upheld by our leaders and defended even at the risk of their lives: religious observances, the auspices,[6] the powers of the magistrates, the authority of the Senate, the laws, ancestral custom, the courts, civil jurisdiction, credit, the provinces, the allies, the glory of empire, the army, the treasury. To be a defender and advocate of so many and such important interests requires a great spirit, great ability, and great resolve. For in such a large number of citizens, there is a great multitude of those who, either from fear of punishment, being conscious of their wrong-doing, seek revolution and the overthrow of the state; or who, because of some inborn madness, feed on civil discord and sedition; or who, because of embarrassment in their finances, prefer to perish in a general conflagration rather than their own. When such men have found advisers and leaders for their criminal enterprises, storms are stirred up in the state, so that those who have demanded for themselves the governance of the state must be vigilant and strive, with all their skill and energy, that they may be able, while safeguarding the foundations and elements I spoke of a little earlier, to hold their course, and arrive at that harbor of peace and dignity.

(136–9) But in order that my speech may have some ending, and that I may finish speaking before you stop listening to me so attentively, I will conclude my remarks about the *optimates*, and their leaders, and the defenders of the state; and you, young Romans, who are nobles, I will exhort to imitate your ancestors; and you who can win nobility by your talent and virtue, I will urge to pursue that career in which many "new men"[7] have distinguished themselves with both honor and glory. This is, believe me, the only way to fame, and distinction, and honor – to be praised and loved by men who are good, and wise, and naturally well-ordered, and to understand the organization of the state most wisely established by our ancestors, who, when they could not tolerate the power of kings, created annual magistracies in such a way that they put the council of the Senate in charge of the state forever, and arranged that the members of that council should be chosen by the whole people, and that admission to that highest of ranks should be open to all citizens of industry and merit. They appointed the Senate to be the guardian, governor, and defender of the state; they wanted the magistrates to rely on the authority of this order, and to be, so to speak, ministers of this highly influential council; and they wanted the Senate itself to be supported by the prestige of the classes immediately below it, and to defend and enlarge the liberty and the interests of the common people.

Those who defend these things to the best of their ability are *optimates*, whatever class they belong to; but those who, more than others, carry such great responsibilities and the government itself on their shoulders, have always been considered to be the leaders of the *optimates*, the advisers and saviors of the state. To this class of men, I confess (as I have already said), many are opposed, hostile, and envious; they are threatened by many dangers; they endure many injustices; they have to undertake and to endure great labors. But my whole speech is about virtue, not about indolence; about honor, not about pleasure; about those who think they were born for country, for their fellow-citizens, for reputation, for glory, not for sleep, and parties, and enjoyment. For if they are drawn to pleasure, and have given themselves up to the seductions of vice and the allurements of desire, they should renounce public office, they should not engage in public affairs, they should be content to enjoy the leisure that they owe to the labor of brave men. But those who seek the respect of good men, which alone can be called true glory, ought to seek security and pleasures for others, not for themselves. They should sweat for the common interests, expose themselves to hostility, often undergo storms for the sake of the state, contend with many audacious, wicked, and sometimes even powerful men. That is what we have heard, what we have been told, what we have read, about the thoughts and actions of the most famous men. Nor do we see as objects of praise those who have ever moved the hearts of the people to sedition, or who have used bribery to cloud the minds of the reckless, or who have sullied the reputation of brave and illustrious men who deserved well of the state. Our people have always considered these men to be untrustworthy, and reckless, and wicked, and pernicious citizens. But those who have checked their attacks and efforts, who have, by their influence, their loyalty, their steadfastness, their greatness of soul, resisted the schemes of the reckless, these have always been considered to be of good character, chiefs, and leaders, and the authors of this our present eminence and sovereignty.

28 QUINTUS CICERO, *HANDBOOK ON CAMPAIGNING FOR OFFICE*

Quintus Cicero was the younger brother of Marcus Tullius Cicero. He held a number of public offices, including a praetorship in 62 BC; he was also governor of Asia, 61–59 (see selection 35). Like Marcus, he died in the proscriptions of the triumvirs in 43 BC.

The *Handbook on Campaigning for Office* (*commentariolum petitionis*) describes Marcus Cicero's campaign for the consulship of 63 BC. Though some scholars have maintained that the work is a clever forgery written a century or so later, it is usually attributed to Quintus. It is an invaluable source of information about political values and institutions in the period of the Late Republic.

Quintus to his brother Marcus.

(1) Although you have everything that men can achieve by talent, or experience, or diligence, nevertheless, I did not think it inconsistent with my affection to write down for you what keeps coming into my mind as I think, day and night, about your candidacy, not that you would learn anything new from it, but that those things which seemed to be disconnected and infinite might be brought under one classification in a methodical arrangement.

(2) Consider what the state is; what you are seeking; who you are. Almost every day, as you go down to the Forum, you should think of this: "I am a new man;[8] I seek the consulship; this is Rome."

You will compensate for the newness of your name mainly by the brilliance of your oratory. That has always carried the greatest distinction; he who is considered worthy to be the advocate of men of consular rank cannot be thought unworthy of the consulship. For that reason, since you start from this reputation, and whatever you are, you are because of this, come prepared to speak as if on each occasion your entire reputation will be judged. (3) See to it that the aids to this ability, which I know you have in reserve, are prepared and ready; and remember often what Demetrius wrote about the hard work and practice of Demosthenes; then make sure that it's apparent that you have both a great many friends and friends of many types; for you have what [few] "new men" have had – all the publicans; almost the whole equestrian order; many municipal towns attached to you; many men, of every rank, who have been defended by you; many of the colleges;[9] and, in addition, a large number of the young men who have been won over by their enthusiasm for oratory, and the large number of friends who visit you religiously every day. (4) Be careful to retain these advantages by commending them, by appealing to them, and by using every possible means to bring it about that those who are in your debt understand that there will never be another time for them to show their gratitude, or for those who so wish to place you under an obligation. It seems also that this could be of much help to a "new man" – the good-will of the nobility, and especially of men of consular rank. It helps that you are thought worthy of that position and rank by those very men whose position and rank you hope to attain. (5) You must diligently ask all these men for their support; people must be sent to persuade them that, in matters of state, you have always sided with the *optimates*, that you have never been a *popularis* in any way;[10] that if we seem to have said anything meant to win popular support, we did it for the purpose of enlisting Gnaeus Pompeius,[11] so that we might have the man of the greatest authority either as a friend in our campaign, or certainly not as an adversary. (6) In addition, you should work hard to win over the young men of the nobility, or hold on to the support of those you already have: they will contribute much to your reputation. You have a great many; make sure that they understand how much you think depends on them. If you bring it about that those who are not unwilling to support you are eager to do so, it will help a great deal.

(7) It also helps to off-set your "newness" that the nobles who are candidates with you are of such a kind that there is no one who would dare to say that their

nobility ought to be of more benefit to them than your virtue is to you. For who is there who would think that Publius Galba and Lucius Cassius, though born to the highest rank, would be candidates for the consulship? You see, therefore, that men of the most distinguished families are, because they lack ability, not your equals. (8) "But Catiline[12] and Antonius[13] are troublesome." On the contrary, I would say that a man of energy, industry, blameless character, eloquence, and popularity among those who judge these matters, should hope for such competitors – both criminals from their childhood, both given over to lust, both impoverished. We have seen the property of one of them[14] auctioned off, and actually heard him swear that at Rome he could not compete with a Greek on equal terms; we know that he was thrown out of the Senate on the judgment of the most excellent censors; in our praetorship we had him as a competitor, with Sabidius and Panthera as his backers, because he had no one else to appear for him at the record-office (yet while holding this office he bought a girlfriend at the slave-market whom he kept openly at his house). And in his campaign for the consulship, he has preferred to rob all the inn-keepers by means of a most disgraceful ambassadorship rather than to be present and to supplicate the Roman people. (9) But the other! Good gods! What is his distinction? Is he of equally noble birth? Is he richer? No. But greater in virtue? How so? Where Antonius fears his own shadow, this man does not even fear the laws – a man born to an impoverished father, educated in the sexual license of his sister, brought up amid the slaughter of citizens, whose first entrance to public life was heralded by the massacre of Roman knights (for Sulla[15] had put Catiline alone in charge of those Gauls whom we remember, who cut off the heads of the Titinii, and Nannii, and Tanusii), among whom was that most excellent man, his sister's husband, Quintus Caecilius, a Roman knight, adherent of no political faction, always quiet by nature, and also because of his age, whom he killed with his own hands.

(10) Why should I now speak of him as your fellow candidate for the consulship, who beat Marcus Marius,[16] a man most dear to the Roman people, with vine-branches, from one end of the city to the other while the Roman people watched, forced him to the tomb, tore him to pieces with every kind of torture, and then, while he was still alive and standing, severed his neck with the sword he held in his right hand, while holding the hairs on the top of his head with his left, and then lifted up the head with his hand, as rivers of blood flowed through his fingers; who afterwards lived with actors and with gladiators on such terms that the former ministered to his lust, the latter to his crimes; who never entered a place so sacred and so holy that he did not leave behind, even if there was no actual crime, a suspicion of dishonor, because of his own debasement; whose closest friends in the Senate were the Curii and the Annii, in the auction-halls, the Sapalae and Carvilii, in the equestrian order, the Pompilii and Vettii; who is so impudent, so vile, in short, so skillful and successful in lasciviousness, that he defiled young men almost in their parents' laps? Why should I write to you now about Africa, about the testimony of the witnesses? It's well-known – read it for yourself, over and over. But nevertheless, it seems that I should not omit to mention that he went away from that court as poor as some of the jurors were before the trial, and so hated that another prosecution against him is called for every

day. His conduct is such that they fear him more, even if he does nothing, than they despise him, if he does start anything.

(11) How much better a fortune has been given to you in your campaign than that which was recently given to the "new man," Gaius Coelius![17] He was campaigning against two men of the highest nobility, who nevertheless possessed qualities more important than nobility itself – the greatest ability, supreme modesty, a great many public services, the best methods of campaigning, and the greatest diligence in carrying them out. And nevertheless, Coelius defeated one of them, though much inferior in birth, and superior in almost nothing. (12) For that reason, if you do what your nature and studies – which you have always put to use – enable you to do, what the exigencies of your situation require, what you are capable of doing, and what you ought to do, you will not have a difficult struggle with those competitors who are not nearly as distinguished for their birth as notorious for their vices. For what citizen can be found so dishonorable as to want to unsheathe two daggers against the state with one vote?

(13) Since I have explained what you have and might have to compensate for your "newness," it seems I ought to speak now about the importance of the campaign. You seek the consulship, an office of which no one thinks you unworthy, but of which there are many who will be jealous; for, though of equestrian rank, you are seeking the highest position in the state, and an office that is so prestigious that it conveys much greater splendor on a man who is brave, eloquent, and pure than on others. Do not imagine that those who have held that office do not see what influence you will have, when you have achieved the same thing. I suspect, however, that those who, though born to families of consular rank, have not achieved the position of their ancestors, will envy you, except for those who are already attached to you. I think that, except for those who are obligated to you, even the "new men" who have been praetors will not want to be surpassed by you in rank. (14) I know it has certainly crossed your mind that in the population at large there are many who are already jealous, many who, because of the experience of recent years, are averse to "new men." It is inevitable that there are some who are angry at you because of the causes which you have taken up. Now carefully consider this – whether, given that you have dedicated yourself with such enthusiasm to promoting the glory of Pompey, you can suppose that some men are your friends for that reason. (15) Consequently, since you are seeking the highest position in the state, and you see that there are sentiments which are opposed to you, you must make use of every method, and all your vigilance, and energy, and diligence.

(16) And a campaign for office is divided into two kinds of activity, one of which is concerned with the support of friends, the other with the feelings of the people. The support of friends is best won by conferring benefits and by performing services, by familiarity, and by an easy-going and pleasant character. But this term "friends" has a wider application in a campaign than at other times in our life. For anyone who shows any favoritism toward you, who cultivates you, who regularly visits your home, is to be included in the category of friends. But nevertheless, it is especially useful to be esteemed and agreeable in the eyes of those who are friends for the more honorable reason of blood-relationship, or of relationship by marriage, or of membership in the same club, or of some other

close connection. (17) Then, you must work especially hard to see to it that, so far as each man is intimate and most closely connected with your household, he loves you and wants you to achieve as much as possible – such as your fellow-tribesmen, neighbors, clients, and, finally, your freedmen and even your slaves; for almost all the talk that shapes one's public reputation emanates from domestic sources. (18) Next, friends must be cultivated, of every type: for appearances, men distinguished by their office and name (who, even if they do not help in the campaign, nevertheless confer some distinction on a candidate); to maintain your rights, magistrates (above all, consuls, then tribunes of the plebs); to secure the centuries,[18] men of unparalleled popularity. You should work very hard to arrange and to secure those who either have or hope to have the vote of a tribe,[19] or of a century, or some other benefit from you. For during recent years ambitious men have labored strenuously with all their determination and energy to be in a position to obtain from their fellow-tribesmen what they were seeking. You must also do your best, by every means you can, to ensure that these men support you from the heart and with absolute dedication. (19) If men were indeed as grateful as they ought to be, all this should be prepared for you, as I trust that it has been. For in the last two years, you have obligated four associations[20] of men who are vitally important to getting elected, those of Gaius Fundanius, Quintus Gallius, Gaius Cornelius, Gaius Orchivius; in entrusting their defense to you, I know what their fellow club-members undertook and confirmed, for I was present. So now is the time for you to arrange to collect from them what they owe, by reminding them, by appealing to them, by assuring them, and by taking care that they understand that they will never have any other opportunity to show their gratitude. Surely these men, hoping for your services in the future, and mindful of the kindnesses recently done to them, will be motivated to act vigorously. (20) And certainly, since your candidacy is most strongly supported by that type of friendship which you have acquired as counsel for the defense, take care that all those who are obligated to you have their individual duties clearly defined and spelled out. And given that you have never been bothersome to any of them in any regard, so be sure that they understand that you have saved for this occasion everything that you think they owe you.

(21) But since men are induced to show good-will and to be eager to vote mainly for three reasons – a kindness received; hope; like-mindedness and affection – careful attention must be paid to how each of these might best be handled. By the smallest favors men are induced to think that they have sufficient reason for giving their support at elections, and surely those whom you have saved (of whom there are a great many) cannot fail to understand that, if they do not do enough for you at this time, they will never be considered trustworthy by anyone. And though this is so, they must nevertheless be appealed to, and even led to the opinion that they, who are still obligated to us, can now make us obligated to them in turn. (22) But to those who are bound to us by hope – a class of men that is also much more diligent and attentive – you must give the impression that your assistance is ready and available; and you must make them understand that you are carefully watching how they perform their duties, and make it clear that you are closely watching and paying attention to how much support is coming from each of them. (23) The third type I mentioned is that of spontaneous supporters,

whom it will be worthwhile to secure by expressing your gratitude, by accommodating your words to the reasons which seem to you to explain why each is
supportive of you; by demonstrating equal good-will toward them; and by im-
plying that your friendship may develop into familiarity and companionship.
And in all these types, consider and weigh up how much influence each possesses, so that you may know both how best to handle each of them, and what
you should expect and demand from each. (24) For certain men are popular in
their own neighborhoods and towns; there are others who are industrious and
wealthy, and who, even if they have not sought such popularity before, can nevertheless easily win it on the spot for someone to whom they owe or want to do
a favor. Attention must be paid to these types of men in such a way that they
themselves understand that you are monitoring what you expect from each of
them, that you appreciate what you are receiving, and remember what you have
received. There are still others who either have no influence at all or are even
disliked by their fellow-tribesmen, and have neither the spirit nor the ability to
exert themselves on the spur of the moment: be certain to distinguish these men,
in case, having placed too much hope in someone, you arrange too little support.

(25) And although it is appropriate to rely on, and to be shored up by, friendships already won and secured, nevertheless, in the campaign itself, a great many
useful friendships are acquired; for though it has other annoyances, a candidacy
has this advantage: you can, without losing dignity – something which you cannot do at other times of life – admit anyone you want to your friendship. If you
were to allow such men to enjoy your friendship at any other time, you would
appear to be acting foolishly; in a campaign, however, if you were not to do this
religiously and with many, you would seem to be no candidate at all. (26) And I
assure you of this, that there is no one, unless perhaps he is attached by some
close tie to one of your competitors, whom you could not easily induce, if you
made the effort, to earn, by his services, your affection, and your indebtedness to
him, provided that he understands that you value him highly, that you act from
the heart, that he is positioning himself well, and that there will develop from it
not a brief and campaign-long friendship, but one that is firm and lasting. (27)
There will be no one, believe me, who has anything in him at all, who will not
seize this opportunity offered to him to establish a friendship with you, especially
when it so happens that the friendship of your competitors is to be spurned or
avoided, and that they are unable not only to procure what I am urging upon
you, but even to begin to do so. (28) For how does Antonius begin to win over,
and welcome to his friendship, those whom he cannot, without help, call by their
own names? Indeed, nothing seems more foolish to me than to think that someone whom you don't recognize is your supporter. The man who could get elected
to office by total strangers, and without backers, would have to possess a kind of
extraordinary fame, and greatness, and an extensive record of public service.
Certainly, that a man who is unprincipled, and lazy, without responsibility, and
without talent, who is discredited, and without any friends, should beat a man
fortified by the support of a great many people, and by a universally good reputation, cannot happen without gross negligence.

(29) So make sure that you have secured all the centuries by means of many
and various friendships. And first – what is most obvious – you should embrace

the Roman senators and knights, and the active and influential men of all the other orders. There are many men in the city who are industrious; there are many freedmen employed in the Forum who are influential and energetic: through your own efforts, and, if possible, through your common friends, see to it, with the utmost attention, that these men eagerly support you, by working on them, by seeking them out, by sending people to them, by showing them that they are doing you the greatest possible favor. (30) Then develop a plan of the whole city, all the colleges, districts, neighborhoods; if the leaders of these are attached to you as friends, you will be able, through them, to keep a hold on the rest of the multitude. After this, see to it that you have committed to memory a mental plan of the whole of Italy divided by tribes, so that there is no municipality, colony, prefecture, in short, any place at all in Italy, in which you do not have as strong a foundation as it is possible to have, (31) and that you may identify and seek out men from every region, get to know them, appeal to them, strengthen their resolve, make sure that in their own neighborhoods they will campaign for you, and be, as it were, candidates on your behalf. They will want you as a friend, if they see that their friendship is being sought by you. Make sure that they understand this by speaking about those things which pertain to this point. Men from the municipalities, and from the countryside, if they are known to us by name, think that they are among our friends. But if they think that they are also securing some protection for themselves, they do not pass up the opportunity to be obliging. Others, and especially your competitors, do not even know of these men; you know them and will easily recognize them, without which friendship is not possible. (32) But this is still not enough (though it is important), if the hope of material advantage and friendship does not follow, so that you might seem to be, not just a *nomenclator*,[21] but a good friend also. So when you have as your supporters in the centuries these very men, who, because of their own campaigning, can exercise the greatest influence among their fellow-tribesmen, and have ensured that others who are influential in some part of their tribe, because of their municipality, or neighborhood, or college, are eager for you to succeed, then you ought to be of the highest hopes.

(33) Now it seems to me that the centuries of the knights can, if you're careful, be won over much more easily: first, get to know the knights, for they are few in number; then appeal to them, for it is much easier to gain the friendship of young men. You have on your side also all the best of the young men, and those who are most devoted to learning. Then too, because the equestrian order is yours, they will follow the authority of that order, if you work diligently to confirm the support of those centuries, not only by the good-will of the order, but also by the friendships of individuals. For the enthusiasm of the young in canvassing for votes, in attendance, in disseminating information, and in accompanying you in public are both surprisingly important and respectable.

(34) And since I have mentioned "attendance," this also should be seen to – that every day you make use of every type, and class, and age; for from their very numbers a guess can be made as to how much strength and support you will have at the election itself. And this business consists of three parts: first, morning-callers, who come to your house; second, those who lead you down to the Forum; third, those who accompany you on your campaign. (35) In respect to the

morning-callers, who are rather ordinary, and, in keeping with the custom that
now exists, come in greater numbers, you must see to it that they think that this
very minor service of theirs is very pleasing to you. Those who come to your
home must be given the impression that you notice it; show your gratitude to
those of their friends who will repeat it to them; mention it often to the men
themselves. It often happens that people, when they visit many candidates, and
see that there is one in particular who pays special attention to their services,
devote themselves to him, abandon the others, gradually become attached to one
instead of being indiscriminate, and turn out to be firm supporters instead of
pretend ones. Carefully remember this also – if you have heard that someone
who has promised you his support is, as they say, "putting on a show," or you
get the feeling that he is, act as if you had not heard it or did not know it; if
anyone wants to prove himself to you, because he is thought to be suspect, announce that you have never doubted his intentions and have no grounds for
doubting them. For he who thinks that he is not satisfying you cannot be a friend
in any way. You should, however, know each man's feelings, so that you can
decide how much you can trust him.

(36) You should indicate and demonstrate that the service done by those who
lead you down to the Forum, as it is greater than that of the morning-callers, is
also more pleasing to you, and, as far as it is possible, you should go down at
fixed times. A large crowd accompanying you every day makes a great impression and confers great distinction. (37) The third category is the crowd that always attends you on your campaign. Among those who do so spontaneously, see
to it that they understand that you are obligated to them forever for their extremely important service; from those who owe you this service, however, openly
demand that, in the case of those whose age and occupation allow it, they themselves constantly be with you, and that, in the case of those who cannot accompany you, they arrange for their relatives to perform this duty. I am very eager,
and think it very important, that you should always be with a large crowd. (38)
Besides, it confers great prestige and the utmost distinction to be accompanied by
those who have been defended by you, and those who have been saved and acquitted in the courts because of you. From them, you must clearly demand that,
because it was through your efforts, and without any expense, that some of them
held onto their property, others their honor, still others their personal safety and
entire fortunes, and because there will never be another time when they can thank
you, they should repay you with this service.

(39) And since this whole discourse is about the loyalties of friends, it seems
that I ought not to pass over one cautionary point in regard to this type. Everything is full of deception, intrigue, and treachery. This is not the time for a long
disquisition about the ways in which a true friend can be distinguished from a
false one: the only appropriate thing at this time is to give you a warning. Your
great virtue compels the same men both to pretend to be your friends and to be
envious of you. For that reason, remember the saying of Epicharmus,[22] "the sin-
ews and bone of wisdom is not to believe anything rashly." (40) And when you
have arranged for the loyalty of your friends, then you must also learn the attitudes and varieties of your detractors and adversaries. These are three: first, those
whom you have harmed; second, those who dislike you for no reason; third,

those who are good friends of your competitors. As for those you attacked when speaking against them on behalf of a friend, openly excuse yourself to them; remind them of your personal ties; give them hope that, if they should make themselves your friends, you will act with the same enthusiasm and concern in respect to their affairs. As for those who dislike you for no reason, work hard to remove that prejudice either by some service, or by holding out hope of it, or by indicating your devotion towards them. As for those whose feelings are against you because of their friendship for your competitors, attach yourself to them by the same methods as with the others, and, if you can convince them of it, show them that you are well-disposed even towards your competitors.

(41) Since I have said enough about establishing friendships, I ought to speak about that other aspect of campaigning, which is concerned with winning over the people. This requires the ability to remember names, flattery, constant attendance, generosity, gossip, and a high profile in the state. (42) First, make it clear that you have the ability to recognize people, and improve it so that it becomes better every day – it seems to me that there is nothing that is so popular or so pleasing. Next, if there is something that you don't have by nature, make up your mind to simulate it, in such a way that you seem to be acting naturally. For you are not lacking that friendliness which is appropriate for a good and polite man, but there is a great need for flattery, which, even if it is shameful and unseemly at other times of life, is nevertheless necessary in a campaign. For when someone is made worse by agreeing with everything, it is improper; when it makes him more friendly, it should not be so disparaged; but it is a necessity for a candidate, whose face and expression and words must be altered and accommodated to the feelings and opinions of everyone he meets. (43) Now there is no general rule for "attendance;" the word itself indicates what the thing is. Of course, it is very important that you not go away anywhere. But the advantage of such attendance is this – not only being at Rome and in the Forum, but campaigning constantly, talking often to the same men, making certain (to the extent that you can) that no one can say that he has not been canvassed by you, and canvassed earnestly and diligently. (44) Generosity also has wide application; it is shown in connection with your own wealth, which, although it does not actually reach the multitude, still, if praised by friends, is pleasing to the multitude; it is shown in banquets, which you must arrange to attend yourself and for your friends to attend, both those that are open to all and those for particular tribes; it is shown also in doing services, which should be made available to all. And see to it that you are accessible to everyone day and night, not only by the doors of your house, but by your face and expression, which is the doorway to the heart: for if that shows that your feelings are hidden and out of sight, it matters little that your doors are open. For men want not only to have promises made to them, especially in what they request from a candidate, but also want to have promises made to them in a generous and respectful way. (45) And so it is easy to prescribe that you should indicate that whatever you are going to do, you will do eagerly and with pleasure; it is more difficult, and more a matter of expediency than something appropriate to your character, that when you cannot do something, you should either graciously decline to do it, or even promise to do it – the former is the conduct of a good man, the latter of a good candidate. For when a request

is made which we cannot grant honorably or without loss to ourselves – if, for example, someone were to ask us to take up a case against one of our friends – it must be refused nicely, and in such a way that you indicate to him that you have no choice, that you demonstrate how sorry you are, that you persuade him that you will make up for it in other ways.

(46) I heard someone say about certain orators, to whom he had offered his case, that the words of the one who refused him were more pleasing than those of the one who accepted. So it is that men are more taken by one's countenance and words than by actual service. But this is quite likely to meet with your approval. It is difficult to recommend that other course of action to a Platonist like you, but nevertheless, I will consider your present circumstances. For even those to whom you refuse your help because of some other obligation may nevertheless leave you mollified and sympathetic. But those whom you turn down by saying only that you are prevented by the affairs of your friends, or by cases that are more important, or by ones previously undertaken, go away feeling hostile, and are all so inclined that they would prefer that you lie to them rather than turn them down. (47) Gaius Cotta,[23] an expert in the art of campaigning, used to say that he was accustomed to promise his services to everyone, provided that he was not asked to do something contrary to duty, and actually to bestow them on those in whom they seemed to be best invested; that he did not refuse anyone, because it often happened that there would be some reason why the person to whom he had made a promise could not make use of it, and it often happened also that he himself was not as busy as he had thought; that someone's house could not be full if he undertook to do only what he thought he would be able to do; that it often happens by accident that things get done which you did not think possible, and that what you believed to be in hand does not get done for one reason or another; finally, that the worst that can happen is that the man you lied to is angry. (48) And this risk, if you do make a promise, is uncertain, in the future, and only applies to a few; but if you refuse, you will definitely alienate many men immediately. For there are many more who ask to be allowed to make use of one's services than there are those who actually do so. So it is better to have some of them angry at you in the Forum some of the time, than all of them always angry at you at your own house, especially when they are much more angry at those who refuse than at someone whom they see is prevented by the sort of reason that is consistent with his wanting to do what he promised, if only he could. (49) But lest I seem to have departed from my own classification, since I am discussing what belongs to the part of the campaign that has to do with winning popular support, I insist on this: that all these things pertain not so much to the support of friends as to your reputation among the people. Although there is something in this that pertains to that other category – answering kindly, helping eagerly with the affairs and the dangers of friends – nevertheless, I am speaking here about those things by which you can win over the populace: that your house is full before day-break, that many are attached to you because they hope for your support; that men should leave you feeling more friendly than when they came; that the ears of as many as possible are full of the most excellent words.

(50) For it follows that I should speak about public reputation, to which the greatest attention must be paid. But what I have said throughout the preceding

discussion applies also to the cultivation of a favorable reputation – praise of your eloquence; the support of the publicans and equestrian order; the good-will of the nobility; a crowd of young men; the constant attendance of those who have been defended by you; the multitude of those who appear to have come from the municipal towns for your sake; that you are good at recognizing men, address them politely, constantly and earnestly seek their support; that they speak and think of you as kind and generous; that your house is full long before dawn; that large numbers of every class are present; that your words are satisfying to everyone, your actions and deeds to many; that everything is done which can be done by hard work, and skill, and diligence, not that your reputation among these men might reach the people, but that the populace might share in these feelings. (51) You have already won over that urban multitude and the support of those who control the public meetings by extolling Pompey, by taking up the cause of Manilius, by defending Cornelius.[24] We must make the most of those advantages, which no one has had before now without at the same time having the support of the most eminent men. We must also ensure that everyone knows that Gnaeus Pompeius is very strongly in your favor, and that it matters a great deal to his purposes that you achieve what you are seeking. (52) Lastly, take care that your whole candidacy is full of display, that it's brilliant, splendid, and accommodated to popular taste, that it has the utmost magnificence and dignity, and that also, if possible, some scandal should arise about your competitors for criminal conduct, or licentiousness, or corruption, such as is in keeping with their characters.

(53) And most of all, in this campaign you must see to it that the state expects good things from you and has an honorable opinion of you. But you must not engage in matters of state while campaigning, either in the Senate or in a public meeting; you must refrain from such things in order that the Senate may judge, from how you have conducted your life, that you will be a defender of its authority; that the Roman knights, and the good men, and the wealthy, may judge, on the basis of your past, that you are a supporter of peace and tranquility; and that the people may conclude, from the fact that in your comments at public meetings, and in court, you have been a *popularis*, that you will not be averse to their interests.

(54) This is what occurred to me about those two morning-reflections, which I said you should think about every day as you go down to the Forum: "I am a new man; I seek the consulship." The third remains: "this is Rome," a city made up of an assemblage of nations, in which there are many plots, much deception, many vices in every aspect of life; in which you have to put up with the arrogance, the obstinacy, the resentments, the overbearing pride, the hatred, and troublesome nature of many. I understand that it requires great wisdom and skill, living amid so many and such serious vices of every kind, to avoid giving offense, to avoid scandal, to avoid treachery, for one person to be adapted to such a variety of character, and of speech, and of feeling. (55) So I urge you again and again, to stay on that road you have embarked upon, by speaking brilliantly; it is by this that men at Rome are captivated, and deterred from obstructing you or causing you harm. And since the state is corrupt especially in this – that it is accustomed to forget virtue and honor when bribery intervenes – be sure that you are well-

informed in this respect, that is, that you understand that you are someone who is capable of inducing in your competitors the greatest fear of legal action and of danger. Make sure that they know that they are being watched and scrutinized by you: when they are afraid of your diligence and of the authority and power of your speech, then they will fear the good-will of the equestrian order towards you. (56) But I do not want you to set this before them in such a way that it appears that you are already thinking about bringing an accusation, but that, because of this fear, you might more easily accomplish what you are doing. And clearly, you should fight with all your energies and faculties in such a way as to achieve what we seek. I observe that there are no elections so corrupted by bribery that there are not at least some centuries which will, without being paid, support those who are connected to them. (57) So if we are as vigilant as the importance of the matter demands, and if we stir up our supporters to give their utmost effort, and if we assign a specific task to each of our influential and enthusiastic supporters, and if we hold before our competitors the prospect of legal action, instill fear in their followers, and somehow restrain the bribe-distributors, it can happen either that there is no bribery or that it has no effect.

(58) These are the things that I thought, not that I knew better than you, but that, given your preoccupations, I could more easily collect in one place and send to you in writing. And although they are written in such a way as to apply, not to all candidates for office, but especially to you and to your campaign, nevertheless, I hope that you will tell me if there is anything that you think ought to be changed or altogether deleted, or if there is anything that has been overlooked. For I want this handbook on campaigning to be considered complete in every respect.

29   TACITUS, *ANNALS* 1.1–15

Cornelius Tacitus was born probably in southern Gaul or in northern Italy about AD 56. He was consul in 97, and later, perhaps in 112–13, governor of the province of Asia. He died sometime after 113. His surviving works include the *Dialogue about Orators*, a pessimistic account of the decline of oratory; the *Agricola*, a biography of his father-in-law, Gnaeus Julius Agricola, who was governor of Britain, AD 78–84 (see also selection 44); the *Germania* (see selection 45), which describes the institutions and customs of the Germanic tribes; the *Histories*, which covered the period AD 69–96 (only Books 1–4, and the beginning of 5, survive); and the *Annals*, a full-scale history of the period AD 14–68, which is only partially preserved – we have the whole of Books 1–4, the beginning of 5, all of 6, the last part of 11, and all of 12–16 (covering the periods AD 14–29, 31–7, and 47–66) – and which is easily our most reliable source of information about a period that forever changed the shape of the Roman world. The following passage, which opens the first book of the *Annals*, describes the last acts of Augustus and the accession of Tiberius.

(1) From the beginning, kings ruled the city of Rome: Lucius Brutus established liberty and the consulship. Dictatorships were assumed only for a fixed length of time; the decemviral power[25] did not last more than two years; nor did the

consular authority of the military tribunes[26] last long. The despotism of neither Cinna nor Sulla was lasting: the power of Pompey and Crassus passed quickly to Caesar, the arms of Lepidus and Antony to Augustus, who, under the name of *princeps*,[27] gathered beneath his empire a world exhausted by civil dissension. But the glories and vicissitudes of the Roman people of old have been recorded by distinguished writers; good minds were not lacking to tell of the times of Augustus, until they were deterred by the growth of sycophancy; the deeds of Tiberius, and Gaius, and Claudius, and Nero, were, while they flourished, falsified because of fear, and, after they died, composed while hatreds were fresh. And so my plan is to relate a few things about the last part of Augustus' reign, then the principate of Tiberius and the rest, without anger and partisanship, from the causes of which I am far removed.

(2) After Brutus and Cassius had been killed, and the state disarmed; after Pompey[28] had been suppressed in Sicily, Lepidus cast off, and Antony cut down, and no general was left, even for the Julian faction, except Caesar;[29] after setting aside the title of triumvir and advertising himself as consul and as content with the authority of a tribune to protect the plebs; after he had seduced the soldiers with gifts, the people with grain, everyone with the amenities of peace, then little by little he began to rise up and to collect in his own person the duties of the Senate, the magistrates, and the laws, with no opposition, since the boldest men had fallen in battle or by proscription, while the rest of the nobility were bought off with wealth and honors, the more so as each was disposed to be servile, and having profited from revolution, preferred the safety of the present to the dangers of the past. Nor did the provinces find fault with that state of affairs, since government by the Senate and people had been discredited by the struggles of the powerful and by the greed of the magistrates, there being almost no help from the laws, which were overwhelmed by violence, by ambition, and, in the last instance, by money.

(3) In the meantime, to consolidate his domination, Augustus promoted Claudius Marcellus, his sister's son, and still a youth, to the office of *pontifex*[30] and of curule aedile,[31] Marcus Agrippa, of humble birth, but a good soldier and the partner of his victory, to consecutive consulships, and then, after Marcellus had died, to be his son-in-law. He honored his step-sons, Tiberius Nero and Claudius Drusus, with the title of *imperator*,[32] though his own family was still intact. For he had admitted Agrippa's children, Gaius and Lucius, into the household of the Caesars, and, while feigning reluctance, had passionately wanted them to be designated consuls and called "First of the Youth,"[33] even before they put aside the toga of boyhood. After Agrippa had departed this world, death, hastened by fate, or by the treachery of their stepmother Livia, removed Lucius Caesar as he was going to the armies of Spain, Gaius, wounded and sick, as he was returning from Armenia. With Drusus long dead, Nero alone of the stepsons survived: everything centered on him. Adopted as son, as colleague of empire, as partner in the tribunician power, he was paraded before all the armies, not, as before, because of his mother's secret scheming, but openly at her insistence. For so firmly had she got hold of the aged Augustus that he banished his only grandson, Agrippa Postumus, to the island of Planasia[34] – admittedly devoid of virtue, and ferocious in his animal-like strength, he had, nevertheless, been convicted of no crime. Yet

he put Drusus' son Germanicus in charge of eight legions on the Rhine, and ordered Tiberius to adopt him, so that he might be surrounded by more defenses, even though there was a grown son in Tiberius' home. At the time, there was no war, except for the one that continued to be waged against the Germans, more for the purpose of erasing the dishonor caused by the loss of the army commanded by Quintilius Varus[35] than from any desire to extend the empire or with the prospect of an adequate reward. At home, all was tranquil. The magistrates had the same titles; the younger men had been born after the victory of Actium, many of the older men during the civil wars – how few were left who had seen the Republic.

(4) So the nature of the state had been altered, and there was nowhere a trace of the old and virtuous Roman character. With equality cast aside, everyone looked to the orders of the *princeps*, and, for the time being, without fear, so long as Augustus was in the prime of his life, and preserved himself, his household, and peace. But afterwards, as old age advanced, and he was worn down by sickness, and the end was near, and new hopes emerging, a few men began idly to discuss the blessings of freedom; more were afraid of war; others desired it. The large majority exchanged gossip about those who were about to become their masters: "Agrippa [Postumus], violent, and burning with humiliation, was not up to so heavy a burden, either in age or experience. Tiberius Nero was mature in years and tested in war, but he possessed the old, in-born arrogance of the Claudian family, and many indications of his cruelty kept emerging, though he tried to repress them. From earliest infancy, he had been raised in a royal household; consulships and triumphs were heaped on him in his youth; even in the years when he lived at Rhodes, ostensibly in retirement but really as an exile, he had thought of nothing except anger, hypocrisy, and secret lusts. Add his mother with her womanly excess: they were to be slaves to a woman, and to two young men as well, who would first oppress the state, and then tear it apart!"

(5) While these and similar things were being discussed, the health of Augustus began to grow worse, and some suspected foul play on the part of his wife. For a rumor had gone around that, a few months before, Augustus, with the knowledge of a chosen few, and accompanied only by Fabius Maximus, had gone to Planasia to see Agrippa; there were many tears there on both sides, and signs of affection such as to create the hope that the young man might be restored to the household of his grandfather, something which Maximus had revealed to his wife Marcia, and she to Livia. It had become known to Caesar. When Maximus died not long afterwards, perhaps by his own hand, Marcia had been heard sobbing at his funeral, and reproaching herself for having been the cause of her husband's destruction. However it really happened, Tiberius had barely entered Illyricum[36] when he was called back by an urgent letter from his mother; and it is not entirely clear whether, on reaching the city of Nola, he found Augustus still breathing or dead. For Livia had carefully closed off the house and streets with guards, while cheerful announcements were periodically issued, until, when the measures required by the situation had been taken, the same report announced simultaneously that Augustus had died and that Nero was in charge of affairs.

(6) The first crime of the new principate was the murder of Agrippa Postumus, whom a determined centurion had difficulty killing, though he was taken by

surprise and unarmed. Tiberius said nothing about the subject in the Senate: he pretended it had been done on his father's orders, by which he had instructed the tribune assigned to guard Agrippa not to delay in killing him, just as soon as he himself should have completed his last day. There was no question that Augustus had complained often and bitterly about the young man's character, to such an extent that his exile was sanctioned by a decree of the Senate; but he never hardened himself to the killing of one of his relatives; nor was it believable that the death of a grandson would have been arranged for the security of a stepson. It was more likely that Tiberius and Livia, the one because of fear, the other because of stepmotherly hatred, hastened the death of the young man whom they suspected and detested. To the centurion who brought the news, as was the military custom, that what he had ordered had been done, Tiberius replied that he had not given any orders, and that the deed would have to be accounted for in the Senate. This later came to the attention of Sallustius Crispus, a partner in his secrets (he had forwarded the note to the tribune); fearing that he might be charged, and that he was at risk whether he lied or spoke the truth, he advised Livia not to make known the secrets of the palace, the advice of her friends, the services of the soldiers, and not to allow Tiberius to weaken the power of the principate by referring everything to the Senate: "this was a condition of exercising sovereignty, that the account did not balance unless rendered to one man."

(7) But at Rome, the consuls, the senators, and the knights rushed headlong into servitude. The more distinguished each was, the greater his hypocrisy and haste; with his expression adjusted, so as not to seem happy at the departure of one emperor or too gloomy at the entrance of another, he mixed tears with joy, regrets with adulation. The oath of allegiance to Tiberius Caesar was taken first by the consuls, Sextus Pompeius and Sextus Appuleius, then, in their presence, by Seius Strabo and Gaius Turranius, the former the prefect of the praetorian cohorts, the latter of the grain-supply; then the senators, the soldiers, and the people. For Tiberius began everything through the consuls, as if the old republic existed, and he himself was uncertain about governing: even the edict by which he summoned the senators to the Senate-house was issued under the title of the tribunician power which he had received under Augustus. The words of the edict were few, and very modest in nature: "he would see to the last rites of his father; he was not leaving the body; this was the one official duty that he was undertaking." But at the death of Augustus he had given the watchword to the praetorian cohorts as *imperator*;[37] he had guards, armed soldiers, and the other trappings of a court; soldiers accompanied him to the Forum, and to the Senate-house. He sent letters to the armies as if he had taken control of the principate; and nowhere did he show any hesitation, except when speaking in the Senate. The main reason was his fear that Germanicus, who had control of so many legions, the vast auxiliary-forces of the allies, and a remarkable degree of support among the people, might prefer to have the imperial power rather than to wait for it. He let it be known also that he wanted to be regarded as the called and chosen of the state, rather than as one who had crept in through a wife's intrigues and a senile adoption. Afterwards, it was realized that his hesitation had also been feigned for the purpose of ascertaining the feelings of the leading men: for he was twisting words and looks into crimes, and storing them away.

(8) At the first meeting of the Senate, he allowed nothing to be done other than what concerned the funeral of Augustus, whose will, brought in by the Vestal Virgins, named Tiberius and Livia as heirs. Livia was to be adopted into the Julian family and the Augustan name; in the second degree, he had written his grandchildren and great-grandchildren; in the third place, the leading men – an ostentatious attempt to secure his reputation for posterity, seeing as he hated most of them. His bequests were not beyond the ordinary civic scale, except that he gave 43,500,000 sesterces to the people and the plebs, 1,000 each to the soldiers of the praetorian cohorts, 500 each to the urban cohorts, and 300 apiece to the legionaries or cohorts of Roman citizens. Then there was discussion about the last honors. The two proposals that were considered to be most notable were those of Asinius Gallus – that the funeral procession should pass under a triumphal gate, and of Lucius Arruntius – that the titles of all the laws that he had passed and the names of all the peoples whom he had conquered should be carried in front of it. Valerius Messalla added that the oath in the name of Tiberius should be renewed every year; asked by Tiberius whether he had expressed that opinion at his urging, he replied that he had spoken of his own free will, and that, in matters pertaining to the state, he would use no counsel other than his own, even at the risk of giving offense – this was the only type of flattery left. The senators shouted that the body should be carried to the funeral-pyre on their shoulders. Caesar excused them, with arrogant moderation, and warned the people in an edict that, as formerly they had spoiled the funeral of the deified Julius by their excessive enthusiasm, so they should not want Augustus to be cremated in the Forum rather than in the Campus Martius,[38] his designated resting-place. On the day of the funeral, soldiers were arrayed as if on guard, to the jeers of those who themselves had seen or who had heard from their fathers of that day of still immature servitude and of freedom inauspiciously recovered, when the killing of the dictator Caesar had seemed to some the worst, to others the most beautiful, of deeds: now an aged *princeps*, of long-standing authority, who had seen to it that not even his heirs would lack resources against the state, actually had to be protected by the military, so as to ensure that his funeral would be undisturbed.

(9) After this, there was much talk about Augustus, with most expressing wonder at the trivial – that the same day he had become *princeps* ["first man"] of the empire was also the last of his life; that he should have ended his life at Nola in the same house and bedroom as his father Octavius. Much was said also about the number of his consulships (by which he had equaled Valerius Corvus and Gaius Marius combined), about the tribunician power he held continuously for thirty-seven years, about the title of *imperator* he had won twenty-one times, and about his other honors, multiplied or new. But among the wise, his life was variously praised and criticized. Some maintained that duty to his father and the needs of the state, in which there was, at the time, no place for laws, had driven him to the weapons of civil war, which could not be fashioned or wielded with honorable methods. He had conceded a great deal to Antony, and to Lepidus, so long as he was avenging his father's assassins. Later, when Lepidus grew old and lazy, and Antony was brought down by his lusts, there had been no other remedy for the dissension of the country than that it be ruled by one man. Nevertheless,

he had organized the state, not as a monarchy or dictatorship, but in the name of *princeps*; the empire had been fenced in by Ocean or far-off rivers; the legions, the provinces, the fleets, everything had been made inter-connected; there had been law among the citizens, modesty among the allies, and the city itself had been marvelously embellished; very few things had been managed by force, and then only so that there might be tranquility for everyone else.

(10) On the other side, it was said that duty to his father and the crisis of the state had been used as a pretext; as for the rest, it was because of his desire to rule that he had stirred up the veterans with bribes, assembled an army while still a youth and a private citizen, seduced the legions of a consul, pretended to be a supporter of the Pompeian party; then after he had usurped, by decree of the Senate, the *fasces*[39] and authority of a praetor, and Hirtius and Pansa[40] had been killed – whether removed by the enemy, or Pansa by poison sprinkled on his wound, Hirtius by his own soldiers and by Caesar, acting as architect of the plot – he had taken over both their armies, extorted a consulship from an unwilling Senate, and turned against the state the arms which he had received for use against Antony; the proscription of citizens and the confiscations of land had been approved not even by those who carried them out. No doubt, Cassius and the Bruti had been sacrificed to inherited enmities (though it would have been proper to subordinate private hatreds to public utility); but Pompeius had been deceived by a phantom peace,[41] Lepidus by a pretended friendship; afterwards, Antony, seduced by the treaties of Tarentum and Brundisium,[42] and by a sister's marriage,[43] had paid with his life the penalty of that deceitful relationship. After this, there had undoubtedly been peace, but a bloody one – the disasters of Lollius[44] and of Varus;[45] a Varro,[46] an Egnatius,[47] a Iullus[48] executed at Rome. His domestic affairs were not spared: the abduction of Nero's wife, and the ludicrous question put to the *pontifices*[49] – whether, with a child conceived but not yet born, she could lawfully marry; the excesses of Vedius Pollio;[50] and finally, Livia – as a mother, a burden to the state; as a stepmother, a burden to the house of the Caesars. He had left nothing for the honor of the gods, when he wanted to be worshipped by the *flamines*[51] and *sacerdotes*[52] in temples and in the image of the gods. Even in adopting Tiberius as his successor, he had acted, not out of affection or concern for the state, but because, having observed his arrogance and cruelty, he had hoped to heighten his own glory by the very worst of comparisons. For Augustus, a few years earlier, when asking the Senate to renew Tiberius' tribunician power, had let slip, although the speech was complimentary, certain remarks about his demeanor, dress, and habits, for the purpose of reproaching them, as if by way of apology. But the funeral was carried out in the usual manner; a temple and celestial rites were decreed.

(11) Then prayers were directed to Tiberius. And he talked variously about the greatness of the empire and about his own diffidence: only the mind of the deified Augustus was equal to such a great burden; he himself, when called by Augustus to share in his anxieties, had learned how arduous, how dependent on fortune, was the task of ruling everything. It followed that, in a state which could rely on so many illustrious men, everything should not be referred to one man; a larger number would more easily carry out the business of the state through a partnership of labor. Such a speech was more dignified than convincing. Besides,

Tiberius' words were, by nature or by habit, always indirect and obscure, even in regard to matters in which he had nothing to hide; but now, in an effort to conceal his feelings completely, they became even more uncertain and ambiguous. The senators, however, whose one fear was that they might seem to understand him, dissolved in pleas, tears, and prayers. They were stretching their hands to the gods, to the image of Augustus, to his own knees, when he ordered a document to be brought in and read aloud. It described the public resources – how many citizens and allies were under arms; how many fleets, kingdoms, and provinces there were; direct and indirect taxes; necessary expenditures and payments. Augustus had written it all out in his own hand, and had added – it was uncertain whether because of fear or jealousy – his advice that the empire should be kept within its present boundaries.

(12) Meanwhile, with the Senate descending to the most abject entreaties, Tiberius casually remarked that, in so far as he was unequal to governing the whole empire, he would undertake the administration of whatever part of it might be assigned to him. Then Asinius Gallus said : "I ask you, Caesar, what part of the government do you want to be assigned to you?" Caught off balance by this unforeseen question, he was silent for a little while, then, recovering himself, he answered that it was not at all in keeping with his modesty either to select or to avoid any part of a burden from which he preferred to be excused altogether. Gallus, who had inferred anger from his expression, spoke again: "the question had been asked of him, not so that he would divide what could not be separated, but that it might be made clear by his own admission that the state was a single organism that ought to be governed by the mind of one man." He added some laudatory remarks about Augustus, and reminded Tiberius himself of his own victories and of the brilliant things he had done as a statesman for so many years. He failed, however, to mollify his anger; he had been hated for a long time, ever since his marriage to Vipsania, the daughter of Marcus Agrippa, who had once been the wife of Tiberius, which had made it appear that he aimed at more than what was appropriate for a private citizen, and that he retained the courage of his father, Asinius Pollio.

(13) After this, Lucius Arruntius, speaking in a way hardly different from that of Gallus, also gave offense, though Tiberius had no long-standing anger against him: but because he was rich, energetic, of distinguished ability, and corresponding popularity, he was suspect. For Augustus, in his last conversations, when he was discussing who might take his place as *princeps* – those who were capable and uninterested; those who were incapable and willing; or those who were at the same time able and eager – had described Manius Lepidus as capable but uninterested, Asinius Gallus as eager but inadequate, Lucius Arruntius as not unworthy and, if the opportunity should present itself, bold enough. About the first two, there is agreement; some have recorded Gnaeus Piso in place of Arruntius; and all, except Lepidus, were soon beset by a variety of charges, instigated by Tiberius. Quintus Haterius and Mamercus Scaurus also offended that suspicious mind, Haterius when he said: "how long, Caesar, will you allow the state to be without a head?"; and Scaurus because he said that, since he had not used the authority of his tribunician power to veto the proposal of the consuls, there was hope that the prayers of the Senate would not be in vain. Tiberius tore into Haterius

immediately; Scaurus, against whom his anger was more implacable, he passed over in silence. Worn down by the general outcry and by individual appeals, he gradually yielded, not so far as to admit that he was taking up the responsibility of governing, but that he ceased to refuse and to be asked. It is well known that Haterius, when he had entered the palace to make his excuses, and had thrown himself at Tiberius' knees as he was walking, was almost killed by the soldiers, because Tiberius, either by accident or because he was impeded by Haterius' hands, had fallen down. That such a man was in danger failed, however, to soften him, until Haterius appealed to the Augusta, and was saved by her most urgent prayers.

(14) The Senate directed much adulation also to the Augusta: some proposed that she be called the "Parent," others the "Mother," of her country; a majority suggested that "son of Julia" should be added to the name of Caesar. Tiberius, declaring that honors for women should be kept within bounds, and that he would act with the same moderation in the case of those that were granted to him (actually, he was moved by jealousy, and considered the elevation of a woman to be a diminishment of himself), did not even allow her to be awarded a lictor,[53] and banned an "Altar of Adoption" and other things of this sort. But he asked for proconsular authority for Germanicus Caesar, and a delegation was sent to confer it, and at the same time to console his grief at the death of Augustus. That the same was not requested on behalf of Drusus was because he was consul-designate and was present. Tiberius nominated twelve candidates for the praetorship, the number handed down by Augustus; and when the Senate urged him to increase it, he declared on oath that he would not exceed it.

(15) Then the elections were transferred for the first time from the Campus to the Senate; for until that day, although the most important were at the discretion of the *princeps*, some of them had still been decided by the preferences of the tribes. Nor did the people complain that the right had been taken away, except for some pointless grumbling; and the Senate, freed from having to pay bribes and from the sordidness of begging for votes, gladly went along, with Tiberius limiting himself to recommending no more than four candidates, who would be appointed without any possibility of their being rejected, and without their having to campaign. At the same time, the plebeian tribunes asked that they be allowed to stage games at their own expense, which would be called the Augustalia,[54] from the name Augustus, and which would be added to the calendar of festivals. But it was decided that the money should come from the treasury; and that the tribunes should be permitted to use triumphal dress in the Circus:[55] they were not to be allowed to ride in a chariot. Responsibility for celebrating the games was soon transferred to the praetor who happened to have jurisdiction between citizens and foreigners.

30   Augustus, *Accomplishments of the Deified Augustus*

Gaius Octavius was born in 63 BC. His mother, Atia, was the niece of Julius Caesar; his father, also named Gaius Octavius, died when he was four. After Julius Caesar adopted him in his will, he was known as Gaius Julius Caesar Octavianus. The title Augustus was given to him by the Senate in 27 BC.

Shortly before he died in August, AD 14, Augustus ordered two bronze pillars to be set up in front of his mausoleum at Rome, and to be inscribed with what he called "a record of his accomplishments" (Suetonius, *Life of Augustus* 4). Though the pillars have disappeared, the document itself survives in a copy that was inscribed on the temple of Rome and Augustus (now a mosque) in what is today Ankara, Turkey. It is divided into four parts: the honors he received and the offices he held (sections 1–14); the expenditures he made for public purposes (sections 15–24); his accomplishments in war and in foreign affairs (sections 25–33); his position in the state (sections 34–5). Its main purpose, it seems, was to secure his reputation in posterity.

Below is a copy of the achievements of the deified Augustus, by which he subjected the entire world to the sovereignty of the Roman people, and of the expenses which he made on behalf of the state and the Roman people, engraved on two bronze pillars, which have been set up at Rome.

(1) At the age of nineteen,[56] on my own initiative and at my own expense, I raised an army, by means of which I restored liberty to the state, when it was oppressed by the tyranny of a faction.[57] Because of this, the Senate enrolled me, through honorary decrees, in its order, when Gaius Pansa and Aulus Hirtius were consuls,[58] at the same time giving me consular status in voting; it also gave me *imperium*.[59] It ordered me, as propraetor, to see to it, together with the consuls, that the state should not suffer any harm. Also in the same year, when both consuls had fallen in battle, the people elected me consul and triumvir for reorganizing the Republic.

(2) Those who murdered my father,[60] I drove into exile, avenging their deed by due process of law, and afterwards, when they waged war on the state, I twice defeated them in battle.

(3) Wars on land and at sea, civil and foreign, I undertook throughout the whole world, and as victor I spared all citizens who asked for pardon. Foreign nations which could safely be spared, I preferred to preserve rather than to destroy. The number of Roman citizens who were bound to me by oath was about 500,000. Of these, I settled in colonies or sent back to their own towns, after they had completed their term of service, somewhat more than 300,000, and to all of them I assigned land or gave money as a reward for military service. I captured 600 ships, not including those that were smaller than triremes.

(4) I twice triumphed with an ovation;[61] three times I celebrated curule triumphs; and I was hailed as *imperator*[62] twenty-one times. And when the Senate decreed more triumphs for me, I declined them. When the vows which I had undertaken in each war had been performed, I deposited the laurel from my

fasces[63] on the Capitol. Because of what was done successfully on land and at sea, by me or by my commanders acting under my auspices, on fifty-five occasions the Senate decreed that supplication should be made to the immortal gods. The number of days on which supplication was made by decree of the Senate was 890. In my triumphs, nine kings or children of kings were led before my chariot. I had been consul thirteen times when I wrote this, and I was in the thirty-seventh year of my tribunician power.[64]

(5) The dictatorship offered to me by the people and the Roman Senate, both when I was absent and when I was at Rome, in the consulship of Marcus Marcellus and Lucius Arruntius,[65] I did not accept. When there was a serious shortage of grain, I did not decline the supervision of the grain-supply, which I administered in such a way that, within a few days, and at my own expense, I freed the entire population from fear and from the danger they were in. The annual and life-long consulship offered to me at that time, I did not accept.

(6) In the consulship of Marcus Vinucius and Quintus Lucretius,[66] and afterwards in that of Publius and Gnaeus Lentulus,[67] and a third time in that of Paullus Fabius Maximus and Quintus Tubero,[68] when the Senate and the Roman people agreed that I should be appointed supervisor of laws and morals, without a colleague, and with supreme power, I did not accept any magistracy offered to me which was not in keeping with the customs of our ancestors. What the Senate wanted me to do at that time, I carried out through my tribunician power; I myself, on my own initiative, five times asked for and received from the Senate a colleague in that power.

(7) For ten consecutive years, I was triumvir for reorganizing the Republic. Up to the day on which I wrote this, I have been *princeps senatus*[69] for forty years. I have been *pontifex maximus*,[70] augur,[71] a member of the board of fifteen for performing sacred rites,[72] a member of the board of seven for sacred feasts,[73] an Arval brother,[74] a *sodalis Titius*,[75] a *fetialis*.[76]

(8) As consul for the fifth time,[77] by order of the people and the Senate, I increased the number of patricians. I revised the roll of the Senate three times, and in my sixth consulship,[78] with Marcus Agrippa as my colleague, I conducted a census of the people. After an interval of forty-one years, I performed a *lustrum*,[79] at which 4,063,000 Roman citizens were registered. Then a second time, I performed a *lustrum*, with consular *imperium*, and without a colleague, in the consulship of Gaius Censorinus and Gaius Asinius;[80] at that *lustrum*, 4,233,000 Roman citizens were registered. And a third time, I performed a *lustrum*, with consular *imperium*, and with my son Tiberius Caesar as my colleague, in the consulship of Sextus Pompeius and Sextus Apuleius;[81] at that *lustrum*, 4,937,000 Roman citizens were registered. By new laws enacted at my suggestion, I restored many traditions of our ancestors which had begun to disappear from our age, and I myself handed down to posterity many kinds of exemplary practices.

(9) The Senate decreed that every fifth year the consuls and the priests should undertake vows for my health. In connection with these vows, games were held often during my life, sometimes by the four most distinguished colleges of priests, sometimes by the consuls. And all of the citizens, individually and on behalf of their municipalities, have unanimously and continuously offered prayers for my health at all the *pulvinaria*[82] of the gods.

(10) By decree of the Senate, my name was included in the Salian hymn, and it was enacted by law that my person should be sacrosanct forever, and that I should have the tribunician power as long as I might live. I declined to be made *pontifex maximus* in place of my colleague who was still alive, when the people offered me that priesthood which my father had held. Some years later, I accepted that priesthood, at the death of the man who had made use of the opportunity afforded by civil war to seize it for himself, and such a multitude came from all over Italy to Rome for my election, in the consulship of Publius Sulpicius and Gaius Valgius,[83] as had never been recorded at Rome before that time.

(11) In honor of my return, the Senate consecrated an altar to Fortuna Redux in front of the temples of Honor and Virtue near the Porta Capena,[84] and ordered the pontiffs and the Vestal Virgins to make a sacrifice there every year on the day on which I had returned to the city from Syria, in the consulship of Lucius Lucretius and Marcus Vinucius,[85] and it named the day the Augustalia, from my *cognomen*.[86]

(12) On the authority of the Senate, some of the praetors and the tribunes of the plebs, together with the consul Quintus Lucretius and the leading men, were sent to Campania to meet me, an honor which up to this time has been decreed to no one except me. When I returned to Rome from Spain and Gaul, in the consulship of Tiberius Nero and Publius Quintilius,[87] having successfully managed the affairs of those provinces, the Senate decreed that an altar of Augustan Peace should be consecrated next to the Campus Martius in honor of my return, and ordered the magistrates and priests and Vestal Virgins to make a sacrifice there every year.

(13) Janus Quirinus,[88] which our ancestors wanted to be closed when victories had secured peace throughout the whole empire of the Roman people, on land and at sea, and which tradition records was closed only twice from the founding of the city down to when I was born, the Senate ordered to be closed three times while I was *princeps*.

(14) My sons, Gaius and Lucius Caesar, whom Fortune stole from me when they were young, the Senate and the Roman people designated as consuls, as an honor to me, when they were fourteen years old, that they might enter on that magistracy after a period of five years, and the Senate decreed that from that day on which they were led down into the Forum, they should take part in the councils of state. And all the Roman knights hailed each of them as *princeps iuventutis*,[89] and presented them with silver shields and spears.

(15) To each of the Roman plebs I gave 300 sesterces[90] in accordance with the will of my father, and in my fifth consulship,[91] I gave each of them 400 sesterces in my own name from the spoils of war; and again, in my tenth consulship,[92] out of my own patrimony, I paid 400 sesterces to each as a gift, and in my eleventh consulship,[93] having bought grain at my own expense, I distributed twelve grain-rations to each, and in the twelfth year of my tribunician power,[94] I gave each of them 400 sesterces for the third time. These gifts of mine never reached fewer than 250,000 people. In the eighteenth year of my tribunician power, when I was consul for the twelfth time,[95] I gave sixty *denarii*[96] to each of the 320,000 urban plebs. And in my fifth consulship,[97] I gave 1,000 sesterces from the spoils of war to each of the colonists drawn from my soldiers; around 120,000 men in the

PLATE 5.1   *Detail from the Altar of Augustan Peace, consecrated in 13 BC on
the Campus Martius at Rome. It depicts members of the imperial family
(photo SCALA).*

colonies received this triumphal gift. When I was consul for the thirteenth time,[98]
I gave sixty *denarii* to each of the plebs who at that time was receiving public
grain; these were a little more than 200,000 people.

(16) I paid money to the municipal towns for the lands which I assigned to
soldiers in my fourth consulship,[99] and afterwards in the consulship of Marcus
Crassus and Gnaeus Lentulus the augur;[100] this sum was roughly 600,000,000
sesterces which I paid for lands in Italy, and about 260,000,000 sesterces which
I paid for lands in the provinces. Of all those who established colonies of soldiers
in Italy or in the provinces, I was, in the memory of my contemporaries, the first
and only one to do this. And later, in the consulship of Tiberius Nero and Gnaeus
Piso,[101] and again in the consulships of Gaius Antistius and Decimus Laelius,[102]
and of Gaius Calvisius and Lucius Pasienus,[103] and of Lucius Lentulus and Marcus
Messalla,[104] and of Lucius Caninius and Quintus Fabricius,[105] I paid cash rewards to the soldiers whom I settled in their own towns after they had completed
their term of service; on this I spent about 400,000,000 sesterces.

(17) Four times I helped the public treasury with my own money, with the
result that I transferred 150,000,000 sesterces to those who were in charge of the
treasury. And in the consulship of Marcus Lepidus and Lucius Arruntius,[106] I
transferred 170,000,000 sesterces from my own patrimony into the military treas-

ury, which was established on my advice for the purpose of giving rewards to soldiers who had completed twenty or more years of service.

(18) From that year in which Gnaeus and Publius Lentulus were consuls,[107] when taxes were insufficient, I made distributions of grain and money from my granary and from my patrimony, sometimes to 100,000 people, sometimes to many more.

(19) I built the Senate-house and the Chalcidicum adjoining it, the temple of Apollo on the Palatine with its porticoes, the temple of the deified Julius, the Lupercal, the portico at the Circus Flaminius which I allowed to be called Octavia, from the name of the man who had built an earlier one on the same site, a *pulvinar* at the Circus Maximus, the temples of Jupiter Feretrius and Jupiter Tonans on the Capitol, the temple of Quirinus, the temples of Minerva and of Queen Juno, and of Jupiter Libertas on the Aventine, the temple of the Lares at the top of the Sacred Way, the temple of the Di Penates in the Velia, the temple of Youth, and the temple of the Great Mother on the Palatine.

(20) I rebuilt the Capitol and the theater of Pompey, both works at great expense, and without inscribing my own name. I rebuilt the channels of the aqueducts, which in many places were falling into disrepair because of age, and by bringing water from a new spring into its channel, I doubled the capacity of the aqueduct which is called Marcia. I completed the Julian Forum and the basilica which was between the temple of Castor and the temple of Saturn, works begun and almost finished by my father, and when the same basilica was consumed by fire, I began to rebuild it, on an enlarged site, to be dedicated in the name of my sons, and in case I do not finish it during my lifetime, I have ordered that it be completed by my heirs. In my sixth consulship,[108] on the authority of the Senate, I rebuilt eighty-two temples of the gods in the city, overlooking none which at that time needed restoring. When I was consul for the seventh time,[109] I rebuilt the Via Flaminia from the city to Ariminum,[110] and all the bridges except the Mulvian and Minucian.

(21) On private ground, from the spoils of war, I built the temple of Mars the Avenger and the Augustan Forum. On ground purchased mostly from private owners, I built the theater adjacent to the temple of Apollo, and arranged that it be under the name of my son-in-law, Marcus Marcellus. From the spoils of war, I consecrated gifts on the Capitol, and in the temple of the divine Julius, and in the temple of Apollo, and in the temple of Vesta, and in the temple of Mars the Avenger, which cost me around 100,000,000 sesterces. In my fifth consulship,[111] I sent back 35,000 pounds of *aurum coronarium*,[112] which had been contributed by the municipalities and colonies of Italy for my triumphs, and afterwards, whenever I was hailed as *imperator*, I did not accept the *aurum coronarium* which the municipalities and colonies voted with the same generosity as they had decreed it before.

(22) Three times I gave gladiatorial shows in my own name, and five times in the name of my sons or grandsons; at those shows, about 10,000 men fought. Twice in my own name, and a third time in the name of my grandson, I provided for the people an exhibition of athletes summoned from all over. I produced shows four times in my own name, and twenty-three times on behalf of other magistrates. On behalf of the board of fifteen, as president of the college, and

with Marcus Agrippa as my colleague, I produced the Secular games in the consulship of Gaius Furnius and Marcus Silanus.[113] When I was consul for the thirteenth time,[114] I produced, for the first time, the games of Mars, which since that time, in each succeeding year, the consuls have produced in accordance with a decree of the Senate and by statute. In my own name, or that of my sons or grandsons, on twenty-six occasions, I have given hunts of African beasts to the people, in the Circus, in the Forum, or in the amphitheater, at which about 3,500 beasts were slaughtered.

(23) As a show for the people, I produced a naval battle across the Tiber, at the place where the grove of the Caesars is now, a site having been excavated 1,800 feet long and 1,200 feet wide. In this show, thirty beaked ships, triremes or biremes, and many smaller ships, fought against each other. Approximately 3,000 men, not including the rowers, fought in these fleets.

(24) After my victory, I replaced in the temples of all the cities of the province of Asia the ornaments which had been stolen from them by that man with whom I had waged war,[115] and who had taken them into his private possession. About eighty silver statues of me, on foot, on horseback, and in chariots had been set up in the city; I myself removed them, and from the money they produced I placed gold offerings in the temple of Apollo, in my own name and in the names of those who had honored me with the statues.

(25) I freed the sea from pirates. About 30,000 slaves, who had run away from their owners and had taken up arms against the state, I captured in that war and handed over to their owners for punishment. The whole of Italy voluntarily swore an oath of allegiance to me, and demanded me as its general in that war in which I was victorious at Actium. The provinces of Gaul, Spain, Africa, Sicily, and Sardinia swore the same oath of allegiance. There were more than 700 senators who served under my standards at that time, including eighty-three who either before or after (up to the day on which this was written) had been appointed consuls, and about 170 priests.

(26) I extended the boundaries of all the provinces of the Roman people which were bordered by nations that were not subject to our empire. I pacified the provinces of the Gauls, the Spains, as well as Germany, throughout the region that is bordered by the Ocean from Gades[116] to the mouth of the Elbe river. I pacified the Alps, from that region which is nearest the Adriatic Sea as far as the Tuscan Sea, without waging war unjustly on any people. My fleet sailed through the Ocean from the mouth of the Rhine eastwards to the territory of the Cimbri, a place to which no Roman had gone before either by land or by sea, and through their ambassadors, the Cimbri, and Charydes, and Semnones, and other German peoples of that region sought my friendship and that of the Roman people. On my order and under my auspices two armies were led, at almost the same time, into Ethiopia and into Arabia, which is called the "Blessed,"[117] and vast enemy forces of both peoples were cut down in battle, and a great many towns captured. Ethiopia was penetrated as far as the town of Nabata, which is next to Meroë; in Arabia, the army advanced into the territory of the Sabaeans to the town of Mariba.

(27) I added Egypt to the empire of the Roman people. Greater Armenia I could have made a province after its king, Artaxes, was killed, but I preferred,

following the example of our ancestors, to hand over that kingdom, through Tiberius Nero, who was then my stepson, to Tigranes, the son of king Artavasdes, and grandson of king Tigranes. And later, when the same people revolted and rebelled, and were subdued by my son Gaius, I handed them over to be ruled by king Ariobarzanes, son of Artabazus, king of the Medes, and after his death to his son, Artavasdes; when he was killed, I sent Tigranes, who had been born into the Armenian royal family, to that kingdom. I recovered all the provinces which extend east beyond the Adriatic Sea, as well as Cyrene, most of them at that time being ruled by kings, and earlier I recovered Sicily and Sardinia, which had been seized in the slave war.

(28) I settled colonies of soldiers in Africa, Sicily, Macedonia, both Spains, Achaia, Asia, Syria, Gallia Narbonensis, Pisidia. Italy also has twenty-eight colonies founded on my authority, which were densely populated during my lifetime.

(29) By conquering enemies, I recovered many military standards – from Spain, Gaul, and the Dalmatians – which had been lost by other generals. I forced the Parthians to return to me the spoils and standards of three Roman armies, and, as suppliants, to seek the friendship of the Roman people. And I deposited those standards in the innermost shrine which is in the Temple of Mars the Avenger.

(30) The Pannonian peoples, whom no army of the Roman people had visited before I was *princeps*, having been conquered through the agency of Tiberius Nero, who was then my stepson and my legate, I subjected to the sovereignty of the Roman people, and I extended the boundaries of Illyricum to the bank of the river Danube. An army of Dacians that crossed the river was defeated and routed under my auspices, and afterwards, my army was led across the Danube and forced the Dacian peoples to submit to the authority of the Roman people.

(31) Delegations from the kings of India were often sent to me, something never seen before with any Roman general. Through their ambassadors, the Bastarnae and the Scythians, and the kings of the Sarmatians who are on both sides of the river Tanais,[118] and the kings of the Albanians, and of the Iberians, and of the Medes sought our friendship.

(32) The following sought refuge with me as suppliants: the Parthian kings Tiridates, and, later, Phraates, son of king Phraates; Artavasdes, king of the Medes; Artaxares, king of the Adiabeni; Dumnobellaunus and Tincommius, kings of the Britons; Maelo, king of the Sugambri; . . .rus, king of the Marcomanni and the Suebi. The Parthian king Phraates, son of Orodes, sent all his sons and grandsons to me in Italy, not because he had been defeated in war, but to seek our friendship by pledging his own children. And many other peoples experienced the good faith of the Roman people while I was *princeps*, who had never before exchanged embassies and friendship with the Roman people.

(33) The Parthian and Median peoples, having sent their leading men as ambassadors to ask for kings, received them from me: for the Parthians, Vonones, son of king Phraates, grandson of king Orodes; for the Medes, Ariobarzanes, son of king Artavasdes, grandson of king Ariobarzanes.

(34) In my sixth and seventh consulships,[119] after I had extinguished civil wars, and when I was, by universal consent, in control of everything, I transferred the republic from my power to the control of the Senate and the Roman people. In return for this service of mine, I was given the name Augustus by decree of the

Senate, and the door-posts of my house were decorated with laurel at public expense, and a civic crown was attached above my door, and a golden shield was placed in the Curia Julia, which the inscription on the shield indicates was given to me by the Senate and the Roman people in honor of my courage, and clemency, and justice, and piety. After that time, I surpassed everyone in authority, but I had no more power than the others who were my colleagues in each magistracy.

(35) In my thirteenth consulship,[120] the Senate and the equestrian order and the entire Roman people gave me the title "Father of the Country," and decreed that it should be inscribed in the entrance-way of my house and in the Curia Julia and in the Augustan Forum under the chariot which had been placed there in my honor by decree of the Senate. When I wrote this, I was in my seventy-sixth year.

Appendix[121]

1 The amount of money which he gave to the treasury or to the Roman plebs or to discharged soldiers: 600,000,000 *denarii*.
2 The new works that he built: the temple of Mars, of Jupiter Tonans and Feretrius, of Apollo, of the deified Julius, of Quirinus, of Minerva, of Queen Juno, of Jupiter Libertas, of the Lares, of the Di Penates, of Youth, of the Great Mother, the Lupercal, the *pulvinar* at the Circus, the Senate-house with the Chalcidicum, the Augustan Forum, the Basilica Julia, the theater of Marcellus, the portico of Octavia, the grove of the Caesars across the Tiber.
3 He restored the Capitol, and sacred buildings, eighty-two in number, the theater of Pompey, the aqueducts, the Via Flaminia.
4 The expenditures he made on theatrical shows, and gladiatorial shows, and exhibitions of athletes, and wild beast-hunts, and the naval battle, and the money he gave to colonies, municipalities, towns destroyed by earthquake and fire, or individually to friends and to senators, whose property qualification he made up, are uncountable.

31 SUETONIUS, *CALIGULA*

Gaius Suetonius Tranquillus was born about AD 69 to a wealthy and politically active family. He became a lawyer and, for a time, a secretary to the emperor Hadrian. He died about AD 150. His surviving works include several biographies of grammarians, rhetoricians, and poets, and *On the Lives of the Caesars*, biographies of Julius Caesar and of the first eleven emperors (from Augustus through Domitian). The following passages are taken from his biography of the emperor Gaius, or Caligula, much of which is given over to describing his life as a "monster" (ch. 22, below).

(8.1) Gaius Caesar was born the day before the Kalends of September in the consulship of his own father and of Gaius Fonteius Capito.[122] Conflicting testimony makes it uncertain where he was born. Gnaeus Lentulus Gaetulicus writes that he was born at Tibur,[123] Plinius Secundus that he was born among the Treveri, in a village above the Confluence[124] called Ambitarvium; he adds as proof that altars are shown there which are inscribed "on account of Agrippina's delivery." Verses that were circulated soon after he became emperor indicate that he was conceived in the winter-quarters of the legions: "Born in the camp, raised amid the arms of his country, from the outset it was a sign that he was destined to become *princeps*."[125]

(9) He derived his *cognomen*[126] Caligula from a camp-joke, because he was brought up among the troops in the dress of a rank-and-file soldier.[127] And how much he was loved and admired by them, from having been raised in their fellowship, is especially evident from the fact that, after the death of Augustus, when they were on the verge of rebelling and of rushing headlong into some act of madness, the very sight of him was unquestionably enough to calm them. For they did not settle down until they saw that he was being led away to the nearest town for protection because of the danger caused by their uprising. Then, at last, they repented, and grabbing hold of his carriage, and not allowing it to proceed, they begged to be spared the disgrace which was coming to them.

(11) Even at that time he was unable to control his natural cruelty and viciousness, but was a very eager witness to the tortures and suffering of those who had been handed over for punishment; at night, he reveled in gluttony and adultery, disguised in a wig and a long robe; and he was passionately interested in the theatrical arts of dancing and singing, in which Tiberius was clearly willing to indulge him, in the hope that in this way his savage nature might be softened. That most perceptive old man was so thoroughly aware of Gaius' nature that he sometimes predicted that allowing him to live would be the ruin of himself and of everyone, and that he was raising a viper for the Roman people, and a Phaethon[128] for the world.

(13) By assuming control of the empire, he fulfilled the prayers of the Roman people, or I might say of the human race – a *princeps* most eagerly desired by the large majority of the provincials and soldiers, because many of them had known him as a child, and by the whole of the urban plebs, because of their memory of his father Germanicus, and their pity for a household that was almost destroyed. And so, when he set out from Misenum, though dressed as a mourner and accompanying the funeral procession of Tiberius, he was met, nevertheless, with altars, and sacrificial victims, and blazing torches, and a dense and joyous crowd, calling him, in addition to other auspicious names, their "star," their "chick," their "boy," and their "nursling."

(16) The male prostitutes who catered to perverse lusts he banished from the city, persuaded only with difficulty not to sink them in the sea. The writings of Titus Labienus, Cremutius Cordus, and Cassius Severus, which had been suppressed by decrees of the Senate, he allowed to be tracked down, and circulated, and read, believing that it was strongly in his interest that whatever happened be handed down to posterity. He published the accounts of the empire, which had usually been made public by Augustus, but discontinued by Tiberius. He granted unrestricted jurisdiction to the magistrates, without right of appeal to himself. He strictly and carefully revised the roster of the Roman knights, and not without moderation, publicly taking their horses from those who were involved in

something wicked or scandalous, while merely omitting to read the names of those who were guilty of minor offenses. To lighten the work of the jurors, he added a fifth division to the four that already existed. He also tried to restore voting to the people by reviving the custom of elections. He faithfully and without dispute paid the legacies described in the will of Tiberius, though it had been declared invalid, as well as in the will of Julia Augusta, which Tiberius had suppressed. He remitted the half a percent tax on auctions in Italy; replaced what many people had lost in fires; and if he restored kingdoms to anyone, he gave them all the taxes and revenue that had accrued in the meantime, such as the 100,000,000 sesterces seized by the treasury which he gave to Antiochus of Commagene. And to make it clearer that he encouraged every sort of good deed, he gave 800,000 sesterces to a freedwoman, because she had refused to say anything about her patron's crimes, though subjected to the most excruciating tortures. Because of these actions, a golden shield, among other honors, was decreed to him; every year, on a specified day, the colleges of priests were to carry it to the Capitol, accompanied by the Senate, and by noble boys and girls singing praises of his virtues in a choral ode. It was also decreed that the day on which he took control of the empire should be called the Parilia,[129] to indicate that the city had been founded a second time.

(19) He also devised a new and unheard of kind of spectacle. For he connected Baiae[130] to the pier at Puteoli,[131] a distance of roughly 3,600 paces, by building across the gap a bridge made of merchant ships brought together from all sides and anchored in a double line, with a mound of earth piled on top of them and arranged to look like the Appian Way. He rode over this bridge back and forth for two straight days, the first day on a richly ornamented horse, himself resplendent in an oak-leaf crown, a Spanish shield, a sword, and a golden cloak, on the next day dressed as a charioteer in a race-chariot pulled by a pair of famous horses, carrying before him a boy named Dareus, one of the Parthian hostages, and accompanied by a large contingent of the Praetorian Guard and by a company of his friends in Celtic war-chariots. I know that many have thought that this kind of bridge was devised by Gaius in emulation of Xerxes, who was admired for bridging the somewhat narrower Hellespont; others, that he was trying to terrorize Germany and Britain, on which he had designs, by reports of some immense undertaking. But when I was a boy, I used to hear my grandfather say that the reason for the work, as revealed by his most intimate courtiers, was that Thrasyllus the astrologer had declared to Tiberius, when he was anxious about a successor and leaning towards his natural grandson, that Gaius was no more likely to become emperor than he was to ride over the gulf of Baiae with horses.

(22) Up until now, I've been speaking about the emperor, as it were; what remains is to tell the story of the monster. After he had assumed various *cognomina* – for he was called "Pious," and "Child of the Camps," and "Father of the Armies," and "Best and Greatest Caesar" – when he happened to hear some kings, who had come to the city to pay their respects, arguing among themselves at dinner about the nobility of their birth, he exclaimed: "Let there be one Lord, one King."[132] And he was not far from putting on a crown immediately, and from converting the pretense of "principate" into the practice of monarchy. But reminded that he had surpassed the station of both a *princeps* and a king, from

that time on he began to lay claim to divine majesty; for after he had ordered that statues of the gods that were famous for their sanctity or their artistic merit, including that of Jupiter of Olympia, should be brought from Greece, so that their heads might be taken off and his own placed on them, he extended part of the Palace to the Forum, and having remodeled the temple of Castor and Pollux into an entrance-hall, he often displayed himself stationed between the divine brothers to be worshipped by those who presented themselves; and some saluted him as Jupiter Latiaris.[133] He also constructed a special temple to his own divinity, with priests and sacrificial victims of the choicest kind. In the temple was a life-sized gold statue, and it was dressed each day in clothes of the sort that he himself was wearing. ... And at night, he was constantly inviting the full and shining moon into his embrace and into his bed, while during the day he would converse secretly with Jupiter Capitolinus, sometimes whispering, and then in turn putting his ear to the god's mouth, at other times speaking more distinctly and even quarreling; for he was heard to threaten: "Lift me up, or I'll lift you."[134]

(23.2) He often called his great-grandmother Livia Augusta "Ulysses in a stole,"[135] and in a letter to the Senate he even dared to accuse her of low birth, alleging that her maternal grandfather had been a decurion[136] at Fundi,[137] though it is clear from public records that Aufidius Lurco held elected offices at Rome. When his grandmother Antonia asked for a private meeting, he refused, unless the prefect Macro was present, and by indignities and annoyances of this sort he brought about her death, though some believe that he also gave her poison. After she was dead, he paid her no honor, and watched her burning funeral-pyre from his dining-room.

(24.1) He routinely had sex with all his sisters, and at a well-attended banquet placed each of them in turn below him, with his wife lying down above him. Of his sisters, he is believed to have violated Drusilla's virginity when he was still a boy, and even to have been caught once in her bed by his grandmother Antonia, at whose home they were brought up together. Later, when she was married to Lucius Cassius Longinus, an ex-consul, he took her away and openly treated her as his lawful wife; and when he was ill, he even made her heir to his property and to the empire. When she died, he decreed a period of public mourning, during which it was a capital offense to laugh, to bathe, or to dine together with one's parents, or wife, or children. After he had suddenly fled the city at night and made his way across Campania, he set out for Syracuse, mad with grief, and quickly returned from there without having cut his beard or his hair. And afterwards, he never swore an oath about really important matters, even before the assembly of the people or among the soldiers, other than by the divinity of Drusilla.

(26.2–5) He was no more respectful or lenient towards the Senate: he allowed some who had held the highest offices to run several miles beside his chariot dressed in their togas, and, when he ate, to stand with a napkin in their hands, sometimes at the back of his couch, sometimes at his feet. Others whom he had secretly executed, he still continued to send for as if they were alive, after a few days falsely announcing that they had committed suicide. When the consuls forgot to announce his birthday, he removed them from office, and for three days the state was without its highest authority. When his quaestor was implicated in a conspiracy, he had him whipped, taking off the man's clothes and spreading them under the feet of the soldiers, so that they might have a firm footing when they beat him. He treated the other orders with similar cruelty and violence. Disturbed by the noise made by those who were occupying the free seats in the Circus in the middle of the night, he drove them all out with clubs; during the confusion, more than twenty Roman knights were crushed, an equal number of matrons, and a countless crowd of others. At plays in the theater, to sow discord between the plebs and the knights, he would give out free tickets ahead of time, so that the seats reserved for the equestrians would be occupied by people of the lowest sort. At a gladiatorial show, he would sometimes have the awnings pulled back when the sun was hottest and announce that no one was allowed to leave; then, with the ordinary equipment removed, he would bring together mangy wild animals, useless and decrepit gladiators, and, for play-fights, fathers who were of good reputation, but distinguished by some physical disability. And sometimes he would close the granaries, and condemn the people to hunger.

(30.1) He normally did not allow anyone to be put to death other than by many small wounds, his constant and soon well-known order being: "Strike in such a way that he feels that he's dying." When a different man than the one that he had intended had been killed, because of a mix-up about their names, he said that that man had also deserved the same thing. He was in the habit of uttering that line of tragedy: "Let them hate me, as long as they fear me."[138]

(33) As examples of his sense of humor, when he was standing next to a statue of Jupiter, and asked the tragic actor Apelles which of the two seemed to him to be greater, and Apelles hesitated, he had him torn to pieces with whips, periodically praising his voice, as he begged for mercy, as rather sweet even in his groans. Whenever he kissed the neck of his wife or girlfriend, he would add: "This beautiful neck comes off just as soon as I give the word." And in fact, he would sometimes say that he was going to find out from his dear Caesonia, by torture if necessary, why he loved her so passionately.

(50) He was tall and extremely pale, with a large body, a very thin neck and legs, hollow eyes and temples, a forehead that was broad and stern, not much hair, and none at all on the top of his head, though the rest of him was hairy. For this reason, to look down on him from above as he passed by, or to mention a goat, for any reason whatsoever, was treated as a capital offense. His naturally frightening and ugly face, he intentionally made even more so, by practicing all sorts of terrifying and horrible expressions in front of a mirror. He was healthy neither in body nor in mind. As a boy, he was plagued with epilepsy; in his youth, he had some endurance, but it was such that sometimes, because of sudden faintness, he could hardly walk, stand up, collect himself, or hold himself up. And he himself was aware of his mental illness, and sometimes thought about retiring and about clearing his brain. It is believed that his wife Caesonia gave him a drug meant to be a love-potion, which had the effect, however, of driving him mad. He was tormented especially by insomnia; for he never slept more than three hours at night, and not even then did he sleep quietly, but was terrified by strange apparitions, once, for example, dreaming that some spirit of the Ocean was talking with him. And so, awake most of the night, and tired of lying in bed, he would sit for a while on his couch, and then wander through the long covered walkways, periodically crying out for the daylight and longing for it to come.

(54) . . . . He appeared as a Thracian gladiator, and as a charioteer, and also as a singer and dancer; he fought with real weapons; he drove a chariot in circuses constructed in many different places; he would get so carried away by his enjoyment of singing and dancing that even at public performances he could not refrain from singing along as the tragic actor spoke his lines, or from openly imitating his gestures as if praising or correcting them. It appears that on the day on which he died, he had decreed a night-long vigil for no other reason than that the license of the occasion would afford an auspicious opportunity to make his first appearance on the stage. Sometimes he even danced at night, and once he summoned three former consuls to the Palace during the second watch,[139] seated them, terrified, on a platform, and then, dressed in a cloak and an ankle-length tunic, suddenly burst forth with a great clamor of flutes and castanets, and after dancing a song, went away. And yet the man who so easily learned other things did not know how to swim.

(55.3) On the day before the games, he would send his soldiers to order silence in the neighborhood, so as not to disturb his horse, Incitatus. Besides a marble stall and an ivory manger, besides purple blankets and a collar made of precious stones, he also gave the horse a house, and slaves, and furniture, so that those who were invited in his name might be entertained more elegantly; it is also said that he intended to make him consul.

(57.1–2) There were many signs of his approaching murder. The statue of Jupiter at Olympia, which he had ordered to be taken apart and transferred to Rome, suddenly emitted such a loud laugh that the scaffolding collapsed and the workmen ran away; and immediately a man named Cassius appeared, claiming that he had been ordered in a dream to sacrifice a bull to Jupiter. The Capitol at Capua was struck by lightning on the Ides of March, and likewise the room of the doorkeeper of the Palace at Rome. There were some who inferred from the latter omen that danger was portended to the owner at the hands of his guards; and from the former, that there would be another murder of a distinguished man, such as had occurred long before on that day. Also, the soothsayer Sulla, when Caligula consulted him about his horoscope, announced that certain death was close at hand.

(58) On the ninth day before the Kalends of February,[140] at about the seventh hour, hesitating whether or not to get up for lunch, with his stomach still weak from an onslaught of food the day before, he finally came out at the urging of his friends. In the underground passage through which he had to pass, some noble boys, who had been summoned from Asia to perform on the stage, were practicing, so he stopped to watch and encourage them; and if the leader of the company had not said that he was getting cold, he would have returned and had the performance given on the spot. From this point, there are two versions of the story: some say that as he was talking with the boys, Chaerea[141] came up from behind, and, with the edge of his sword, struck him violently in the neck, having first cried out, "Take that!" and then another of the conspirators, the tribune Cornelius Sabinus, stabbed him in the breast from the other side. Others say that Sabinus, having gotten rid of the crowd with the help of some centurions who were in on the plot, asked him for the watchword, as was the military custom, and that when Gaius said "Jupiter," he shouted "So be it!"[142] and when Gaius looked

around, he split his jawbone with his sword. As he lay writhing on the ground, calling out that he was still alive, the others finished him off with thirty wounds; for everyone's signal was "Strike again." Some even ran their swords through his privates. At the beginning of the disturbance, his sedan-carriers ran to help him with their poles, and then his German body-guards, who cut down several of his assassins, as well as some harmless senators.

32   DIOCLETIAN, *PRICE EDICT*

The Roman world experienced rapid inflation during the third century AD (perhaps especially in the 260s and 270s), because of spending on the army and bureaucracy, and because of inept fiscal and monetary policies. Diocletian issued the Price Edict in 301 to set a limit on what could be charged for goods and services. The wording of the edict has been reconstructed from several fragmentary Latin and Greek copies found mostly in the eastern part of the empire. Diocletian retired in AD 305, and died, probably in 313 or 316, in Salona, near modern Split, Croatia.

The Emperor Caesar Gaius Aurelius Valerius Diocletianus Pius Felix Invictus Augustus, *pontifex maximus*,[143] Germanicus Maximus for the sixth time, Sarmaticus Maximus for the fourth time, Persicus Maximus for the second time, Brittannicus Maximus, Carpicus Maximus, Armenicus Maximus, Medicus Maximus, Adiabenicus Maximus, holding the tribunician power for the eighteenth year, consul seven times, *imperator*[144] for the eighteenth time, father of his country, proconsul; and the Emperor Caesar Marcus Aurelius Valerius Maximianus Pius Felix Invictus Augustus, *pontifex maximus*, Germanicus Maximus for the fifth time, Sarmaticus Maximus for the fourth time, Persicus Maximus for the second time, Brittannicus Maximus, Carpicus Maximus, Medicus Maximus, Adiabenicus Maximus, holding the tribunician power for the seventeenth year, consul six times, *imperator* for the seventeenth time, father of his country, proconsul; and Flavius Valerius Constantius, Germanicus Maximus for the second time, Sarmaticus Maximus for the second time, Persicus Maximus for the second time, Brittannicus Maximus, Carpicus Maximus, Armenicus Maximus, Medicus Maximus, Adiabenicus Maximus, holding the tribunician power for the ninth year, consul three times, most noble Caesar; and Galerius Valerius Maximianus, Germanicus Maximus for the second time, Sarmaticus Maximus for the second time, Persicus Maximus for the second time, Brittannicus Maximus, Carpicus Maximus, Armenicus Maximus, Medicus Maximus, Adiabenicus Maximus, holding the tribunician power for the ninth year, consul three times, most noble Caesar, declare:

In memory of the wars which we have successfully waged, we ought to be grateful to the fortune of our state, next only to the immortal gods, for a tranquil world that is situated in the embrace of the most profound quiet, and also for the blessings of peace, for the sake of which we have labored mightily. And that

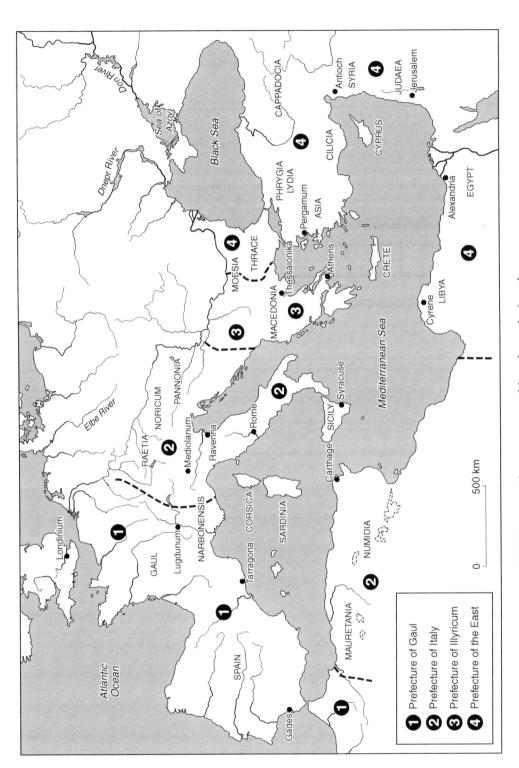

FIGURE 5.1 *The Roman world in the early fourth century* AD.

this fortune be carefully managed and honorably adorned is desired by the law-abiding public and by the dignity and majesty of Rome. So we, who, by the kind favor of the gods, previously suppressed the raging devastation of barbarian peoples by destroying their very nations, should protect, by the defenses of justice, the quiet which we have established for eternity.

If the actions of those who burn with unlimited and frenzied greed, without consideration for the human race, scrambling for gain and profit with no thought for mankind, not annually or monthly or daily, but almost hour to hour and minute to minute, could be held in check by some measure of self-restraint, or if the general welfare could endure with equanimity this riotous license by which, in its miserable condition, it is being injured every day, perhaps there would seem to be some room left for dissembling and reticence, in the hope that human patience might improve the execrable and pitiable situation. But because the only desire of the uncontrolled madman is to give no thought to the common need, and among the unscrupulous and the immoderate, swelling with greed and consumed by fierce desires, it is considered to be a kind of principle, as it were, to desist from plundering the wealth of everyone, not voluntarily, but when forced to by necessity, and those who have been brought, by extreme poverty, to an awareness of this most unfortunate situation can no longer pretend not to notice it, we, who are the parents of the human race, are, as we look at the situation, agreed that legal intervention is required, so that what people have desired for a long time, and what human nature itself could not provide, may, by our provident remedies, be established for the general betterment of everyone. . . .

We hasten, therefore, to apply the remedies which have long been demanded by the situation, confident that no one can complain that the intervention of our regulations is untimely or unnecessary, or too lenient or too meager against the wicked, who have perceived in our silence of so many years a lesson in restraint which, nevertheless, they have been unwilling to imitate. For who is so hard-hearted and so devoid of human feeling as to have ignored or indeed not to have been aware that, in the sales which take place in the markets or in the daily business of the cities, unrestrained prices have become so widespread that the uncontrolled passion for profiteering is lessened neither by the abundance of supplies nor by the fruitfulness of our times? So there is no doubt that the men who are engaged in such businesses intend to control the very winds and weather, even by the movements of the stars, and because of their iniquity, cannot tolerate, in regard to their hopes for future harvests, that the fertile fields be inundated by waters from above. So they judge the abundance of things produced by the moderation of the sky itself to be their personal loss.

And those who are always scheming to derive profit from divine generosity and to limit the occurrence of public prosperity, both by means of the food-shortages that come with reduced harvests, and by means of the trading activities of their agents; who, already overflowing personally with immense riches that could easily support entire peoples, try to acquire small profits and pursue ruinous rates of interest; the common interest of humanity persuades us to establish, O our provincials, a limit to their avarice. . . .

Who does not know that, wherever the common safety requires our armies to be sent, they insolently and covertly attack the public welfare for the sake of profiteering, not only in villages or towns, but on every road, extorting prices for merchandise, not fourfold or eightfold, but such that human language cannot supply words to describe their profit and their actions? That sometimes, in fact, a soldier is deprived of his bonus and his pay in a single transaction? And that what the whole world contributes to the support of the armies becomes the loathsome profits of these plunderers? And so our soldiers seem to confer the rewards of their military service and their veterans' bonuses on the profiteers, with the result that the pillagers of the state itself seize every day as much as they know how to hold.

Justly and righteously disturbed by all these matters, which have been described above, and when humanity itself appears to be praying, we have decided, not to fix the prices of products for sale, for we do not consider it just to do that, since many provinces sometimes enjoy the welcome good fortune of low prices and a sort of privilege, as it were, of prosperity, but that a limit should be set. So when the pressure of high prices develops anywhere – may the gods avert such a possibility! – avarice, which, as if spread across some vast expanse of territory, cannot be checked, will be restrained by the boundaries of our statute and by the moderating limits of our law.

It is our pleasure, therefore, that the prices which are indicated in the brief list below be observed across the whole of our empire, so that everyone may understand that the freedom to exceed them has been ended, but that the blessing of low prices has not been impeded in those places where an abundance of things overflows, special provision having been made for this, so long as greed is held in check. Between buyers and sellers, moreover, who are accustomed to visit ports and far-off provinces, this universal edict ought to be a moderating influence, so that when they themselves also know that, at a time of scarcity, the prices laid down for things cannot be exceeded, they will, at the time of sale, take into account the costs of the localities, of transportation, and of all the rest, whereby it will be clear how just our decision is that those who transport things may not sell anywhere at higher prices. . . .

It is our pleasure that anyone who dares to resist the provisions of this statute shall be subject to capital punishment. Nor should anyone consider the statute harsh, since the means of avoiding danger are at hand in the observance of moderation. And that man will also be subject to the same penalty, who, because of his desire for profit, and in contravention of the statute, has conspired with the greed of the seller. Neither will he be held immune from the same penalty who, having the things necessary for eating and for daily use, comes to the conclusion, after this moderating legislation, that they should be withdrawn, for there ought to be an even more serious penalty for someone who causes poverty than for one who, contrary to the statute, increases it. . . .

The prices which no one is allowed to exceed in the sale of individual items are indicated below.

Grain, one army-*modius*,[145] [?] *denarii*.[146]
Barley, one army-*modius*, 100 *denarii*.
Centenum[147] or *sicale*, one army-*modius*, 60 *denarii*.

Ground millet, one army-*modius*, 100 *denarii*.
Un-ground millet, one army-*modius*, 50 *denarii*.
Panic-grass, one army-*modius*, 50 *denarii*. . . .

Likewise for wines:

Picene, one Italian *sextarius*,[148] 30 *denarii*.
Tiburtine, one Italian *sextarius*, 30 *denarii*.
Sabine, one Italian *sextarius*, 30 *denarii*.
Aminaean, one Italian *sextarius*, 30 *denarii*.
Saitic, one Italian *sextarius*, 30 *denarii*.
Surrentine, one Italian *sextarius*, 30 *denarii*.
Falernian, one Italian *sextarius*, 30 *denarii*.
Likewise for old wine of the first tasting, one Italian *sextarius*, 24 *denarii*.
Old wine of the second tasting, one Italian *sextarius*, 16 *denarii*.
Country wine, one Italian *sextarius*, 8 *denarii*. . . .

Likewise for oil:

Oil of the highest quality, one Italian *sextarius*, 40 *denarii*.
Oil of the second quality, one Italian *sextarius*, 24 *denarii*.
Ordinary oil, one Italian *sextarius*, 12 *denarii*.
Radish-oil, one Italian *sextarius*, 8 *denarii*.
Wine-vinegar, one Italian *sextarius*, 6 *denarii*.
Fish-sauce of the first quality, one Italian *sextarius*, 16[?] *denarii*.
Fish-sauce of the second quality, one Italian *sextarius*, 12[?] *denarii*.
Salt, one army-*modius*, 100 *denarii*. . . .

Likewise for meat:

Pork, one Italian pound, 12 *denarii*.
Beef, one Italian pound, 8 *denarii*.
Goat, one Italian pound, 8 *denarii*. . . .
Sow's udder, one Italian pound, 20 *denarii*.
Liver of the best quality, one Italian pound, 16 *denarii*.
Bacon of the best quality, one Italian pound, 16 *denarii*.
Ham of the best quality, or Menapian[149] or Cerretanian[150] pork-shoulder, one
   Italian pound, 20 *denarii*.
Marsic,[151] one Italian pound, 20 *denarii*.
Fresh lard, one Italian pound, 12 *denarii*.
Suet, one Italian pound, 12 *denarii*. . . .

Likewise for fish:

Rough-scaled fish from the ocean, one Italian pound, 24 *denarii*.
Fish of the second quality, one Italian pound, 16 *denarii*.

River-fish of the best quality, one Italian pound, 12 *denarii*.
River-fish of the second quality, one Italian pound, 8 *denarii*. . . .

For wages:

Farm-laborer, with maintenance, daily, 25 *denarii*.
Stone-mason, as above, daily, 50 *denarii*. . . .
Carpenter, as above, daily, 50 *denarii*.
Blacksmith, as above, daily, 50 *denarii*.
Baker, as above, daily, 50 *denarii*.
Shipwright, on a sea-going ship, as above, daily, 60 *denarii*. . . .
Shepherd, with maintenance, daily, 20 *denarii*.
Muleteer, with maintenance, daily, 25 *denarii*.
Mule-doctor, for clipping and tending to feet, per animal, 6 *denarii*.
For blood-letting and head-cleaning, per animal, 20 *denarii*.
Barber, per person, 2 *denarii*. . . .
Scribe, for the best writing, 100 lines, 25 *denarii*. . . .
Tutor, per boy, monthly, 50 *denarii*. . . .
Teacher of Greek or Latin grammar and geometry, per student, monthly, 200
    denarii.
Teacher of oratory, or sophist, per student, monthly, 250 *denarii*.
Advocate or jurist, fee for handling a claim, 250 *denarii*.
Trial-fee, 1,000 *denarii*. . . .
Private bath-keeper, per bather, 2 *denarii*.

33   AMMIANUS MARCELLINUS, *HISTORY*

Ammianus Marcellinus was born about AD 330 to a moderately wealthy family at Antioch,
Syria. A career military officer, he died probably about AD 395. His only surviving work is a
history of the period from the accession of the emperor Nerva in AD 96 to the death of the
emperor Valens in 378, which he wrote in Latin, though his native language was Greek, and of
which only the last eighteen books, covering the period 353–78, are preserved. A pagan, who
greatly admired the emperor Julian, he nevertheless writes tolerantly of Christianity (for example, at 25.4.20, below).

(14.6) *Vices of the Senate and Roman people.*

(1) . . . . Orfitus was governing the eternal city with the rank of prefect, behaving
arrogantly, beyond the limit of the authority conferred upon him, a wise man,
certainly, and very well informed in legal matters, but less equipped with the
splendor of the liberal arts than was suitable for a man of noble rank. During his
administration, serious riots broke out because of a scarcity of wine: the people,
greedily intent on consuming it, are roused to violent and frequent disturbances.
(2) And because I think that some foreigners who may read this (if I am fortu-

nate) might wonder why it is that when my account turns to describing what was going on at Rome, nothing is reported other than conflicts, taverns, and other similar vulgarities, I will briefly touch on the causes, nowhere departing intentionally from the truth.

(3) At the time when Rome first began to rise to world-wide renown, destined to last as long as there will be men, in order that she might grow to the highest position, Virtue and Fortune, which are usually at odds, agreed to a treaty of eternal peace; if either one of them had failed, Rome would not have come to total supremacy. (4) Her people, from the cradle to the last period of childhood, which covers nearly 300 years, conducted wars around her walls; then, having entered upon adulthood, after many troublesome wars, they crossed the Alps and the sea; having grown to youth and manhood, from every region which the immense world includes they brought back laurels and triumphs; and now, slipping into old age, and often conquering only in name, they have come to a much quieter time of life. (5) So the venerable city, after bending the proud necks of wild peoples, and passing laws, the eternal foundations and moorings of liberty, like a frugal parent, both wise and wealthy, has handed over her inheritance to be managed by the Caesars, as if by her children. (6) And although the tribes[152] are now inactive and the centuries[153] are at peace, and there are no contests for votes, but the security of Numa's time has returned, nevertheless, through all the regions and parts of the earth she is accepted as mistress and queen; and everywhere the white hair of the senators is revered, together with their authority, and the name of the Roman people is respected and honored.

(7) But this magnificent splendor of the assemblies is harmed by the uncouth worthlessness of a few, who do not take into account where they were born, but, as if license had been granted to vices, sink into wrong-doing and licentiousness. For as the lyric poet Simonides reveals, one who is going to live happily and with perfect reason should, before everything else, have a glorious fatherland. (8) Some of these men, thinking that they can be commended to eternity through statues, eagerly pursue them, as if they would acquire a greater reward from senseless bronze images than from consciousness of honorable and virtuous achievements, and they are careful to have them overlaid with gold, a practice first introduced by Acilius Glabrio, when he had overcome King Antiochus by planning and by arms.[154] But how beautiful a thing it is, spurning these small and trivial matters, to reach for the long and steep ascent to true glory, as the poet of Ascra puts it,[155] is demonstrated by Cato the Censor. For when he was asked why he alone among many did not have a statue, he replied: "I prefer that good men wonder why I did not deserve one than – what is much worse – that they grumble about why I obtained one."

(9) Others, attaching great importance to four-wheeled coaches that are higher than what is customary, and to the ostentatious appearance of their clothes, sweat under the weight of their cloaks, which, fastened around their necks, they tie around their very throats, while the wind blows through them because of the excessive thinness of the material; and they lift them up with both hands and wave them about with frequent gestures, especially with their left hands, so as to make conspicuous the overly long fringes and the tunics embroidered with many-colored threads in multi-form figures of animals. (10) Others, even when no one

questions them, put on a serious expression and greatly exaggerate their wealth, multiplying the annual yields of their well-cultivated (so they think) fields, which they boast that they possess in abundance from the rising to the setting sun,[156] clearly unaware that their ancestors, by whom the greatness of Rome was so widely spread, stood out, not by wealth, but through the harshest wars, and overcame all obstacles by courage, not differing from the rank-and-file soldiers in wealth, way of life, or the commonness of their clothing. . . .

(12) But now, if, as a respectable stranger, you enter for the first time to pay your respects to someone who is well off and therefore swollen with pride, you will be greeted as if you had been expected, and after being asked many questions and forced to lie, you will wonder why such a great man, who has never seen you before, is so anxious to attend to you, a humble man, so that you will, given this special kindness, as it were, regret that you had not seen Rome ten years before. (13) Emboldened by this friendliness, when you do the same thing the following day, you will hang around unrecognized and unexpected, while the man who encouraged you the day before counts up his people, all the while wondering who you are or where you came from. But recognized at last, and admitted to his friendship, if you devote yourself to calling on him assiduously for three years without interruption, and then are away for the same number of days, and return to complete an equal term, you will not be asked where you were, and unless you go away from there despondent, you will waste your entire life in cultivating a blockhead to no purpose. . . .

(16) I pass over the gluttonous banquets and the various enticements to pleasure, lest I go on too long, and I will move on to the fact that some people hurry through the wide spaces of the city and over the upturned paving-stones without fear of danger, as if they were driving public horses with hoofs of fire (as the saying goes), dragging armies of slaves like bands of robbers behind them, not leaving even Sannio at home (as the comic writer puts it).[157] A great many matrons imitate them, rushing about in enclosed sedan-chairs through all parts of the city with their heads covered. (17) And just as skillful directors of battles situate dense crowds of troops and the brave men in front, then the light-armed troops, after them the javelin-throwers, and finally, the reserves, ready to assist the battle-line if chance should require it, so those who are in charge of an urban slave-household, distinguished by the wands they hold in their right hands, thoughtfully and carefully draw them up; then, as if a signal had been given in camp, all the weavers march near the front of the carriage; next to them the blackened kitchen-servants, then all the rest of the slaves willy-nilly, joined by the idle plebeians of the neighborhood; lastly, a multitude of eunuchs, starting with the old men and ending with the boys, pale and disfigured by the deformed arrangement of their features; so that, wherever anyone goes, seeing the crowds of mutilated men, he would curse the memory of that ancient queen Samiramis,[158] who was the first to castrate young males, doing violence, as it were, to nature, and twisting her away from her intended course, for from the very beginning of life, through the primeval fountains of the seed, by a certain kind of secret law, she reveals the ways to propagate posterity. . . .

(19) It has finally reached such a state of vileness, that when, not so long ago,[159] foreigners were driven headfirst from the city because of a shortage of food, and

those who practiced the liberal arts were, though few in number, expelled without a chance to catch their breath, the genuine attendants of the mime-actresses, and those who pretended to be such for the occasion, were kept, and 3,000 dancing girls, without even being questioned, remained, together with their choruses, and an equal number of instructors. (20) And wherever you turn your eyes, you can see a large crowd of women with curled hair, who, had they married, are old enough that they could already have produced three children, and who polish the pavement with their feet to the point of exhaustion, throwing themselves around in rapid gyrations, while they portray the countless characters that the theatrical plays have concocted. . . .

(25) But of the multitude of the lowest rank and greatest poverty, some stay up all night in the wine-taverns, some lurk in the shade of the awnings of the theaters, which Catulus, in his own aedileship, was the first to put up, in imitation of Campanian licentiousness; or they rowdily compete at dice, making a disgusting sound by drawing the breath back up into their snorting nostrils; or – what is the greatest of all amusements – they stand with their mouths open, from sunrise until evening, in the sun or in the rain, minutely scrutinizing the merits or the defects of charioteers and their horses. (26) And it's certainly amazing to see a huge number of plebeians, their minds infused with a kind of passion, hanging on the outcome of the chariot races. These and similar things allow nothing memorable or serious to be done at Rome. . . .

(22.4) *Julian Augustus expels all the eunuchs, and barbers, and cooks from the palace. And about the vices of the court-eunuchs, and about the corruption of military discipline.*

(1) . . . . Having turned his attention to the palace attendants, the *princeps*[160] dismissed all who were or could be part of that group, but not like a philosopher claiming to investigate the truth. (2) For he might have been praised if he had at least kept those, although they were few, who practiced moderation and were known for the integrity of their character. And yet it must be admitted that the large majority of them maintained a vast seed-bed of all the vices, to such a degree that they infected the state with depraved desires, and harmed many, more by their example than by their license for wrong-doing. (3) For some of them, fattened on the spoils of temples, and smelling out profit at every opportunity, having been elevated, at one bound, from abject poverty to enormous riches, observed no limit to either bribery, or robbery, or extravagance, accustomed always to seize the property of others. (4) From here sprouted the seeds of a dissolute life, and lack of respect for a good reputation; and their demented pride stained their trustworthiness with shameful profits. (5) Meanwhile, gluttony and steep abysses of banquets multiplied, and banquet-triumphs replaced those won by victories, and the widespread use of silk and the textile arts increased, and more anxious attention to the kitchen. . . .

(6) To these shameful circumstances was added the disgraceful condition of military discipline, when, instead of the war-whoop, the soldiers practiced effemin-

ate ditties, and the warrior's bed was not a stone (as it had been before), but feathers and folding couches, and their cups were heavier than their swords (for they were now ashamed to drink from earthenware), and they even sought out marble houses, although it is written in the ancient records that a Spartan soldier was severely punished because during a campaign he had dared to be seen under a roof. . . .

(9) It happened at the same time that a barber, who had been summoned to cut the emperor's hair, came dressed in an ostentatious sort of way. When he saw him, Julian was stunned, and said: "I gave orders for a barber to be summoned, not an accountant." Nevertheless, he asked the man how much he made from his skill, to which the barber replied, "twenty allowances[161] of bread a day, and the same amount of fodder for pack-animals (which they commonly call *capita*), and a large annual salary, as well as many rich perquisites." (10) Angered by this, Julian expelled all who were of that type (on the grounds that he had no need for them), as well as the cooks and other similar servants, who were accustomed to receive almost the same things, giving them permission to go wherever they wanted.

(25.4) *Julian's merits and defects, his bodily shape and stature.*

(1) He was certainly a man to be numbered among the heroes, distinguished for the illustriousness of his deeds and for his inborn majesty. For since there are, as the wise define it, four principal virtues – moderation, wisdom, justice, and courage – and corresponding to these, other external characteristics, such as knowledge of military affairs, authority, good luck, and generosity, he cultivated them, together and separately, with absolute devotion. (2) And first of all, he was so conspicuous for untarnished chastity that, after he lost his wife, it is agreed that he never thought at all about sex, recalling what we read in Plato, that Sophocles, the writer of tragedies, when he was asked, at a time when he was very old, whether he still had sex with women, said no, and added that he was glad that he had escaped from the love of such things as from some mad and cruel master. (3) Similarly, in order to shore up this principle, Julian often repeated a saying of the lyric poet Bacchylides, whom he read with pleasure, and who asserts that, as a skillful painter gives a face beauty, so chastity embellishes a life elevated to a higher level. He so carefully avoided this stain on the mature strength of youth that even his most intimate ministers did not (as often happens) accuse him of even a suspicion of any lustfulness.

(4) And this sort of temperance he made even more conspicuous by practicing moderation in eating and sleeping, which he assiduously observed both at home and abroad. For the frugality of his life-style and of his table in a time of peace – as if he was about to put his philosopher's cloak back on – won the admiration of those who judge correctly; and throughout his various campaigns, he was seen to eat only a little food, and that of an ordinary kind, sometimes even while standing, as was the military custom. (5) And when he had refreshed his body, which was hardened by labor, by a brief period of sleep, he awoke and observed in person the changing of the watch and of the guards, and after these serious ac-

tivities, took refuge in the arts of learning. (6) And if the night-lamps among which he worked could have testified with a voice, they would certainly have indicated that there was a great deal of difference between him and some other emperors, for they knew that he did not indulge in pleasures, not even to the extent that nature required.

(7) Then there were a great many indications of his wisdom, of which it will be enough to mention a few. He was very knowledgeable of the arts of war and peace, greatly devoted to civility, and arrogated to himself only what he thought preserved him from contempt and insolence; he was older in virtue than in years. He was very interested in all things legal, and was sometimes an inflexible judge; a very strict censor in regulating morality, quietly contemptuous of wealth, despising everything mortal; finally, he used to say that it was shameful for a wise man, since he had a soul, to win praise by his body. (8) And by what good qualities of justice he was distinguished, there are many indications: first, because, by taking account of circumstances and people, he was frightening but without cruelty; secondly, because he controlled wrong-doing by singling out a few; then also because he threatened people with the sword more often than he used it. (9) Finally, to be brief, it is agreed that he behaved so mercifully towards some openly hostile enemies who plotted against him, that he censured the harshness of their punishment by his genuine mildness.

(10) His bravery is shown by the great number of battles he fought and by his conduct of wars, and by his endurance of great cold and heat. And although bodily duty is required of a soldier, mental duty of a commander, he himself boldly confronted a savage enemy and struck him down with a blow, and several times, when our men were giving way, he, acting alone, held them back by placing his breast in their way. And when destroying the kingdoms of the crazed Germans, and on the burning sand of Persia, he increased the confidence his soldiers had in him by fighting among the men in front. (11) There are many well-known proofs of his knowledge of military affairs: the sieges of cities and fortresses, carried out amid the greatest of dangers; the various forms in which he drew up his battle-lines; the camps carefully laid out in healthful locations; the frontier troops and field-guards stationed according to the dictates of safety. (12) Deeply loved, and at the same time feared, partner in their dangers and hardships, he had so much authority that he both ordered cowards to be punished in the middle of the fiercest battles, and, while still a Caesar, controlled his soldiers without pay, when they were fighting against wild peoples. . . . (13) Finally, it will be enough to know this, as representative of many things – that simply by a speech he persuaded his Gallic soldiers, who were accustomed to snow and to the Rhine, to journey over long stretches of territory and to travel across burning Assyria to the very borders of the Medes. . . .

(15) There are many proven indications of his generosity, among which are the very light tribute he imposed; the crown-tax[162] he remitted; the many debts, enlarged by the passage of time, that he forgave; the disputes between the treasury and private persons that he dealt with even-handedly; the tax-revenues he restored to states, along with their lands, which previous rulers had sold off under the pretense of law; and that he was never eager to increase his wealth, which he thought would be more secure in the hands of its owners, frequently remarking

that Alexander the Great, when he was asked where his treasures were, had benevolently replied, "with my friends."

(16) Having described as many of his good qualities as I could know, let me turn now to elaborating his faults, although they can be discussed briefly. His personality was rather inconsistent, but he tempered this by the excellent habit of allowing himself to be corrected when he diverted from good practice. (17) He was rather talkative, and too infrequently silent; too devoted to inquiring about omens and portents, so that in this respect he seemed to be the same as the emperor Hadrian. Superstitious rather than genuinely religious, he sacrificed countless animals without concern for what it cost, to such an extent that one might conclude that, if he had returned from the Parthians, there would soon have been a shortage of cattle; like the Caesar Marcus[163] about whom we have heard it was written: "We, the white cattle, salute Marcus Caesar; should you win again, we will all have to die." (18) He was delighted by the applause of the mob, and immoderately anxious to be praised for the slightest things; and his desire for popularity often led him to speak with those who were unworthy. (19) But nevertheless, although this was so, it could be thought (as he himself used to say) that the ancient goddess, Justice, whom Aratus[164] raised to the heavens because she was offended by the vices of men, would have returned to earth while he was emperor, if he had not done some things arbitrarily, and sometimes seemed to be unlike himself. (20) For the laws he enacted were not bothersome, but, with a few exceptions, clearly indicated what was to be done or not to be done; among them was a harsh law which forbade Christian rhetoricians and grammarians to teach, unless they agreed to worship the pagan gods. (21) And it was also barely tolerable that he unjustly allowed certain men to be made members of the municipal councils, who, either because they were foreigners, or because of community privileges or origin, were altogether exempt.

(22) The appearance and structure of his body were as follows. He was of medium height, with hair that was soft as if it had been combed; he had a full beard, that was arranged so as to end in a point; his eyes were attractive and sparkling with fire, an indication of how acute his mind was. He had handsome eyebrows, and a very straight nose, a mouth that was a little larger than normal, with a lower lip that hung down. His neck was thick and curved, his shoulders large and broad. From the top of his head to his toes, he had a straight frame, as a result of which he was strong and good at running.

(23) And since his detractors claim that he stirred up new outbreaks of war, to the ruin of the commonwealth, they should clearly understand, with truth as their teacher, that it was not Julian, but Constantine who inflamed the passions of the Parthians, when he acquiesced too greedily in the lies of Metrodorus, as I earlier explained at length.[165] (24) It was because of this that our armies were annihilated, that companies of soldiers were so often captured, that cities were destroyed, that fortresses were captured or demolished, that the provinces were exhausted by heavy expenses, and that the Persians, making threats they later brought into effect, claimed everything right up to Bithynia and the shores of the Propontis. (25) But in Gaul, where barbarian arrogance was growing, with the Germans pouring across our territories, and the Alps about to break through to devastate Italy, nothing (after men had suffered so many unspeakable things) was left except tears and terror, since recalling the past was bitter and the pros-

pect of what threatened was even sadder. Sent to the western region, a Caesar in name only, that young man completely fixed all this with almost incredible speed, driving kings before him like low-born slaves. (26) And in order to restore the Orient with equal resolve, he attacked the Persians, and he would have brought back from there a triumph and a *cognomen*,[166] if the decrees of the heavens had coincided with his plans and illustrious accomplishments.

34   *THEODOSIAN CODE*

On the *Theodosian Code*, see the introduction to selection 8. The following passages illustrate some of the characteristics, as well as the failings, of imperial government in the later empire; the last (14.3.8) describes the development of an hereditary guild of bread-makers at Rome.

1.32.5. Emperors Gratian, Valentinian, and Theodosius, Augustuses, to Eusignius, Praetorian Prefect.

Since the superintendents of the mines in Macedonia, Middle Dacia, Moesia, and Dardania, who are normally appointed from the ranks of the *curiales*[167] to collect the customary taxes, have abandoned this compulsory service, on the pretense of being afraid of the enemy, they must be dragged back to fulfill their duty, and thereafter no one is to be granted the freedom to seek undeserved honors before he has faithfully, and with the customary exactitude, completed the superintendency he has been required to undertake.

Issued at Mediolanum[168] the fourth day before the Kalends of August, in the consulship of Honorius and Evodius [July 29, AD 386].

6.27.18. Emperors Honorius and Theodosius to Helion, Master of Offices.

Many men from all over are flocking to the department of the secret service as if to a sort of refuge, but their criminal lives and low-born origins indicate that they have burst forth from the dregs of servility. Since we have granted your Eminence the power that it had sought, suitable remedies must be applied, so that, having conducted a careful investigation, you may remove them from their position, and punish them; and after these degraded and worthless criminals have been removed, the imperial service will be restored to its pristine condition, and the college will be filled with good men.

Issued at Constantinople the thirteenth day before the Kalends of February, in the consulship of the Augustus, Theodosius, for the seventh time, and of Palladius [January 20, AD 416].

8.10.4. Emperors Honorius and Theodosius, Augustuses, to Eucharius, Proconsul of Africa.

We decree that every kind of tax-collector is to be expelled from the provinces of Africa, of course with those things restored which they may have appropriated through their lawlessness.

Issued at Ravenna the sixth day before the Ides of August, in the consulship of the Augustuses, Honorius, for the ninth time, and Theodosius, for the fifth time [August 8, AD 412].

9.4.1. Emperors Theodosius, Arcadius, and Honorius, Augustuses, to Rufinus, Praetorian Prefect.

If anyone, ignorant of decency and modesty, should imagine that our names may be attacked with wicked and impudent slander, and if, boisterous with drunkenness, he should criticize our times, we do not want him to be punished or to suffer anything severe or harsh, since, if it is the result of light-mindedness, it should be treated with contempt, if the result of madness, it is most worthy of pity, if meant to injure, it should be pardoned. Therefore, it is to be referred to our knowledge with everything unchanged, so that we may weigh the words with regard to the man's character, and decide whether the offense should be overlooked or righteously prosecuted.

Issued at Constantinople the fifth day before the Ides of August, in the consulship of the Augustus, Theodosius, for the third time, and of Abundantius [August 9, AD 393].

14.3.8. Emperors Valentinian and Valens, Augustuses, to Symmachus, Prefect of the City.

The office of your Sincerity shall see to it that, if anyone has at any time been assigned to the association of bread-makers, he will not, for any reason, be given the opportunity or ability to withdraw from it, even if all the bread-makers try to obtain his release, and it appears that they are in agreement. It will not even be permitted to anyone to move from one workshop to another.

Issued at Mediolanum eighteen days before the Kalends of February, in the consulship of the Augustuses, Valentinian and Valens [January 15, AD 365].

Suggestions for Further Reading

F. Millar, "The political character of the classical Roman republic," *Journal of Roman Studies*, 74 (1984), pp. 1–19, is an excellent introduction to the practice of government in the time of Polybius. For Polybius himself, see F. W. Walbank, *Polybius* (Berkeley and Los Angeles, 1972). On the political life of the period, H. H. Scullard, *Roman Politics, 220–150 BC*, 2nd edn (Oxford, 1973). On citizenship: A. N. Sherwin-White, *The Roman Citizenship*, 2nd edn (Oxford, 1973); C. Nicolet, *The World of the Citizen in Republican Rome*, 2nd edn, trans. P. S. Falla (Berkeley and Los Angeles, 1980).

The classic work on the period of the late Republic is R. Syme, *The Roman Revolution* (Oxford, 1939). There is much that is relevant also in his *Roman Papers*, 7 vols (New York, 1979–91). T. P. Wiseman (ed.), *Roman Political Life, 90 BC–AD 69* (Exeter, 1985), is a short and highly readable introduction. On the fall of the Republic, see P. A. Brunt, *The Fall of the Roman Republic and Related Essays* (Oxford, 1988); E. S. Gruen, *The Last Generation of the Roman Republic* (Berkeley and Los Angeles, 1974); R. Seager (ed.), *The Crisis of the Roman Republic: Studies in Political and Social History* (Cambridge, 1969). On elections and electioneering, L. R. Taylor, *Party Politics in the Age of Caesar* (Berkeley and Los Angeles, 1949); *Roman Voting Assemblies* (Ann Arbor, 1966).

On the period of Augustus, see K. Raaflaub and M. Toher (eds), *Between Republic and Empire: Interpretations of Augustus and his Principate* (Berkeley, 1990). There is a wonderfully detailed commentary on the *Accomplishments of the Deified Augustus* in P. A. Brunt and J. M. Moore, *Res Gestae divi Augusti: The Achievements of the Divine Augustus* (Oxford, 1967). On the duties of emperors, see F. Millar, *The Emperor in the Roman World, 31 BC–AD 337* (Ithaca, NY, 1977). On their slaves and freedmen, P. R. C. Weaver, *Familia Caesaris: A Social Study of the Emperor's Freedmen and Slaves* (Cambridge, 1972). For the Senate, R. J. A. Talbert, *The Senate of Imperial Rome* (Princeton, 1984).

The most important book about Tacitus is R. Syme, *Tacitus*, 2 vols (Oxford, 1958). Worth reading also is R. Mellor, *Tacitus* (New York and London, 1993). For an interesting attempt to understand Caligula, see A. A. Barrett, *Caligula: The Corruption of Power* (New Haven, 1989). On Suetonius, A. Wallace-Hadrill, *Suetonius: The Scholar and His Caesars* (New Haven, 1983).

On Diocletian and his reforms, see especially T. D. Barnes, *The New Empire of Diocletian and Constantine* (Cambridge, Mass., 1982); S. Corcoran, *The Empire of the Tetrarchs: Imperial Pronouncements and Government, AD 284–324* (Oxford, 1996). The best biography of Julian is G. W. Bowersock, *Julian the Apostate* (Cambridge, Mass., 1978); see also P. Athanassiadi, *Julian: An Intellectual Biography*, rev. edn (London, 1992). On Ammianus Marcellinus, see J. Matthews, *The Roman Empire of Ammianus* (Baltimore, 1989); R. C. Blockley, *Ammianus: A Study of his Historiography and Political Thought* (Brussels, 1975).

Six

ROME AND THE PROVINCES

Editor's introduction

In the period of the Republic, the provinces were governed by former magistrates (consuls and praetors), who were selected each year by the Senate and then assigned to a province by lot. Because governors were given only a single assistant – a quaestor responsible for dealing with financial matters – they normally took with them also an advisory group of friends, as well as a number of their own freedmen and slaves. A governor's main duties were to maintain order and to oversee the administration of justice. Taxes were collected in the provinces, not by the governors, but by the publicans, private syndicates formed by men of equestrian rank who bid on contracts let out annually by the Senate, and who acquired a reputation, apparently well-earned, for greed and profiteering. According to Cicero (selection 35, below), a governor's most serious challenge was to rein in their predatory behavior. The evidence indicates that most were not very successful at it. In fact, not a few governors seem to have viewed their own position as an opportunity to compensate themselves for their years of unpaid public service. The thievery exhibited by Gaius Verres, governor of Sicily in 73 BC, was probably atypical, but not uncommon.

The broad objectives of provincial government – to keep order and to collect taxes – did not change in any significant way under the emperors, who were inclined to govern, as much as possible, through existing local elites. There is no reason to suppose either that the Romans had a deliberate policy of Romanizing provincial populations. Those who would have us believe otherwise can point to only a single passage in the whole of Latin literature, Tacitus' account (*Agricola* 21) of Gnaeus Julius Agricola's programme, when governor of Britain in the late 70s AD, that arranged for the sons of the leading Britons to be taught Latin, and that encouraged the natives to build "temples, fora, houses." There is no evidence to show that Agricola's programme was ever duplicated in Britain or in any of the other provinces.

From 27 BC, the provinces were categorized either as senatorial provinces, which continued to be governed by former magistrates chosen by the Senate, or as imperial provinces, which fell under the emperor's jurisdiction (and in which, not coincidentally, most of the legions were stationed). The governors of the imperial provinces were chosen by the emperor. Many of them were also former magistrates, though some, like the prefect of Egypt, were equestrians. They reported directly to the emperor, and remained in office until he chose to replace them. The duties of the provincial governors were not much different than they had been in the time of the Republic: they handled financial matters, heard legal cases, and settled disputes between cities. But their ability to act independently was eroded, especially after the emperors began to provide them with formal instructions (*mandata*). It is clear also, from an inscription recovered at Cyrene (now Shahhāt, Libya), which records five edicts issued by Augustus in 7/6 and 4 BC, that, almost from the beginning, the emperors did not hesitate to intervene even in those provinces, like Crete and Cyrene, which were deemed to be under the Senate's jurisdiction. In fact, the distinction between senatorial and imperial provinces probably mattered a great deal more to the Senate than to anyone else.[1] In practice, probably the biggest difference between them was that the governors of the imperial provinces tended to stay longer in office.

The Republican system of letting out contracts for the collection of taxes was gradually phased out, first in the imperial provinces, and then in the senatorial ones. Instead, cities were made liable for collecting taxes in the areas which they controlled. Elsewhere, taxes were collected mostly by government officials. The main forms of direct taxation were unchanged from the time of the Republic: a capitation tax, and a tax on land, which was often, but not always, paid as a lump sum (in Sicily it was paid as a proportion of the harvest), and from which certain privileged cities were, like Italy, exempt. Various indirect taxes were also collected, probably the most lucrative of which were the dues charged on goods transported across provincial boundaries or brought into the empire. The tax-rate applied to inter-provincial trade generally ranged between 2 and 5 percent; on luxury goods imported from India, it ran as high as 25 percent. Roman citizens in the provinces were also required to pay a tax on inheritance, and another on the manumission of slaves.

It seems now to be widely agreed that the quality of provincial government improved in the time of the emperors. The provincial population, it is said, was better protected against the abuse of power, in part because governors themselves began to be paid a regular salary. It is, however, hard to believe that corruption was reduced in any really significant way. In the period from Augustus to Trajan, there were no fewer than forty trials for provincial maladministration and extortion.

35   CICERO, *LETTERS TO HIS BROTHER QUINTUS* 1.1.8–35

On Cicero, see the introduction to selection 19. The following passage is taken from a letter
that he wrote to his brother Quintus (see also selection 28), probably in December, 60 BC or
early in 59, shortly after the Senate had decided to extend Quintus' term as governor of the
province of Asia for a third year. It describes both the duties of a provincial governor and some
of the challenges that he might be expected to confront.

(8) It is a mark of distinction that you have been in Asia for three years with the
highest authority, conducting yourself in such a way that no statue, or picture, or
dish, or clothes, or slave, or anyone's beauty, or any financial proposal (the sorts
of things in which that province of yours abounds) has led you away from the
utmost integrity and self-restraint. (9) And what could be found so excellent or
so desirable as that your virtue, your self-control, your temperance, should not
lurk in the shadows or be hidden away, but be positioned in the light of Asia,
before the eyes of that most distinguished province, and in the ears of all the
peoples and nations; that men are not trampled by your journeys, not exhausted
by expenditure, not disturbed at your approach; that, wherever you go, there is
the utmost joy, both in public and in private, since the city seems to have received
a protector, not a tyrant, the home a guest, not a plunderer?

(10) In these matters, however, experience itself has by this time certainly taught
you already that it is not enough that you yourself possess these virtues, but that
you must diligently watch around you so that in this guardianship of your province, it may appear that you are responsible to the allies, the citizens, and the
state, not only for yourself, but for all the officials of your government. And yet
you have as your assistants men who themselves will, on their own initiative,
consider their reputation; among them, Tubero[2] stands out, in rank, and position, and age; for my part, I imagine, especially since he writes history, that he
can choose many men from his own annals whom he might want and be able to
emulate; and Allienus[3] is one of us in spirit and kindness, and also in emulating
our approach to life. And what can I say about Gratidius?[4] I am certain that he is
so concerned about his own reputation that, because of his fraternal affection for
us, he is also concerned about ours.

(11) You have a quaestor who was not chosen by you, but instead was assigned
to you by lot. It is best that he be naturally self-controlled, and that he comply with
your policies and instructions. If any of these men should be somewhat disreputable, you should put up with him only to the extent that he ignores the laws that
bind him as a private person, but not if he uses, for the purpose of private gain, the
power that you had entrusted to him for his position. I am certainly not of the
opinion, especially when today's morality so heavily favors leniency and self-ag-
grandizement, that you should investigate every sordid thing, and examine each
and every one of these men, but that you should attach as much loyalty to each one
of them as each possesses of trustworthiness. And among them, you will be responsible for those whom the state itself has given to you as your aides and assistants in public business only within the limits that I laid down above.

(12) But those whom you have chosen to be with you, either among your household companions or among your personal attendants, who are customarily referred to as a sort of "praetor's cohort" – we have to be responsible not only for their actions, but for everything they say. But you have with you the sort of men whom you can easily praise when they act correctly, and very easily reprove when they show too little consideration for your reputation, who could have taken advantage of your generosity when you were new to the job, for the better a man is, the more difficult it is for him to suspect others of being dishonest. But now, let this third year manifest the same integrity as the preceding ones, and an even greater degree of caution and diligence.

(13) Let your ears be such as are judged to hear what they actually hear, and not such as are whispered into, falsely and insincerely, for the sake of profit. Let your signet-ring not be a sort of utensil, but your very self, as it were, not the agent of another man's desires, but the witness of your own. Let your *accensus*[5] be in the station which our ancestors wanted him to be in; for they did not want that post to be a sinecure, but one of work and duty, and hesitated to confer it on anyone other than their own freedmen, whom they governed not much differently than their slaves. Let your lictor be the dispenser not of his own, but of your kindness, and let him carry the *fasces* and axes before him as symbols more of rank than of power.[6] In short, let it be known to the province that the welfare, children, reputation, and fortunes of all whom you govern are most dear to you. Finally, let there be the impression, not only among those who have taken a bribe, but also among those who have given one, that you will be hostile, if you should learn of it. No one, in fact, will give when it is clear that, ordinarily, nothing is obtained from you through those who pretend to have a lot of influence with you.

(14) But these remarks of mine are not such that I would want you to be excessively harsh or suspicious toward your subordinates. For if there is one of them, who, in the space of two years, has never caused you to suspect him of greed (and I not only hear this, but, because I know them, believe it of Caesius and Chaerippus and Labeo), I should think that there is nothing which is not most properly entrusted and confided to them, or anyone else of the same type. But if there is anyone whom you already suspect, or about whom you have sensed something, do not trust him at all, and entrust no part of your reputation to him. (15) But in the province itself, if you have found someone who has entered deeply into your intimate acquaintance, and who was not known to us before, be careful how much you trust him; not that many provincials are unable to be good men, but though we may hope for this, it is dangerous to be confident. For each person's character is concealed under covers, and spread over, so to speak, with a kind of curtain; the forehead, the eyes, the face very often lie, but speech most often. Among the sort of men, therefore, who, induced by their desire for money, would abandon all those things from which we ourselves cannot be torn away, how can you find anyone who genuinely cares for you, a stranger, and is not just pretending to do so for his own advantage? In fact, it seems to me to be very difficult, especially when all of those same men feel affection for hardly any private citizen, but are always very fond of praetors. If you have found someone from that class to be fonder of you than of your present circumstances (for it

could have happened), gladly add him to the list of your people; but if you aren't certain about it, there is, in regard to familiarity, no class which you will have to guard against more, because they know all the ways to make money, and do everything for the sake of money, and have no consideration for the reputation of someone with whom they are not going to spend their lives.

(16) And also among the Greeks themselves, you must carefully guard against certain intimacies, except among a very few men, if there are any who are worthy of ancient Greece. But in that province of yours, there are a great many men who are deceitful and fickle, and trained by a long period of servitude to be excessively flattering, all of whom I am saying ought to be treated courteously, but only the best of them attached to you by ties of hospitality and friendship; too great an intimacy with them is not to be so trusted (for they don't dare to oppose our wishes), and they envy not only us, but also their own people.

(17) Now, since I should want to be cautious and diligent in matters of this sort, in which I fear that I am actually too strict, what do you think my feelings are in regard to slaves? We ought to control them everywhere, but especially in the provinces. In connection with this, many things can be prescribed, but this is both the shortest and the easiest to apply – that they should conduct themselves on your travels in Asia as if you were making a trip along the Appian Way; nor should they think that it makes any difference whether they are going to Tralles[7] or Formiae.[8] Nevertheless, if any of your slaves is especially trustworthy, let him be employed in your domestic and private affairs; what business pertains to your duties as governor, and to any part of the state, he should have nothing to do with. For there are many things which can properly be entrusted to loyal slaves, which, nevertheless, in order to avoid rumors and criticism, should not be entrusted to them.

(18) . . . . So let these things be the foundations of your reputation – your integrity and self-restraint; the modest conduct of those who are with you; a very cautious and careful choice in respect to your intimate acquaintances, both provincials and Greeks; and the strict and consistent discipline of your slaves. (19) For since these things are honorable in our private and daily affairs, in so important a position of command, where morals are so depraved, and the province is so corrupting, they must necessarily appear to be divine. These principles and this discipline can justify that severity in settling and deciding affairs which you have practiced in those matters, as a result of which we have taken upon ourselves some animosities, to my great delight. Unless, perhaps, you think that I am bothered by the complaints of someone like Paconius, who is not even Greek, but rather Mysian or Phrygian, or by the sniping of Tuscenius, a crazy and sordid man, from whose exceedingly filthy jaws you, acting with the utmost justice, snatched away the object of his most dishonorable greed.

(20) These and the other things full of severity that you have established in that province of yours, we would not easily justify without the utmost integrity. So let there be the greatest severity in administering justice, provided that it is not varied according to influence, but equitably upheld. But still, it matters little that you yourself administer justice fairly and carefully, unless this is done also by those to whom you have committed any part of that responsibility. And in fact, it seems to me that there is not a great variety of business in the administration of

Asia, but the whole thing depends mainly on the administration of justice; so that the very practice, especially of provincial government, is easily handled; what needs to be applied is consistency and firmness, which can stand up not only to influence, but also to the suspicion of it. (21) In addition to this, there must be a willingness to listen, compassion in deciding, and diligence in giving satisfaction and in settling disputes. It was because of these things that Gaius Octavius[9] recently made himself very popular; it was at his court, for the first time, that the lictor kept quiet, the *accensus* was silent, and everyone spoke whenever he wished, and for as long as he wanted. Because of this, he perhaps seemed to be too gentle, except that this gentleness counter-balanced his severity. The "men of Sulla"[10] were forced to restore what they had stolen through violence and intimidation. Those who, in their magistracies, had passed unjust decrees, were themselves, as private citizens, subjected to the same laws. This severity of his might seem to be harsh, except that it was mitigated by many seasonings of kindness.

(22) But if this leniency is popular at Rome, where there is so much arrogance, such unrestrained freedom, such infinite license in society, and finally, so many magistrates, so many sources of help, such power of the people, and such authority of the Senate, how pleasing indeed can a praetor's friendliness be in Asia, where so large a multitude of citizens, so many allies, so many cities, so many communities, wait expectantly on the nod of a single man? Where there is no help, no means of complaining, no Senate, no popular assembly? And so it is the mark of a great man, and one who is self-restrained by his very nature, but also refined by learning and by the study of all the best arts, to conduct himself, in possession of so much power, in such a way that no other power is desired by those whom he himself governs. . . . (24) And it seems to me, at least, that those who govern others ought to evaluate everything in relation to this – whether those who are under their authority are as happy as possible; and that this was your view long ago, and has been from the beginning, from when you first set foot in Asia, has been made known by your unchanging reputation and by what everyone is saying. And it is the duty, not only of the man who governs allies and citizens, but also of the man who governs slaves and voiceless animals, to be a slave to the interests and well-being of those whom he governs.

(25) And in this respect I see that there is universal agreement that the greatest diligence is being applied by you; that no new debt is being contracted by the states; that in fact many have been freed by you from a great and burdensome debt of long standing; that a great many cities, ruined and almost deserted (of which one – Samos – is the most famous in Ionia, another – Halicarnassus – the most famous in Caria) have been restored through your agency; that there are no insurrections, no civil disorder in the towns; that you are seeing to it that the states are administered by councils of the best men; that brigandage has been eliminated in Mysia; murder suppressed in many places; that peace has been established throughout the province; that thefts and robberies, not only on the roads and in the countryside, but also – and they are much more common and serious – in towns and temples, have been stopped; that the reputations, and the fortunes, and the peace of mind of the rich have been freed from that harshest instrument of praetorian greed – false prosecution; that expenditures and taxes in the states are distributed equally across all who live within the boundaries of

those states; that it is very easy to get access to you; that your ears are open to the complaints of all; that no one's poverty and isolation has prevented him from approaching you, not only in public and on the tribunal, but even in your house and bed-room; finally, that in the whole of your administration, there is nothing harsh, nothing cruel, and that everything is full of clemency, gentleness, and kindness.

(26) But how great is that service of yours, that you have freed Asia from the iniquitous and heavy taxation of the aediles, though at the cost of great animosities toward us! For if a single man of noble rank openly complains that, because you decreed "that no monies are to be voted for games," you have robbed him of 200,000 sesterces,[11] how much money, do you suppose, would be paid out if it was spent in the name of all who have put on games at Rome – a practice which in fact had already been established? Anyway, we suppressed the complaints of our "friends" by that decision, which – I don't know how it may have been received in Asia – was greeted at Rome with no small measure of praise and admiration – that when the states had voted money for a temple and a monument in our honor; and though they had done this with the utmost good-will in return for my great accomplishments and your greater services; and though the law made a specific exception, "that it is permitted to receive money for a temple and a monument;" and though what was given was not going to be wasted, but spent on the decoration of a temple, so that it seemed to be given not so much to myself as to the people of Rome and to the immortal gods; nevertheless, this, in which there was dignity, law, and the good-will of those who were doing it, I did not think should be accepted, both for other reasons, but also in order that those to whom such an honor was neither due nor permitted might bear it with equanimity.

(27) So apply yourself with all your heart and all your energy to this policy, which you have practiced until now – that you cherish those whom the Senate and people of Rome have committed and handed over to your trust and power, that you protect them by every means, and that you want them to be as happy as possible. If chance had put you in charge of Africans or Spaniards or Gauls, uncouth and barbarous nations, it would nevertheless be incumbent upon your humanity to watch out for their interests, and to serve their welfare and security. But since we are governing the kind of men in whom there is not only civilization itself, but from whom it is thought to have spread to others, we certainly ought to give them, most of all, what we have received from them. (28) For I am not embarrassed to say now, especially since in my life and accomplishments there can be no space for any suspicion of laziness or frivolity, that what I have accomplished has been achieved because of the studies and arts handed down to us in the records and teachings of Greece. And that – in addition to the common honesty that is owed to all, and what seems to be our special indebtedness to that race of men – is the reason why, among those very people by whose teachings we have been educated, we should be willing to admit what we have learned from them. (29) And indeed, that leading man of genius and learning, Plato, thought that states would be happy only when learned and wise men had begun to rule them, or when those who ruled them had devoted all their attention to learning and wisdom.[12] He evidently believed that this combination of power and wisdom could be the salvation of states, something which some day perhaps will befall

our whole state, as now indeed it has certainly befallen that province of yours, in so far as he holds supreme power there, who, from boyhood, devoted as much enthusiasm and time as he could to learning philosophy, and virtue, and humanity. (30) So see to it that this year, which has been added to your labors, may seem to have been added also for the welfare of Asia. Since Asia has been more successful in keeping you than I have been in bringing you back, manage things in such a way that the joy of the province may lighten my sense of loss. . . .

(31) . . . . Since you are exercising the highest authority and power in those cities in which you see that your virtues are revered and ranked among the attributes of the gods, in all things – what you decide, what you decree, what you do – you will think about what you owe to the high opinions men have of you, to their favorable judgments about you, to the honors conferred upon you. And it will be this – that you consider everyone's interests, that you remedy the sufferings of men, that you provide for their welfare, that you want to be both called and considered, "the father of Asia."

(32) And yet, to that good-will of yours and devotion to duty, the publicans[13] constitute a serious obstacle; if we should go against them, we would separate from ourselves and from the state an order that has deserved extremely well of us, and that, through us, has been closely linked to the state; but if we should give in to them on everything, we would be acquiescing in the utter destruction of those whose security and also interests we ought to be watching out for. This is the one difficulty (if we are willing to face the truth) in the whole of your administration. For to be unselfish, to restrain all passions, to keep one's people in line, to maintain an even-handed policy in applying the law, to be good-natured in investigating things and in listening to men and giving them access, is more a mark of distinction than it is difficult. For it is not so much a matter of physical effort, but rather of purpose of mind, as it were, and of intention.

(33) How bitterly the allies feel about this issue of the publicans, we understand from those citizens who recently, in abolishing import-taxes in Italy, complained not so much about the taxes as about certain injustices perpetrated by the tax-collectors. So I am not ignorant of what happens to the allies in far-off lands, since I have heard the complaints of citizens in Italy. To conduct yourself in such a way as both to satisfy the publicans, especially when they have overbid in contracting to collect the taxes, and not to allow the allies to be ruined, seems to require a sort of divine virtue, that is, yours. And first, in respect to the Greeks: what is most bitter for them – that they are subject to taxation – ought not to seem so harsh, given that, even without the governance of the Roman people, they themselves were in that position on their own initiative, and by their own prescription. And they cannot disdain the name of "publican," who, without "the publican," could not have paid the tax imposed on everyone by Sulla. And that the Greeks are no more lenient in exacting the payment of taxes than our own publicans can be inferred from the fact that recently the Caunians,[14] and everyone from the islands that Sulla had made subject to the Rhodians, fled to the Senate, to ask that they be allowed to pay us rather than the Rhodians. So those who have always been subject to taxation should not shudder at the name of "publican;" nor should those who were unable to pay the taxes themselves disdain it; nor should those who have asked for them reject it.

(34) And at the same time, let Asia keep this in mind, that if it was not subject to our government, there is no disaster either of foreign war or domestic discord from which it would have been spared. And since this government cannot possibly be maintained without taxes, it ought not to resent having to purchase for itself, with some part of its profits, perpetual peace and tranquility. (35) But if they can accept without resentment the existence of such a class, and the name of "publican," everything else, because of your counsel and wisdom, can appear to them to be less oppressive. In making agreements, they have the power to look, not to the censorian law, but rather to their own convenience in arranging their business and freeing themselves from nuisance. You also can do what you have done so well, and are doing – that you remind everyone how much authority there is among the publicans, and how much we owe to that order, so that you, by your influence and authority, leaving aside your sovereignty and the force of your power and of the *fasces*, may unite the publicans with the Greeks, and that from those whom you have served so well, and who owe you everything, you request that, relying on their good nature, they allow us to maintain and preserve the close bond which exists between us and the publicans.

36   *British Museum Papyrus* 1912

When news of Caligula's assassination (which is described in selection 31) reached Alexandria in Egypt, long-standing tensions between the city's Greek and Jewish populations erupted into armed conflict and rioting. On Claudius' accession, the Alexandrians sent a delegation to Rome to ask the new emperor for various favors, including his help in resolving some of the issues that divided the Greek and Jewish communities. The following letter, which is preserved on papyrus, is Claudius' official response. It illustrates, among other things, how an emperor might be expected to settle local disputes. The translation is from N. Lewis and M. Reinhold, *Roman Civilization: Selected Readings*, 3rd edn (New York, 1990), vol. 2, pp. 285–8.

Lucius Aemilius Rectus[15] declares: since the whole of the city, owing to its [size], was unable to be present at the reading of the most sacred and most beneficent letter to the city, I have deemed it necessary to display the letter publicly, in order that reading it individually you may admire the majesty of our god Caesar and feel gratitude for his good will toward the city. Year 2 of the Emperor Tiberius Claudius Caesar Augustus Germanicus,[16] [the] 14th of New Augustus.

The Emperor Tiberius Claudius Caesar Augustus Germanicus, *pontifex maximus*,[17] holder of the tribunician power, consul-designate, to the city of Alexandria, greeting. Tiberius Claudius Barbilus, Apollonius, son of Artemidorus, Chaeremo, son of Leonidas, Marcus Julius Asclepiades, Gaius Julius Dionysius, Tiberius Claudius Phanias, Pasio, son of Potamo, Dionysius, son of Sabbio, Tiberius Claudius Archibius, Apollonius, son of Aristo, Gaius Julius Apollonius, Hermaiscus, son of Apollonius, your envoys, delivered your resolution to me and discoursed at length concerning the city, directing my attention to your good will toward us, which from long ago, you may be sure, had been stored up to your advantage in my memory; for you are by nature reverent toward the emperors, as I have come to know well from many [indications], and in particular you have taken a warm interest – warmly reciprocated – in my [household], of which fact (to mention the latest instance, passing over the others) the supreme witness is my brother, Germanicus Caesar, when he addressed you in franker tones. . . .

Wherefore I gladly accepted the honors given to me by you, though I am not partial to such things. And first I permit you to keep my birthday as an Augustan day in the manner you have yourselves proposed, and I agree to the erection by you in their several places of the statues of myself and my family; for I see that you were zealous to establish on every side memorials of your reverence for my [household]. Of the two golden statues, the one made to represent the Claudian Augustan Peace, as my most honored Barbillus suggested, and persisted in, when I wished to refuse for fear of being thought too offensive, shall be erected at Rome, and the other, according to your request, shall be carried in procession on my name days in your city; and it shall be accompanied in the procession by a throne, adorned with whatever trappings you wish. It would perhaps be foolish, while accepting such great honors, to refuse the institution of a Claudian tribe, and the establishment of sacred groves after the manner of Egypt; wherefore I grant you these requests as well, and if you wish, you may also erect the equestrian statues given by Vitrasius Pollio, my procurator. As for the erection of the statues in four-horse chariots which you wish to set up to me at the entrance to the country, I consent to let one be placed at the town called Taposiris, in Libya, another at Pharus, in Alexandria, and a third at Pelusium, in Egypt. But I deprecate the appointment of a high priest for me and the building of temples, for I do not wish to be offensive to my contemporaries, and my opinion is that temples and the like have by all ages been granted as special honors to the gods alone.

Concerning the requests which you have been eager to obtain from me, I decide as follows. All those who have become ephebes[18] up to the time of my principate, I confirm and maintain in the possession of the Alexandrian citizenship, with all the privileges and indulgences enjoyed by the city, [except for] those who, by fraud, have contrived to become ephebes, though born of slaves. And it is equally my will that all the other privileges shall be confirmed which were granted to you by the emperors before me, and by the kings and by the prefects, as the deified Augustus also confirmed them. It is my will that the overseers of the temples of the deified Augustus in Alexandria shall be chosen by lot in the same way as those of the same deified Augustus in Canopus are chosen by lot. With regard to the municipal magistrates being made triennial, your proposal seems to me to be very good; for through fear of being called to account for any [misgovernment], your magistrates will behave with greater circumspection during their term of office. Concerning the city council, what your custom may have been under the ancient kings I have no means of saying, but that you had no council under the former emperors you are well aware. As this is the first broaching of a novel project, whose utility to the city and to my interests is not evident, I have written to Aemilius Rectus to hold an inquiry, and inform me whether in the first place it is right that the body should be constituted, and, if it should be right to create one, in what manner this is to be done.

As for which party was responsible for the riot and feud (or rather, if the truth must be told, the war) with the Jews, although your envoys, particularly Dionysius, son of Theo, confronting [your opponents], put your case with great zeal, nevertheless, I was unwilling to make a strict inquiry, though guarding within me a store of immutable indignation against any who renewed the conflict; and I tell you once [and] for all that, unless you put a stop to this ruinous and obstinate enmity against each other, I shall be driven to show what a benevolent emperor can be when turned to righteous indignation. Wherefore, once again I [urge] you that, on the one hand, the Alexandrians show themselves forbearing and kindly toward the Jews, who for many years have [lived] in the same city, and dishonor none of the rights observed by them in the worship of their god, but allow them to observe their customs as in the time of the deified Augustus, which customs I also, after hearing both sides, have confirmed. And, on the other hand, I explicitly order the Jews not to agitate for more privileges than they formerly possessed, and in the future not to send out a separate embassy as if they lived in two separate cities – a thing unprecedented – and not to force their way into gymnasiarchic or cosmetic games,[19] while enjoying their own privileges and sharing a great abundance of advantages in a city not their own, and not to bring in or admit Jews from Syria or those who sail down from Egypt, a proceeding which will compel me to conceive serious suspicions; otherwise I will proceed against them by all means as fomenters of what is a general plague of the whole world. If, desisting from these courses, you both consent to live with mutual forbearance and kindliness, I, on my side, will exercise a solicitude of very long standing for the city, as one bound to us by ancestral friendship. I bear witness to my friend Barbillus of the solicitude which he has always shown for you in my presence, and of the extreme zeal with which he has now advocated your cause, and likewise to my friend, Tiberius Claudius Archibius. Farewell.

37   CHARTER OF URSO (*CORPUS INSCRIPTIONUM LATINARUM* 1.594)

The Romans routinely founded colonies, both in Italy and in the provinces, for veterans and for the urban poor. Sometimes also, existing towns were reconstituted as colonies. Both types were given elaborate charters, which were normally drawn up by commissioners sent out from Rome, and which were later inscribed on bronze tablets. Parts of about half a dozen charters have been recovered from various locations in Italy and in southern Spain. The following passages are taken from the charter of Urso (mod. Osuna, Spain), which was known formally as the *colonia* Genetiva Julia, and which was founded by Julius Caesar in 44 BC. The translation is based on the text in M. H. Crawford (ed.), *Roman Statutes* (London, 1996), vol. 1, pp. 400–17.

(64) Whoever will be duoviri[20] after the colony has been founded, they, within ten days of when they have begun to hold that magistracy, shall discuss with the decurions,[21] when not less than two-thirds [of them] are present, which and how many days ought to be festivals, and which sacrifices should be publicly per-

formed, and who should perform those sacrifices. And in regard to those matters, what a majority of the decurions who are then present have decreed and decided, is to be legal and binding, and there are to be those sacrifices and those festival days in that colony.

(70) Whoever will be duoviri, they, except for those who will first be appointed after this statute, are to organize, during their term of office, and at the direction of the decurions, an exhibition or theatrical shows for Jupiter, Juno, Minerva, and the gods and goddesses, for four days, for the greater part of the day, so far as [is possible], and each of them is to spend not less than 2,000 sesterces[22] from his own money on those shows and on that exhibition, and it is to be lawful for each duovir to take and to spend up to 2,000 sesterces from the public money, and it is to be lawful for them to do so without personal liability, provided that no one takes or makes assignment from that money, which money, in accordance with this statute, can properly be given or assigned for those sacrifices which are conducted publicly in the colony or in any other place.

(73) No one is to bring a dead man within the boundaries of a town or of a colony, where it has been drawn around by a plow, nor is he to bury him there, or burn him, or build the tomb of a dead person. If anyone has acted contrary to these rules, he is to be condemned to pay 5,000 sesterces to the colonists of the colony Genetiva Julia, and anyone who wishes will have the right to claim and to bring suit for that money. And a duovir or aedile[23] shall see to it that whatever has been built is demolished. If a dead body has been brought in or deposited contrary to these regulations, they are to make expiation in whatever way is appropriate.

(75) No one in the town of the colony Julia is to un-roof or demolish or take apart a building, unless he has furnished guarantors, at the discretion of the duoviri, that he will rebuild it, or unless the decurions have [so] decreed, provided that not less than fifty [of them] are present when that matter is discussed. If anyone has acted contrary to these regulations, he is to be condemned to pay to the colonists of the colony Genetiva Julia as much money as the matter is worth, and anyone who wishes will have the right to claim and bring suit for that money in accordance with this statute.

(78) Whatever public roads or public pathways there are or have been within those boundaries which have been assigned to the colony, whatever boundaries and whatever roads and whatever pathways there are or shall be or have been across those lands, those roads and those boundaries and those pathways are to be public.

(99) Whatever public waters shall be brought into the town of the colony Genetiva, those who are then duoviri are to discuss with the decurions, when two-thirds [of them] are present, through which lands it will be permitted to bring water. To whatever place the majority of the decurions who are then present have decreed that it is to be brought, there is to be the right and power to bring water through those lands, provided that the water is not brought through that building which has not been built for that purpose; and no one is to act in such a way as to prevent the water from being brought.

(100) If any colonist wishes to bring overflow water into private use, and he has approached a duovir and demanded that he discuss it with the decurions,

then that duovir, of whom it has been so demanded, is to discuss it with the decurions, when not less than forty [of them] are present. If the decurions, the majority who are then present, have decided that the overflow water is to be brought into private use, there is to be the right and power that he use that water in that way, to the extent that it can be done without damage to private persons.

(105) If anyone says that any of the decurions is unworthy of his place or of the order of the decurionate, other than on the grounds that he is a freedman, and it is demanded of a duovir that a trial be granted concerning that matter, the duovir who has been approached for a hearing concerning that matter is to administer the law and grant trials. And that decurion, who has been condemned in a trial, is afterwards not to be a decurion, nor to speak his opinion among the decurions, nor to seek a duovirate or an aedileship; nor is any duovir to take account of him in an assembly or at a vote, nor is he to announce him as a duovir or aedile, nor is he to allow him to be announced.

(127) Whatever theatrical shows are performed for the colony Genetiva Julia, no one [is to sit] in the *orchestra*[24] for the sake of watching the shows, except a magistrate or promagistrate of the Roman people, or whoever is in charge of administering the law, and whoever is or will be or has been a senator of the Roman people, and whoever is or will be or has been the son of a senator of the Roman people, and whoever is a *praefectus fabrum*[25] of that magistrate or promagistrate who governs the further of the Spanish provinces, and for whomever it is or will be appropriate to sit in the place of the decurions in accordance with this statute and by decree of the decurions – except for those who are written down above, no one is to sit in the *orchestra* for the sake of watching the shows, nor is any magistrate or promagistrate of the Roman people or whoever is in charge of administering the law to lead them; nor is anyone to lead anyone to sit; nor is anyone to allow anyone to sit in that place, as he will want it to be done properly, without wrongful intent.

(132) After this statute has been granted, no candidate in the colony Genetiva – whoever seeks a magistracy in the colony Genetiva Julia, for the sake of seeking a magistracy in that year, in which year each candidate seeks or is about to seek a magistracy – is to provide banquets for the sake of seeking a magistracy, or invite anyone to dinner, or hold a banquet, or knowingly and with wrongful intent arrange for someone to hold a banquet, or invite anyone to dinner for the sake of his candidacy, except that the candidate himself, in that year in which he seeks a magistracy, may invite up to nine men a day, and may hold a banquet, if he wishes, without wrongful intent. Nor may any candidate give or distribute a gift or a present or anything else for the sake of his candidacy knowingly and with wrongful intent. Nor is anyone, for the sake of another person's candidacy, to provide banquets, or invite anyone to dinner, or hold a banquet; nor is anyone, for the sake of another person's candidacy, to give or donate or distribute any gift or present or anything else knowingly and with wrongful intent. If anyone has acted contrary to these regulations, he is to be condemned to pay 5,000 sesterces to the colonists of the colony Genetiva Julia, and in accordance with this statute, there is to be, for whomever of them wishes, the right and power [to bring] an action, claim, and suit for that money in a recuperatorial trial before the duovir [or] prefect.

38   AELIUS ARISTIDES, *TO ROME*

Aelius Aristides was born to a land-owning family in the province of Mysia, in what is today western Turkey, in AD 117 or 129. He studied for a time at Athens, but lived mainly in the port-city of Smyrna, now Izmir, Turkey. He died probably in 181. His surviving works include numerous speeches, essays, hymns, and the *Sacred Teachings*, which record the dream-revelations made to him by Asclepius, the god of healing.

The speech *To Rome* was delivered there probably in AD 144 or 156. It is not an objective assessment of the city or of its empire. It does, however, indicate what qualities of Roman rule most appealed to the wealthy and educated elite of the Greek-speaking cities of the eastern empire. The translation is from J. H. Oliver, "The ruling power: A study of the Roman empire in the second century after Christ through the Roman oration of Aelius Aristides," *Transactions of the American Philosophical Society*, n.s. 43, pt. 4 (1953), pp. 895–907.

(1) It is a time-honored custom of travelers setting forth by land or sea to make a prayer pledging the performance of some vow – whatever they have in mind – on safe arrival at their destination. . . . As for me, the vow that I made as I journeyed [here] was not of the usual stupid and irrelevant kind, nor one unrelated to the art of my profession, merely that if I came through safely, I would salute your city with a public address. (2) But since it was quite impossible to pledge words commensurate with your city, it became evident that I had need of a second prayer. It is perhaps really presumptuous to dare [to] undertake an oration to equal such majesty in a city. However, I have promised to address you, and I can speak only as I can. . . . (3) But you who are at home in the great city, if you share the hope that I not prove false to my vow, join your prayers to mine for the success of my boldness. [Allow] me to say at once, before I come to the praise of your city, that here I found men – in a phrase of Euripides – "able to inspire one, though he was speechless before, to eloquence and skill," to discourse on things quite beyond his natural gifts.

(10) Some chronicler, speaking of Asia, asserted that one man ruled as much land as the sun passed, and his statement was not true because he placed all Africa and Europe outside the limits where the sun rises in the East and sets in the West. It has now, however, turned out to be true. Your possession is equal to what the sun can pass, and the sun passes over your land. Neither the Chelidonean nor the Cyanean promontories[26] limit your empire, nor does the distance from which a horseman can reach the sea in one day; nor do you reign within fixed boundaries; nor does another dictate to what point your control reaches; but the sea like a girdle lies extended, at once in the middle of the civilized world and of your hegemony. (11) Around it lie the great continents greatly sloping, [always] offering to you in full measure something of their own. . . . For whatever is grown and made among each people cannot fail to be here at all times and in abundance. And here the merchant vessels come carrying these many products from all regions in every season and even at every equinox, so that the city appears [to be] a kind of common emporium of the world.

(12) Cargoes from India and, if you will, even from Arabia the [Blessed], one

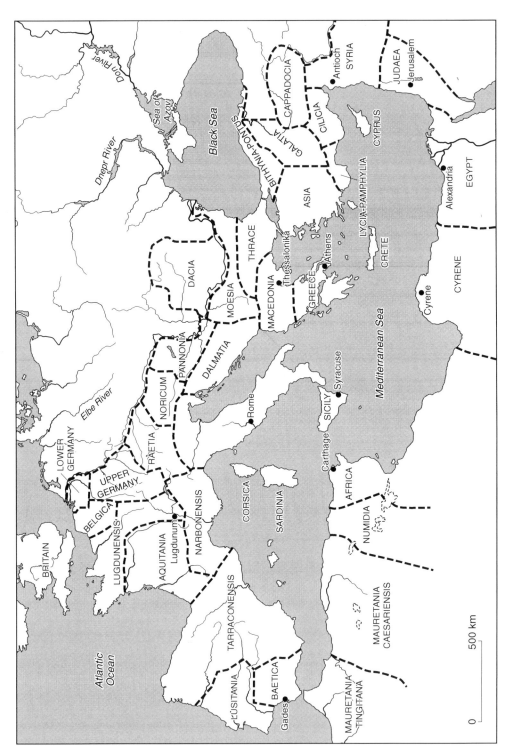

FIGURE 6.1   *The Roman provinces in the time of Hadrian.*

can see in such numbers as to surmise that in those lands the trees will have been stripped bare, and that the inhabitants of these lands, if they need anything, must come here and beg for a share of their own. Again, one can see Babylonian garments and ornaments from the barbarian country beyond arriving in greater quantity and with more ease than if shippers from Naxos or from Cythnos,[27] bearing something from those islands, had [only] to enter the port of Athens. Your farms are Egypt, Sicily, and the civilized part of Africa. (13) Arrivals and departures by sea never cease, so that the wonder is, not that the harbor has insufficient space for merchant vessels, but that even the sea has enough, [if] it really does. And just as Hesiod said about the ends of the Ocean, that there is a common channel where all waters have one source and destination,[28] so there is a common channel to Rome and all meet here, trade, shipping, agriculture, metallurgy, all the arts and crafts that are or ever have been, all the things that are engendered or grown from the earth. And whatever one does not see here neither did nor does exist.

(28) . . . . Now the present empire has been extended to boundaries of no [little] distance, to such, in fact, that one cannot even measure the area within them . . . . The Red Sea and the cataracts of the Nile and Lake Maeotis,[29] which formerly were said to lie on the boundaries of the earth, are like the courtyard walls to the house which is this city of yours. On the other hand, you have explored Ocean. Some writers did not believe that Ocean existed at all, or did not believe that it flowed around the earth; they thought that poets had invented the name and had introduced it into literature for the sake of entertainment. But you have explored it so thoroughly that not even the island [in it] has escaped you.

(31) All directions are carried out by the chorus of the civilized world at a word or gesture of guidance more easily than at some plucking of a chord; and if anything needs [to] be done, it [is enough] to decide, and there it is already done. The governors sent out to the city-states and ethnic groups are each of them rulers of those under them, but in what concerns themselves and their relations to each other, they are all equally among the ruled, and in particular, they differ from those under their rule in that it is they – one might assert – who first show how to be the right kind of subject. So much respect has been instilled in all men for him who is the great governor, who obtains [everything] for them. (32) They think that he knows what they are doing better than they do themselves. . . . And if the governors should have even some slight doubt whether certain claims are valid in connection with either public or private lawsuits and petitions from the governed, they straightaway send to him with a request for instructions what to do, and they wait until he renders a reply, like a chorus waiting for its trainer. (33) Therefore, he has no need to wear himself out traveling around the whole empire nor, by appearing personally, now among some, then among others, to make sure of each point when he has the time to tread their soil. It is very easy for him to stay where he is, and manage the entire civilized world by letters, which arrive almost as soon as they are written, as if they were carried by winged messengers.

(39) There is an abundant and beautiful equality of the humble with the great and of the obscure with the illustrious, and, above all, of the poor man with the rich and of the commoner with the noble, and the words of Hesiod come to pass,

"For he easily exalts, and the exalted he easily checks,"[30] namely this judge and *princeps*,[31] as the justice of the claim may lead, like a breeze in the sails of a ship, favoring and accompanying, not the rich man more, the poor man less, but benefiting equally whomever it meets.

(59) But there is that which very [definitely] deserves as much attention and admiration now as all the rest together. I mean your magnificent citizenship with its grand conception, because there is nothing like it in the records of all mankind. Dividing into two groups all those in your empire – and with this word I have indicated the entire civilized world – you have everywhere appointed to your citizenship, or even to kinship with you, the better part of the world's talent, courage, and leadership, while the rest you recognized as a league under your hegemony. (60) Neither sea nor intervening continent are bars to citizenship, nor are Asia and Europe divided in their treatment here. In your empire, all paths are open to all.

(63) It was not because you stood off and refused to give a share in it to any of the others that you made your citizenship an object of wonder. On the contrary, you sought its expansion as a worthy aim, and you have caused the word Roman to be the label, not of membership in a city, but of some common nationality, and this not just one among all, but one balancing all the rest. For the categories into which you now divide the world are not Hellenes and Barbarians, and it is not absurd, the distinction which you made, because you show them a citizenry more numerous, so to speak, than the entire Hellenic race. The division which you substituted is one into Romans and non-Romans. To such a degree have you expanded the name of your city. (64) Since these are the lines along which the distinction has been made, many in every city are fellow-citizens of yours no less than of their own kinsmen, though some of them have not yet seen this city. There is no need of garrisons to hold their citadels, but the men of greatest standing and influence in every city guard their own fatherlands for you. . . . (65) No envy sets foot in the empire, for you yourselves were the first to disown envy, when you placed all opportunities in view of all. . . .

(70) Wars, even if they once occurred, no longer seem real; on the contrary, stories about them are interpreted more as myths by the many who hear them. If anywhere an actual clash occurs along the border, as is only natural in the immensity of a great empire, because of the madness of Getae[32] or the misfortune of Libyans or the wickedness of those around the Red Sea, who are unable to enjoy the blessings they have, then simply like myths, they themselves quickly pass and the stories about them. (71a) So great is your peace, though war was traditional among you.

(72a) Now it is time to speak about the army and military affairs. . . . (71b) . . . . The shoemakers and masons of yesterday are not the hoplites and cavalry of today. On the stage a farmer appears as a soldier after a quick change of costume, and in poor homes the same person cooks the meal, keeps the house, makes the bed. But you were not so undiscriminating. You did not expect that those engaged in other occupations would be made into soldiers by [necessity], nor did you leave it to your enemies to call you together.

(75) Who then have been assembled and how? Going over the entire league, you looked about carefully for those who would perform this [service], and when

you found them, you released them from the fatherland and gave them your own city. . . . Having made them fellow-citizens, you made them also soldiers, so that the men from this city would not be subject to the levy, and those performing military service would nonetheless be citizens, who together with their enrollment in the army had lost their own cities, but from that very day had become your fellow-citizens and defenders.

(80) You did not forget walls, but these you placed around the empire, not the city. And you erected walls splendid and worthy of you, as far away as possible, visible to those within the circuit, but, for one starting from the city, an outward journey of months and years if he wished to see them. (81) Beyond the outermost ring of the civilized world, you drew a second line, quite as one does in walling a town, another circle, more widely curved and more easily guarded. Here you built the walls to defend you, and then erected towns bordering upon them, some in some parts, others elsewhere, filling them with colonists, giving these the comfort of arts and crafts, and in general establishing beautiful order.

(87) In respect to military science, furthermore, you have made all men look like children. For you did not prescribe exercises for soldiers and officers to train for victory over the enemy only, but for victory over themselves first. Therefore, every day the soldier lives in discipline and no one ever leaves the post assigned to him, but as in some permanent chorus, he knows and keeps his position, and the subordinate does not on that account envy him who has a higher rank, but he himself rules with precision those whose superior he is.

(92) How far you surpass all in total extent of your empire and in firmness of grip and plan of civil administration is set forth in what has already been said; but now, it seems to me that one would not miss the mark if he said the following: all those of the past who ruled over a very large part of the earth ruled, as it were, naked bodies by themselves, mere persons composing the ethnic groups or nations. (93) For when were there so many cities both inland and on the coast, or when have they been so beautifully equipped with everything? Did ever a man of those who lived then travel across country as we do, counting the cities by days, and sometimes riding on the same day through two or three cities as if passing through sections of merely one? . . . Those whom the others ruled did not as individuals have the equality of civil rights and privileges, but against the primitive organization of an ethnic group in that time, one can set the municipal organization of the same group's city of today. It might very well be said that while the others have been kings, as it were, of open country and strongholds, you alone are rulers of civilized communities.

(99) Cities gleam with radiance and charm, and the whole earth has been beautified like a garden. Smoke rising from plains, and fire signals for friend and foe have disappeared, as if a breath had blown them away, beyond land and sea. Every charming spectacle and an infinite number of festal games have been introduced instead. Thus, like an ever-burning sacred fire, the celebration never ends, but moves around from time to time and people to people, always somewhere, a demonstration justified by the way all men have fared. Thus it is right to pity only those outside your hegemony, if indeed there are any, because they lose such blessings. (100) It is you again who have best proved the general assertion, that Earth is mother of all and common fatherland. . . . Neither Cilician Gates nor

narrow sandy approaches to Egypt through Arab country, nor inaccessible mountains, nor immense stretches of river, nor inhospitable tribes of barbarians cause
terror, but for security it [is enough] to be a Roman citizen, or rather to be one of
those united under your hegemony.

(101) Homer said, "Earth common of all,"[33] and you have made it come true.
You have measured and recorded the land of the entire civilized world; you have
spanned the rivers with all kinds of bridges, and hewn highways through the
mountains, and filled the barren stretches with posting-stations; you have accustomed all areas to a settled and orderly way of life. . . . Though the citizens of
Athens began the civilized life of today, this life in its turn has been firmly established by you, who came later but who, men say, are better. (102) There is no
need whatsoever now to write a book of travels and to enumerate the laws which
each country uses. Rather you yourselves have become universal guides for all;
you threw wide all the gates of the civilized world and gave those who so wished
the opportunity to see for themselves; you assigned common laws for all and you
put an end to the previous conditions which were amusing to describe but which,
if one looked at them from the standpoint of reason, were intolerable; you made
it possible to marry anywhere, and you organized all the civilized world, as it
were, into one family.

(108) But the trial which we undertook at the beginning of our speech is beyond any man's power, namely to compose the oration which would equal the
majesty of your empire, for it would require just about as much time as time
allotted to the empire, and that would be all eternity. Therefore, it is best to do
like those poets who compose dithyrambs and paeans, namely to add a prayer
and so close the oration. (109) Let all the gods and the children of the gods be
invoked to grant that this empire and this city flourish forever, and never cease
until stones [float] upon the sea and trees cease to put forth shoots in spring, and
that the great governor and his sons be preserved and obtain blessings for all. My
bold attempt is finished. Now is the time to register your decision whether for
better or for worse.

SUGGESTIONS FOR FURTHER READING

On Roman provincial administration, see D. C. Braund (ed.), *The Administration of the Roman Empire, 241 BC–AD 193* (Exeter, 1988); A. W. Lintott, *Imperium Romanum: Politics and
Administration* (London and New York, 1993); F. Millar, et al., *The Roman Empire and its
Neighbors*, 2nd edn (New York, 1981). G. H. Stevenson, *Roman Provincial Administration
till the Age of the Antonines* (Oxford, 1939) is still useful. The standard work on the publicans
is E. Badian, *Publicans and Sinners: Private Enterprise in the Service of the Roman Republic*,
rev. edn (London, 1983). There are a number of good biographies of Cicero: E. Rawson,
Cicero: A Portrait (Ithaca, NY, 1975); D. R. Shackleton Bailey, *Cicero* (New York, 1971); D.
Stockton, *Cicero: A Political Biography* (London, 1971).

On Alexandria, see D. Sly, *Philo's Alexandria* (London and New York, 1996). The best
book on Claudius is B. Levick, *Claudius* (New Haven, 1990). The classic work on municipal
administration is F. F. Abbott and A. C. Johnson, *Municipal Administration in the Roman
Empire* (Princeton, 1926). There is much that is relevant also in M. Crawford (ed.), *Roman

Statutes, 2 vols (London, 1996). On Aelius Aristides and his speech *To Rome*, see J. H. Oliver, "The ruling power: A study of the Roman empire in the second century after Christ through the Roman oration of Aelius Aristides," *Transactions of the American Philosophical Society*, n.s. 43, pt. 4 (1953), pp. 871–1003.

Seven

THE ARMY

Editor's introduction

The history of the Roman army is difficult to reconstruct before the time of Polybius, whose *Histories*, written about the middle of the second century BC, provide the earliest surviving account of its organization (see selection 40). From the beginning, the army functioned as a kind of citizen militia. Military service was required of all citizens between the ages of 17 and 46. In practice, however, the right to serve was restricted to those who possessed a certain property-qualification, which varied over time, and which generally excluded the poor. The army normally campaigned only part of the year, usually from about March to October. Pay was introduced sometime around the beginning of the fourth century BC.

The army consisted originally of four legions, each of which was made up of about 3,000 heavily armed foot soldiers, who were drawn up in three lines of *hastati*, *principes*, and *triarii*, approximately 1,200 light-armed infantry (*velites*), who included the youngest and poorest of the eligible citizens, and 300 cavalrymen, who were drawn exclusively from the wealthiest classes. Each legion was divided into maniples, which in turn were divided into centuries, each of which seems to have consisted of about eighty men.

The nature of the army was radically altered at the end of the second century BC and in the early part of the first, through a series of reforms which the sources attribute mainly to Gaius Marius. For the first time, the opportunity to serve was extended to those without property (*proletarii*), with the result that the army was gradually transformed into one made up mostly of volunteers. The cohort replaced the maniple as the main tactical unit of the legion, which was now divided into ten cohorts, each consisting of six centuries. The cavalry and the light-armed *velites* of the legion were also replaced, their functions taken over by troops recruited from outside of Italy and organized into units called *auxilia*.

The professionalization of the army was completed under Augustus, who turned it into a standing force made up almost entirely of volunteers. Terms of service were standardized, probably in 13 BC. Legionaries, for example, were required to serve at least twenty years before they could obtain an honorable discharge, and the retirement bonuses that were now routinely awarded to them. The Praetorian Guard was established in 27 BC to act as the emperor's escort. It consisted originally of 9,000 men, who were required to serve for sixteen years. Augustus also created the urban cohorts, three units of 1,000 men each, who were charged with keeping order in Rome, and who were placed under the command of the prefect of the city (*praefectus urbi*). Two permanent naval bases were founded, one at Misenum (on the bay of Naples), the other at Ravenna. Auxiliary fleets were established in Britain, Mauretania (mod. Morocco), Egypt, Syria, and on the Black Sea; river flotillas were created to patrol the Rhine and the Danube. The principal function of the imperial navy was logistical – to transport troops, horses, arms, food, and dignitaries.

Over the course of the first two centuries AD, the number of legions deployed in the provinces was remarkably constant, ranging between twenty-five and thirty, each with a nominal strength of 5,400 (at any given time, therefore, the number of legionaries was roughly 150,000). In the period from Augustus to Vespasian, the legions were recruited mainly from Italy, southern Gaul, and Spain, in part because recruits were required to be Roman citizens. From about the beginning of the second century AD, they were recruited increasingly from the areas in which the legions were stationed. Higher-ranking officers continued to be selected from the senatorial and equestrian orders; they were generally young men, who had little, if any, training, and no intention of spending their careers in the army. The real officers of command were the centurions, who appear to have been promoted mostly from the ranks or from the Praetorian Guard.

According to Tacitus (*Annals* 4.5), the number of auxiliaries, who were generally not Roman citizens, was about equal to that of the legionaries. At least from the time of Claudius (AD 41–54), they were, it seems, normally awarded the Roman citizenship after they had completed their term of service, which came to be standardized at twenty-five years. The *auxilia* was divided into units of 500 or 1,000 men, which were of three types – infantry, cavalry, or a combination of the two. Other provincial troops were organized into units which the Romans called *numeri*, and which were allowed to retain much of their ethnic character (in their style of weapons, for example, or in their uniforms).

It is often said that the chief function of the imperial army was to defend the empire against external aggression. In many provinces, however, it seems to have acted primarily as an internal security force (in Benjamin Isaac's words, as an army "of conquest and occupation"),[1] whose deployment was intended at least as much to tame the local population as to protect it. From the time of Hadrian (AD 117–38), the army constructed an increasingly complex system of fortifications along the frontiers – forts, watchtowers, roads, and, in some areas, linear barriers, like Hadrian's wall in Britain, or the so-called *fossatum* in north Africa, which, for the most part, consisted of a low wall and a ditch. It is unlikely, however, that the frontiers were intended to serve a strictly defensive purpose, or that the Romans ever considered them to be lines of defense. The location and discontinuous nature of the *fossatum*, for example, indicate that it was designed to control and to channel movement across the frontier, not to prevent it. In fact, it could be argued that the purpose of the frontier-fortifications was as much administrative as military – to enable the authorities to control trade, collect customs duties, and check smuggling.

It seems now to be generally agreed that the army also played an important role in the social and economic development of the frontier zones. For one thing, it acted as an agent of social mobility, by providing young indigenous males with the opportunity to acquire prestige and influence through military service. We might imagine that the army's presence served to enrich the local craftsmen who produced goods that the soldiers wanted. It can also be expected to have increased demand for local agricultural products (by how much it is hard to say), and to have stimulated the development of long-distance trade, in so far as soldiers with cash to spend will have created new and ready markets for goods that could not be produced locally. It is sometimes supposed that the army acted also as an instrument of Romanization in the provinces, through its building programmes, for example, or by establishing veteran colonies. It is likely enough, I suppose, that the army disseminated some Roman ideas and practices in some parts of the empire (though probably not as a matter of policy). It might also be remarked, however, that the frontier army appears to have built mainly for itself. And there is no evidence of any kind to show that it acted as a bridge between the occupying and indigenous populations.

The army of the second century AD was not changed in any really significant way until the time of Gallienus (AD 253–68), who created a substantial cavalry corps and a large, mobile field army, which was positioned behind the frontier-lines, and which was meant to act as a rapid intervention force against large-scale invasion. The army was reformed again by Diocletian, who built an extensive system of defensive works and fortresses on the frontiers, and increased the strength of the stationary frontier armies, apparently at the expense of the field army (*comitatus*), which was later restored by Constantine. Volunteers continued to make up the majority of recruits; many, it seems, were soldiers' sons, who are frequently recorded as having been "born in the camps." By the end of the fourth century AD, a significant proportion of recruits were drawn from the so-called "federated" tribes, like the Goths, who were loosely bound to Rome by treaties.

39   VEGETIUS, *EPITOME OF MILITARY SCIENCE*

Little is known about either the life or career of Publius Flavius Vegetius Renatus. A Christian, and a prominent horse-breeder, who lived probably in Spain or in Gaul, he appears also to have been a high-ranking member of the imperial bureaucracy. Besides the *Epitome of Military Science*, we possess also his *Digest of the Art of Caring for the Diseases of Mules*, a veterinary work on the ailments of horses and cattle.

The *Epitome of Military Science* was written sometime between AD 383 and 450, possibly for the emperor Theodosius I or for Valentinian III. It was intended to remedy what Vegetius considered to be contemporary failings in military recruitment, training, strategy, arms, and equipment. It borrows heavily from earlier treatises on military science, including a now lost work by Cato the Elder. The following selections are taken from Book 1, which deals mainly with the recruitment and training of legionaries. The translation is from N. P. Milner, *Vegetius: Epitome of Military Science*, 2nd edn (Liverpool, 1996), pp. 4–13, 18, 25–6.

(1.3) *Whether recruits from the country or from the city are more useful.*

The next question is to consider whether a recruit from the country or from the city is more useful. On this subject, I think it could never have been doubted that the rural populace is better suited for arms. They are nurtured under the open sky in a life of work, enduring the sun, careless of shade, unacquainted with bathhouses, ignorant of luxury, simple-souled, content with a little, with limbs toughened to endure every kind of toil, and for whom wielding iron, digging a fosse, and carrying a burden is what they are used to from the country. . . .

(1.4) *At what age recruits should be approved.*[2]

Next let us examine at what age it is appropriate to levy soldiers. Indeed, if ancient custom is to be retained, everyone knows that those entering puberty should be brought to the levy. For those things are taught not only more quickly but even more completely which are learned from boyhood. Secondly, military alacrity, jumping, and running should be attempted before the body stiffens with age. For it is speed which, with training, makes a brave warrior. Adolescents are the ones to recruit, just as Sallust says: "Directly as soon as youth was able to endure war, it learned military practice in camp through labor."[3]

(1.6) *That the potentially better recruits are recognized at selection from the face and physical posture.*

He who is charged with carrying out the levy procedure should take great pains to choose those able to fill the part of soldiers from the face, from the eyes, from the whole conformation of the limbs. For quality is indicated not only in men, but even in horses and dogs, by many points. . . . So let the adolescent who is to be selected for martial activity have alert eyes, straight neck, broad chest, muscular shoulders, strong arms, long fingers; let him be small in the stomach, slender in the buttocks, and have calves and feet that are not swollen by surplus fat, but firm with hard muscle. When you see these points in a recruit, you need not greatly regret the absence of tall stature. It is more useful that soldiers be strong than big.

(1.7) *Of what trades recruits should be selected or rejected.*

The next matter is for us to examine from what crafts soldiers should be selected or rejected utterly. Fishermen, fowlers, pastry-cooks, weavers, and all who shall seem to have dealt in anything pertaining to textile-mills should, in my view, be banned far from camp. Masons, blacksmiths, wainwrights, butchers and stag- and boar-hunters may usefully be joined to the military. . . .

(1.8) *When recruits should be marked.*

The recruit should not be tattooed with the pin-pricks of the official mark as soon as he has been selected, but first be thoroughly tested in exercises so that it may be established whether he is truly fitted for so much effort. Both mobility and strength are thought to be required of him, and whether he is able to learn the discipline of arms, whether he has the self-confidence of a soldier. For very many, though they seem not unacceptable in appearance, are yet found unsuit- able in training. Therefore, the less useful ones should be rejected, and in their place the most energetic should be substituted. For in any conflict it is not so much numbers as bravery that pays off. So once the recruits have been tattooed, the science of arms should be shown them in daily training. . . .

(1.9) *Recruits should be trained in the military step, in running, and in jumping.*

So, at the very start of the training, recruits should be taught the military step. For nothing should be maintained more on the march or in battle than that all soldiers should keep ranks as they move. The only way that this can be done is by learning through constant training to maneuver quickly and evenly. For a divided and disordered army experiences danger from the enemy which is al- ways most serious. So at the military step, twenty miles[4] should be covered in five hours, at least in summer time. At the full step, which is faster, twenty-four miles[5] should be covered in the same time. If you add anything to this, it now becomes running, for which a distance cannot be defined. . . . The soldier should also be trained at jumping, whereby ditches are vaulted, and hurdles of a certain height surmounted, so that when obstacles of this kind are encountered, he can cross them without effort. Furthermore, in actual conflict and clash of arms, the soldier coming on by a running jump makes the adversary's eyes flinch, fright- ens his mind, and plants a blow before the other can properly prepare himself . . . .

(1.10) *Recruits should be trained in the art of swimming.*

Every recruit without exception should, in the summer months, learn the art of swimming, for rivers are not always crossed by bridges, and armies both when advancing and retreating are frequently forced to swim. Torrents often tend to flood after sudden falls of rain or snow, and ignorance of swimming incurs risk not only from the enemy but the water also. Therefore, the ancient Romans, who were trained in the whole art of warfare through so many wars and continual crises, selected the Campus Martius[6] next to the Tiber in which the youth might wash off sweat and dust after training in arms, and lose their fatigue from running in the exercise of swimming. . . .

(1.11) *How the ancients trained recruits with wicker shields and with posts.*

The ancients, as one finds in books, trained recruits in this manner. They wove shields from withies, of hurdle-like construction, and circular, such that the hurdle had twice the weight that a government shield normally has. They also gave recruits wooden foils, likewise of double weight, instead of swords. So equipped, they were trained not only in the morning but even after noon against posts. Indeed, the use of posts is of very great benefit to gladiators as well as soldiers. Neither the arena nor the [practice]-field ever proved a man invincible in armed combat, unless he was judged to have been thoroughly trained at the post. Each recruit would plant a single post in the ground so that it could not move, and protruded six feet. Against the post, as if against an adversary, the recruit trained himself using the foil and hurdle like a sword and shield, so that now he aimed at, as it were, the head and face, now threatened the flanks, then tried to cut the hamstrings and legs, backed off, came on, sprang, and aimed at the post with every method of attack and art of combat, as though it were an actual opponent. In this training, care was taken that the recruit drew himself up to inflict wounds without exposing any part of himself to a blow.

(1.19) *Recruits should be trained in carrying a burden.*

Recruits should very frequently be made to carry a burden of up to sixty pounds,[7] and route-march at the military step, since on arduous campaigns they have necessarily to carry their rations together with their arms. This should not be thought hard, once the habit has been gained, for there is nothing that continual practice does not render very easy. We know that the ancient soldiers used to do this exercise from the evidence of Vergil himself, who says: "Just as the bold Roman in his national arms cruelly laden takes the road, and before the enemy expects it, stands in formation, having pitched camp."[8]

(1.26) *How recruits are trained to keep ranks and intervals in the line.*

. . . . Recruits should be led out constantly to the exercise-field and drawn up in line following the order of the roll, in such a way that, at first, the line should be single and extended, having no bends or curvatures, and there should be an equal and regular space between soldier and soldier. Then the command should be given that they at once double the line, so that in an actual assault that arrangement to which they are used to conform may be preserved. Thirdly, the command should be given suddenly to adopt a square formation, and after this the line itself should be changed to triangular formation, which they call a "wedge." This formation is usually of great advantage in battle. Next, they are commanded to form circles, which is the formation commonly adopted by trained soldiers to resist a hostile force that has breached the line, to prevent the whole army being turned to flight and grave peril ensuing. If recruits learn these maneuvers by continual practice, they will observe them more easily in actual battle.

40   POLYBIUS, *HISTORIES*

On Polybius, see the introduction to selection 26. The following passages, taken from Book 6 of his *Histories*, describe the Roman army around the middle of the second century BC. A legion consisted of sixty centuries, each of which comprised about eighty men. It was commanded by a *legatus*, who was of senatorial rank, and who was assisted by junior officers called military tribunes. The translation is from I. Scott-Kilvert, *Polybius: The Rise of the Roman Empire* (Harmondsworth, 1979), pp. 318–22, 324–8, 333–5.

(6.19) After they have elected the consuls, they proceed to appoint military tribunes; fourteen are drawn from those who have seen five years' service, and ten from those who have seen ten. As for the rest, a cavalryman is required to complete ten years' service and an infantryman sixteen before he reaches the age of forty-six, except for those rated at less than 400 *drachmae*[9] worth of property, who are assigned to naval service. In periods of national emergency, the infantry are called upon to serve for twenty years, and no one is permitted to hold any political office until he has completed ten years' service. When the consuls are about to enroll soldiers, they announce at a meeting of the popular assembly the day on which all Roman citizens of military age[10] must report for service, and this is done every year. On the appointed day, when those who are liable for service have arrived in Rome and assembled on the Capitoline hill, the fourteen junior military tribunes divide themselves into four groups, according to the order in which they have been appointed by the people or the consuls; this is because the main and original division of the Roman forces is into four legions.

(6.21) When the enrolment has been carried out in this fashion, the ones who have been assigned to this duty then parade the conscripts, and each of them selects from the whole body one man whom they consider the most suitable; he is then ordered to take the oath that he will obey his officers and carry out their commands to the best of his ability. Then the rest of the conscripts come forward, and each swears that he will do the same as the first man. At the same time, the consuls send out orders to the magistrates of the allied cities in Italy from which they wish to raise troops, stating the numbers required, and the day and the place at which the men selected for service must appear. The authorities then choose the men and administer the oath by means of a similar procedure, appoint a commanding officer and a paymaster, and dispatch the contingent to Rome.

After the conscripts have been sworn in, the military tribunes at Rome announce for each legion a day and a place for the men to present themselves without arms, and then dismiss them. When they report on the given date, the youngest and those with the lowest property qualification are posted to the *velites*,[11] the next group to the *hastati*,[12] those in the prime of life to the *principes*,[13] and the oldest to the *triarii*.[14] These are the names used by the Romans for the four classes in each legion which are distinguished from one another both in age and in equipment. They are divided so that the senior, the *triarii*, number 600, the *principes* 1,200, and the *hastati* 1,200, the remainder being made up of *velites*. If the strength of the legion exceeds 4,000, the numbers of each of these classes are increased in proportion, except for the *triarii*, whose strength remains constant at 600.

(6.22) The youngest soldiers, the *velites*, are ordered to carry a sword, javelins, and a target. This last is circular, three feet in diameter, strongly made and large enough to protect a man. They also wear a plain helmet,[15] which is sometimes covered with a piece of wolf's skin or something similar, which serves both to protect and to identify the soldier; this enables the officers to recognize the man and to observe whether or not he shows courage in the face of danger. The wooden shaft of the javelins which they carry is about three feet in length and a finger's breadth in diameter. The head is a span[16] in length, and is hammered out thin and so finely sharpened that it is inevitably bent at the first impact, thus making it useless for the enemy to hurl back; otherwise the weapon would be equally serviceable for both sides.

(6.23) The next age group, known as the *hastati*, are ordered to wear a complete panoply. The Roman panoply consists in the first place of a long shield (*scutum*). The surface is convex; it measures two and a half feet in width and four in length, and the thickness at the rim is a palm's breadth. It consists of two layers of wood fastened together with bull's hide glue; the outer surface is then covered first with canvas and then with calf-skin. The upper and lower edges are bound with iron to protect the shield both from the cutting strokes of swords and from wear when resting on the ground. In the center is fixed an iron boss, which turns aside the heavy impact of stones, pikes, and weighty missiles in general. Besides the shield, they also carry a sword, which is worn on the right thigh and is called a Spanish sword. This has a sharp point, and can deal an effective blow with either edge, as the blade is very strong and unbending.

In addition, the *hastati* carry two throwing spears (*pila*), a bronze helmet, and greaves. The spears are of two kinds, the slender and the thick. Of the thicker kind, some are round and a palm's breadth in diameter; others are a palm square. The slender spears which they carry, as well as the thicker variety, are like medium-sized hunting spears, the length of the wooden shaft being about four and a half feet. The iron head is barbed, and is of the same length as the shaft. They take great pains to ensure the utility of this weapon by attaching the iron firmly to the shaft. It is fastened into the wooden shaft half-way up its length, and riveted with a series of clasps, so that in action it will break rather than come loose, although its thickness at the socket where it meets the wood measures only a finger and a half. Finally, the *hastati* wear as an ornament a plume of three purple or black feathers standing upright about a foot and a half in height. These are placed on the helmet, and the general effect, combined with the rest of the armor, is to make each man look about twice his real height, and gives him an appearance which strikes terror into the enemy. Besides this armament, the private soldiers also wear a brass breast-plate a span square, which is placed in front of the heart, and called a heart-protector (*pectorale*). This item completes their panoply, but those who are rated at a property qualification of above 10,000 *drachmae* wear instead a coat of chain-mail (*lorica*). The *principes* and *triarii* are armed with the same weapons, except that instead of the throwing-spear, the *triarii* carry long thrusting-spears (*hastae*).

(6.24) The *principes*, *hastati*, and *triarii* each elect ten centurions according to merit, and then a second ten. All these have the title of centurion, and the first man elected is a member of the military council. The centurions in their turn appoint an equal number of rear-rank officers (*optiones*). Together with the centurions, these officers then divide each of the classes into ten companies, leaving out the *velites*, each company being allotted two centurions and two *optiones*. The *velites* are then divided into equal groups among all the companies, 120 of them to each company. These companies are known as orders (*ordines*), maniples (*manipuli*),[17] or standards (*signa*), and their officers as centurions (*ordinum ductores*). These officers then choose from the ranks two of their bravest and most soldierly men to be the standard-bearers (*signiferi*)[18] for each maniple. . . . When both centurions are present, the senior commands the right half of the maniple and the junior the left; otherwise the one who is present commands the whole. In choosing their centurions, the Romans look not so much for the daring or fire-eating type, but rather for men who are natural leaders and possess a stable and imperturbable temperament, not men who will open the battle and launch attacks, but those who will stand their ground even when worsted or hard-pressed, and will die in defense of their posts.

(6.38) If it ever happens that a large body of men break and run, . . . and whole maniples desert their posts under extreme pressure, the officers reject the idea of beating to death or executing all who are guilty, but the solution they adopt is as effective as it is terrifying. The tribune calls the legion on parade and brings to the front those who are guilty of having left the ranks. He then reprimands them sharply, and finally chooses by lot some five or eight or twenty of the offenders, the number being calculated so that it represents about a tenth of those who have shown themselves guilty of cowardice. Those on whom the lot has fallen are mercilessly clubbed to death. . . . The rest are put on rations of barley instead of wheat, and are ordered to quarter themselves outside the camp in a place which has no defenses. The danger and the fear of drawing the fatal lot threatens every man equally, and since there is no certainty on whom it may fall, and the public disgrace of receiving rations of barley is shared by all alike, the Romans have adopted the best possible practice both to inspire terror and to repair the harm done by any weakening of their warlike spirit.

(6.39) The Romans also have an excellent method of encouraging young soldiers to face danger. Whenever any have especially distinguished themselves in a battle, the general assembles the troops and calls forward those he considers to have shown exceptional courage. He praises them first for their gallantry in action and for anything in their previous conduct which is particularly worthy of

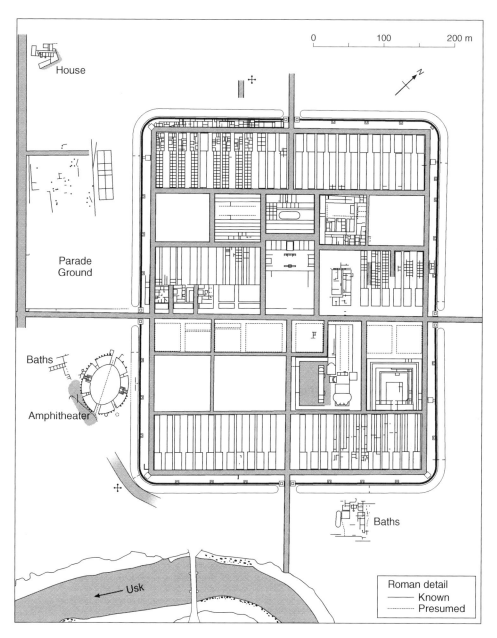

FIGURE 7.1 *Plan of the legionary fortress at Caerleon (Roman* Isca
Silurum*), Wales (from G. Webster,* The Roman Imperial Army of the First
and Second Centuries AD, *3rd edn, Totowa, NJ, 1985).*

The following labels appear on the plan:

House

0   100   200 m

N

Parade
Ground

Baths

Amphitheater

Baths

Usk

Roman detail
——— Known
·········· Presumed

mention, and then he distributes gifts such as the following: to a man who has wounded one of the enemy, a spear; to one who has killed and stripped an enemy, a cup if he is in the infantry, or horse-trappings if in the cavalry – originally the gift was simply a lance. These presentations are not made to men who have wounded or stripped an enemy in the course of a pitched battle, or at the storming of a city, but to those who during a skirmish or some similar situation in which there is no necessity to engage in single combat, have voluntarily and deliberately exposed themselves to danger.

At the storming of a city, the first man to scale the wall is awarded a crown of gold. In the same way, those who have shielded and saved one of their fellow-citizens or of the allies are honored with gifts from the consul, and the men whose lives they have preserved present them of their own free will with a crown; if not, they are compelled to do so by the tribunes who judge the case. Moreover, a man who has been saved in this way reveres his rescuer as a father for the rest of his life, and must treat him as if he were a parent. And so, by means of such incentives, even those who stay at home feel the impulse to emulate such achievements in the field no less than those who are present and see and hear what takes place. For the men who receive these trophies not only enjoy great prestige in the army and soon afterwards in their homes, but they are also singled out for precedence in religious processions when they return. On these occasions, nobody is allowed to wear decorations [except] those who have been honored for their bravery by the consuls, and it is the custom to hang up the trophies they have won in the most conspicuous places in their houses, and to regard them as proofs and visible symbols of their valor. So when we consider this people's almost obsessive concern with military rewards and punishments, and the immense importance which they attach to both, it is not surprising that they emerge with brilliant success from every war in which they engage.

For his pay, the infantryman receives two *obols*[19] a day, the centurion twice this amount, and the cavalryman a *drachma*. The infantry receive a ration of wheat equal to about two-thirds of an Attic *medimnus*[20] a month, and the cavalry seven *medimni* of barley and two of wheat. Among the allies, the infantry receive the same, and the cavalry one and one-third *medimni* of wheat and five of barley. These rations are provided free to the allies, but in the case of the Roman troops, the quaestor deducts from their pay the price of the wheat and their clothes, and any additional arms they may need.

41   R. O. Fink, *Roman Military Records on Papyrus,* no. 63

The following document, which was recorded on papyrus, is the strength report of a cohort of soldiers (known as *I Veterana Hispanorum*), which was made up partly of cavalry, and which was stationed at Stobi in Macedonia. The document, which was found in Egypt, dates to AD 105 or 106. The translation is adapted from J. B. Campbell, *The Roman Army, 31 BC–AD 337* (London and New York, 1994), pp. 114–15.

September 16.

[According to ?], the *pridianum*[21] of the first cohort of Spaniards *Veterana*, at Stobi.

[. . . .] Arruntianus, prefect.

[Total of soldiers], December 31 – 546, including six centurions, four decurions;[22] cavalry – 119, including [. . . .] men on double pay, three men on pay and a half, one infantryman on double pay, and [. . . .] men on pay and a half.

Additions after January 1.

. . . .

[Total] – 596, including six centurions, four decurions; cavalry – [. . . .], including two men on double pay, three on pay and a half, [. . . .] infantrymen on pay and a half.

From these there have been lost:

given to the Fleet Flavia Moesica [. . . .], on the orders of Faustinus the legate;[23]
[. . . .] on the orders of Justus the legate, including one cavalryman [. . . .];
sent back to Herennius Saturninus;
transferred to the army of Pannonia;
died by drowning;
killed by bandits, one cavalryman;
killed in battle, [. . . .]
Total lost, including [. . . .]
Restored from the stragglers.

The remainder, net total – [. . . .], including six centurions, four decurions; cavalry – 110 (or more), including two men on double pay, and three on pay and a half, infantrymen on double pay [. . . .], six men on pay and a half.

From these absent:

in Gaul to obtain clothing;
similarly to obtain [grain?];
across the river(?) Erar(?) to obtain horses, including [. . . .] cavalrymen;
at Castra in the garrison, including two cavalrymen;
in Dardania[24] at the mines.
Total absent outside the province, including [. . . .] cavalrymen.

Inside the province:

guards of Fabius Justus the legate, including Carus, decurion [. . . .];

in the office of Latinianus, procurator[25] of the emperor;

at Piroboridava in the garrison;

at Buridava in the detachment;

across the Danube on an expedition, including [. . . .] men on pay and a half,
   twenty-three cavalrymen, two infantrymen on pay and a half;

similarly across (the river) to protect the grain supply;

similarly on a scouting mission with the centurion A[. . .]vinus, [. . . .] cavalrymen;

in [. . . .] at the grain ships, including one(?) decurion;

at headquarters with the clerks;

to the Haemus (mountains) to bring in cattle;

to guard beasts of burden, including [. . . .] men on pay and a half;

similarly on guard duty [. . . .].

Total absent of both types, including one centurion, three decurions; cavalry,
including [. . . .] two infantrymen on pay and a half.

The remainder present, including five centurions, one decurion; cavalry, including [. . . .] men on double pay, one infantryman on double pay, [. . . .] men on pay
and a half.

From these sick, among them [. . . .].

42   ANONYMOUS, ON MILITARY MATTERS

The author of *On Military Matters* is unknown. The work appears to have been written in the
period AD 366–75, perhaps in 368 or 369, probably for the emperors Valens and Valentinian
I. It was intended to provide solutions to what the author considered to be the most pressing
problems of empire, including the currency and the army. The reforms that he proposes include a variety of mechanical contrivances, like the *ascogefyrus* described below in chapter 16.
There is nothing to indicate that the work was read by Valens or Valentinian I (or by any other
emperor).

Preface.

(1) Most sacred emperors: in order that your divine policies might prosper with
divine successes, proposals should be advanced at appropriate times for the
benefit of your commonwealth, always flourishing under the guidance of heaven.
(2) Wherefore, to the extent that my ability allows, I have composed one chapter
in this little book on the subject of public grants, not that that is enough for so
vast a subject, but I hope that, with this evidence of my modest ability placed
first, you may have confidence in the usefulness of what follows. . . . Let no
praise or [reward?][26] be granted to me, since it is more than enough in this section to dodge your indignation at my audacity. (3) But it will be proper for the
head of state to learn of desirable things from a private person, since useful things

sometimes lie hidden from his inquiries. (4) That is why those who have been shown to understand something correctly should occasionally be called upon, for as the best of orators says: "the majority of men turn to that man whom nature has endowed with ability." In this regard, one should always consider what someone thinks more than what he says, for everyone agrees that the usefulness of the arts, which includes the invention of weapons, is advanced, not by those of the highest birth, or immense wealth, or the power that is inherent in public office, or eloquence derived from literary studies, but solely by great intellect (which is the mother of all virtues), based on the good fortune of nature – something, in fact, which we see happen without regard to status. For though the barbarian nations are neither powerful in eloquence nor made illustrious by public honors, nevertheless, with the assistance of nature, they are hardly considered to be strangers to the invention of things. (5) Wherefore, most merciful emperors, who, in your everlasting good fortune, cherish the glory of a good reputation, and hand down to your sons the affection due to the Roman name, deign to consider the useful things which divine providence has placed in my mind.

(6) . . . . I shall describe how, with half the taxes remitted, the provincial farmer can be restored to his former strength; (7) how also, with the exaction of taxes [reduced?], and the affront to our frontiers ended, the settler, with military fortifications erected, might develop uninhabited lands without worry; in what way also the amount of gold and silver might be doubled without hardship to taxpayers, or by what means the soldier might be pleased, with honors piled on him beyond your customary generosity. To these things also, I thought it necessary to add what might be useful in acquiring victories on land and at sea in the exigencies of war. From these, I shall describe a few mechanical inventions, for the sake of alleviating your boredom. I shall demonstrate, therefore, how a very fast type of warship can, because of the brilliance of its design, prevail over ten ships, such that it sinks them by itself without the help of a large crew of men. (8) And a clever thing has been devised for land-engagements, whereby a horse, whether attacking the line to break it, or in pursuit of fleeing troops, is equipped with a device such that, lashing itself, without need of anyone's direction, it inflicts great destruction on the enemy. (9) Also, a new type of bridge, which is not at all burdensome to transport, has been invented to handle the problems associated with crossing rivers. For this bridge, which is essential for rivers and swamps, can be carried by a very small number of men and approximately fifty pack-animals.

(10) With what I have related serving, I think, as an indication of what is to come, I would ask your leave to say that I am, by divine permission, bringing you a great gift, and I assert that, through the providence of your piety, the vigor of your arms and the entire state will be sustained by the above-mentioned remedies. These are certainly not unknown to those closest to your clemency, who are harassed by many other things to which I am a stranger. But because much escapes the attention of those busy men, I, prompted by leisure, and not a complete stranger to the advantages of things, have wanted to gather together from all over what might be of use to your good fortune. But if my speech has, in view of the exigencies of the situation, advocated anything too freely, I think that I should be protected by your forgiveness, since for the sake of fulfilling my promise, I must be given help because of the freedom of inquiry.

1. *On Controlling Public Spending.*

(1) The interests of the treasury always imitate the praise of war and the glory of triumphs, . . . so that extravagant expenditure should not further excite the seeds of war.[27] If the providence of the imperial majesty restrains this expenditure, the shamefulness of war will no longer flourish, but the inadequate resources of the taxpayers will instead be restored. But if immoderate expenditure dissipates what ought to be saved, the great pleasure of wealth will no longer be able to support our needs, as it did in ancient times. . . .

2. *In Which Periods Extravagance or Greed Began.*

(1) In the time of Constantine, extravagant expenditure assigned gold in place of bronze (which before had been considered to be of great value) to petty commercial transactions; but the origin of this greed is thought to have arisen from the following. For when the gold and silver of ancient times and the great quantity of precious stones that had been stored in temples had reached the public, they increased everyone's desire to give and to possess. And although the expenditure of bronze itself – which, as I said, had been stamped with the heads of kings – seemed already enormous and burdensome, nevertheless, from a kind of blindness, there was a more extravagant desire to spend gold, which is considered more precious. (2) Because of this abundance of gold, the private homes of the powerful were full, and their greater splendor contributed to the destruction of the poor, the poorer people, of course, being oppressed by violence. (3) But the poor, afflicted and driven into various criminal enterprises, and losing sight of any respect for the law or feeling of piety, entrusted their revenge to evil arts. For they often inflicted very serious damage on the empire, by destroying fields, by breaking the peace with brigandage, and by stirring up hatreds; and passing through the grades of crime, they supported usurpers, who were brought forth for the glory of your virtue more than they were inspired by audacity. (4) It will, therefore, be required of your care and prudence that you, the best of emperors, limit public expenditure, and look out for the taxpayer, and hand down to posterity the glory of your name. (5) Finally, reflect for a little while on the memory of those happy times, and consider the famous kingdoms of long-ago poverty, which knew how to cultivate the fields and abstain from riches; how their uncorrupted frugality commends them to every age with praise of their honor. Certainly, we call "golden" those times which did not have any gold at all.

3. *Concerning the Fraudulent Practices of the Mint and their Correction.*

(1) Among the intolerable injuries to the state, the debasement of the *solidus*,[28] occasioned by the fraudulent practices of certain persons, harms people in a variety of ways, and cheapens the likeness of the royal majesty, in that it is repudi-

ated through the fault of the Mint. For the fraudulent cunning of the purchaser of the *solidus* and the injurious situation of the seller have together introduced some difficulty into the contracts themselves, so that there is no possibility of business being straightforward. (2) Therefore, the correction of your majesty must be applied in this area also, as in all things, in such a way that the workers of the Mint are brought back from all over, concentrated in a single island, so as to improve the utility of the coinage and of the *solidi*, and forbidden, obviously, to have any association with the neighboring land forever, so that freedom of association, which provides opportunity for fraudulent practices, may not spoil the integrity of the public service. (3) For confidence in the Mint will be maintained intact in that place because of its isolation; nor will there be any room for fraud where there is no opportunity for profit. . . .

4. *Concerning the Corruption of the Provincial Governors.*

(1) Then to these disadvantages, which injure the provinces with the arts of greed, is added also the execrable greed of the provincial governors, which is inimical to the interests of the taxpayers. For these men, despising the reverence owed their office, think that they have been sent into the provinces as merchants, and are all the more burdensome because injustice originates in those from whom a remedy ought to have been expected. And as if their own iniquity were not enough, in ruining things, every single one of them directs tax-collectors of the sort that they exhaust the resources of the taxpayers by various methods of extortion; evidently, they believe that they would be insufficiently distinguished if they alone were committing wrong-doing. For what opportunity afforded by the collection of taxes remains unexploited by the tax-collectors? When do judicial proceedings occur without plunder? The buying of recruits, the purchase of horses and grain, the expenditure intended for walls, are all routine sources of profit for those men, and the pillaging they hope for. But if those who are pure, and jealous of their integrity, were to govern the provinces, there would be no place left anywhere for fraud, and the state would be enriched and strengthened with morality.

5. *On Lessening Military Expenditures.*

(1) Having described, as I intended, the misfortunes of the state, which should properly be removed by imperial measures, let us turn to the enormous expenditures on soldiers, which must be restrained in a not dissimilar way, for this is why the entire system of tax collection is suffering. (2) But in order that the imperial industriousness not grow weary from a mass of such confusion, I shall briefly explain the solution to this problem of such long standing. Someone of the military class, after he has completed a certain number of years of service, and has achieved the benefit of five or more *annonae*,[29] in order that he not burden the state by receiving these any longer, should be honorably discharged and released to enjoy his retirement. By having the next in rank take his place, the entire

company will, at fixed intervals, be relieved of very heavy expenses. (3) But if the subsequent soldiers of the army-colleges, who are summoned to take the place of those retiring, are too numerous, let them also go into retirement with an equally generous bonus, or be assigned to another unit for which soldiers are lacking, in order to supplement its strength. This procedure will not only relieve a state weighed down by its expenses, but will also diminish the worries of the imperial providence. It will also attract more men to military service, who were discouraged by the slowness of promotion. (4) The usefulness of a provision of this kind will augment the population of the provinces with veterans who have been enriched by imperial gifts, and who are still strong enough to cultivate the land. They will live on the frontiers, they will cultivate the places which they recently defended, and having obtained the goal of their labors, they will be taxpayers instead of soldiers. (5) But because full strength is sometimes reduced by the disasters of war or by desertion from military service because of boredom with camp duties, the losses must be made good by some such remedy as this: one hundred or fifty younger men, beyond those included on the rolls, should be trained in weapons and held in readiness, and maintained at a lower rate of pay (seeing as they are new recruits), and, if the situation should require it, substituted for those who have been lost. When these arrangements have been made, the integrity of the army will safely be maintained, and trained reserves will not be lacking to make up losses quickly.

6. *Concerning Machines of War.*

(1) In the first place, it must be recognized that wild nations are pressing against and howling around the Roman empire on all sides, and treacherous barbarism, protected by natural locations, is attacking all along the frontiers. (2) For the above-mentioned nations are generally either covered by forests, or high up in the mountains, or defended by snow; some are nomadic and protected by deserts and excessive sun. There are some that are defended by marshes and rivers and cannot easily be tracked down, and yet they mangle our peace and quiet by unexpected incursions. (3) Nations of this type, therefore, which are protected by such defenses or by city- and fortress-walls, should be attacked by a variety of new military machines. . . .

16. *Description of the Ascogefyrus.*

(1) In case a river barrier should sometimes impede a necessary journey of the army, as often happens, ingenious necessity has devised a very simple and extraordinarily useful remedy for this matter, which is put together in the following way: (2) when calf-skins have been softened by the Arabian process – for they are exceptionally skilled in their preparation, on account of having to draw water from wells with skin-buckets – when these then, as was said, have been carefully stitched together, they become bladders three and a half feet in length, such that, when they have been inflated with air and swell up, they do not swell into a

paunch, but because they are full on both sides, with a kind of equal tension, they produce level surfaces. Their sides are tied together by thongs attached underneath them; and above, there are projecting circles on one side, with hooks hanging down on the other. And when the parts are joined in this way, the whole is unfolded into the form of a bridge. But because of the motion of the current, this machine will be more easily extended to the opposite bank when at an angle to the river. If iron stakes are fixed on each bank, and strong ropes are stretched beneath the skins themselves in the middle to sustain the weight of those walking across them, but above the skins on the edges so as to make them firm, it will provide a ready means of crossing a river in a short period of time by a new and exotic kind of travel-equipment. (3) We should be reminded also that goat-hair mats should be scattered above the joints of the bladders under the feet of those walking across them, so that the slippery leather-work may provide a firm surface for those who step on it. (4) On each bank, however, hand-*ballistae*[30] will have been deployed, in case a band of the enemy should obstruct those constructing the bridge.

20. *On Frontier Fortifications.*

(1) Also among the things that are beneficial to the state is care of the frontier-works surrounding all the borders of the empire, whose safety will be better provided for by a continuous line of forts constructed so that they are at intervals of one mile, with firm walls and very strong towers. Landowners should be made responsible for the construction of these fortifications without public expenditure, of course with guards and sentries stationed in them, so that the peace of the provinces, surrounded by a kind of belt of defenses, may rest unimpaired.

SUGGESTIONS FOR FURTHER READING

There are several good books on the Roman army: E. Birley, *The Roman Army: Papers, 1929–1986* (Amsterdam, 1988); J. B. Campbell, *The Emperor and the Roman Army, 31 BC–AD 235* (New York, 1984); L. Keppie, *The Making of the Roman Army: From Republic to Empire* (Totowa, NJ, 1984); G. Webster, *The Roman Imperial Army of the First and Second Centuries AD*, 3rd edn (Totowa, NJ, 1985). J. B. Campbell, *The Roman Army, 31 BC–AD 337* (London and New York, 1994) is an excellent collection of primary sources.

On patterns of recruitment, see J. C. Mann, *Legionary Recruitment and Veteran Settlement during the Principate*, ed. M. M. Roxan (London, 1983). On the conditions of military service, see especially R. W. Davies, *Service in the Roman Army*, ed. D. Breeze and V. A. Maxfield (New York, 1989); G. R. Watson, *The Roman Soldier* (London, 1969). On soldiers' equipment, H. R. Robinson, *The Armour of Imperial Rome* (New York, 1975). The best introduction to Vegetius is N. P. Milner, *Vegetius: Epitome of Military Science*, 2nd edn (Liverpool, 1996).

On officers, see D. J. Breeze and B. Dobson, *Roman Officers and Frontiers* (Stuttgart, 1993). For the imperial guard, M. Speidel, *Riding for Caesar: The Roman Emperors' Horse Guards* (Cambridge, Mass., 1994). On the origins and organization of the *auxilia*, see D. B. Saddington,

The Development of the Roman Auxiliary Forces from Caesar to Vespasian (49 BC–AD 79) (Harare, 1982). The role of the cavalry is examined in K. R. Dixon and P. Southern, *The Roman Cavalry: From the First to the Third Century AD* (London, 1992). For the navy, C. G. Starr, *The Roman Imperial Navy, 31 BC–AD 324* (Ithaca, NY, 1941).

Discussions of military strategy now start with E. N. Luttwak, *The Grand Strategy of the Roman Empire: From the First Century AD to the Third* (Baltimore, 1976). But see also B. Isaac, *The Limits of Empire: The Roman Army in the East*, rev. edn (Oxford, 1992), on the lack of military planning. On warfare, see A. K. Goldsworthy, *The Roman Army at War, 100 BC–AD 200* (Oxford, 1996), and for the period of the later empire, H. Elton, *Warfare in Roman Europe, AD 350–425* (Oxford, 1996). On the social and economic impact of the army in the later empire, R. MacMullen, *Soldier and Civilian in the Later Roman Empire* (Cambridge, Mass., 1963). For a comprehensive discussion of *On Military Matters*, see E. A. Thompson, *A Roman Reformer and Inventor, Being a New Text of the Treatise De Rebus Bellicis* (Oxford, 1952).

Eight

BEYOND THE FRONTIER

Editor's introduction

In the period that begins with Julius Caesar's conquest of Gaul (which was more or less complete by 52 BC), we are presented with a constantly shifting and almost bewildering array of peoples who were, at one time or another, beyond the Roman frontier. Because the frontier-lines were inherently fluid and unstable – often little more than the forward lines of advance established during military campaigns – it might be unclear even to the Romans whether certain peoples, like the highland tribes of the Middle Atlas mountains in Mauretania Tingitana (now Morocco), were within the empire. In the eyes of Roman writers like Tacitus (selections 44–5, below), those who lived beyond the frontiers were backward and primitive, but at the same time superior, in their very simplicity, to the Romans. The characterization is in some ways reminiscent of the myth of the "noble savage," which for a long time informed, and poisoned, European relations with the indigenous peoples of north America. What little survives to describe those who were beyond the reach of Roman military and political control, and whom the Romans were inclined to call barbarians, is characterized also by an unsophisticated tendency to portray their cultural traits as eternally fixed and unchanging.

We are probably most poorly informed about the peoples who lived beyond (that is, south of) the frontier in north Africa, which in the time of the Severan emperors (AD 193–235), when Roman territorial expansion in the region achieved its fullest expression, coincided more or less with the 150–millimeter isohyet, where the semi-arid lands that can support the dry-farming cultivation of cereals begin to give way to the vast sand dunes of the Sahara. The Romans, it can safely

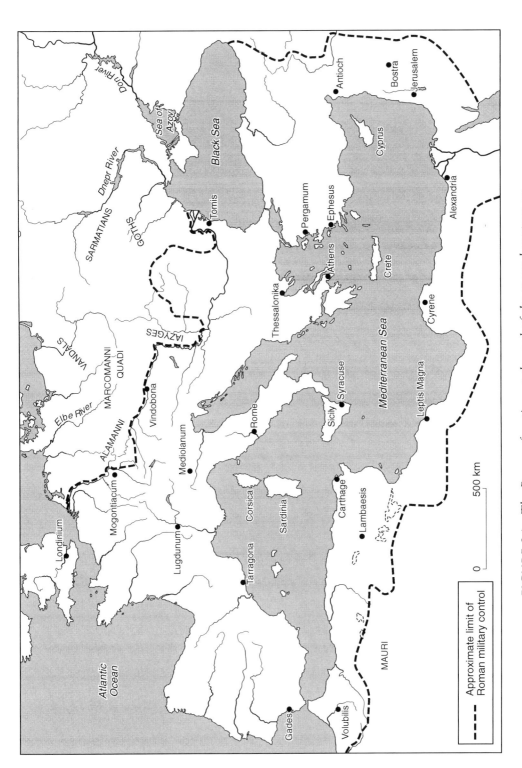

FIGURE 8.1   *The Roman frontiers at the end of the second century* AD.

be said, had very little interest in the desert, or in the semi-nomadic peoples who lived there, and who, because they were not politically united, posed no serious threat to the frontier (at least in the period before about AD 250). There are indications that the desert-based tribes who practiced seasonal transhumance, driving their flocks and herds north in the spring and early summer, occasionally came into conflict with the urbanized inhabitants of the frontier-zone, mostly over access to pasture. Roman policy in the area, as in other parts of the empire, aimed at co-opting indigenous elites, like the leading family of the semi-nomadic Zegrenses, who, according to an inscription recovered at Banasa (about 20 miles north-east of Rabat, Morocco), were given the Roman citizenship in the time of Marcus Aurelius (AD 161–80).

Initially, at least, Roman policy in the East was to create dependent or client kingdoms which could act as a buffer against the Parthians, the only really large and well-organized state on any of Rome's frontiers. Over the course of the first century AD, however, the client kingdoms were gradually absorbed into the system of Roman provincial government, so that by the time of the Flavian emperors (AD 70–96), there were none at all, for example, in Asia Minor. In AD 224, Parthian rule was replaced by the highly centralized government of the Sassanid Persians, who established an empire which stretched from Syria to India, and which lasted until AD 636, when it was overthrown by the Arabs. The Sassanids were generally hostile to Roman interests in the region, especially, it seems, in Armenia, which became a source of almost constant tension between them, and occasionally of conflict. The Romans grudgingly acknowledged the cultural and political sophistication of the Persians. But if Ammianus Marcellinus is any guide (selection 46, below), they were also inclined to portray them as cruel and over-sexed.

We are somewhat better informed about the peoples who lived beyond Rome's European frontier, which, from the early part of the first century AD, came to be fixed, almost by default, along the Rhine and the Danube rivers. What Tacitus called *Germania* extended from the Danube to the North Sea and the Baltic, and from the Rhine as far east as the Vistula river. Until about the early part of the third century AD, the Germans consisted of a great many small and sometimes mutually hostile tribes. Roman policy in the frontier-zone aimed at developing friendly relations with those who lived just beyond it, in the hope that they would supply the Romans with raw materials such as cattle and slaves, and serve as a buffer against the tribes who lay still further to the north and east. For reasons that are not entirely clear, the Germans eventually began to form large confederations, like the Marcomanni, who broke through the Danubian frontier in the second century AD, and the Alamanni, who appeared along the upper Rhine in the early part of the third. It is difficult now to determine whether confederations like the Alamanni possessed any shared traditions, ancestry, or sense of communal identity.[1] By the late third century AD, the Romans had begun to make treaties with some of the Germanic confederations, according to which they were classified as "federates" (*foederati*), and expected to supply troops for the Roman army.

The Germans lived in villages made up mostly of herders and farmers. The basic unit of social organization was the nuclear family, which was ruled by the husband or father. Households were grouped into larger kindred units, which moderns generally call clans, and which seem to have formed the basis for military defense and for the carrying out of feuds. Villages were governed by assemblies of free men under the leadership of chiefs whose position, it seems, was a product mostly of wealth, family influence, and the ability to wage war. Local economies were built primarily on raiding, which was normally directed against neighboring tribes, and on a combination of agriculture and animal husbandry. Status was determined mainly by military prowess and by wealth, which was sometimes measured in cattle.

Of all the peoples who threatened the security of the frontier, the Romans were probably most afraid of the Huns, a confederation of central Asian warriors who shared a nomadic way of life and a common tradition of mounted warfare, and who showed up suddenly in the region of the Black Sea in AD 375. The Huns were held together mostly by the promise of booty, and by annual subsidies – bribes really – which the Roman authorities hoped would deter them from attacking the frontier. Attila (ruled AD 444–53) led two raids against the western empire: the first, in AD 451, was turned back in Gaul at the battle of the Catalaunian plains near modern Troyes; the second, in 452, reached the gates of Rome, where the Huns were bought off by Pope Leo I. After the death of Attila in 453, the confederation of the Huns rapidly disintegrated.

43   CAESAR, *GALLIC WAR* 6.13–23

Julius Caesar (100–44 BC) wrote mainly to defend his actions and policies. Besides his *Civil War*, a transparently partisan record of the events of 49–48 BC, we possess also his *Gallic War*, which narrates his conquest of Gaul in the period 58–52 BC. It is the earliest surviving account of the institutions and customs of the Gauls and Germans. The following passage is taken from Book 6, which describes his military operations in Gaul in 53 BC.

(13) In the whole of Gaul there are two classes of men who are distinguished by their position and rank. For the plebs are treated almost like slaves; they do not dare to do anything on their own; their advice is never taken. Most of them, oppressed either by debt, or by the magnitude of the tribute, or by the wrongdoing of the more powerful men, give themselves in slavery to the nobles, who have all the same rights over them as masters over slaves. But of these two classes, one consists of Druids, the other of knights. The former are involved in divine matters: they arrange public and private sacrifices; they interpret ritual matters; a great number of young men go to them for schooling; and they are greatly honored among the people. For they make decisions about nearly all public and private disputes; and if any crime has been committed, if any murder has been done, if there is any dispute about inheritance or boundaries, the same men adjudicate it. They determine rewards and penalties: if any private person or group of people does not abide by their decision, they ban them from sacrifices. This is their most serious penalty. Those who are banned in this way are considered to

be among the ranks of the impious and the criminal; everyone shuns them, and flees from their approach and conversation, for fear of acquiring some disadvantage from being associated with them; and legal redress is not made available to them when they seek it, and no kind of honor is shared with them. And of all these Druids, one is preeminent, who has the highest authority among them. When he dies, if there is anyone who is preeminent in rank, he succeeds to the position, or if there are several who are of equal rank, they compete for the leadership by the vote of the Druids, sometimes even with weapons. At a certain time of the year, they meet in the territory of the Carnutes,[2] whose land is considered to be the center of all Gaul, and they sit together in a consecrated place. Those who have disputes come there from all over, and they obey the decisions and judgments of the Druids. It is believed that their way of life was discovered in Britain, and transferred from there to Gaul; and today those who want to study it in more detail often travel to Britain to learn it.

(14) The Druids are normally not involved in warfare, and they do not pay tribute like the others; they are excused from military service and exempt from all duties. Tempted by such great rewards, many come together, on their own initiative, to be trained; many are sent by parents and relatives. There they are said to learn a great number of verses. And so some remain in training for twenty years. And they do not think it right to commit these verses to writing, although in nearly all other matters, and in their public and private financial records, they use Greek letters. It seems to me that this has been instituted for two reasons – because they do not want their ways to become widely known, and because those who are learning them would, if they relied on writing, pay less attention to memorization; and, in fact, it does often happen that, with the assistance of writing, they lose their enthusiasm for learning and memorizing. Above all, they want to persuade them of this – that souls do not die, but after death pass from one person to another; and they think that, with the fear of death put aside, this is the greatest incentive to bravery. They also have many discussions about the stars and their motions, about the size of the universe and of the earth, about the nature of things, about the strength and the power of the immortal gods, and they hand this down to the young. (15) The other class consists of the knights. These, when the need arises, and some war happens (and before Caesar's coming, this used to happen nearly every year, in the sense that either they themselves would launch attacks on others or repulse attacks made against them), are all engaged in war; and the more important each of them is in birth and resources, the more dependents and clients he has around him. This is the one kind of influence and power they recognize.

(16) The whole nation of the Gauls is greatly devoted to religious observances, and for that reason, those who are afflicted with more serious illnesses and those who are engaged in the dangers of battle either sacrifice human beings as victims or vow that they will sacrifice them, and they employ the Druids to administer these sacrifices, because they think that, unless a human life is paid for with a human life, the spirit of the immortal gods cannot be placated; and in public life they observe a sacrificial practice of the same kind. Others have images of immense size, whose limbs, woven together out of twigs, they fill with living men; when these have been set on fire on all sides, the men die in the flames. They

think that the execution of those who have been apprehended in the act of theft or robbery or some criminal wrong-doing is more pleasing to the immortal gods; but when the supply of these runs out, they descend to executing even the innocent.

(17) Of the gods, they most worship Mercury. There are a great many images of him; they consider him to be the inventor of all arts, the guide for all roads and journeys, and they think he has the greatest influence on money-making and trade. After him, they worship Apollo, Mars, Jupiter, and Minerva. About them they have nearly the same opinion as other peoples: Apollo drives away diseases, Minerva hands down the foundations of arts and crafts, Jupiter rules the celestial empire, Mars governs war. To Mars, when they have decided to fight a battle, they often dedicate whatever they might capture. After they have won, they sacrifice the living things that they have captured, and collect everything else in one place. In many states, mounds of these things can be seen piled up in consecrated places; nor does it happen often that someone disregards religion and dares to hide the spoils in his house or to remove them from where they have been placed, and the most serious punishment, with torture, is prescribed for such an offense. (18) The Gauls claim that they are all descended from father Dis,[3] and they say that this is passed down by the Druids. For that reason, they measure all periods of time by the number, not of days, but of nights; they observe birthdays and the beginnings of months and years in such a way that day follows night. In other institutions of life, they are different from nearly everyone else in this – that they do not allow their own sons to approach them in public until they have grown to the point where they can undertake the burden of military service, and they consider it disgraceful for a son who is still a boy to stand in the presence of his father in public.

(19) . . . . Men have the power of life and death over their wives, as over their children; and when a *paterfamilias*[4] of distinguished birth has died, his relatives assemble, and if there is anything suspicious about his death, they hold an inquiry about his wives just as they would about his slaves, and if something is discovered, they execute them with fire and all kinds of excruciating tortures. Their funerals, considering the culture of the Gauls, are magnificent and sumptuous. They throw into the fire everything which is thought to have been special to them during their lifetimes, even living things. And only a little before our time, slaves and dependents who were known to have been cherished by them were cremated with them after the funeral rites had been completed. (20) Those states which are judged to conduct their public business more skillfully have it prescribed by law that if anyone has learned anything about the state from his neighbors by rumor or report, he must bring it to a magistrate and not communicate it to anyone else, because it is understood that imprudent and ignorant men are often terrified by false rumors, and are driven to crime and to make decisions about the most important matters. Magistrates conceal whatever they choose, and reveal to the multitude what they judge to be appropriate. It is not permitted to speak about the state, except by means of an assembly.

(21) The Germans have a much different way of life. For they do not have Druids to preside over divine matters; nor are they enthusiastic about sacrifices. They rank among the gods only those whom they see and by whose assistance they are openly helped – the Sun, Vulcan,[5] and Luna;[6] they have learned of the

others not even by report. Their whole life consists of hunting expeditions and military pursuits; from early boyhood they are eager for labor and hardship. Those who remain celibate the longest win the greatest praise among their relatives; some think that this contributes to stature, others that it contributes to strength and muscle. Certainly, they consider it to be among the most disgraceful things to have had knowledge of a woman before the age of twenty; there is no secrecy in this matter, since both sexes bathe in the rivers and wear skins or small cloaks of reindeer hide, leaving a great part of the body naked.

(22) They have no enthusiasm for agriculture, and the greater part of their food consists of milk, cheese, and meat. No one has a definite amount of land or his own estate, but every year the magistrates and leading men assign land, in an amount and location that seems best to them, to peoples and clans who have assembled together, and they force them to move somewhere else after a year. They cite many reasons for this practice – the fear that, tempted by continuous habit, they might substitute agriculture for their enthusiasm for conducting war; that they might become eager to acquire large estates, with the result that the more powerful would drive the more humble from their holdings; that they might build with greater care to avoid the cold and the heat; that some desire for money might develop, from which factions and quarrels would arise; that they might keep the common people content, when each of them sees that his own wealth is equal to that of the most powerful.

(23) The greatest distinction for states is to have empty areas around them as wide as possible by devastating their borders. They consider it to be a particular mark of bravery when their neighbors are forced to withdraw from their lands, and no one dares to settle nearby; at the same time, they think they will be safer because of this, with the fear of sudden incursion removed. When a state makes war or resists one made against it, magistrates are chosen to preside over the war, with the power of life and death. In time of peace, there is no general magistrate, but the leading men of the regions and districts administer justice among their people and settle disputes. Brigandage committed outside the borders of each state is not considered to be disgraceful, and they claim that it is done to exercise the young men and to lessen indolence. And when any of the leading men has said at an assembly that he will be a commander – "Let those who want to follow, declare it" – those who approve of both the cause and the man rise up together for him, and promise their own help, and are praised by the multitude. Any of these who have not followed are reckoned to be deserters and traitors, and afterwards trust is denied to them in everything. They think it wrong to injure a guest; those who have come to them for any reason they protect from harm, and treat as sacred, and the homes of all are open to them, and food is shared with them.

44   TACITUS, *AGRICOLA*

On Tacitus, see the introduction to selection 29. The two passages below are taken from his biography of Gnaeus Julius Agricola, who was Tacitus' father-in-law, and governor of Britain,

AD 78–84. The second (chapters 29–30), which is set in AD 83–4, includes a speech that he puts in the mouth of a Caledonian chieftain named Calgacus.

(10) The location and peoples of Britain have been recorded by many writers: I shall describe them, not for the purpose of comparing accuracy or talent, but because it was at that time[7] that it was first completely tamed; so where earlier writers relied on their eloquence to embellish what was not yet well-known, I shall provide a faithful account of the facts. Britain is the largest of the islands known to the Romans. In respect to its size and location, it extends toward Germany in the east, Spain in the west; on the south, it can actually be seen from Gaul; its northern parts, with no land opposite them, are beaten by the vast and empty sea. Livy and Fabius Rusticus, the most eloquent of ancient and recent authors respectively, have compared the shape of Britain as a whole to a rather long shoulder-blade or to a double-edged axe. And this is its appearance as far as Caledonia,[8] as a result of which the notion has been extended to the whole of it; but when you cross into Caledonia, a vast and irregular zone of land running ahead to the farthest shore is eventually shaped into a kind of wedge. At that time a Roman fleet first sailed around this coast of the farthest sea, and confirmed that Britain is an island, and it discovered and conquered islands which had been unknown until that time, and which they call the Orcades.[9] Thule[10] also was observed, because they had been instructed to go only that far, and winter was approaching. But they reported that the sea was sluggish, and heavy for the oarsmen, and not even raised by the wind – I imagine because land and mountain, the cause and origin of storms, are relatively rare, and because the deep mass of continuous water is slower to be set in motion. It is beyond the scope of this work to investigate the nature and the motions of Ocean, and many have reported on them; I would add one thing – that nowhere is the sea as powerful across as wide an area; there are many currents moving in all directions; nor do the tides extend only to the shore and then recede, but flow far into the land and cover it, and even creep into the hills and mountains, as if in their own environment.

(11) As for the rest, which people first inhabited Britain, and whether they were indigenous or immigrants, have barely been investigated, as one might expect among barbarians. There are various body-types, from which various inferences are made. Certainly, the red hair and large limbs of the inhabitants of Caledonia testify to their Germanic origin; the swarthy faces and generally curly hair of the Silures,[11] and the fact that Spain is situated opposite, indicate that Iberians long ago crossed over and occupied these districts; and those who are nearest to the Gauls are similar to them, either because of the lasting influence of a common origin, or because, with their lands projecting in opposite directions towards each other, the nature of the climate has given their bodies a certain appearance. But on the whole, it is believable that the Gauls occupied the neighboring island. You would observe Gallic rites and religious beliefs; their language is not much different; there is the same recklessness in searching out danger, and, when it has come, the same terror in fleeing it. But the Britons display more courage, since they have not yet been softened by many years of peace. For we hear that the Gauls also used to flourish in war; then laziness crept in with peace,

and courage and liberty were lost together. This has happened to those of the Britons who were conquered long ago; the rest remain as the Gauls once were.

(12) Their strength is in infantry; some tribes also fight from chariots. To be a chariot-driver is more honorable; dependents do the fighting. At one time the people were ruled by kings; now they are torn apart by the factions and ambitions of their leaders. Nor is there anything more useful for us against the stronger tribes than that they have no common purpose. Rarely do two or three states cooperate to repulse a common danger: so they fight individually and are all conquered. The sky is darkened by constant rain and clouds; bitter cold is absent. The length of the days is beyond the measure of our world; the night is clear and, in the farthest part of Britain, brief, such that you would notice very little difference between the end and the beginning of daylight. And they say that if there are no clouds in the way, the light of the sun can be seen throughout the night; nor does it set and then rise again, but passes across. Evidently, the flat and farthest parts of the earth, with their low shadows, do not raise up the darkness, and night does not fall within the sky and the stars.

The soil supports crops, except for the olive, and the vine, and the other things that are customarily grown in warmer lands, and is fertile for cattle; they ripen slowly, but sprout quickly, in each case for the same reason – that there is a lot of moisture in the ground and the sky. Britain produces gold and silver and other metals – the price of conquest. And the Ocean produces pearls, but ones that are somewhat cloudy and lead-colored. Some think that those who harvest them lack skill, for in the Red Sea they are torn alive and still breathing from their shells; in Britain they are gathered only when they have been thrown up on shore; for my part, I could more easily believe that quality was lacking in the pearls than that greed was lacking in us.

(29) The Britons, not at all broken by the outcome of the previous battle, . . . and having learned at last that a common danger must be resisted by cooperation, had called up the forces of all their states by means of envoys and treaties . . . . Pre-eminent among the many generals in courage and in birth was one named Calgacus. To the multitude that had assembled and was demanding battle, he is reported to have spoken in the following way: (30) "Whenever I consider the causes of this war and our circumstances, I have great hopes that this very day and this unity of yours will be the beginning of liberty for the whole of Britain. For you have come together still untouched by slavery; there is no land beyond, and not even the sea is secure, with the Roman fleet threatening us. So battle and arms, honorable for the brave, are at the same time safest for the cowardly. Earlier battles, which were fought with varying success against the Romans, put hope of assistance in our hands, because we, the noblest men in all of Britain, the inhabitants of its inner shrine, not seeing any shores of slavery, kept our very eyes inviolate from the desecration of tyranny. Remoteness itself, and the obscurity of our reputation, have, up until this day, defended us, the last outpost of land and of liberty. Now the end of Britain is exposed, and everything that is unknown is magnified: but there are no more tribes now, nothing except waves and rocks, and the more deadly Romans, whose arrogance you cannot escape through obedience and self-restraint. Plunderers of the world, after they have run out of earth

to devastate, they now search the sea: if their enemy is wealthy, they are greedy; if he is poor, they are ambitious; not the East, not the West, has satiated them; alone of all men they covet riches and poverty with equal passion. To plunder, to butcher, to steal – to these they give the false name of empire, and where they create desolation, they call it peace."

45   TACITUS, *GERMANIA*

On Tacitus, see the introduction to selection 29. The *Germania* was published probably in AD 98. Its sometimes idealized description of the customs and institutions of the Germanic tribes was intended, at least in part, to illustrate what Tacitus considered to be the moral degeneration of the Romans. A good deal of what it reports he is likely to have learned second-hand, from earlier writers like Pliny the Elder, or from observations made by merchants and soldiers.

(2) I should believe that the Germans themselves are indigenous and barely intermingled with immigrants and visitors from other races, because in the past, those who sought to change their homes were transported, not over land, but by fleets, and the immense Ocean on the far and, as it were, opposite side, is rarely approached by ships from our world. Besides, not to mention the danger of an awful and unknown sea, who would have left Asia or Africa or Italy to search out Germany, misshapen in its geography, harsh in its climate, unpleasant in its culture and appearance, unless it was his fatherland? In their ancient hymns – which is their only type of remembrance and history – they celebrate a god Tuisto, born of the soil. To him they attribute a son, Mannus, the originator of their race, and to Mannus, three sons, its founders; from whose names those nearest the Ocean are called the Ingaevones,[12] in the middle, the Herminones,[13] the rest, the Istaevones.[14] Some, relying on the license that pertains to antiquity, assert that there were more sons of the god, and a greater number of names for the race – Marsi, Gambrivii,[15] Suebi,[16] Vandilii[17] – and that these are the real and ancient names. They also claim that the name "Germany" is a new and recent addition, because those who first crossed the Rhine and expelled the Gauls, and are now known as the Tungri,[18] were then called Germans: so the name of a tribe, not of a race, slowly prevailed, with the result that all were called by the invented name "Germans," at first by the victor,[19] for the sake of intimidation, afterwards also by themselves.

(4) I myself lean towards the opinion of those who think that the peoples of Germany, uncontaminated by intermarriage with other races, are a unique and pure race, similar only to themselves, which is why the appearance also of their bodies, even in such a large number of men, is the same for all: fierce and dark-blue eyes, red hair, bodies that are large and strong only for attacking; they do not have the same endurance for labor and hard work, and are barely able to tolerate thirst and heat; because of their climate and soil, they are accustomed to endure cold and hunger.

(6) Not even iron is abundant, as may be inferred from the nature of their

weapons. They rarely use swords or the longer kind of lance: they carry short spears,[20] in their own language, *frameae*, with a narrow and short iron tip, but so sharp and so useful that they fight with the same weapon, as circumstances demand, either hand-to-hand or from a distance. And even the cavalryman is content with a shield and a *framea*; foot-soldiers also launch missiles, many each, and they hurl them a great distance, naked, or wearing a light cloak. There is no boasting in their dress: their shields are distinguished only by the colors they pick out. Few have breast-plates; barely one or two have helmets of metal or hide. Their horses are conspicuous neither for their appearance nor for their speed. But they are not trained like our horses to run in various directions: they ride them straight ahead or with a single bend to the right, with the whole joined so closely together that no one is left behind. On the whole, they are thought to have more strength in their infantry, and so they fight mixed together, the speed of the infantrymen, whom they select from the entire body of young men and place at the front of the battle-line, being adapted and suited to a cavalry engagement. And their number is fixed: a hundred from each district, and this is what they themselves call them,[21] so that what was at first a number is now a title and an honor. The battle-line is arranged in wedges. To withdraw from a place, provided that you attack again, is considered to be a matter more of tactics than of cowardice. They carry off the bodies of their men even in battles where the outcome is uncertain. To have abandoned a shield is the height of disgrace; anyone disgraced in this way is not allowed to be present at religious ceremonies or to attend an assembly: many who have survived wars have ended their infamy with a noose.

(11) On lesser matters, the leaders consult, on more important issues, the whole of them, but in such a way that even those things which are for the people to decide are first dealt with by the leaders. They assemble, unless something unforeseen and sudden happens, on certain days, when the moon is either new or full, for they believe this is the most auspicious occasion for conducting business. They count, not the number of days, as we do, but of nights. This is how they make arrangements and reach agreements: the night seems to lead in the day. It is a fault of their liberty that they do not assemble all at once or as they have been commanded, but a second and a third day is wasted by their delay in coming together. When it pleases the crowd, they sit down together armed. Silence is demanded by the priests, who thereafter possess also the power of coercion. Then a king or a chief is listened to, in order of their age, birth, distinction in war, and eloquence, relying more on their authority to persuade than on the power to command. If an opinion is displeasing, it is rejected by groans; but if it is pleasing, they bang together their shields: to praise with weapons is the most honorable kind of consent.

(14) . . . . If the state in which they were born becomes sluggish because of a long period of peace and quiet, many of the noble young men voluntarily seek out those tribes which are at the time engaged in some war, because quiet is displeasing to the race, and because they can distinguish themselves more easily among uncertainties, and you cannot maintain a large retinue other than by violence and war, for it is from their leader's generosity that they demand that famous war-horse, and that blood-stained and triumphant spear: banquets and a somewhat rough but lavish equipment serve as their salary. The material for this

munificence comes through war and plunder. You would not so easily persuade them to plow the land and wait for the harvest as to challenge the enemy and earn wounds. Indeed, they think it lazy and indolent to acquire with sweat what you can obtain with blood.

(15) Whenever they are not engaged in wars, they spend much of their time hunting, even more in idleness, devoted to sleep and food, each of the bravest and most war-like doing nothing, having delegated the care of their home, of their household, and of their fields to the women, and the old men, and whoever is weakest in the family: they themselves lounge about, with that strange diversity of temperament, whereby the same men so passionately love laziness and hate quiet. . . .

(16) It is well known that none of the German peoples live in cities, that they do not even allow their houses to touch each other. They live separated and scattered, as spring, or field, or grove appeals to them. They lay out their villages, not in our way, with buildings connected and touching: everyone surrounds his house with an open space, either as a precaution against the accident of fire, or because of ignorance of building. They do not even use stone or tiles; the timber they use for everything is shapeless, and without ornamentation or attractiveness. Certain places they rather carefully cover with earth so pure and glittering that it imitates painting and frescoes. They are also accustomed to dig underground pits, over which they pile up a mass of dung, as a refuge from the winter and a storage-place for crops, because places of this kind mitigate the intensity of the cold, and if an enemy should ever come, the open places are laid waste, but the hidden and buried places are either ignored or escape detection for the very reason that they have to be searched for.

(18) . . . . Marriage there is strict; there is no part of their character you would praise more. For nearly alone among the barbarians, they are content with a single wife, with a few exceptions, who are sought out for additional marriages, not because of lust, but because of their nobility. The wife does not bring a dowry to the husband, but the husband to the wife. The parents and relatives are present, and approve the gifts – gifts sought not for womanly pleasures, nor for the sake of adorning the new bride, but oxen, and a horse and bridle, and a shield, with a spear and sword. . . .

(21) . . . . No other race indulges more lavishly in feasting and hospitality. To bar the door against any human being is considered to be a crime. Everyone receives guests at a well-prepared feast according to his means. When it has come to an end, the man who just now had been the host points out the place of entertainment and comes along. They go to the nearest house uninvited. It doesn't matter; they are received with equal courtesy. . . .

(25) . . . . They employ their slaves not as we do, with duties defined throughout the household: each rules his own house and hearth. The owner demands a certain amount of grain or cattle or clothing, as if from a tenant,[22] and to that extent, the slave is subservient; the owner's wife and children carry out the other duties of the household. To beat a slave and to coerce him with chains and labor is rare: if they are killed, it is not normally for the sake of discipline and severity, but because of impulsiveness and anger, as if they were enemies, except that there is no penalty. . . . To strive for profit and to increase it by

interest are unknown, and so the principle is upheld more than if they had been forbidden.

(45) Beyond the Suiones[23] is another sea, sluggish and almost motionless, by which the earth is circled and enclosed. . . . And the rumor is true that the world reaches only to that point, and no further. Next, therefore, are the tribes of the Aestii, who are washed by the right shore of the Suebic Sea;[24] their customs and appearance are Suebic, their language more like that of Britain. They worship the mother of the gods. As an emblem of the superstition, they wear the figures of wild boars: this takes the place of weapons and of human protection, and renders the worshipper of the goddess calm even among the enemy. They use swords rarely, clubs frequently. Grain and other crops they work at with a patience not in keeping with the customary lethargy of the Germans. But they also search the sea, and alone among the Germans gather amber (which they call *glesum*) in the shallow waters and on the shore itself. Nor have they, being barbarians, inquired into or learned what material or process produces it: indeed, for a long time it actually lay there among the other things tossed up the sea, until our luxurious-ness made it famous. For them, it has no use: it is collected raw and exported unshaped; they are astonished at being paid for it. You may conclude, nonethe-less, that it is the sap of trees, because certain terrestrial and even winged crea-tures are often embedded in it, having been entangled in its liquid form, and then, as the material hardens, trapped. I should imagine, therefore, that, as in the se-cluded places of the East, where frankincense and balsam are exuded, so in the islands and lands of the West there are groves and thickets more fertile than usual, which, wrung out and liquefied by the approaching sun, seep into the nearest sea, and are washed up by the force of storms on the opposite shores. If you test the nature of the sap by setting fire to it, it kindles like a torch and emits an oily and scented flame; afterwards, it dissolves into something like pitch or resin. Next to the Suiones are the tribes of the Sitones.[25] They are similar to them in other respects, different only in this – that the woman is dominant; to such a degree have they degenerated not only from liberty but also from servitude.

(46) This is the end of Suebia. I am uncertain whether to assign the tribes of the Peucini, Venethi,[26] and Fenni[27] to the Germans or Sarmatians,[28] although the Peucini, whom some call the Bastarnae,[29] behave like Germans in their language, way of life, habitation, and house-building. They are all dirty and their leaders are lethargic; because of intermarriage, their appearance is disfigured, somewhat like that of the Sarmatians. The Venethi have adopted many Sarmatian habits; for they commit acts of brigandage all over the forests and mountains that rise between the Peucini and the Fenni. And yet they are more properly included among the Germans, because they have fixed homes, and carry shields, and de-light in using their feet and in running fast, all of which are opposite to the Sarmatians, who live in wagons and on horseback. The Fenni are characterized by astonishing barbarism and disgusting poverty: no arms, no horses, no house-hold; wild plants for their food, skins for their clothing, the ground for their beds; their only hopes are in arrows, which they equip with bone because of the lack of iron. And again, hunting supports the men and women, who accompany the men everywhere, and seek a share of the spoil. Nor is there any protection for their infants against wild animals and rain, except that they are covered by a kind

of fastening of branches – there the young men return; this is the sanctuary of the old. But they think it happier than to mourn over fields, to work on houses, to involve their own and others' fortunes in hope and fear. Unconcerned towards men, unconcerned towards the gods, they have achieved a very difficult thing – that they have no need even for wishes. All the rest beyond is legendary – that the Hellusii and Oxiones have the faces and features of men, the bodies and limbs of wild animals; as something unknown, I shall leave it undecided.

46   AMMIANUS MARCELLINUS, *HISTORY* 23.6.75–84

For Ammianus, see the introduction to selection 33. The following passage, which is taken from Book 23 of his *History*, describes the customs of the Persians, who constituted the most serious threat to the security of the eastern frontier.

(75) Among the many and different peoples, there are varieties also of persons and of places. But to describe their bodily characteristics and their customs in general, they are nearly all slender, somewhat dark or pale with a leaden color, grim-looking, with goats' eyes and eyebrows joined and curved in the shape of a half-circle, not unattractive beards, and long, shaggy hair. Every single one of them, even at banquets and on festival days, is seen wearing a sword, an old Greek custom which, according to the very distinguished author Thucydides, the Athenians were the first to abandon. (76) Most of them are immoderately devoted to sex, and are barely content with a multitude of concubines; they do not engage in sexual relations with boys. Each, according to his wealth, contracts many or a few marriages, as a result of which their affections, scattered across various sexual relationships, are dissipated. They avoid splendid and luxurious banquets like the plague, and most of all, excessive drinking. (77) Nor do they have any fixed hour for eating, except at the king's tables, but each one's belly is, so to speak, his sundial; at its urging, they eat whatever happens to be there, and no one piles on superfluous food after he is satiated. (78) They are exceedingly self-restrained and cautious, so much so that when they happen to march through an enemy's gardens and vineyards, they neither desire nor touch anything, because of fear of poison and magical arts.

(79) In addition to this, a Persian is rarely seen stopping to urinate, or stepping aside to do nature's business; so religiously do they avoid these and other shameful things. (80) But they are so fluid and loose-limbed, flinging themselves about with a rambling gait, that you would think them to be effeminate, although they are very fierce warriors, but more crafty than courageous, fearsome at long range, overflowing with empty words, saying crazy and wild things, boastful, and harsh, and repulsive, equally threatening in adversity and prosperity, crafty, overly proud, cruel, claiming the power of life and death over slaves and the mass of commoners. They peel off the skin of living men, bit by bit or all at once; nor is a servant who waits on them or stands at their table permitted to open his mouth, either to speak or to spit – to such an extent do they bind each person's mouth after the

skins have been spread.[30] (81) They are greatly afraid of the laws, among which those directed against ingrates and deserters are conspicuous for their severity; and some, which provide that, because of a single person's wrong-doing, all his relatives must die, are despicable. (82) And to serve as judges, honest men of proven experience are chosen, who have little need for the advice of others, and for that reason they ridicule our custom, which sometimes places eloquent men, very skilled in public law, behind the backs of the unlearned.[31] But the story that one judge was forced to sit on top of the hide of a judge who had been convicted of injustice[32] is a fiction of antiquity, or, if it was the accepted custom at one time, it has been given up.

(83) As a result of their military training and discipline, and constant maneuvers and exercises with weapons, which I have often described, they are to be feared even by great armies, relying especially on the bravery of their cavalry, in which all the nobles and men of rank train hard. For the foot-soldiers, equipped in the manner of the *murmillones*,[33] obey orders like servants. The crowd of them always brings up the rear, as if doomed to perpetual servitude, never supported by either pay or gifts. And this nation, so bold and so well trained for the dust of Mars, would have brought many more peoples under the yoke, in addition to those whom they thoroughly subdued, if they were not constantly harassed by civil and foreign wars. (84) Most of them are so covered with clothes gleaming with shimmering colors that, although they leave the fronts and sides open to flutter in the breeze, still nothing is to be seen uncovered from their shoes to the top of their heads. After Lydia and Croesus had been conquered,[34] they became accustomed to the use of golden bracelets, and necklaces, and gems, and especially pearls, which they have in abundance.

47 AMMIANUS MARCELLINUS, *HISTORY* 31.2.1–11

For Ammianus, see the introduction to selection 33. The following passage, which is taken from Book 31 of his *History*, describes the customs of the Huns, a nomadic people of central Asia who appeared in eastern Europe around AD 375.

(1) .... The race of the Huns, little known from ancient records, living near the ice-covered ocean beyond the Maeotic Sea,[35] exceeds every degree of savagery. (2) Because the cheeks of the children are deeply furrowed with steel from their very birth, in order that the growth of hair, emerging at the proper time, might be held back by the wrinkled scars, they grow old there without beards and without any beauty, like eunuchs. They all have compact and strong limbs, and thick necks, and are so prodigiously ugly and bowed, that one might think they were two-legged beasts or mistake them for the stumps, roughly fashioned into images, which are used in making the sides of bridges. (3) But though they are in the shape of men, however unattractive, they are so rugged in their way of life that they have no need of either fire or flavorful food, but eat the roots of wild plants and the half-raw flesh of any sort of animal, which, placing between their thighs

and the backs of their horses, they warm up a little. (4) They are never covered by any buildings, but avoid these like tombs set apart from everyday use. For not even a hut roofed with reed can be found among them. But wandering widely across the mountains and woods, they become accustomed from infancy to endure cold, hunger, and thirst. Away from home, they never enter buildings, unless compelled by extreme necessity, for they think that they are not safe when staying under a roof. (5) They wear clothes made of linen cloth or the skins of forest-mice sewn together; nor do they have one set of clothes to wear inside, another for outdoors. But once a faded tunic has been put on their necks, it is not taken off or changed until, falling apart from daily wear and tear, it has been reduced to rags. (6) They cover their heads with round caps, and protect their hairy legs with goat-skins; and because their shoes are not made with any patterns, they prevent them from walking with a free step. For this reason, they are little suited to battles on foot, but they are almost glued to their horses, which are certainly hardy, but ugly; and sometimes, to perform their customary tasks, they sit on them as women do. From their horses, night and day, every person in that nation buys and sells, takes food and drink, and bent over the narrow neck of the animal, relaxes into a sleep deep enough to be accompanied by a variety of dreams.

(7) And when deliberation is proposed about serious matters, they all consult together in that fashion.[36] They are, however, not subject to any royal severity; instead, content with the tumultuous government of their leading men, they break through whatever they encounter. (8) And sometimes they fight when provoked, entering battles in wedge-shaped groups, their combined voices making a savage sound. And because they are lightly equipped for swift movement, and quick to act, they intentionally separate suddenly and attack, and with their irregular battle-line rush about in all directions, with great loss of life; and because of their extraordinary speed, they are never seen attacking a rampart or pillaging an enemy's camp. (9) And for that reason, you would readily say that they are the most terrible of all warriors, because they fight from far away with missiles, which, instead of sharp points on their tips, have sharp bone attached to them with wonderful skill; and riding across the intervening spaces, they fight hand-to-hand with swords, without any concern for themselves; and while the enemy are protecting themselves against wounds from the swords, they tie them up with twisted strips of cloth, in such a way that their opponents' limbs are ensnared, and they lose the ability to ride or walk.

(10) None of them ever plows or touches a plow-handle. For they are all without fixed homes, and without hearth, or law, or settled way of life; they are always roaming from one place to another, like fugitives, with the wagons in which they live, where their wives weave their vile clothing for them, and have sex with their husbands, and give birth, and raise their children to the age of puberty. When asked, none of them can say where he comes from, having been conceived in one place, and born far away, and brought up even farther away. (11) In respect to truces, they are untrustworthy and unreliable, easily bent to every breeze of new hope that develops, sacrificing everything to a momentary impulse. In the manner of unreasoning animals, they are completely ignorant of the difference between right and wrong; they are deceitful and secretive, never bound by any reverence for religion or superstition, burning with an immense

desire for gold, so fickle and easily angered that they often quarrel with their allies several times on the same day, for no particular reason, and are won over in the same way, without anyone to conciliate them.

SUGGESTIONS FOR FURTHER READING

On the Roman frontiers, see C. R. Whittaker, *Frontiers of the Roman Empire: A Social and Economic Study* (Baltimore, 1994); V. A. Maxfield, et al., "The frontiers," in *The Roman World*, ed. J. Wacher (London, 1987), vol. 1, pp. 139–325.

The best introduction to Roman Gaul is J. F. Drinkwater, *Roman Gaul: The Three Provinces, 58 BC–AD 260* (Ithaca, NY, 1983); see also E. M. Wightman, *Gallia Belgica* (Berkeley, 1985), and for the period of the later empire, J. F. Drinkwater, *The Gallic Empire: Separatism and Continuity in the North-western Provinces of the Roman Empire* (Stuttgart, 1987); J. F. Drinkwater and H. Elton (eds), *Fifth-century Gaul: A Crisis of Identity?* (Cambridge, 1992).

On the history of Roman Britain, see S. S. Frere, *Britannia: A History of Roman Britain*, 3rd edn (London, 1987); P. Salway, *Roman Britain* (Oxford, 1981); for the period of the later empire, S. Johnson, *Later Roman Britain* (London, 1980). The archeological record is reviewed in R. G. Collingwood and I. A. Richmond, *The Archaeology of Roman Britain*, rev. edn (London, 1969); M. Todd (ed.), *Research on Roman Britain, 1960–1989* (London, 1989). On Romanization, see M. Millett, *The Romanization of Britain: An Essay in Archaeological Interpretation* (Cambridge, 1990).

On the Germans, see E. A. Thompson, *The Early Germans* (Oxford, 1965); M. Todd, *The Early Germans* (Oxford, 1992), and *The Northern Barbarians, 100 BC–AD 300*, rev. edn (New York, 1987). For the Goths, P. Heather, *Goths and Romans, 332–489* (New York, 1991). On the material culture of the Germans, see now P. S. Wells, *The Barbarians Speak: How the Conquered Peoples Shaped Roman Europe* (Princeton, 1999).

The standard history of the Persians is A. Olmstead, *History of the Persian Empire* (Chicago, 1948). On the Sassanid empire and its relations with Rome, see M. H. Dodgeon and S. N. C. Lieu, *The Roman Eastern Frontier and the Persian Wars (AD 226–363): A Documentary History* (London and New York), 1994. On the Huns, O. Mänchen-Helfen, *The World of the Huns: Studies in their History and Culture*, ed. M. Knight (Berkeley, 1973); E. A. Thompson, *The Huns*, rev. by P. Heather (Oxford, 1996).

Nine

PAGANS AND
CHRISTIANS

Editor's introduction

The Romans believed that their security and prosperity depended on the support
of the gods, which they thought they could win by performing certain rituals, by
making offerings to the gods, for example, or by celebrating annual festivals like
the Lupercalia (described in selection 49). The practice of the state religion centered on sacrifice and divination. Senior magistrates routinely consulted the gods
before taking action or making major decisions. The gods, it was believed, showed
their displeasure by causing plague, famine, or natural disasters like earthquakes
and floods; phenomena that were believed to be indications of divine wrath were
interpreted by professional diviners, and expiated by various, sometimes dire,
procedures.

The earliest gods were generally chthonic deities, mostly of fertility and of
fruitfulness. In the early and middle Republic, other gods and goddesses were
taken over from the Etruscans and from the Greeks, and incorporated into the
state religion. So Ceres, who was imported from Sicily to watch over cereal crops,
was a rather transparent disguise for the Greek goddess Demeter. At an official
level, the adoption of foreign gods ended in 204 BC, during the second Carthaginian

war, when the goddess Cybele (or *Magna Mater*, "Great Mother") was brought to Rome from Asia Minor.

From the beginning of the Republic, the supervision of the state religion was monopolized by the political authorities. The priesthoods, which were said to have been created in the time of the kings, were generally filled by the same men who held political office.[1] Many of the priesthoods were collegial, like the Virgins who were consecrated to the service of Vesta, goddess of fire and of the hearth (see selection 48), the augurs, who specialized in observing the heavens and in interpreting auspices, and the *haruspices*, Etruscan experts in interpreting lightning and the entrails of sacrificial animals.

The traditional practices of the state religion changed hardly at all in the time of the emperors. Probably the most far-reaching innovation was the creation of the imperial cult, which can be traced back to the time of Augustus (27 BC–AD 14), who publicly discouraged its development, but made no real effort to suppress it. In the eastern half of the empire, where there was a long tradition of ruler-worship, the growth of the imperial cult appears to have been the product mostly of local initiative. In the West, the political authorities played a much more active role in its dissemination, largely, it seems, as a way of promoting allegiance to Rome and to the person of the emperor.

The Roman gods came to be worshipped also in the provinces, particularly in the western half of the empire, where the Capitoline triad of Jupiter, Juno, and Minerva is widely attested, especially after the time of the emperor Trajan (AD 98–117). In some places, Roman and native gods were assimilated, in north Africa, for example, where Shadrapa came to be identified with Bacchus, Melkart with Hercules. From the last part of the first century BC, a number of eastern religions (which moderns sometimes call the "mystery cults") gained a following in Italy and in parts of the West. One of the most popular, it appears, was the cult of Isis, an Egyptian goddess of fertility, who was worshipped in secret and emotional rites, and at festivals, where she was honored with music, dancing, and elaborate processions (see selection 52). The Roman elite considered the cult to be disreputable. But in the time of the Flavians (AD 70–96), it acquired the backing even of the emperors. In fact, the only religious custom that the state was not prepared to countenance was human sacrifice. So in Gaul, where it was associated with the Druids, and in north Africa, where it was connected with the worship of Saturn, the practice was suppressed, in part because the Romans considered it to be morally repugnant, probably also as a way to undermine the authority of local religious leaders.

From time to time, the Roman authorities took action also against the Christians, though generally not as a matter of policy, at least until about the middle of the third century AD. It is difficult now to reconstruct the history of the persecutions of the Christians, because the non-Christian sources typically have very little to say about them. The first occurred in Rome in AD 64, after fire had destroyed a large part of the city. Faced with rumors that he had started the fire or ordered it to be set, Nero tried to shift the blame onto the Christian community (see selection 54). The persecution that followed did not result in any general measures against the Christians. About thirty years later, the emperor Domitian executed his cousin, Flavius Clemens, and another man named Acilius Glabrio (consul in

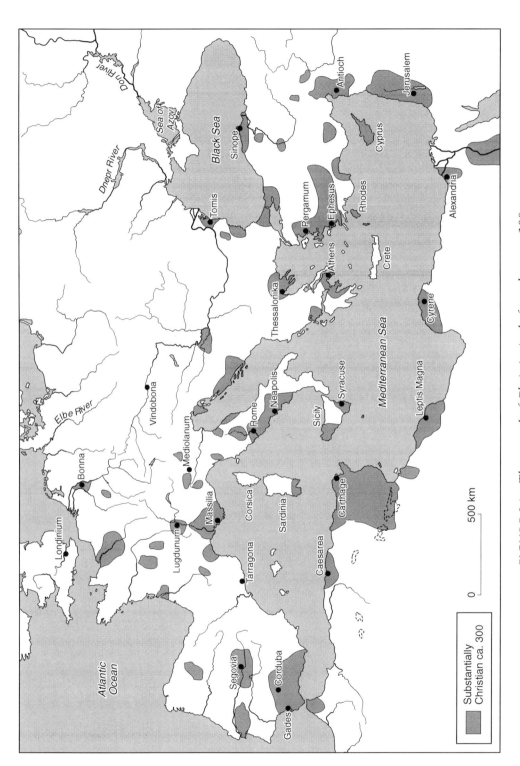

FIGURE 9.1 *The spread of Christianity before about* AD *300.*

Substantially
Christian ca. 300

0   500 km

AD 91), on the grounds that they were "atheists" (Cassius Dio, *History of Rome* 67.14). It is possible, though far from certain, that they were Christians: an early Christian cemetery at Rome was named after Flavius Clemens' wife, Flavia Domitilla; the family of Acilius Glabrio had a crypt in the Christian cemetery of Priscilla.

In AD 111/12, when he was governor of the province of Bithynia-Pontus (in what is now northern Turkey), Pliny the Younger found himself in the position of having to decide what he should do with a number of Christians who had been brought before him. In the end, he ordered some of them to be executed, more, he tells us (selection 55), because of their "stubbornness" and "obstinacy" than because of their beliefs, which he judged to be nothing more than "a depraved and extravagant superstition." Another forty-eight Christians were martyred at Lugdunum (now Lyons, France) in AD 177, on the orders of the governor, and with the approval of the emperor, Marcus Aurelius (see selection 56).

There was still no general law against being a Christian, however. It is reasonably clear also that the persecutions were often instigated, not by the authorities, but by ordinary Romans. For reasons that are not entirely clear, the Christians were generally unpopular. Perhaps because they appeared to be secretive and exclusive, it was often assumed that their ceremonies served merely as a cover for depraved and even criminal conduct (see selection 53). It was widely believed also that their refusal to worship the gods of Rome or to take an oath by the guardian spirit of the emperor was likely to provoke the wrath of the gods, and therefore to harm the community as a whole. And to those who witnessed their sometimes ostentatious defiance of authority, it seemed that the Christians were only too eager to be martyred.

It was not until the time of the emperor Decius (AD 249–51) that the Roman state set out to get rid of Christianity altogether. Perhaps because he believed that the unity of the empire was threatened (though Christians were still a small minority), Decius issued two edicts against them in AD 250: the first ordered the arrest of senior clergy; the second required a general sacrifice to the Roman gods. The Christians were persecuted again under the emperor Valerian, from AD 257 until he was captured by the Persians in 259/60. The last of the persecutions occurred under Diocletian, who is said to have been put up to it by his anti-Christian junior colleague (Caesar), Galerius. In February, AD 303, Diocletian ordered the destruction of churches and Christian writings, and demanded that the clergy sacrifice to the gods. The following spring, he ordered a universal sacrifice (see selection 57). In the western half of the empire, the persecution ended with Diocletian's abdication in AD 305; in the East, it dragged on until 311. Two years later, Constantine, the first Christian emperor, issued the Edict of Milan, which declared that Christianity was to be officially tolerated. By AD 325, when the Council of Nicaea was convened, it had become, for all intents and purposes, the official religion of the empire.

48 DIONYSIUS OF HALICARNASSUS, *ROMAN ANTIQUITIES* 2.67

Dionysius was born at Halicarnassus (mod. Bodrum, Turkey) ca. 60/55 BC (he died sometime after 7). In 30, he moved to Rome, where he became a teacher of rhetoric. The *Roman Antiquities* is an antiquarian and moralizing history of Rome from its foundation to 264 BC. The whole of Books 1–10 and most of 11 (to 446 BC) are extant; the rest survives in fragments.

The following passage discusses the responsibilities of the Vestal Virgins, who were devoted to the service of Vesta, goddess of fire and of the hearth. They were chosen from noble families when they were between six and ten years of age. Their principal duty was to tend the sacred and eternal fire that burned on the altar in the Temple of Vesta at Rome. The translation is from J. Shelton, *As the Romans Did: A Sourcebook in Roman Social History*, 2nd edn (Oxford and New York, 1998), p. 386.

The Virgins who serve the goddess Vesta were originally four in number, and chosen by the king in accordance with the regulations which Numa[2] established. Later, their number was increased to six, because of the multitude of sacred duties which they perform, and it has remained at six up to our own time. They live in the sanctuary of the goddess, which no one can be prevented from entering, if he wishes, during the day. It is forbidden, however, for any man to stay there at night. These priestesses must remain pure and unmarried for thirty years, offering sacrifices and performing other religious rites in accordance with the law. During the first ten years, they must learn these rites; during the second ten, they perform them; and during the remaining ten, they must teach others. When the thirty years have been completed, there is no law which prohibits those who so wish from putting aside the headbands and other insignia of the priestly service and marrying. Only a few, however, do so, and they have, during their remaining years, lives which are neither enviable nor very happy. And therefore, taking the unhappy fates of these few as a warning, the rest of the Virgins remain in service to the goddess until their deaths, at which time another virgin is appointed by the *pontifices*[3] to take the place of the deceased.

The Vestal Virgins receive many fine honors from the city, and do not, therefore, yearn for children or marriage. In any case, the penalties imposed for misbehavior are heavy. According to the law, the *pontifices* are the investigators and the punishers of the misdeeds. They whip with rods those priestesses who have committed some lesser offense, but they sentence those who have lost their virginity to a most shameful and most pitiable death. For while they are still alive, they are carried on a bier in a funeral procession such as that arranged for dead men, and their friends and relatives join the procession and mourn for them. They are taken as far as the Colline Gate,[4] and placed in an underground cell, which has been constructed within the walls of the gate. They are dressed in funeral attire but do not receive a monument or funeral offerings or any other customary rites. There are apparently many clues which indicate that a priestess who is performing holy rites is no longer a virgin, but the principal clue is the extinction of the fire, an occurrence which the Romans fear more than all catastrophes, since they believe that, whatever the cause of the extinction, it is a sign warning of the destruction of the city. They reintroduce fire into the temple with many rites of atonement.

49 PLUTARCH, *LIFE OF ROMULUS* 21.3–5

On Plutarch, see the introduction to selection 2. Romulus was the mythical founder and first king of Rome. The following passage describes the annual festival of the Lupercalia, a purification and fertility rite that was celebrated on February 15. The translation is from J. Shelton, *As the Romans Did: A Sourcebook in Roman Social History*, 2nd edn (Oxford and New York, 1998), p. 382.

The Lupercalia would appear, because of its date, to be a purification ceremony, since it is celebrated on the *dies nefasti*[5] of the month of February, a word which may be interpreted to mean "purifying;" indeed, the day on which this festival occurs used to be called *Februata* a long time ago. However, the name of the festival means the same as the Greek *Lukaia*,[6] and therefore the festival seems very ancient and to have been brought to Italy by the Arcadians under Evander.[7] And this is the widely accepted explanation, for the word can then be derived from the she-wolf of early Roman history.[8] In fact, the *Luperci*[9] begin their run around the city, as we see, at that spot where legend says Romulus was abandoned. However, the procedures at the festival offer no help in determining its origin. Goats are slaughtered. Then two young men of noble birth are brought before the priests. Some of the priests touch the boys' foreheads with the bloody knife; others immediately wipe clean their foreheads with wool soaked in milk. The young men must laugh after their foreheads are wiped. Then they cut the hides of the goats into strips and run through the city, naked except for a loin covering, lashing anyone in their way with the strips of goat-hide. However, women of childbearing age do not avoid the lashings, since they think they aid in fertility, pregnancy, and childbirth. A peculiar feature of this festival is that the *Luperci* also sacrifice a dog.

50 CATO, *ON AGRICULTURE* 139–41

For Cato, see the introduction to selection 2; on his work *On Agriculture*, see selection 20. The following passage describes three agricultural prayers – for thinning a grove, for digging, and for purifying land – and the animal sacrifices that accompanied them. The Romans prayed to the gods, not so much to appease them, but in the expectation that they would thereby win their favor.

(139) To thin a grove according to Roman custom, it is best to do the following. Make an offering of a pig; utter the following words: "If you are a god or a

goddess to whom this is sacred, as it is right to sacrifice a pig to you for the sake of thinning this sacred place, and toward that end, whether it is done by me or by someone acting on my orders, may it be done correctly, and for that purpose, in sacrificing this pig to you, I humbly pray that you will be kind and propitious to me, my house, my household, and my children, and toward that end, accept this pig which I am offering to you."

(140) If you want to dig, make a second offering in the same way; say this in addition: "for the sake of doing the work." As long as the work continues, do it every day on some part of the land. If you miss a day, or if public or household feast-days intervene, make another offering.

(141) To purify land, it is best to do the following. Order the *suovitaurilia*[10] to be led around: "With the gods willing, and that it may turn out well, I enjoin you, Manius,[11] to take care to purify my farm, my land, and my ground with this *suovitaurilia*, in whatever part you think they ought to be led around or carried around." Make a preliminary prayer with wine to Janus and Jupiter; speak in the following way: "Father Mars, I pray and beg you that you be kind and propitious to me, my house, and my household, toward which end I have ordered the *suovitaurilia* to be led around my land, my ground, and my farm, that you keep away, ward off, and remove sickness, seen and unseen, barrenness and destruction, disasters and bad weather; and that you allow my crops, my grain, my vineyards, and my thickets to grow and to turn out well, that you keep safe my shepherds and my cattle, and that you give good health and strength to me, my house, and my household, and for that purpose, for the sake of purifying my farm, my ground, and my land, and of carrying out the purification, as I have said, accept the offering of this suckling *suovitaurilia*; Father Mars, for the same purpose, accept this suckling *suovitaurilia*." And arrange the pile of offering-cakes with the knife, and see to it that the oblation-cake is nearby, then make the offering. When you sacrifice the pig, the lamb, and the calf, it is best to do so in the following way: "For that purpose, accept the offering of the *suovitaurilia*." It is forbidden to name Mars or the lamb and the calf.[12] If not all of the omens are favorable, speak in the following way: "Father Mars, if anything in that suckling *suovitaurilia* has not pleased you, I make atonement with this *suovitaurilia*." If there is doubt about one or two, speak in the following way: "Father Mars, because that pig was not pleasing to you, I make atonement with this pig."

51   AUGUSTINE, *CITY OF GOD* 4.8

Aurelius Augustinus was born at Thagaste (mod. Souk Ahras, Algeria) in AD 354 (he died in 430). He taught rhetoric at Carthage, Rome, and Milan, where he became a Christian. From AD 395, he was bishop of Hippo (mod. Bône, Algeria). His surviving works, which number more than a hundred, include many letters and sermons; the *Confessions*, an account of his life to AD 388, and of his conversion; and the *City of God*, a reply (in twenty-two books) to anti-Christian propaganda, which includes this derisive denunciation of the multiplicity of the pagan gods and of the division of labor that was thought to exist among them.

With the help of which gods the Romans think that their empire was increased and preserved, when they could hardly believe that the safeguarding of individual things should be entrusted to a single god.

Let us ask next, if you please, out of the large crowd of gods the Romans worship, which god or gods they believe was most important in extending and preserving that empire. For in this achievement, so glorious and so full of great distinction, they do not dare to assign any part to Cluacina,[13] or to Volupia, who is named for pleasure (*voluptas*), or to Lubentina, whose name comes from lust (*libido*), or to Vaticanus, who presides over the crying (*vagitus*) of infants, or to Cunina, who supervises their cradles (*cunae*). But how can all the names of the gods and goddesses be recorded in one section of this book, when, dividing up the gods' particular responsibilities for individual things, they were barely able to include them all in huge volumes? Nor did they think that responsibility for the fields should be entrusted to one god, but they assigned farms (*rura*; sing. *rus*) to the goddess Rusina, mountain ridges (*iuga*) to the god Iugatinus, hills (*colles*) to the goddess Collatina, valleys (*valles*) to Vallonia. They were not even able to find a single Segetia such that she could be entrusted once and for all with the grain in the fields, but they wanted to have the goddess Seia in charge of the sown grain, as long as it was under ground, then when it was above ground and producing a crop (*seges*), the goddess Segetia, but when the grain had been harvested and stored away, in order that it might be guarded safely (*tuto*), they put the goddess Tutulina in charge. . . . They put Proserpina in charge of germinating the grain,[14] the god Nodutus in charge of the joints and knots (*nodi*; sing. *nodus*) of the stems, the goddess Volutina in charge of the covers (*involumenti*) of the husks; when the husks open (*patesco*), so that the ears may emerge, the goddess Patelana; when the grain stands level with new ears, because the ancients said *hostire* to mean "to make level," the goddess Hostilina; when the grain was flowering (*floreo*), the goddess Flora; when it was becoming milky (*lactesco*), the god Lacturnus; when it was ripening (*maturesco*), the goddess Matuta; when it was mowed (*runco*), that is, removed from the field, the goddess Runcina. Nor am I recording them all, for what does not embarrass them bores me.

But I have mentioned these very few in order that it might be understood that they in no way dare to say that the Roman empire was established, extended, and preserved by these gods, who were so busy, each with their own duties, that nothing was entirely entrusted to any one of them. So how could Segetia care for the empire, when she was not allowed to look after the grain and the trees at the same time? How could Cunina think about weapons, when her stewardship was not allowed to go beyond the cradles of babies? How could Nodutus help in war, when he was involved, not with the husk of the ear, but only with the knot of the joint? Everyone appoints a single doorkeeper for his house, and because he is a man, that is altogether sufficient: they appoint three gods, Forculus for the doors (*fores*), Cardea for the hinges (*cardines*), Limentinus for the threshold (*limen*). So Forculus was unable to guard both the hinge and the threshold at the same time.

52 APULEIUS, *METAMORPHOSES* 11

Apuleius was born about AD 123 to a wealthy family at Madaurus, north Africa. Educated at Carthage, Athens, and Rome, he became a lawyer, poet, rhetorician, philosopher, and lecturer. His *Metamorphoses* (or *Golden Ass*) is the only Latin novel to have survived intact. It is the story of a young man named Lucius, who, having been turned into an ass, endures a series of strange and amusing adventures until, in the sections of Book 11 translated below, he is restored to human form by the Egyptian goddess Isis and initiated into her cult. The procession described in chapter 8 took place every year at the beginning of the sailing season to honor Isis, who was a goddess both of fertility and of sailing.

(8) Now the prelude to the great procession slowly marched past, everyone beautifully dressed according to his own tastes and desires. One, having strapped on a sword-belt, was playing the role of a soldier; another, wearing a tucked-up cloak, was shown by his boots and spears to be a hunter; another, who twirled as he walked, and who was dressed in gilded slippers, a silk dress, and precious ornaments, with curls fastened to his head, was pretending to be a woman. Still another, distinguished by greaves, shield, helmet, and sword, you would suppose was coming from a gladiatorial school. Not missing either was someone playing at being a magistrate, with *fasces*[15] and a purple toga; and someone with a cloak, a staff, woven shoes, and a goat's beard, pretending to be a philosopher; and two with different kinds of rods, one with bird-lime[16] representing a bird-catcher, the other with hooks representing a fisherman. I also saw a tame bear that was dressed like a matron and carried in a sedan-chair, and a monkey with a Phrygian cloth cap and a saffron-colored dress, looking like the shepherd Ganymede, carrying a golden cup,[17] and an ass with wings glued on it, walking alongside some decrepit old man, so that you would say the latter was Bellerophon[18] and the former Pegasus,[19] but laugh at both.

(9) In the midst of these joyous, crowd-pleasing displays, which wandered all over the place, the special procession of the savior goddess was now beginning. There were women shining with white garments, rejoicing in their different costumes, garlanded with spring wreaths, who scattered flowers from their laps along the path on which the sacred company was proceeding; there were others who held shining mirrors reversed behind their backs to demonstrate reverence to the goddess as she passed, and others who carried ivory combs, and who, by the movement of their arms and bending of their fingers, pretended that they were shaping and combing the royal hair; and other women sprinkled the streets, shaking out drops of pleasant balsam and other perfumes; in addition, a great crowd of both sexes carried lamps, torches, candles, and other sorts of artificial light to honor the source of the celestial stars. After this, a charming orchestra of pipes and flutes played the sweetest of melodies. They were followed by a lovely chorus of carefully chosen youths, brightly shining in their white holiday clothes, repeating a charming song, which a skilled poet had composed and set to music with the help of the Muses, the words of which sometimes referred to the preludes of the "greater vows."[20] Flute-players dedicated to the great Sarapis[21] also

came, with transverse pipes held close to their right ears, repeating the familiar song of the temple and its god; and public heralds who kept warning people to make way for the sacred procession.

(10) Then the crowds of those initiated into the divine rites poured in, men and women of every rank and every age, shining with the pure radiance of their linen garments, the women's hair anointed and wrapped up in a transparent covering, the men's heads shaved and their skulls gleaming brightly – terrestrial stars of the great religion. Together they made a shrill ringing sound with their sistrums[22] of bronze and of silver, indeed even of gold. And the leading priests of the sacred rites, wearing ankle-length, white linen robes tightly clasped at their breasts, carried before them the distinguishing insignia of the most powerful gods. . . . (11) Without delay came the gods, who deigned to walk with human feet, first, that awe-inspiring messenger between the gods above and those below, with a face now black, now gold, tall, lifting his dog's neck aloft, Anubis, carrying a staff in his left hand, brandishing a green palm-branch in his right. Immediately in his footsteps followed a cow that had been raised to an upright posture, a cow, the fertile symbol of the divine parent-of-all, which one of the priests carried on his shoulders with a happy and rhythmic step. Another carried a large basket of secret things, concealing within it hidden objects of magnificent sanctity. Another carried the venerable image of the supreme deity in his happy arms. . . .

(12) And now the blessings promised to me by the most benevolent goddess drew near, and the priest who carried my destiny and my very salvation was approaching, holding in his right hand a sistrum for the goddess, a crown for me, decorated exactly in accordance with the prescription of the divine promise; and by Hercules, a crown was appropriate, seeing that, after enduring so many great labors and undergoing so many dangers, I would, by the providence of the great goddess, overcome Fortune, which was so cruelly fighting against me. Exhilarated with sudden joy, I did not, however, rush forward in a mad dash, fearing, obviously, that the peaceful order of the rites might be upset by the sudden approach of a four-footed beast. Instead, moving slowly, little by little, with my body turned sideways, and with the crowd yielding, no doubt because of divine guidance, I gently crept forward. (13) But the priest, remembering, as far as I could tell, the oracle that he had received in his dream, and marveling at how things coincided with the instructions he had been given, immediately stopped, and with his right hand spontaneously extended, he held the crown in front of my very face. Then with my mouth I greedily lifted the crown, which shone with the lovely roses woven into it, and trembling, with my heart pounding and beating rapidly, anxious for the promise to be fulfilled, I most eagerly devoured it. Nor did the heavenly promise deceive me: immediately, my ugly and animal form slipped away from me. And first, my rough bristles disappeared, and then my thick hide was thinned, my fat belly shrunk, the soles of my feet grew out through their hoofs into toes, my hands were no longer feet, but were extended into their upright functions, my long neck was shortened, my face and head were rounded, my enormous ears returned to their original size, my rock-like teeth went back to their human smallness, and what had tortured me most of all before, my tail, was no more. The people were amazed, and the religious venerated this evidence of the power of the great deity, her magnificence that was so much like that of my

dreams, and the ease of my transformation; with a single clear voice, stretching their hands toward the sky, they gave witness to the marvelous beneficence of the goddess. . . .

(17) When we arrived at the temple itself, the chief priest and those who were carrying the divine images and those who had already been initiated into the awe-inspiring inner sanctuary, had been admitted into the chamber of the goddess, and were arranging the breathing images in their proper places. Then one of them, whom they all called the scribe, stood before the doors and summoned the company of the *pastophori* – which is the name of a consecrated college – as if for an assembly. Then, from a high platform, having first recited from a book vows for the prosperity of the great Emperor, the Senate, the knights, and the entire Roman people, the sailors, and the ships which are under the rule of our world empire, he announced, in the Greek language and custom, the opening of the navigation season.[23] The chanting of the crowd that followed indicated that his words had been happily received by everyone. Then, anointed in joy, the people brought boughs, branches, and garlands, and kissed the feet of the goddess, who stood, fashioned from silver, on the steps, and then they went away to their own homes. My heart, however, would not allow me to move more than a finger-nail's breadth away; but I stared at the image of the goddess, and thought about my former misfortunes.

(22) . . . . One dark night, with clear commands, (the goddess) plainly indicated that the day that I had always hoped for had come, when she would grant me my greatest wish, and she indicated how much I ought to spend on the ceremonies, and she decreed that Mithras himself, her high priest, who, as she said, was joined to me by a kind of divine conjunction of the stars, would administer the rites. My spirit revived by these and other kind instructions from the supreme goddess, I shook off sleep, and even before the day was completely light, I hurried straightaway to the residence of the priest, and meeting up with him just as he was coming out of his room, I greeted him. I had decided to demand, more insistently than usual, that I take part in the rites, on the grounds that they were now owed to me. But as soon as he saw me, he said first, "Lucius, how fortunate you are, how blessed you are, that the august deity so greatly favors you with her propitious will." And he added, "Why are you now standing around doing nothing, and delaying yourself? The day has come for you, that you have been hoping for with constant prayers, the day on which, by the divine commands of the goddess of many names, you will be initiated, through these very hands of mine, into the holiest secrets of our rites." Then the kindly old man took my hand and led me straight to the doors of the most splendid temple. And after the ceremony of opening had been celebrated with the customary ritual, and the morning sacrifice had been completed, from the secret parts of the sanctuary he brought out some books covered with mysterious letters, some in the shapes of every kind of animal to represent abridged words of religious language, others knotted and curved like wheels and woven together like clumps of vines to protect their meaning from the curiosity of the uninitiated. From them he read aloud to me what I would have to get ready for the initiation.

(23) And immediately, I eagerly and somewhat extravagantly set about buying these things, some of them myself, others through my friends. And then, because,

as the priest said, the occasion demanded it, he led me, surrounded by a cohort of devotees, to the nearest baths, and after I had taken the customary bath, he first asked for the favor of the gods, and then, sprinkling me all over, washed me most purely. He led me back to the temple, with two-thirds of the day now complete, and stationed me before the very feet of the goddess. And having secretly given me certain instructions, too holy to be spoken, he openly commanded, with all as witnesses, that I restrain my pleasure in food for the next ten days, not eat animal food, and eat without wine. I religiously observed these things with reverent abstemiousness. The day fixed for my appearance before the gods had now come, and the Sun, curving down, was dragging in the evening. Then suddenly, in keeping with the ancient custom of the sacred rites, crowds flowed in from every direction, each of them honoring me with various gifts. Then, with all the uninitiated sent far away, I was covered in a new linen robe, and the priest seized my hand, and led me to the innermost part of the sanctuary itself.

Perhaps, eager reader, you are rather anxious to learn what was said then, and what was done. I would tell if I were permitted to tell; you would learn if you were permitted to hear. But ears and tongue would incur equal guilt, the latter because of its impious talkativeness, the former because of their unbridled curiosity. But because you are, perhaps, in suspense with religious longing, I will not torment and torture you any longer. Listen, therefore, but believe – these things are true. I arrived at the boundary of death and, having stepped upon the threshold of Proserpina,[24] I traveled through all the elements and returned; in the middle of the night, I saw the sun flashing with bright light; I came face to face with the gods below and the gods above and worshipped them up close. Behold, I have told you things, which, although you have heard them, it is necessary, nevertheless, that you not know. . . .

53   MINUCIUS FELIX, *OCTAVIUS*

Almost nothing is known of Marcus Minucius Felix, whose only surviving work, the *Octavius*, was written probably early in the third century AD. It takes the form of a debate, which the author claims to have witnessed, between a Christian, Octavius Januarius, and a pagan, Quintus Caecilius Natalis.[25] The debate is set in Ostia, Rome's port-city. In the passage below, Caecilius Natalis indignantly recites many of the charges that were commonly leveled against the Christians.

(8) . . . . Is it not lamentable that men (you will forgive me for advocating rather vehemently the cause that I have undertaken), men, I say, who belong to a deplorable, illicit, and desperate faction, are attacking the gods? Men who, having gathered together the more ignorant members of the dregs of society and credulous women made unstable by the volatility of their sex, have organized a rabble of profane conspirators, bound together by nocturnal meetings and ritual fasts and inhuman meals, not for some sacred purpose but for wickedness, a secretive tribe that shuns the light, silent in public, talkative in corners, who despise tem-

ples as if they were tombs, spit on the gods, laugh at our sacred rites, pitiful themselves, pity (if it is possible) our priests, despise honors and offices, themselves half-naked. What wondrous stupidity and incredible audacity! They disdain this world's tortures, while they dread those that are uncertain and in the future; and while they are afraid to die after death, they are not afraid to die in the meantime; so for them false hope mitigates fear with the promise of a life to come.

(9) And already – for wrong-doing grows rather plentifully – with morality declining every day throughout the whole world, the abominable sanctuaries of that impious confederacy multiply. This conspiracy must be utterly exterminated and accursed. They recognize themselves by secret signs and marks, and they fall in love almost before they know each other; everywhere, a kind of religion of lust, as it were, is shared among them, and they promiscuously call themselves "brothers" and "sisters," so that even ordinary sex becomes, under cover of a sacred name, incest. So their vain and demented superstition boasts about crimes. . . . I hear that, because of some unfathomably idiotic notion, they worship the consecrated head of an ass, the foulest of animals – a suitable thing for a religion sprung from such morals. Others say that they worship the private parts of their very overseer and priest, and revere his organs as if they were their parent. I don't know whether this is false; certainly suspicion adheres to their secret and nocturnal rites. To say that a man who was executed for his crimes, and the deadly wood of the cross, are their sacred rites is to assign suitable altars to the abandoned and the criminal, such that they worship what they deserve. The story of how recruits are initiated is as disgusting as it is notorious. An infant, covered in dough, so as to deceive the unsuspecting, is placed next to the person who is to be initiated into the rites. When the recruit has been induced to deliver what seem to be harmless blows on the surface of the dough, the infant is killed by the unseen and hidden wounds. Its blood – how wicked! – they greedily lap up; its limbs they fight to tear to pieces; by this victim they are bound together; by their consciousness of criminality they are pledged to mutual silence. These rites are more foul than any sacrilege. And everyone knows about their banquets; everyone everywhere talks about them, as the speech of our friend from Cirta[26] also indicates. On a specified day, they gather for a banquet with all their children, sisters, mothers, people of both sexes and every age. There, after much feasting, when the banquet grows hot and drunkenness inflames the passions of incestuous lust, a dog, which has been tied to a lamp, is, by means of a scrap thrown beyond the range of his leash, tempted to bound forward in a rush. So with the observant light overturned and extinguished, in the shameless dark they are indiscriminately caught up in the bond of unnatural lust; and though not all of them are actively involved, still they are, by their complicity, equally incestuous. . . .

(10) . . . . Why do they have no altars, no temples, no recognized images? Why do they never speak in public, never meet openly, unless what they worship and conceal is either punishable or shameful? From where, or who, or where is that one and only god, solitary, forlorn, whom no free nation, no kingdom, not even a Roman superstition knows? The solitary and wretched race of the Jews also worshipped one god, but openly, with temples, altars, victims, and ceremonies; but one so without strength and power that he and his beloved nation are captive

to the Romans. But furthermore, what omens, what portents the Christians invent – that that god of theirs, whom they can neither show nor see, inquires diligently into the morality and actions of all, indeed, into their words and hidden thoughts, apparently hurrying all over, and present everywhere: they want him to be bothersome, restless, shameless, and interfering. . . .

(11) What of the fact that they threaten the whole world and the universe itself and its stars with fire, and that they are trying to destroy them, as if the eternal order of nature established by divine laws could be overthrown. . . . Not content with this insane notion, they construct and embellish ridiculous stories: they say that they are born again after death from the ashes and the embers, and with a strange sort of inexplicable confidence believe in each other's lies – you might think they had already come to life again. . . . This, no doubt, is why they denounce funeral pyres and condemn cremation, as if the whole body, though removed from the flame, would not over the years and ages be resolved into earth; and as if it makes a difference whether wild beasts tear them to pieces, or the sea swallows them up, or the ground covers them, or the flame carries them off, seeing that for corpses, if they feel anything, every burial is a punishment, while if they do not feel anything, speed in getting it over with is the best treatment. Deluded by this mistake, they promise themselves, whom they consider to be virtuous, a blessed and eternal life after death, others, whom they judge to be unjust, everlasting punishment. . . . But I should like to know whether resurrection occurs with bodies or without bodies, and with what bodies, their own or restored ones? Without a body? In that case, there is, as far as I know, neither mind, nor soul, nor life. With the same body? But it has already fallen apart. With another body? In that case, a new man is born, not the former one renewed. And yet so much time has gone past, so many ages have flowed by: what single person has ever returned from the underworld or with the privilege of Protesilaus, who was permitted a furlough at least of a few hours, such that we might trust in even one example? All those figments of your unhealthy imagination and the empty comforts invented by fanciful poets to sweeten their song have been shamefully reworked by your exceeding credulity into the service of your god.

(12) . . . . Behold, for you there are threats, punishments, tortures, crosses – to be not worshipped but undergone – even the flames which you both foretell and fear; where is that God who can help you in the next life, but cannot help you in this one? Do the Romans not have an empire and rule without your god, enjoy the blessings of the whole world, and dominate you? But you, doubtful and anxious in the meantime, abstain from honest pleasures: you do not attend the shows or take part in processions or public banquets; you abhor the sacred games, the sacrificial foods, the drinks poured in libation on the altars. So frightened are you of the gods whom you deny! You do not adorn your heads with flowers, your bodies with perfumes; you save your ointments for funerals, deny garlands even for graves; pale, trembling, worthy of pity, but the pity of our gods! So, wretched, you neither rise again nor live in the meantime.

54   Tacitus, *Annals* 15.44

On Tacitus, and on the *Annals*, see the introduction to selection 29. In AD 64, fire destroyed a large part of the city of Rome. It was rumored that Nero had either started the fire or ordered it to be set (allegedly so that he would have room to build his *domus aurea* or Golden House). In the following passage, Tacitus describes how Nero tried to dispel the rumors by shifting the blame onto the Christian community at Rome.

.... Soon means were sought for propitiating the gods, and the Sibylline books[27] were consulted, in accordance with which supplication was made to Vulcan, and Ceres, and Proserpina; and Juno was propitiated by the matrons, first on the Capitol, then at the nearest sea-shore, from which water was drawn and sprinkled in the temple and on the image of the goddess; and women who had husbands celebrated ritual banquets and all-night vigils. But neither human help, nor the emperor's largess, nor the efforts to appease the gods could dispel the scandal or the belief that the fire had been ordered. So, to do away with the rumor, Nero substituted as defendants, and subjected to the most carefully contrived tortures, those who were hated for their crimes, and whom the ordinary people called Christians. The originator of this name, Christus, had been executed in the reign of Tiberius, through the agency of the procurator Pontius Pilatus.[28] Suppressed for a time, this pernicious superstition kept breaking out again, not only in Judaea, the origin of this evil, but also in the city, where everything awful or shameful in the world flows together and is celebrated. First, therefore, those who confessed were arrested; then, because of their disclosures, a huge multitude was convicted, not so much for the crime of arson as for hatred of the human race.[29] And ridicule was added to their dying: covered with the skins of wild animals, they were torn to death by dogs; or they were attached to crosses and set on fire; and when daylight failed, they were burned to provide light during the night. Nero had offered his gardens for this spectacle, and put on an exhibition in the Circus, mingling with the plebs in the costume of a charioteer, or standing on his race-chariot. It was for this reason that, though directed against the guilty and those who deserved the most extreme punishments, a feeling of pity arose, on the grounds that they were being sacrificed, not to the public good, but to the cruelty of one man. yikes

55   Pliny, *Letters* 10.96–7

On Pliny, see the introduction to selection 15. The tenth book of his *Letters* consists of his correspondence with the emperor Trajan when he was governor of the province of Bithynia-Pontus (what is now northern Turkey) in about AD 111/12. The first of the two letters below describes how Pliny handled a number of Christians who were brought before him; the second is Trajan's official reply to Pliny's request for guidance.

Gaius Plinius to the emperor Trajan.

It is my custom, my lord, to refer to you everything about which I am in doubt.
For who else can better guide my hesitation and instruct my ignorance? I have
never been present at the trials of Christians, so I do not know how or to what
extent they are normally punished or interrogated. Nor am I at all certain whether
some distinction should be observed in respect to age, or all should be treated no
differently than the adults; whether those who repent should be pardoned, or it
should be of no benefit to someone who was once a Christian to have ceased to
be one; whether it is the name itself which is to be punished, if free of crimes, or
the crimes associated with the name.

Meanwhile, in regard to those who have been denounced to me as Christians,
I have followed this procedure. I asked them whether they were Christians. Those
who admitted it, I asked a second and a third time, at the same time threatening
them with punishment; those who persisted, I ordered to be led away.[30] For I had
no doubt that, whatever it was they were confessing, their stubbornness and
inflexible obstinacy certainly ought to be punished. There were others possessed
of a similar madness, who, because they were Roman citizens, I directed to be
sent to the city.

Now, as often happens, the charge is becoming more widespread because of
the investigation itself, and more varieties are cropping up. An anonymous pamphlet has been circulated containing the names of many. I thought that I ought to
dismiss those who denied that they were or had ever been Christians, when,
following my example, they had invoked the gods and had made offerings of
incense and wine to your statue – which I had ordered to be brought in for that
purpose, together with images of the gods – and, in addition, had cursed Christ,
none of which, it is said, those who are true Christians can be forced to do.
Others, named by an informer, said that they were Christians and later denied it;
they said that they had once been Christians, but had ceased to be, some within
the previous three years, others many years earlier, a few of them even twenty
years ago. And all of them both venerated your statue and the images of the gods
and cursed Christ. And they asserted that this had been the sum total of their
wrong-doing or error: that they were accustomed to assemble before dawn on a
predetermined day to take turns singing hymns to Christ, as if to a god, and to
bind themselves by oath, not for some criminal purpose, but that they would not
commit theft, and robbery, and adultery, that they would not violate a trust, and
that they would not deny a deposit when it was demanded. After these things had
been done, it had been their custom to disperse and then to reassemble to take
food, but of an ordinary and innocent sort; but they had ceased to do even this
after my edict, by which, in accordance with your instructions, I had banned
political associations. For that reason, I believed it even more necessary to learn
the truth, through torture, from two slave-women whom they called deacon-
esses. I found nothing other than a depraved and extravagant superstition.

Having therefore postponed the investigation, I hastened to consult you. For it
seemed to me that the matter is worthy of your consideration, especially given
the number of those who are endangered. For many of every age and of every

rank, and of both sexes, are, and will be, called into danger. The contagion of this superstition has spread, not only through the towns, but also through the villages and rural areas; but it seems to me that it can be stopped and corrected. Certainly, it is quite clear that the temples, which recently had been almost deserted, have begun to be frequented, and the sacred rites, which had been interrupted for a long time, are being performed again, and the flesh of sacrificial animals, for which, until now, a buyer could very rarely be found, is being sold everywhere. From this, it is easy to infer how large a number of people could be reformed, if there should be an opportunity for repentance.

Trajan to Pliny.

You have followed the procedure that you should have, my Secundus, in examining the cases of those who have been brought before you as Christians. For nothing can be prescribed for every case, such that it would have, as it were, a fixed form. They must not be hunted out; if they are brought before you and accused, they must be punished, but in such a way that he who denies that he is a Christian, and makes this clear by his actions, that is, by supplicating our gods, should be pardoned as a result of his repentance, although he has been suspect in the past. But pamphlets circulated anonymously ought to have no place in any accusation. For it is both the worst sort of precedent and not in keeping with our age.

[handwritten margin note: who is punished & why]

56   EUSEBIUS, *ECCLESIASTICAL HISTORY* 5.1–31

Eusebius was born about AD 260, probably in Caesarea, Palestine, where he was elected bishop around 314 (he died ca. 340). He wrote an adulatory *Life of Constantine*, a chronology of universal history (which survives in an Armenian version and in a Latin adaptation by Jerome), and the *Ecclesiastical History*, which recounts, in ten books, the history of the Church to AD 324. The opening chapters of Book 5 describe, in sometimes excruciating detail, the persecution of Christians that occurred at Lugdunum (mod. Lyons) in AD 177, mainly, it seems, because of their refusal to worship the pagan gods. In all, forty-eight Christians were martyred. The translation is from G. A. Williamson, *Eusebius, The History of the Church from Christ to Constantine* (New York, 1965), pp. 193–8.

Gaul was the country in which the arena was crowded with these people.[31] Her capital cities, famous and held in higher repute than any in the land, are Lyons and Vienne, both situated on the river Rhône, whose broad stream flows through the whole area. A written account of the martyrs was sent by the most important churches there to those of Asia and Phrygia, relating what had happened in their midst. . . . They begin their story thus:

"The severity of our trials here, the unbridled fury of the heathen against God's people, the untold sufferings of the blessed martyrs, we are incapable of describing in detail: indeed no pen could do them justice. The adversary swooped on us with all his might, giving us now a foretaste of his advent, which undoubtedly is imminent. He left no stone unturned in his efforts to train his adherents and equip them to attack the servants of God, so that not only were we debarred from houses, baths, and the forum, they actually forbade any of us to be seen in any place whatever. . . .

To begin with, [the martyrs] heroically endured whatever the surging crowd heaped on them, noisy abuse, blows, dragging along the ground, plundering, stoning, imprisonment, and everything that an infuriated mob normally does to hated enemies. Then they were marched into the forum and interrogated by the tribune and the city authorities before the whole population. When they confessed Christ, they were locked up in jail to await the governor's arrival. Later, when they were taken before him and he treated them with all the cruelty he reserves for Christians, Vettius Epagathus, one of our number, full of love towards God and towards his neighbor, came forward. . . . He found the judgment so unreasonably given against us more than he could bear: boiling with indignation, he applied for permission to speak in defense of the Christians, and to prove that there was nothing godless or irreligious in our society. The crowd round the tribunal howled him down, as he was a man of influence, and the governor dismissed his perfectly reasonable application with the curt question: 'Are you a Christian?' In the clearest possible tones, Vettius replied: 'I am.' And he, too, was admitted to the ranks of the martyrs. . . .

Then the rest fell into two groups. It was clear that some were ready to be the first Gallic martyrs: they made a full confession of their testimony with the greatest eagerness. It was equally clear that others were not ready, that they had not trained and were still flabby, in no fit condition to face the strain of a struggle to the death. . . . However, in spite of the agonies they were suffering, these people stayed with the martyrs and did not desert them. But at the time we were all tormented by doubts about their confessing Christ: we were not afraid of the punishments inflicted, but looking to the outcome and dreading lest anyone might fall away. But the arrests went on, and day after day those who were worthy filled up the number of the martyrs, so that from the two dioceses were collected all the active members who had done most to build up our church life. Among those arrested were some of our heathen domestics, as the governor had publicly announced that we were all to be hunted out. These were ensnared by Satan, so that fearing the tortures which they saw inflicted on God's people, at the soldiers' instigation they falsely accused us of Thyestean banquets[32] and Oedipean incest, and things we ought never to speak or think about, or even believe that such things ever happened among human beings. When these rumors spread, people all raged like wild beasts against us, so that even those who, because of blood-relationship, had previously exercised restraint, now turned on us, grinding their teeth with fury. So was proved true the saying of our Lord: 'The time will come when whoever kills you will think he is doing a service to God.'[33]

. . . . The whole fury of crowd, governor, and soldiers fell with crushing force on Sanctus, the deacon from Vienne; on Maturus, very recently baptized but heroic in facing his ordeal; on Attalus, who had always been a pillar and support[34] of the church in his native Pergamum; and on Blandina, through whom Christ proved that things which men regard as mean, unlovely, and contemptible are by God deemed worthy of great glory. . . . When we were all afraid, and her earthly mistress (who was herself facing the ordeal of martyrdom) was in agony lest she should be unable even to make a bold confession of Christ because of bodily weakness, Blandina was filled with such power that those who took it in turns to subject her to every kind of torture from morning to night were exhausted by their efforts, and confessed themselves beaten – they could think of nothing else to do to her. They were amazed that she was still breathing, for her whole body was mangled and her wounds gaped; they declared that torment of any one kind was enough to part soul and body, let alone a succession of torments of such extreme severity. But the blessed woman, wrestling magnificently, grew in strength as she proclaimed her faith, and found refreshment, rest, and insensibility to her sufferings in uttering the words: 'I am a Christian: we do nothing to be ashamed of.'

Sanctus was another who, with magnificent, superhuman courage, nobly withstood the entire range of human cruelty. Wicked people hoped that the persistence and severity of his tortures would force him to utter something improper, but with such determination did he stand up to their onslaughts that he would not tell them his own name, race, and birthplace, or whether he was slave or free; to every question he replied in Latin: 'I am a Christian.' . . . Consequently, the governor and his torturers strained every nerve against him, so that when they could think of nothing else to do to him, they ended by pressing red-hot copper plates against the most sensitive parts of his body. These were burning, but Sanctus remained unbending and unyielding, firm in his confession of faith, bedewed and fortified by the heavenly fountain of the water of life that flows from the depths of Christ's being. . . . A few days later, wicked people again put the martyr on the rack, thinking that now that his whole body was swollen and inflamed, a further application of the same instruments would defeat him, unable as he was to bear even the touch of a hand; or that by dying under torture he would put fear into the rest. However, nothing of the sort happened: to their amazement, his body became erect and straight as a result of these new torments, and recovered its former appearance and the use of the limbs; thus through the grace of Christ his second spell on the rack proved to be not punishment but cure. Biblis again, one of those who had denied Christ, was handed over to punishment by the devil, who imagined that he had already devoured her,[35] and hoped to damn her as a slanderer by forcing her to say wicked things about us, being (so he thought) a feeble creature, easily broken. But on the rack she came to her senses, and, so to speak, awoke out of deep sleep, reminded by the brief chastisement of the eternal punishment in hell.[36] She flatly contradicted the slanderers: 'How could children be eaten by people who are not even allowed to eat the blood of brute beasts?'[37] From then on she insisted that she was a Christian, and so she joined the ranks of the martyrs.

When the tyrant's instruments of torture had been utterly defeated by Christ through the endurance of the blessed saints, the devil resorted to other devices – confinement in the darkness of a filthy prison; clamping the feet in the stocks, stretched apart to the fifth hole; and the other agonies which warders when angry and full of the devil are apt to inflict on helpless prisoners. Thus the majority were suffocated in prison. . . . Some, though tortured so cruelly that, even if they received every care, it seemed impossible for them to survive, lived on in the prison, deprived of all human attention, but strengthened by the Lord and fortified in body and soul, stimulating and encouraging the rest. But the young ones who had been recently arrested and had not previously undergone physical torture could not bear the burden of confinement, and died in prison.

Blessed Pothinus, who had been entrusted with the care of the Lyons diocese, was over ninety years of age and physically very weak. He could scarcely breathe because of his chronic physical weakness, but was strengthened by spiritual enthusiasm because of his pressing desire for martyrdom. Even he was dragged before the tribunal, and though his body was feeble from age and disease, his life was preserved in him, that thereby Christ might triumph. He was conveyed to the tribunal by the soldiers, accompanied by the civil authorities and the whole populace, who shouted and jeered at him as though he were Christ Himself. But he bore the noble witness.[38] When the governor asked him, 'Who is the Christians' god?' he replied, 'If you are a fit person, you shall know.' Thereupon he was mercilessly dragged along beneath a rain of blows, those close by assailing him viciously with hands and feet, and showing no respect for his age, and those at a distance hurling at him whatever came to hand, and all thinking it a shocking neglect of their duty to be behind-hand in savagery towards him, for they imagined that in this way they would avenge their gods. Scarcely breathing, he was flung into prison, and two days later he passed away."

57   H. Musurillo, *The Acts of the Christian Martyrs*, no. 22

The following document records the martyrdom of Agapê, Irenê, and Chionê, three young women of Thessalonica (or Saloniki), Macedonia,[39] who, together with four companions, were arrested in AD 304 for having failed to comply with an edict of the emperor Diocletian, according to which everyone in the empire was to make a sacrifice to the pagan gods. Three hearings take place before the Roman prefect Dulcitius. After the first, Agapê and Chionê are executed; at the second and third hearings, Irenê appears alone. The document originated probably in the Christian community at Thessalonica; the Greek manuscript by which it is preserved (*codex Vaticanus graecus 1660*) dates to AD 916. The translation is from H. Musurillo, *The Acts of the Christian Martyrs* (Oxford, 1972), pp. 281–93.

The Martyrdom of Saints Agapê, Irenê, and Chionê at Saloniki

(1) Since the advent and the presence on earth of our Lord and Savior Jesus Christ, the greater the grace of the men of old, so much the greater was the victory of holy men. For instead of those visible enemies, we have now begun to crush enemies that cannot be seen with bodily eyes, and the invisible substance of the demons has been handed over to the flames by pure and holy women who were full of the Holy Spirit. Such were the three saintly women who came from the city of Thessalonica, the city that the inspired Paul celebrated when he praised

its faith and love, saying, "Your faith in God has gone out to every place."[40] And elsewhere he says, "Of charity for your brothers I have no need to write to you; for you yourselves have learned from God to love one another."[41] When the persecution was raging under the Emperor Maximian, these women, who had adorned themselves with virtue, following the precepts of the Gospel, abandoned their native city, their family, property, and possessions, because of their love of God and their expectation of heavenly things, performing deeds worthy of their father Abraham. They fled the persecutors, according to the commandment, and took refuge on a high mountain.[42] There they gave themselves to prayer: though their bodies resided on a mountain top, their souls lived in heaven.

(2) At any rate, they were here captured and brought to the official who was conducting the persecution,[43] that, by thus fulfilling the rest of the divine commands, and loving their Master even unto death, they might weave for themselves the chaplet of immortality. Of these girls, one had preserved the shining purity of her baptism according to the holy prophet who said: "You will wash me and I shall be whiter than snow,"[44] and she was called Chionê. The second girl possessed the gift of our God and Savior within herself, and manifested it to everyone according to the word, "My peace I give you,"[45] and she was called Irenê by everyone. The third girl possessed the perfection of the Gospel, loving God with her whole heart and her neighbor as herself, in accord with the holy Apostle who says, "The aim of our charge is love,"[46] and she was appropriately named Agapê. When these three girls were brought before the magistrate and refused to sacrifice, he sentenced them to the fire, in order that thus, by a short time in the fire, they might overcome those that are devoted to fire, that is, the Devil and all his heavenly host of demons, and, attaining the incorruptible crown of glory, they might endlessly praise along with the angels the God who had showered this grace upon them. The record that was taken down in their case is the material of our account.

(3) The prefect Dulcitius was sitting on the tribunal, and the court clerk Artemisius spoke: "With your permission, I shall read the charge which was sent to your Genius by the *stationarius*,[47] here present, in connection with the parties in court."

"You may read it," said the prefect Dulcitius.

And the charge was duly read: "To you, my lord, greetings from Cassander, *beneficiarius*.[48] This is to inform you, Sir, that Agatho, Irenê, Agapê, Chionê, Cassia, Philippa, and Eutychia refuse to eat sacrificial food, and so I have referred them to your Genius."

"What is this insanity," said the prefect Dulcitius, "that you refuse to obey the order of our most religious emperors and Caesars?" And turning to Agatho, he said: "When you came to the sacrifices, why did you not perform the cult practices like other religious people?"

"Because I am a Christian," said Agatho.

The prefect Dulcitius said: "Do you still remain in the same mind today?"

"Yes," said Agatho.

The prefect Dulcitius said: "What do you say, Agapê?"

"I believe in the living God," replied Agapê, "and I refuse to destroy my conscience."

"What do you say, Irenê?" asked the prefect Dulcitius. "Why did you disobey the command of our lords, the emperors and Caesars?"

"Because of my fear of God," said Irenê.

"What do you say, Chionê?" asked the prefect.

"I believe in the living God," replied Chionê, "and I refuse to do this."

The prefect said: "And how about you, Cassia?"

"I wish to save my soul," said Cassia.

The prefect said: "Are you willing to partake of the sacrificial meat?"

"I am not," said Cassia.

The prefect said: "And what say you, Philippa?"

"I say the same," said Philippa.

"What do you mean, the same?" said the prefect.

Said Philippa: "I mean, I would rather die than partake."

"Eutychia," said the prefect, "what do you say?"

"I say the same," said Eutychia; "I would rather die."

The prefect said: "Do you have a husband?"

"He is dead," said Eutychia.

"When did he die?" asked the prefect.

"About seven months ago," said Eutychia.

The prefect said, "How is it then that you are pregnant?"

Eutychia said: "By the man whom God gave me."

The prefect said: "But how can you be pregnant when you say your husband is dead?"

Eutychia said: "No one can know the will of almighty God. So God willed it."

The prefect said: "I urge Eutychia to cease this madness and to return to sound reason. What do you say? Will you obey the imperial command?"

"No, I will not," said Eutychia. "I am a Christian, a servant of almighty God."

The prefect said: "Since Eutychia is pregnant, she shall be kept meanwhile in jail."

(4) Then he added: "What say you, Agapê? Will you perform all the actions which religious persons perform in honor of our lords the emperors and Caesars?"

Agapê replied: "It is not at all in Satan's power. He cannot move my reason; it is invincible."

The prefect said: "What say you, Chionê?"

Chionê said: "No one can change my mind."

The prefect said: "Do you have in your possession any writings, parchments, or books of the impious Christians?"

Chionê said: "We do not, Sir. Our present emperors have taken these from us."

"Who was it who gave you this idea?" asked the prefect.

"God almighty," said Chionê.

The prefect said: "Who was it who counseled you to commit such folly?"

"It was almighty God," answered Chionê, "and his only begotten Son, our Lord Jesus Christ."

The prefect Dulcitius said: "It is clear to all that you are all liable to the crime of treason against our lords, the emperors and Caesars. But seeing that you have persisted in this folly for such a long time, in spite of strong warnings and so many decrees, sanctioned by stern threats, and have despised the command of our lords, the emperors and Caesars, remaining in this impious name of Christian, and seeing that even today when you were ordered by the soldiers and officials to deny your belief and signify this in writing, you refused – therefore you shall receive the punishment appropriate for you."

Then he read the sentence written on a sheet: "Whereas Agapê and Chionê have, with malicious intent, acted against the divine decree of our lords, the Augusti and Caesars, and whereas they adhere to the worthless and obsolete worship of the Christians, which is hateful to all religious men, I sentence them to be burned." Then he added: "Agatho, Irenê, Cassia, Philippa, and Eutychia, because of their youth, are to be put in prison in the meanwhile."

(5) After the most holy women were consumed in the flames, the saintly girl Irenê was once again brought before the court on the following day.

Dulcitius said to her: "It is clear from what we have seen that you are determined in your folly, for you have deliberately kept even till now so many tablets, books, parchments, codices, and pages of the writings of the former Christians of unholy name; even now, though you denied each time that you possessed such writings, you did show a sign of recognition when they were mentioned. You are not satisfied with the punishment of your sisters, nor do you keep before your eyes the terror of death. Therefore you must be punished. It would not, however, seem out of place to show you some measure of mercy: if even now you would be willing to recognize the gods, you will be released from all danger and punishment. Now what do you say? Will you do the bidding of our emperors and Caesars? Are you prepared to eat the sacrificial meats and to sacrifice to the gods?"

"No," said Irenê, "I am not prepared, for the sake of the God almighty who 'has created heaven and earth and the seas and all that is in them.'[49] For those who transgress the word of God, there awaits the great judgment of eternal punishment."

The prefect Dulcitius said: "Who was it that advised you to retain those parchments and writings up to the present time?"

"It was almighty God," said Irenê, "who bade us to love him unto death. For this reason, we did not dare to be traitors, but we chose to be burned alive or suffer anything else that might happen to us rather than betray the writings."

The prefect said: "Was anyone else aware that the documents were in the house where you lived?"

"No one else," said Irenê, "saw them, save almighty God who knows all things. But no stranger. As for our own relatives, we considered them worse than our enemies, in fear that they would denounce us. Hence we told no one."

"Last year," said the prefect, "when this edict of our lords the emperors and Caesars was first promulgated, where did you hide?"

"Wherever God willed," said Irenê. "We lived on the mountains, in the open air, as God is my witness."

"Whom were you living with?" asked the prefect.

Irenê answered: "We lived out of doors in different places among the mountains."

The prefect said: "Who supplied you with bread?"

Irenê answered: "God, who supplies all men."

"Was your father aware of this?" asked the prefect.

Irenê answered: "I swear by almighty God, he was not aware; he knew nothing at all about it."

"Were any of your neighbors aware of this?" asked the prefect.

Irenê answered: "Go and question our neighbors, and inquire about the area to see whether anyone knew where we were."

The prefect said: "Now after you returned from the mountain where you had been, as you say, were any persons present at the reading of these books?"

Irenê answered: "They were in our house and we did not dare to bring them out. In fact, it caused us much distress that we could not devote ourselves to them night and day as we had done from the beginning until that day last year when we hid them."

Dulcitius the prefect said: "Your sisters, in accordance with my commands in their regard, have received their sentence. Now you have been guilty even before you ran away, and before you concealed these writings and parchments, and hence I do not wish you to die immediately in the same way. Instead, I sentence you to be placed naked in the brothel, with the help of the public notaries of this city and of Zosimus the executioner; and you will receive merely one loaf of bread from our residence, and the notaries will not allow you to leave."

(6) And so, after the notaries and the slave Zosimus, the executioner, were brought in, the prefect said: "Be it known to you that if ever I find out from the troops that this girl was removed from the spot where I have ordered her to be, even for a single instant, you will immediately be punished with the most extreme penalties. The writings we have referred to, in the cabinets and chests belonging to Irenê, are to be publicly burned."

After those who were put in charge had taken the girl off to the public brothel in accordance with the prefect's order, by the grace of the Holy Spirit which preserved and guarded her pure and inviolate for the God who is the lord of all things, no man dared to approach her, or so much as tried to insult her in speech. Hence the prefect Dulcitius called back this most saintly girl, had her stand before the tribunal, and said to her: "Do you still persist in the same folly?"

But Irenê said to him: "It is not folly, but piety."

"It was abundantly clear from your earlier testimony," said the prefect Dulcitius, "that you did not wish to submit religiously to the bidding of the emperors; and now I perceive that you are persisting in the same foolishness. Therefore, you shall pay the appropriate penalty." He then asked for a sheet of papyrus and wrote the sentence against her as follows: "Whereas Irenê has refused to obey the command of the emperors and to offer sacrifice, and still adheres to a sect called the Christians, I therefore sentence her to be burned alive, as I did her two sisters before her."

(7) After this sentence had been pronounced by the prefect, the soldiers took the girl and brought her to a high place, where her sisters had been martyred before her. They ignited a huge pyre, and ordered her to climb up on it. And the holy woman Irenê, singing and praising God, threw herself upon it, and so died. It was in the ninth consulship of Diocletian Augustus, in the eighth of Maximian Augustus, on the first day of April, in the kingship of our Lord Christ Jesus, who

reigns for ever, with whom there is glory to the Father with the Holy Spirit for ever. Amen.

SUGGESTIONS FOR FURTHER READING

There are several good books about Roman religion: R. MacMullen, *Paganism in the Roman Empire* (New Haven, 1981); R. M. Ogilvie, *The Romans and their Gods in the Age of Augustus* (London, 1969); H. H. Scullard, *Festivals and Ceremonies of the Roman Republic* (Ithaca, NY, 1981); A. Wardman, *Religion and Statecraft among the Romans* (London, 1982). The standard work on the imperial cult is S. R. F. Price, *Rituals and Power: The Roman Imperial Cult in Asia Minor* (Cambridge, 1984).

On Augustine, see Peter Brown's wonderful biography, *Augustine of Hippo* (London, 1967). The cult of Isis is discussed in F. Solmsen, *Isis among the Greeks and Romans* (Cambridge, Mass., 1979); S. A. Takács, *Isis and Sarapis in the Roman World* (Leiden and New York, 1995); R. E. Witt, *Isis in the Graeco-Roman World* (London, 1971); on its appeal to women, S. K. Heyob, *The Cult of Isis among Women in the Graeco-Roman World* (Leiden, 1975). On Apuleius, see S. J. Harrison, *Apuleius: A Latin Sophist* (Oxford, 2000); J. Tatum, *Apuleius and the Golden Ass* (Ithaca, NY, 1979).

The best book about relations between pagans and Christians is R. Lane Fox, *Pagans and Christians in the Mediterranean World from the Second Century* AD *to the Conversion of Constantine* (New York, 1987). Worth reading also: S. Benko, *Pagan Rome and the Early Christians* (Bloomington, 1984); E. R. Dodds, *Pagan and Christian in an Age of Anxiety* (Cambridge, 1965); A Momigliano (ed.), *The Conflict between Paganism and Christianity in the Fourth Century* (Oxford, 1963); R. L. Wilcken, *The Christians as the Romans Saw Them* (New Haven, 1984). For the history of the persecutions, W. H. C. Frend, *Martyrdom and Persecution in the Early Church: A Study of Conflict from the Maccabees to Donatus* (Oxford, 1965). For anything to do with Pliny's *Letters*, A. N. Sherwin-White, *The Letters of Pliny: A Historical and Social Commentary* (Oxford, 1985). On martyrdom, see G. W. Bowersock, *Martyrdom and Rome* (Cambridge and New York, 1995); R. MacMullen, *Christianizing the Roman Empire* (AD *100–400)* (New Haven, 1984).

NOTES

1 THE SOCIAL ORDER

1   A *sestertius* (sesterce) was a small silver coin; see also Appendix 2.
2   A place of assembly adjacent to the Forum.
3   An *as* (pl. *asses*) was a large copper coin; see also Appendix 2.
4   A *lanx* was a large, perforated dish that the searcher held in front of his face so as not to be recognized; he wore only a small girdle (*licium*).
5   A coarse kind of grain widely eaten in early Rome, either roasted or ground into meal.
6   It's unclear whether it was the debtor's property or person that was to be cut up.
7   Anyone (e.g. a son or daughter) who was in the power (*potestas*) of the decedent at the time of his death.
8   A blood-relative on the father's side.
9   Members of the same *gens*, for which see ch. 2, n. 79.
10 At nominal sales (which had a variety of legal purposes), the *libripens* held a balance, as if to weigh out money; he was evidently considered also to be a kind of witness.
11 A *drachma* was a Greek coin; see also Appendix 2.
12 The first of its kind in Latin, his history of Rome (*Origines*) does not survive.
13 Situated on the Campanian coast. It was famous for its Sibyl, a female prophet or soothsayer.
14 A small town on the Campanian coast, near Cumae; it was a favorite resort of wealthy Romans.
15 A small island off the coast of Italy near Misenum.
16 A street at Rome, known for being exceptionally noisy.
17 The Porta Capena was located beneath the Marcian aqueduct on the Appian way.
18 The legendary second king of Rome.
19 A nymph; wife of Numa.
20 Mythical Athenian architect of the time of Theseus and Minos.
21 One of the three Fates.
22 A spear was stuck in the ground at public auctions, apparently to symbolize booty.
23 A river in Spain, famous for its golden sands.
24 The principal river of Syria.
25 Largest of the seven hills of Rome.
26 The Viminal, another of the seven hills of Rome; it was named for a thicket of willows that stood there.
27 An Assyrian rhetorician.
28 A member of a college of priests who ascertained the future by observing lightning, the flight and song of birds, the feeding-habits of the sacred chickens, and other phenomena.
29 Daedalus; see n. 20.

30   One of the seven hills of Rome.
31   A Libyan giant (killed by Hercules).
32   A famous Athenian prostitute.
33   These are all names of Greek actors.
34   The old Stoic is Publius Egnatius Celer. The death of Barea Soranus is described in Tacitus, *Annals* 16.23, 33.
35   At Tarsus on the river Cydnus.
36   A magistrate's attendant. He walked in front of the magistrate, calling out for people to make way.
37   A goddess; mother of Autotycus (by Mercury) and Philammon (by Apollo).
38   Publius Cornelius Scipio received the image of the goddess Cybele when it was brought to Rome from Asia Minor in 204 BC.
39   Lucius Caecilius Metellus; see ch. 2, n. 45.
40   An island off the coast of Thrace, now Samothráki.
41   According to Otho's law of 67 BC, only knights could sit in the first fourteen rows of seats in the theater behind the *orchestra* (where only senators were allowed to sit).
42   A people of the region of Latium, widely reputed to be wizards and snake-charmers.
43   All were small towns near Rome.
44   A centaur, son of Saturn and Philyra.
45   All were small towns in the region of Latium.
46   Pythagoreans were vegetarians.
47   Possibly the allegedly sleepy-headed emperor Claudius.
48   Liburnia was a region on the east coast of the Adriatic Sea (in what is today Croatia).
49   Gnaeus Domitius Corbulo, a general under Claudius and Nero, who forced him to commit suicide in AD 66.
50   In Campania, near Cumae.
51   The meaning is uncertain; it may have something to do with the Helvii, a Gallic tribe.
52   Lucania was a region of southern Italy, named for the Lucani.
53   From the island of Cos, mod. Kós.
54   Caecuban and Chian were reputed to be among the finest wines of Italy and Greece, respectively.
55   Large drinking-vessels manufactured at Allifae in Samnium.
56   A town in Samnium famous for its olive-oil; now Venafro.
57   From the island of Lesbos, mod. Lésvos.
58   A sorcerer.
59   Home to a famous temple of Ceres; now San Giovanni.
60   Mod. Catania.
61   Also called Agrigentum, now Agrigento.
62   Publius Rupilius, consul in 132 BC, a friend of Publius Cornelius Scipio Aemilianus.
63   Ancient Tauromenium.
64   Mod. Morgantina.
65   See n. 1.
66   Goddess of corpses. Burial-equipment could be bought or rented at her temple, which also housed the registers of deaths.
67   An ax bound with twigs; it was carried in front of magistrates as a symbol of their authority to have citizens killed or beaten.
68   The sun and the planets Mercury, Venus, Earth, Mars, Saturn, and Jupiter.
69   Clothes colored with Tyrian (purple) dye were very expensive.
70   A grain-measure; see also Appendix 2.
71   Mod. Taranto, on the south coast of Italy.
72   When a slave was freed, his owner slapped him on the cheek, to symbolize his former power over him.

73 Mod. Terracina, about half-way between Rome and Naples.
74 A lively and lascivious dance often performed in Greek comedies; it was regarded as a sign of drunkenness or licentiousness (or both).
75 The meaning is unknown.
76 See n. 13.
77 See n. 14.
78 A cake of obscene design, named for the god of procreation.
79 Protective gods of the household.
80 The meaning of the word *bacciballum* is uncertain (it is not otherwise attested).
81 A large city in Campania, famous for its luxury; now Santa Maria Capua Vetere.
82 God of the underworld.
83 God of merchants, from whom, it appears, he claimed a kind of tithe.
84 A gladiator.
85 Something, presumably the part of the monument on which the ships were to be located, is missing from the manuscript.
86 A *denarius* (pl. *denarii*) was a silver coin; see also Appendix 2.
87 The order (or division) of society from which the lower public offices were filled, e.g., scribes and heralds.
88 A region of south-east Italy.
89 See n. 3.
90 There is no way now to determine how often this may have occurred.
91 Now Milan.
92 Peasant-farmers tied to the land they worked under contract (i.e., in some sense, "unfree"): see now M. I. Finley, *Ancient Slavery and Modern Ideology*, rev. edn, ed. B. Shaw (Princeton, 1998), esp. at pp. 35–7.

2 WOMEN, MARRIAGE, AND FAMILY

1 *Patriarchy, Property and Death in the Roman Family* (Cambridge, 1994).
2 Plutarch, *Life of Cato the Elder* 17.7.
3 Probably a reference to the story of Hypsipyle, who is said to have rescued her father, the king of Lemnos, when women murdered all the other men on the island; the story is in Herodotus 6.138 and Hyginus, *Fabulae* 15.
4 In 494 BC.
5 The reference is to the Romans' refusal to ransom the soldiers who had been captured at the battle of Cannae in 216 BC (Livy 22.61.3).
6 The "Idaean Mother" is the goddess Cybele, who was worshipped on Mount Ida in Phrygia. When she was imported to Rome in 204 BC, women received the stone that symbolized her (Livy 29.10.5).
7 In 212 BC, after the city was captured by Marcus Claudius Marcellus.
8 Pyrrhus of Epirus was hired in 280 BC to defend Tarentum (mod. Taranto) against the Romans.
9 The law, which was enacted in 367 BC, declared, among other things, that no one should possess more than 500 *iugera* (about 125 hectares or 315 acres) of public land (*ager publicus*).
10 Enacted in 204 BC, the law forbade advocates to charge fees or to accept gifts from their clients.
11 The woman to whom Propertius addresses a series of love-poems, and whose real name is said to have been Hostia.

12   The Lesbia to whom Catullus addresses his love-poetry; in real life, she was Clodia, the sister of Publius Clodius, tribune in 58 BC.

13   Goddess of justice, who lived on earth during the golden age.

14   The tutelar deity of a person or place.

15   One of the Furies.

16   A small town in Latium, twelve miles from Rome; mod. Castiglione.

17   A small town in Latium, on the left bank of the Tiber river, five miles from Rome; mod. Castel Giubileo.

18   A famous pantomime of Alexandria.

19   Daughter of Thestius and wife of Tyndarus; impregnated by Jupiter while she was in the form of a swan, she later produced two eggs, from which came Castor, Helen, Pollux, and Clytemnestra.

20   The Megalesian games were held in early April, the Plebeian games in early November.

21   An ivy-and-vine-covered staff carried by the god Bacchus and by his worshippers, the Bacchantes.

22   A farcical kind of comedy that originated in Atella, a town in Campania near mod. Aversa.

23   Daughter of Cadmus, and mother of Actaeon.

24   Marcus Fabius Quintilianus, author of the *Institutes of Oratory*.

25   Specifically, a *murmillo*, a type of gladiator who displayed the image of a fish on the crest of his helmet.

26   An island off the coast of Egypt, near Alexandria.

27   The father of Ptolemy I.

28   An island-city at the mouth of the Nile.

29   An actor; he was a freedman of Domitia, wife of the emperor Domitian.

30   Hyacinthus was a beautiful young Spartan, much loved by Apollo.

31   Perhaps the name of her husband.

32   A *sestertius* (sesterce) was a small silver coin; see also Appendix 2.

33   Canusia was a town in Apulia famous for its high-quality wool.

34   The Falernian region of Campania, at the foot of Mt. Massicus, was famous for its wines.

35   Berenice, sister of Agrippa II, who lived at the court of the emperor Claudius until he was made king of Chalcis (in Syria) in AD 49/50.

36   Venusia (mod. Venosa) was a town on the border between Apulia and Lucania. It was the birthplace of Horace.

37   King of Numidia during the second Carthaginian war.

38   A town in central Italy; mod. Sulmona. It was the birthplace of Ovid.

39   Haemus and Carpophorus were actors.

40   A popular physician of the time.

41   Probably either a jurist or a rhetorician.

42   That is, from Tyre, a city in Phoenicia that was famous for its purple dye.

43   Games in honor of the goddess Flora, at which women were permitted an unusual degree of freedom. They were held in late April and early May.

44   The Aemilii Lepidi were a distinguished family; exactly which Lepidus is meant here is unclear.

45   Lucius Caecilius Metellus, who rescued a statue of Minerva from the temple of Vesta when it caught fire in 241 BC.

46   Quintus Fabius Maximus Gurges, consul in 292 BC, and again in 276.

47   Apparently, a gladiator.

48   Bona Dea was the goddess of chastity and fertility. Men were forbidden to enter her temple.

49   The god of procreation (also of gardens and vineyards).

50   Kings of Troy and Pylos, respectively, at the time of the Trojan war.

51   A lengthy reply to a pamphlet (*Cato*) written by Cicero in praise of Cato the Younger.

52   For Numa, see ch. 1, n. 18.

53   Publius Clodius, who was later (in 58 BC) tribune, is alleged to have profaned the rites of Bona Dea (above, n. 48) in 62, by attending them dressed as a she-lutist.

54   It was widely believed that eclipses of the moon were caused by the incantations of witches, and that such spells could be rendered inaudible by beating on pots, pans, etc.

55   Men's tunics were shorter than those worn by women.

56   A god of the forest, Silvanus was worshipped exclusively by men.

57   Literally, "for a *quadrans*," a small bronze coin, the nominal fee charged for admission to the baths.

58   A work on grammar by Quintus Remmius Palaemon, who lived in the time of Tiberius and Claudius.

59   Named for Poppaea Sabina, wife of the emperor Nero.

60   The *acta diurna*, which was begun by Julius Caesar, was a public record of the acts of the Senate, the assemblies, and the courts, and of personal events, such as births, deaths, marriages, and divorces.

61   An allusion probably to Phalaris, tyrant of Agrigentum (mod. Agrigento) in the sixth century BC.

62   An Egyptian goddess; wife of Osiris, mother of Horus.

63   Wife of Hector, daughter of king Eëtion of Thebe.

64   Apparently, a sign of satisfaction or approval.

65   A defensive earth-work located between the Esquiline and Colline gates, said to have been built by king Servius Tullius.

66   They were used to indicate the number of laps in a chariot-race.

67   See, e.g., D. Engels, "The problem of female infanticide in the Greco-Roman world," *Classical Philology*, 75 (1980), pp. 112–20.

68   See esp. W. V. Harris, "The theoretical possibility of extensive female infanticide in the Graeco-Roman world," *Classical Quarterly*, 32 (1982), pp. 114–16.

69   The name of a government official charged with approving legal contracts.

70   I.e., the emperor Augustus.

71   Gaius Musonius Rufus (ca. AD 30–100) of Volsinii (mod. Bolsena), in Etruria, was twice banished from Rome, first by Nero, the second time by Vespasian. Several of his discourses are extant.

72   The same story is told in Plutarch, *Aemilius Paullus* 5.2–3.

73   The mercenaries who fought for Cyrus when he tried to seize the Persian throne in 401 BC.

74   King of Macedonia, 359–336 BC, and father of Alexander the Great.

75   Plutarch's wife.

76   The inscription is *Corpus Inscriptionum Latinarum* 6.1527, 31670, 37053 (= *Inscriptiones Latinae Selectae* 8393).

77   Turia, for example, is said to have rescued her husband during the proscriptions of the triumvirs in 43 BC (Appian, *Civil Wars* 4.44; Valerius Maximus, *Memorable Deeds and Sayings* 6.7.2).

78   A form of marriage accomplished by fictitious sale, as a consequence of which the wife came under the authority of her husband.

79   A group of families united by a common name and by shared religious rites (loosely, a "clan").

80   Titus Annius Milo, tribune in 57 BC.

81   The emperor Augustus.

82 Marcus Aemilius Lepidus was Augustus' (at that time, Octavian's) colleague in the second Triumvirate, from 43 BC until 36, when he was stripped of his triumviral powers, and forced into retirement.

83 The Sequani lived along the river Sequana, which is now the Seine.

3   ECONOMY

1   The idea (like many of the others that follow) is borrowed from P. Garnsey and R. P. Saller, *The Roman Empire: Economy, Society and Culture* (Berkeley, 1987).

2   *Novus homo*, a term used to describe someone who was the first of his family to reach the consulship.

3   He is said also to have written a history and ethnology of Italy from the founding of Rome to 149 BC (*Origines*); an encyclopedic handbook on morality, sanitation, oratory, military science, and agriculture (among other things); and an account of the second Carthaginian war that extolled the bravery of a Carthaginian elephant named Surus (Pliny the Elder, *Natural History* 8.11). Cicero claimed (*Brutus* 67) to have read more than 150 of his speeches.

4   Roughly 25 hectares or 65 acres.

5   Literally, *paterfamilias*, a term normally used to designate the male head of a household.

6   Specifically, spelt (*far*), on which, see ch. 1, n. 5.

7   That is, against the integrity of the accounts.

8   An annual festival in honor of the *Lares*, tutelar gods normally associated with households and cross-roads.

9   About 60 hectares or 150 acres.

10 A large liquid measure; see Appendix 2.

11 A small liquid measure; see Appendix 2.

12 A liquid measure; see Appendix 2.

13 The meaning of *semuncias* is uncertain; a measure, of unknown capacity, is implied.

14 A grain-measure; see also Appendix 2.

15 A thin wine made from grape-husks.

16 A liquid measure; see Appendix 2.

17 A large liquid measure; see Appendix 2.

18 An annual festival in honor of Saturn that began on December 17.

19 For (Mars) Silvanus, see ch. 2, n. 56.

20 A very small liquid measure; see Appendix 2.

21 A town in Latium, now ruins.

22 See ch. 1, n. 56.

23 The first day of the month.

24 The thirteenth day of the month, except in March, May, July, and October, when it was the fifteenth day.

25 The fifth day of the month, except in March, May, July, and October, when it was the seventh day.

26 An inscription, possibly funerary, found at Tarentum (mod. Taranto) in southern Italy, is addressed to "Lucius Iunius Moderatus Columella, son of Lucius, of the Galerian tribe, military tribune of the sixth legion Ferrata" (*Corpus Inscriptionum Latinarum* 9.235 = *Inscriptiones Latinae Selectae* 2923).

27 Extant also is a single book *On Trees*.

28 See ch. 1, n. 67.

29 The (legendary) first king of Rome.

30   The Campus Martius, or "Field of Mars," a large plain in Rome along the Tiber, used as a place of assembly.

31   The Circus Maximus, said to have been built by king Tarquinius Priscus; it was located between the Palatine and Aventine hills.

32   Marcus Terentius Varro of Reate, in central Italy, is said to have written seventy-four works, of which only two survive: the *De re rustica* (which Columella entitles *Res rusticae*), a manual on farm-management published in 37 BC; and a partly extant treatise *On the Latin Language*.

33   A liquid measure; see Appendix 2.

34   A city in Cisalpine Gaul (what is now northern Italy), famous for the quality of its cloth.

35   A district of eastern Italy in the region of what is now Ancona.

36   A city in central Italy (in the territory of the Sabines); mod. Mentana.

37   Lucius Annaeus Seneca, or Seneca the Younger, served as tutor and adviser to the emperor Nero until AD 65, when he was forced to commit suicide. He wrote various works on philosophy and ethics; the *Natural Questions*, on physics and cosmology; eight (perhaps nine) tragedies; and the *Apocolocyntosis*, a satire on the deification of the emperor Claudius.

38   A very large liquid measure; see Appendix 2.

39   The name that Columella gave to one of his farms, which was perhaps in the region of Caere (mod. Cervetri), in Etruria.

40   Xenophon, *Oeconomicus* 20.16.

4   SCIENCE AND MEDICINE

1   The other "wandering stars" are the planets Mercury, Venus, Mars, Saturn, and Jupiter.

2   I.e., eclipsed.

3   114 BC.

4   461 BC.

5   In south-west Italy.

6   Crassus was killed in 53 BC.

7   49 BC.

8   A town in Samnium; mod. Conza.

9   Tribune of the plebs in 57 BC.

10   Now the Don.

11   I.e., the Mediterranean.

12   Now the Rock of Gibraltar.

13   Mod. Cádiz, Spain.

14   Now Gierace, Italy.

15   The term *Scythae* was used generically to describe a number of nomadic tribes north of the Black Sea.

16   A race of giants, each with one eye in the middle of its forehead, who are said to have inhabited the coast of Sicily.

17   A people of Italy, originally of Campania, and later of Sicily.

18   The Arimaspi are mentioned at 3.116, 4.13, and 4.27.

19   The Himalayas.

20   Now the Dnepr.

21   A cubit was the distance from the elbow to the end of the middle finger.

22   The *Annales Maximi*, an annual record of events maintained, from a very early period, by the chief priest (*pontifex maximus*).

23 See ch. 3, n. 21.
24 171 BC.
25 Now Izmir, Turkey.
26 The Dead Sea.
27 A town in Latium; now Circello.
28 Perhaps a poet of that name who is known to have lived in Egypt.
29 A town in the western Peloponnese, near Olympia.
30 Legendary king of Phrygia, and later of Elis, father of Atreus and Thyestes, grandfather of Agamemnon and Menelaus.
31 Epilepsy.
32 A type of resinous gum.
33 A city in what is now western Turkey.
34 A very small liquid measure; see Appendix 2.
35 At 1.36–42.
36 From Cimolus, one of the Cyclades islands; today Kimolos.
37 A drachma was equivalent in weight to about 4.3 grams.
38 An obol was equivalent in weight to about 0.7 grams.

5 POLITICS AND GOVERNMENT

1   See also M. Crawford, *The Roman Republic* (Cambridge, Mass., 1982), esp. at pp. 30–7.
2   P. Garnsey and R. Saller, *The Roman Empire: Economy, Society and Culture* (Berkeley and Los Angeles, 1987), p. 26.
3   Now Naples (Napoli).
4   A town in Latium, celebrated for its roses and nuts; now Palestrina.
5   A town in Latium; now Tivoli.
6   Magistrates possessed the right to take the auspices, a method of divining the will of the gods that was accomplished by observing the flight of birds.
7   See ch. 3, n. 2.
8   See ch. 3, n. 2.
9   Associations mainly of people who shared an office or occupation.
10 On *optimates* and *popularis*, see the introduction to selection 27.
11 I.e., Pompey the Great (*Magnus*).
12 Lucius Sergius Catilina, who, after losing the election to Cicero, allegedly tried to overthrow the state.
13 Gaius Antonius, who allegedly intended to stir up a slave rebellion if he was not elected.
14 Antonius.
15 Lucius Cornelius Sulla Felix, the dictator.
16 Marcus Marius Gratidianus, a supporter of Gaius Marius, was killed at the tomb of Catulus in 82 BC.
17 Gaius Coelius Caldus was consul in 94 BC.
18 Voting units of the Centuriate Assembly, which elected consuls and other senior magistrates.
19 The citizen body was divided into thirty-five tribes, which functioned also as voting units.
20 Literally, *sodalitates*, societies or clubs formed usually for religious purposes or to organize feasts and banquets.

21 A slave who accompanied his owner to remind him of the names of people they might encounter on the street.
22 A Pythagorean philosopher and comic poet of Cos and later of Syracuse.
23 Consul in 75 BC.
24 Manilius sponsored a bill which gave Pompey a special command in the East in 66 BC; Cornelius was another of Pompey's supporters.
25 According to Roman tradition, the constitution was suspended in 451 BC, and ten men (*decemviri*) were appointed to prepare a code of law (see also selection 1); they were forced to resign in 449.
26 The senior officers of the Republican army; they were invested with consular authority and functioned as the highest officials of state in the period 444–367 BC.
27 Literally, "first man."
28 Sextus Pompeius, son of Pompey the Great, and pirate-king of Sicily from 39 BC.
29 The emperor Augustus, who took the name Caesar after he had been adopted by Julius Caesar in his will.
30 One of a college of priests that exercised a general responsibility for the administration of the state religion.
31 Curule aediles were entitled to the curule chair, a symbol of office enjoyed also by consuls and praetors.
32 The title symbolized the authority, possessed by certain magistrates, including consuls, to command an army. From the time of Augustus, it was the semi-official title of the emperors.
33 Literally, *principes* (*iuventutis*).
34 Mod. Pianosa, about half-way between Corsica and the coast of Tuscany.
35 The husband of Augustus' grand-niece, Claudia Pulchra; three legions under his command were destroyed in Germany in AD 9.
36 What is now Croatia and Bosnia (more or less).
37 See n. 32.
38 On the Campus Martius, where Augustus' mausoleum was located, see ch. 3, n. 30.
39 See ch. 1, n. 67.
40 Aulus Hirtius and Gaius Pansa were consuls in 44 BC.
41 Late in 39 BC, Sextus Pompeius (above, n. 28) met with the triumvirs – Octavian (Augustus), Antony, and Lepidus – at Misenum (near Naples); they agreed to let him keep control of Sicily, and gave him Corsica and the Peloponnese as well.
42 Agreed to by the triumvirs in October, 40 BC, the treaty of Brundisium added Transalpine Gaul to Octavian's command in the West, and confirmed both Antony's control of the East and Lepidus' position in Africa. Its terms were renewed at Tarentum in 37.
43 The marriage of Antony to Octavian's sister, Octavia, in 40 BC.
44 Marcus Lollius Palicanus, defeated in Germany in 16 BC.
45 See n. 35.
46 Varro Murena was executed in 23 BC for conspiring against Augustus.
47 Egnatius Rufus was executed in 19 BC for conspiring against Augustus.
48 Iullus Antonius; the son of Mark Antony, he was forced to commit suicide in 2 BC, ostensibly for having committed adultery with Augustus' daughter, Julia.
49 See n. 30.
50 A knight, and friend of Augustus, who is said to have enjoyed feeding his slaves to his lampreys.
51 Priests assigned to the worship of a particular god.
52 "Priests," generically.
53 See ch. 1, n. 36.
54 They were celebrated every year in October.

55   The Circus Maximus, on which see ch. 3, n. 31.
56   In 44 BC.
57   The "faction" he had in mind was Mark Antony.
58   In 43 BC.
59   The right to command an army.
60   Julius Caesar.
61   A lesser triumph, in which the victorious general entered Rome on foot or on horseback, rather than in a chariot.
62   See n. 32.
63   See ch. 1, n. 67.
64   AD 14.
65   22 BC.
66   19 BC.
67   18 BC.
68   11 BC.
69   "First man of the Senate;" the title, which was Republican in origin, was given to the senator who was first asked his opinion by the presiding magistrate; Augustus assumed it in 28 BC.
70   Head of the college of *pontifices*, on which see n. 30.
71   See ch. 1, n. 28.
72   They supervised foreign, and especially Greek, cults that had been adopted at Rome.
73   They organized public banquets in honor of the gods.
74   Originally responsible for an agricultural rite, the Arval brothers' main function in the imperial period was to offer prayers and sacrifices for the well-being of the emperor's household.
75   What a *sodalis Titius* did is unclear.
76   The *fetiales* dealt mainly with treaties and with declarations of war.
77   29 BC.
78   28 BC.
79   A purification ceremony conducted by the censors after they had completed the census.
80   8 BC.
81   AD 14.
82   Cushioned couches, on which statues of the gods were laid.
83   12 BC.
84   See ch. 1, n. 17.
85   19 BC.
86   An honorary or distinguishing name (in this case Augustus, on which see below, section 34).
87   13 BC.
88   An arched gate, apparently; near the Palatine.
89   "First of the Youth."
90   A *sestertius* (sesterce) was a small silver coin; see also Appendix 2.
91   29 BC.
92   24 BC.
93   23 BC.
94   11 BC.
95   5 BC.
96   A *denarius* (pl. *denarii*) was a silver coin; see also Appendix 2.
97   29 BC.
98   2 BC.
99   30 BC.

100 14 BC.
101 7 BC.
102 6 BC.
103 4 BC.
104 3 BC.
105 2 BC.
106 AD 6.
107 18 BC.
108 28 BC.
109 27 BC.
110 Mod. Rimini.
111 29 BC.
112 Literally, "gold for crowns;" a kind of tax.
113 17 BC.
114 2 BC.
115 Mark Antony.
116 Mod. Cádiz, Spain.
117 Here (Greek) *Eudaemon*; in Latin, usually *Felix*.
118 Now the Don.
119 28, 27 BC.
120 2 BC.
121 What follows was not written by Augustus; its purpose is unclear.
122 August 31, AD 12.
123 See n. 5.
124 Of the Rhine and Moselle.
125 On *princeps*, see n. 27.
126 See n. 86.
127 The word *caligula* was used to denote a small military boot.
128 The son of Helios; when he lost control while driving his father's chariot, he was struck down by Zeus.
129 The festival (or feast) of Pales; it was celebrated on April 21, the anniversary of the founding of Rome.
130 See ch. 1, n. 14.
131 For Puteoli, see the introduction to selection 6.
132 Homer, *Iliad* 2.204.
133 Guardian deity of the Latins.
134 Homer, *Iliad* 23.724.
135 The *stola* was the characteristic garment of Roman matrons.
136 A member of the local Senate.
137 A town on the coast of Latium; mod. Fondi.
138 Accius, *Trag.* 203.
139 A watch was a fourth part of the night.
140 January 24 (AD 41).
141 Cassius Chaerea, tribune of the Praetorian Guard.
142 Jupiter was, among other things, the god of sudden death.
143 See n. 70.
144 See n. 32.
145 A grain-measure; see also Appendix 2.
146 See n. 96.
147 A type of grain so called because it yielded a hundredfold.
148 A liquid measure; see Appendix 2.

149   The Menapii were a people of Belgic Gaul.
150   The Cerretani lived in the Pyrenees.
151   The Marsi lived in Germany, between the Rhine and Lippe rivers.
152   See n. 19.
153   See n. 18.
154   At Thermopylae, in 191 BC.
155   Hesiod (*Works and Days* 289–92).
156   Literally, "from the first to the last sun."
157   Terence (*Eunuchus* 780).
158   A queen of Assyria.
159   In AD 383.
160   See n. 27.
161   In this case, loaves.
162   *Coronarium*, on which see n. 112.
163   The emperor Marcus Aurelius.
164   A Greek poet from Cilicia, who lived about 250 BC; he wrote an astronomical poem
      entitled *Phenomena*.
165   In a part of his *History* that has not survived.
166   See n. 86.
167   The members of town-councils.
168   Mod. Milan.

6   ROME AND THE PROVINCES

1   C. M. Wells, *The Roman Empire*, 2nd edn (Cambridge, Mass., 1992), p. 131.
2   Lucius Aelius Tubero; elsewhere described by Cicero as "my relative."
3   Aulus Allienus, praetor in 49 BC, and proconsul in Sicily in 46.
4   A Marcus Gratidius was the brother of Cicero's grandmother; the Gratidius mentioned
     here may be his grandson (and therefore Cicero's cousin).
5   An official of low rank (often an ex-slave) who attended a magistrate.
6   For lictor, see ch. 1, n. 36; for *fasces*, ch. 1, n. 67.
7   A city in Asia.
8   A city in Latium (mod. Mola di Gaeta).
9   Father of the future emperor, Augustus.
10   Those who had been given land confiscated (unlawfully) by Sulla.
11   A *sestertius* (sesterce) was a small silver coin; see also Appendix 2.
12   *Republic* 473 D.
13   Men of equestrian rank who formed associations to bid for the right to collect taxes in
     the provinces; see also the introduction to this chapter.
14   Caunus was a large city on the south coast of Asia; it was famous for its dried figs.
15   The prefect of Egypt.
16   AD 41.
17   See ch. 5, n. 70.
18   The term, which was normally used to describe young men (aged 18–20), here means
     something like "citizens."
19   Games presented by the Alexandrian officials known as gymnasiarchs and *cosmetae*,
     who supervised the city's gymnasia.
20   The two highest officials in each of the colonies.
21   See ch. 5, n. 136.

22   See n. 11.
23   A magistrate subordinate in rank to the duoviri; he was responsible for maintaining public property and for enforcing municipal ordinances.
24   The part of the theater normally reserved for senators and similar dignitaries.
25   Superintendent of military engineers.
26   The Chelidonean islands were off the coast of Cilicia; the Cyanean islands were at the mouth of the Bosporus.
27   Greek islands in the Aegean Sea.
28   *Theogony* 736–41.
29   The Sea of Azov.
30   *Works and Days* 5.
31   See ch. 5, n. 27.
32   The Dacians.
33   *Iliad* 15.189.

7   THE ARMY

1   *The Limits of Empire: The Roman Army in the East*, rev. edn (Oxford, 1992), p. 2.
2   Their identity, status, and height were also checked; see R. W. Davies, "Joining the Roman army," in R. W. Davies, *Service in the Roman Army*, ed. D. Breeze and V. A. Maxfield (New York, 1989), pp. 3–30.
3   *Catilinarian War* 7.4.
4   Roughly 18.4 miles or 29.6 kilometers (one Roman mile = about 1,617 yards = 1,478.5 meters).
5   About 22.1 miles or 35.5 kilometers.
6   See ch. 3, n. 30.
7   Roughly 43 pounds or 19.7 kilograms (one Roman pound = about 12 ounces = 327.5 grams).
8   *Georgics* 3.346–8.
9   Roughly 1,600 sesterces; see also Appendix 2.
10   I.e., between the ages of 17 and 46.
11   Light-armed infantry soldiers.
12   So named for the thrusting-spear known as a *hasta*, though the *hastati* themselves carried throwing-spears (*pila*). They fought in the front line of the battle-formation.
13   Despite their name – "leading men" – they formed the second line of the battle-formation.
14   The third line of the battle-formation.
15   I.e., without a crest or plume.
16   About nine inches.
17   Each maniple therefore consisted of about 420 soldiers, or one-tenth of a legion.
18   A standard was a kind of pole (or staff) which was carried in front of the soldiers as they marched into battle. It was decorated usually with representations of animals. It served both as a rallying-point, and as something for the soldiers to watch and to follow in battle; it also had important religious functions in the society of the legion.
19   Equivalent to about 1.3 sesterces; see also Appendix 2.
20   One *medimnus* (pl. *medimni*) was equivalent to roughly 6 *modii* or about 1.5 bushels.
21   An annual strength report.
22   Officers who commanded cavalry units (*decuriae*).
23   The legionary commander.

24   Roughly modern Kosovo.
25   An imperial official in charge of revenues.
26   Here, and at other places below (indicated also by square brackets), a word seems to be missing from the text.
27   Part of the sentence is missing; what remains makes little sense.
28   A gold coin, originally called an *aureus*; when it was first issued, it was equivalent in value to about 25 *denarii* (see Appendix 2).
29   Daily allowances of bread.
30   Machines for hurling stones or other projectiles.

8   BEYOND THE FRONTIER

1   The idea is taken from P. J. Geary, "Barbarians and ethnicity," in *Late Antiquity: A Guide to the Postclassical World*, ed. G. W. Bowersock, P. Brown, and O. Grabar (Cambridge, Mass. and London, 1999), p. 108.
2   Their principal town was Autricum, now Chartres.
3   God of the underworld (the Greek Pluto), here identified with the Celtic god of night.
4   See ch. 3, n. 5.
5   God of fire.
6   The moon.
7   I.e., during Agricola's tenure as governor (AD 78–84).
8   I.e., to the Clyde–Forth isthmus.
9   The Orkneys.
10   Perhaps the Shetland islands.
11   The inhabitants of what is now south Wales.
12   Of Scandinavia; they included, according to Pliny the Elder (*Natural History* 6.99), the Cimbri, Teutones, and Chauci.
13   They included the Hermunduri, Chatti, Cherusci, and Suebi (discussed below, *Germania* 45).
14   Located, it seems, mainly near the Rhine.
15   The exact location of the Marsi and the Gambrivii is unknown.
16   See below, *Germania* 45.
17   The later Vandals of eastern Germany.
18   They settled near what is now Liège, Belgium.
19   I.e., the Tungri.
20   Literally, *hastae*, for which see also ch. 7, n. 12.
21   I.e., "the hundred."
22   Literally, *colonus*, on which see also ch. 1, n. 92.
23   A people of what is now Sweden.
24   The Baltic.
25   Their exact location is unknown. They may be associated with the later Kvaens of north-eastern Scandinavia.
26   Thought to be ancestors of the Slavs, they inhabited the region east and north-east of modern Warsaw.
27   They lived north of the Aestii, along the east coast of the Baltic sea.
28   A Slavic people, who occupied the region between the Vistula and Don rivers (what is now eastern Poland and the Ukraine).
29   Actually, they were part of the Bastarnae, who inhabited the eastern Carpathian mountains and the province of Lower Moesia (mod. Bulgaria).

30   I.e., over the couches around the table.
31   To advise judges who knew little about the law.
32   The custom is reported also by Diodorus of Sicily (15.10), Herodotus (5.25), and Valerius
     Maximus (6.3).
33   Gladiators who wore a Gallic helmet, the crest of which was the image of a fish.
34   In 546 BC.
35   Now the Sea of Azov.
36   I.e., on horseback.

9   PAGANS AND CHRISTIANS

1   P. Garnsey and R. Saller, *The Roman Empire: Economy, Society and Culture* (Berkeley
     and Los Angeles, 1987), p. 163.
2   See ch. 1, n. 18.
3   See ch. 5, n. 30.
4   In the north-east part of Rome, near the Quirinal hill.
5   Days on which public business was suspended.
6   A festival in honor of Lycaean (i.e., Arcadian) Zeus.
7   He is said to have brought Greek settlers to Italy not long before the Trojan war.
8   The wolf that was thought to have suckled Romulus and Remus.
9   The young men of noble birth mentioned below.
10   A sacrificial offering consisting of a swine, a ram, and a bull.
11   A Roman *praenomen* (like Gaius); who Manius might be is uncertain.
12   Something has gone wrong with the Latin text at this point.
13   Goddess of sewers.
14   The verb *proserpo* means "to emerge slowly."
15   See ch. 1, n. 67.
16   Made from mistletoe berries.
17   Ganymede was Jupiter's cup-bearer.
18   Son of Glaucus, grandson of Sisyphus, he slew the Chimaera, a fire-breathing monster
     (part lion, part goat, and part dragon).
19   Bellerophon's flying horse.
20   Perhaps the prayers described below in chapter 17.
21   An Egyptian god routinely worshipped together with Isis, and often identified with her
     husband, Osiris.
22   Metallic rattles used in celebrating the rites of Isis.
23   Greek *ta ploiaphesia* (literally, "ship-launching").
24   Daughter of Jupiter and Ceres, and wife of Pluto, who carried her off to the underworld.
25   The name is attested on inscriptions found at Cirta, North Africa (mod. Constantine,
     Algeria), that date to around AD 210.
26   Marcus Cornelius Fronto. He was the leading orator of his day (ca. AD 100–66), and, for
     a time, tutor of the future emperor, Marcus Aurelius. His speech against the Christians
     does not survive. For Cirta, see n. 25.
27   The Sibyl was a female soothsayer, who is said to have lived in the time of Tarquinius
     Superbus (the last of the Roman kings), and whose written prophesies, kept in the Capi-
     tol, were consulted by a special college of priests in times of crisis.
28   Governor of the province of Judaea, AD 26–36.
29   Alternatively, the Latin here (*odio humani generis*) could be taken to mean, not that the
     Christians hated the human race, but that they were hated by everyone else.

30 I.e., to be executed.
31 I.e., martyrs.
32 Thyestes (inadvertently) ate his sons.
33 The quotation is from John 16.2.
34 1 Timothy 3.15.
35 1 Peter 5.8.
36 Matthew 25.46.
37 Acts 15.29.
38 There is an allusion to 1 Timothy 6.13.
39 Mod. Thessaloniki (Salonika), Greece.
40 The quotation is from 1 Thessalonians 1.8.
41 1 Thessalonians 4.9.
42 The mountain cannot be identified.
43 The prefect Dulcitius, mentioned below.
44 Psalms 51.7.
45 John 14.27.
46 1 Timothy 1.5.
47 A guard or police officer.
48 A military officer who sometimes exercised police functions.
49 Acts 4.24.

APPENDIX 1   ROMAN EMPERORS, TO AD 395

Augustus, 27 BC–AD 14

(AD)

Tiberius, 14–37
Gaius (Caligula), 37–41
Claudius, 41–54
Nero, 54–68
Galba, 68–9
Otho, 69
Vitellius, 69
Vespasian, 70–9
Titus, 79–81
Domitian, 81–96
Nerva, 96–8
Trajan, 98–117
Hadrian, 117–38
Antoninus Pius, 138–61
Marcus Aurelius, 161–80
Commodus, 180–92
Pertinax, 193
Didius Julianus, 193
Septimius Severus, 193–211
Caracalla, 211–17
Macrinus, 217–18
Elagabalus, 218–22
Severus Alexander, 222–35
Maximinus, 235–8
Gordian III, 238–44
Philip, 244–9

Decius, 249–51
Trebonianus Gallus, 251–3
Valerian, 253–60
Gallienus, 253–68
Claudius II, 268–70
Aurelian, 270–5
Tacitus, 275–6
Probus, 276–82
Carus, 282–3
Numerian, 283–4
Carinus, 283–5
Diocletian, 284–305
Maximian, 286–305
Maxentius, 306–12
Constantine, 306–37
Licinius, 308–24
Constantine II, 337–40
Constans, 337–50
Constantius II, 337–61
Julian, 361–3
Jovian, 363–4
Valentinian I, 364–75
Valens, 364–78
Gratian, 367–83
Valentinian II, 375–92
Theodosius I, 378–95

APPENDIX 2 COINS, WEIGHTS, AND MEASURES

COINS

As (pl. *asses*). A large copper coin, weighing one Roman pound (about 12 ounces).

Denarius (pl. *denarii*). A silver coin. By the time of Diocletian, it had become a small copper coin with a nominal value of 756 to one gold *aureus*, of which there were 60 to a pound.

Quadrans (pl. *quadrantes*). A small bronze coin.

Sestertius (sesterce). A small silver coin. It was the most commonly used Roman currency.

Equivalencies: 1 *denarius* = 1 (Greek) *drachma* = 4 *sestertii* (sesterces) = 6 (Greek) *obols* = 16 *asses* = 64 *quadrantes*.

WEIGHTS

One Roman pound = 0.7219 pound avoirdupois = about 12 ounces = 327.5 grams.

MEASURES

Distance. One Roman mile = about 1,617 yards = 1,478.5 meters.

Grain. *Modius*. Equivalent to one peck (i.e., one-quarter of a bushel), or to about one-sixth of an (Attic) *medimnus*. An army-*modius* is estimated to have been 1.3 to 1.5 times larger than a regular *modius*.

Land. *Iugerum* (pl. *iugera*). 1 *iugerum* = 0.25 hectare = 0.625 acre.

Liquid. Rough equivalencies: 1 *sextarius* (pl. *sextarii*) = 12 *cyathi* (sing. *cyathus*) = 2 *heminae* (sing. *hemina*) = 1/6 *congius* (pl. *congii*) = 1/24 *urna* (pl. *urnae*) = 1/48 *quadrantal* (pl. *quadrantales*) = 1/48 *amphora* (pl. *amphorae*) = 1/960 *culleus* (pl. *cullei*) = 1 British pint = 20 fluid oz.

CHRONOLOGICAL TABLE

Political and Military Events	Cultural Developments
BC	BC
753 Traditional date for founding of Rome	
753–509 Period of kings	
509 Traditional date for founding of Republic	509 Temple of Jupiter constructed on the Capitoline
496 Latins defeated at battle of Lake Regillus	
494–287 Struggle of the Orders	
451/50 Twelve Tables	
405–396 Romans besiege, capture Veii	
390 Rome sacked by Gauls	
	348 Secular games first celebrated
341 First Samnite war (against Samnites in central Apennines)	
338 Campania incorporated into Roman state	
327–304 Second Samnite war	
298–290 Third Samnite war	
280–272 War against Pyrrhus of Epirus; Tarentum surrenders	280–275 Earliest Roman coinage
264–241 First Carthaginian war	264 First gladiatorial show at Rome
	240–207 Livius Andronicus, first Roman poet and playwright, active
	236 First play of Naevius produced
227 Sicily and Sardinia are made provinces	
219 Hannibal besieges, captures Saguntum	
218–201 Second Carthaginian war	
216 Hannibal defeats Romans at Cannae	
215 Alliance between Carthage and Philip V of Macedonia	
214–205 First Macedonian war between Rome and Philip	
	204 Plautus' *Miles Gloriosus* performed
202 Scipio Africanus defeats Hannibal at battle of Zama	202 Fabius Pictor writes first prose history of Rome (in Greek)

201–191 Romans conquer Cisalpine Gaul
200–197 Second Macedonian war between
Rome and Philip
197–133 Wars in Spain
192–188 War against Antiochus III of Syria

179 Basilica Aemilia, Aemilian Bridge built
at Rome

171–167 Third Macedonian war between
Rome and Perseus; Macedonia divided into
four republics

167 Polybius comes to Rome as hostage
166–159 Plays of Terence produced
149 Cato the Elder's history of Rome
published

149–146 Third Carthaginian war; Africa
made a province
148 Fourth Macedonian war; war against
Achaean league; Corinth sacked; Macedonia
made a province

144 Stoic philosopher Panaetius comes to
Rome

135–132 First slave war in Sicily
133 Tribunate of Tiberius Gracchus; Attalus
III of Pergamum bequeaths kingdom to
Rome
129 Kingdom of Pergamum becomes
province of Asia
123–122 Tribunates of Gaius Gracchus
121 Gallia Narbonensis made a province

120–110 Circular temple constructed in the
Forum Boarium

112–106 War against Jugurtha of Numidia
107–100 Gaius Marius consul six times

106 Cicero born

104–101 Second slave war in Sicily
102–101 Marius defeats Teutones, Cimbri

99 Lucretius born

91–88 War between Rome and Italian allies
88 Sulla marches on Rome
88–85 First war against Mithridates VI of
Pontus

87–51 Posidonius, historian and
philosopher, active
84 Catullus born

83–82 Civil war at Rome; second war
against Mithridates
82–80 Dictatorship of Sulla

81 Cicero's earliest surviving speech
78 Tabularium constructed on the
Capitoline

74–63 Third war against Mithridates
73–71 Slave revolt of Spartacus
70 Trial of Gaius Verres

70 Cicero's *Verrine Orations*; Vergil born

67 Pompey campaigns against pirates
66–63 Pompey defeats Mithridates, establishes provinces of Bithynia, Cilicia, Syria, Crete

65 Horace born

63 Consulship of Cicero; "conspiracy" of Catiline

63 Cicero's *Catilinarian Orations*

60 First Triumvirate formed by Pompey, Caesar, and Crassus

60–30 Diodorus of Sicily writes *Historical Library*
59–54 Catullus' poems to Lesbia (Clodia)

58–52 Caesar conquers Gaul

55 Theater of Pompey, first stone-built theater at Rome, completed

53 Crassus killed by Parthians at battle of Carrhae
52 Publius Clodius murdered

51 Caesar's *Gallic War* published

49–48 Civil war between Caesar and Pompey; battle of Pharsalus; Pompey is murdered in Egypt
47–44 Dictatorship of Caesar

46 Forum of Caesar begun

44 (March 15) Caesar assassinated

44 Cicero's *Philippics*

43 Second Triumvirate formed by Antony, Octavian, and Lepidus

43 Ovid born

42 Battle of Philippi; Brutus and Cassius commit suicide
40 Marriage of Antony and Octavia; treaty of Brundisium

38 Vergil's *Eclogues* published

36–35 Octavian campaigns against Sextus Pompeius
31 Octavian defeats Antony at battle of Actium
30 Antony and Cleopatra commit suicide; Egypt is annexed

28–23 Vitruvius writes *On Architecture*

27 Octavian's first constitutional settlement; he is given the name Augustus

24–23 First three books of Horace's *Odes* published

23 Conspiracy against Augustus; second constitutional settlement

19 Death of Vergil

18 Augustus' laws on marriage and adultery

17 Secular games celebrated
13–11 Theater of Marcellus constructed

9 Altar of Augustan Peace dedicated
8 Death of Horace

12 Augustus becomes *pontifex maximus*

6 Tiberius retires to Rhodes

2 Forum of Augustus dedicated

AD

AD

2–4 Deaths of Lucius and Gaius Caesar;
Tiberius given tribunician power

3 Maison Carrée built at Nîmes

6 Judaea made a province

8 Ovid exiled to Black Sea

9 Disaster of Quintilius Varus in Germany
14 Death of Augustus; accession of Tiberius

17 Death of Ovid

19 Death of Germanicus (Tiberius' nephew)

Celsus, Valerius Maximus active

23 Death of Drusus (Tiberius' son)
26 Tiberius retires to Capri
31 Praetorian prefect Sejanus executed
37 Death of Tiberius; accession of Caligula
(Gaius)
41 Assassination of Caligula; accession of
Claudius
43 Britain invaded

49 Seneca the Younger appointed tutor to
Nero

54 Death of Claudius; accession of Nero
58–9 War against Parthians
59 Agrippina murdered

60–5 Columella writes *On Agriculture*

61 Revolt in Britain under Boudicca

64 Fire at Rome; Christians persecuted
65 Conspiracy of Piso   65 Suicide of Seneca the Younger
66–73 Jewish rebellion   66 Suicide of Petronius
68 Suicide of Nero; accession of Galba
69 Year of the four emperors: Galba, Otho,
Vitellius, Vespasian
70 Temple at Jerusalem destroyed
78–84 Agricola's campaigns in Britain
79 Death of Vespasian; accession of Titus   79 Eruption of Mt. Vesuvius; destruction of
Pompeii, Herculaneum; death of Pliny the
Elder
80 Colosseum dedicated

81 Death of Titus; accession of Domitian
86–92 Domitian campaigns against Dacians
96 Assassination of Domitian; accession of
Nerva
98 Death of Nerva; accession of Trajan

100 Pliny the Younger consul
100–110 Tacitus writes *Histories* and
Annals

101–6 Trajan conquers Dacia

Plutarch active

106 Arabia is annexed

112–13 Forum of Trajan and Trajan's column dedicated

114–17 Trajan campaigns against Parthians
115–17 Jewish rebellion in the East
117 Death of Trajan; accession of Hadrian

118 Hadrian's villa at Tibur (Tivoli) begun

122–8 Hadrian's Wall built

Juvenal, Suetonius active

132–5 Revolt of Bar Kochba

134 Temple of Rome and Venus dedicated

138 Death of Hadrian; accession of Antoninus Pius

144 (or 156) Aelius Aristides' speech *To Rome*

161 Death of Antoninus Pius; accession of Marcus Aurelius; Parthians invade Syria, Armenia

Apuleius active

162–6 Lucius Verus campaigns against Parthians

165–7 Plague spreads through empire

168–75 Marcus Aurelius campaigns against Germans

174–80 Marcus Aurelius writes *Meditations*

177 Commodus made co-emperor

177 Christians martyred at Lugdunum (Lyons)

180 Death of Marcus Aurelius; accession of Commodus
192 Commodus assassinated
193 Septimius Severus proclaimed emperor
193–7 Civil wars

193 Column of Marcus Aurelius completed

197 Tertullian writes *Apology*

208–11 Septimius Severus campaigns in Britain
211 Death of Septimius Severus; accession of Caracalla and Geta; assassination of Geta
212 Caracalla gives Roman citizenship to all inhabitants of empire, except slaves

216 Baths of Caracalla completed

217 Assassination of Caracalla; accession of Macrinus
218 Death of Macrinus; accession of Elagabalus
222 Assassination of Elagabalus; accession of Severus Alexander
224 Sassanid dynasty established in Persia
235 Assassination of Severus Alexander; accession of Maximinus

249–51 Christians persecuted under Decius

253 Franks and Alamanni invade Gaul

259/60 Valerian captured by Persians
267 Heruli invade Greece
271 Dacia evacuated
284 Accession of Diocletian
286 Maximian made co-emperor

258 Cyprian martyred

271 Aurelian walls at Rome built

301 Price Edict promulgated
303–5 Final persecution of Christians

305 Abdication of Diocletian and Maximian
306 Constantine proclaimed emperor
312 Constantine defeats Licinius at battle of
the Milvian Bridge

313 Edict of Milan
313–22 First Christian basilica at Rome
built
ca. 314 Eusebius becomes bishop of
Caesarea

324 Founding of Constantinople

325 Council of Nicaea

337 Death of Constantine
357 Alamanni defeated at battle of
Strasbourg
361 Accession of Julian
363–4 Campaigns against Persians; death of
Julian; accession of Jovian

373/4 Ambrose becomes bishop of Milan

378 Romans defeated by Visigoths at battle
of Adrianople; accession of Theodosius I

Ammianus Marcellinus, Vegetius active
395 Augustine becomes bishop of Hippo

395 Empire divided between sons of
Theodosius

397–400 Augustine writes *Confessions*

410 Rome captured, sacked by Visigoths

430 Death of Augustine
438 *Theodosian Code* promulgated

455 Rome sacked by Vandals
476 Romulus Augustulus, last Roman
emperor in West, is deposed

INDEX

84086222R00157

Made in the USA
Middletown, DE
17 August 2018